South-South Solidarity and the Latin American Left

D1715406

Critical Human Rights

Scott Straus and Tyrell Haberkorn, Series Editors;
Steve J. Stern, Editor Emeritus

Books in the series Critical Human Rights emphasize research that opens new ways to think about and understand human rights. The series values in particular empirically grounded and intellectually open research that eschews simplified accounts of human rights events and processes.

South-South Solidarity and the Latin American Left

Jessica Stites Mor

The University of Wisconsin Press

The University of Wisconsin Press
728 State Street, Suite 443
Madison, Wisconsin 53706
uwpress.wisc.edu

Gray's Inn House, 127 Clerkenwell Road
London ECIR 5DB, United Kingdom
eurospanbookstore.com

Copyright © 2022 by Jessica L. Stites
All rights reserved. Except in the case of brief quotations embedded in critical articles and reviews, no part of this publication may be reproduced, stored in a retrieval system, transmitted in any format or by any means—digital, electronic, mechanical, photocopying, recording, or otherwise—or conveyed via the internet or a website without written permission of the University of Wisconsin Press. Rights inquiries should be directed to rights@uwpress.wisc.edu.

Printed in the United States of America
This book may be available in a digital edition.

Library of Congress Cataloging-in-Publication Data

Names: Stites Mor, Jessica, author.
Title: South-South solidarity and the Latin American left / Jessica Stites Mor.
Other titles: Critical human rights.
Description: Madison, Wisconsin : The University of Wisconsin Press, [2022] |
    Series: Critical human rights | Includes bibliographical references and index.
Identifiers: LCCN 2021023502 | ISBN 9780299336103 (hardcover)
Subjects: LCSH: Political activists—Latin America—International cooperation. |
    Right and left (Political science)—Latin America—International cooperation. |
    Solidarity—Latin America. | Solidarity—Developing countries. | International cooperation. |
    Latin America—Relations—Developing countries. | Latin America—Politics and government—
    20th century.
Classification: LCC F1414 .S75 2022 | DDC 980.04—dc23
LC record available at https://lccn.loc.gov/2021023502

ISBN 9780299336141 (paperback)

Contents

Illustrations

Acknowledgments

As anyone who has ever written an academic monograph can attest, this is decidedly collaborative work. So many people have helped and encouraged me over the years that it has taken to complete this project that my debts of gratitude run exceedingly deep. It is impossible to imagine completing a project like this without the support of family, colleagues, and friends or without the tremendous generosity of an intellectual community actively willing to share their resources and knowledge along the way. I would like to thank as many of them here as I am able, though I will certainly not be able to capture the full extent of what this support has meant to me over the years.

This project began as an idea, an argument, that first came to me as an undergraduate student. I had been working with the Africa Faith and Justice Network in Washington, DC, where I had the great fortune to spend hours talking with two women, Sister Mary Agnes and Sister Francine, about the time they had spent in Africa. The job consisted of receiving reports that were sent to us from Catholic activists in the region and sending out a regular news bulletin. My French at the time was better than it is now, and I had gotten the job just out of high school, in my first year living away from home. My first intellectual debt, as such, is to a number of wonderful teachers in high school, including Larry Spotts, who not only taught French but also did his part to inform his students of what was at stake in our public education. Because he had been so dedicated to his students' linguistic competence before they went off to college, I was able to convince the organization to give me the task of translating the reports from French-speaking West Africa. At a certain point, the sisters got together to purchase a Lonely Planet travel guide for me and helped convince me to take a job in Abidjan.

When I arrived there, I was a curious nineteen-year-old, translating for nurses and physicians who had come to work in a free clinic in one of the Côte d'Ivoire's most impoverished neighborhoods. While they spent the day attending to the health needs of the community and giving vaccines, I taught a conversational English class to a group of theology students preparing to head to Kenya. My class was attended by some other regulars, a dozen children from the neighborhood, many of whom were migrants that had fled the Liberian civil war. I spent time with two families of missionaries who tried to carefully explain local politics and the connections they saw between their work and that of other international humanitarian outfits in town. When I came back to the United States, I had a head full of thoughts, which I was lucky enough to be able to share with Tony Rosenthal, who became an adviser and a lifelong friend and co-conspirator. Tony encouraged me to think about what these ties of solidarity between the Americas and Africa meant and how they had developed. He also encouraged me to think about transnational history, the ways people and ideas traveled across borders, and the importance of comparing historical experience across distance and time. The argument he convinced me to pursue—that this history is important even if it is very difficult to reconstruct—is what has driven this research project. I would like to extend my deepest gratitude to Tony for his encouragement over the years. No one has spent more time listening to my research stories, plotting with me to take them further, and helping me sort through their meaning.

Over the years, the scholars I have had the pleasure of meeting as an undergraduate and graduate student provided a source of constant reassurance and many important models of how one might eventually try to contribute to this field. I am extremely grateful to Leonardo Villalón, Charles Stansifer, Chris Crandall, Kirk Shaffer, Paul Sutter, and Bill Tsutsui, with whom I studied at the University of Kansas, for their many kindnesses. Hodgie and Jack Bricke were a lighthouse to me long after I moved from Lawrence to New Haven. When I arrived to study at Yale, I could not have found myself in a more welcoming and nurturing environment. Working with Gil Joseph, James Scott, Vicky Murrillo, and Arun Agrawal, I felt as if I had landed in the most advantageous spot imaginable to continue asking questions and finding guidance. Gil went to great lengths and extended boundless patience to my research on the spread of political ideas through communities of activist filmmakers. His flexibility allowed me to explore and build connections from Mexico to the Southern Cone and, later, from Havana to Hanoi. I have been able to call on many of these connections over the years for support in researching this book, and I am incredibly appreciative of the time and attention with which Gil helped me get started down this path. James Scott provided early critical feedback and inspiration for the project, in addition to connecting me with a wonderful community of scholars interested in similar subjects. The Agrarian Studies program and the many events surrounding its workshop were a remarkable intellectual incubator in so many ways. During this time, I worked closely with Arun Agrawal, who not only helped me think about how to organize a project of these dimensions but also gave advice that helped me refine my research questions and secure research funding at a crucial moment. I cannot express how much the support of these long-term mentors has meant to me.

I also wish to thank the many scholars that helped with various stages of preparing this research. I am grateful for the insightful suggestions and constructive advice of Daniela Spencer, Pablo Yankelevich, Eric Zolov, Luis Roniger, Alberto Gilly, Alejandro Velasco, Cynthia Milton, Catherine LeGrande, Emilio Ferrín, Edward Wright-Rios, Alejandra Bronfman, Jadwiga Pieper-Moody, Sandra McGee-Deutsch, Adam Howard, Aiyaz Husein, Pablo Palomino, Steven Hyland, Bill Beezley, Bill French, María Muñoz, Douglas Smith, Marian Schlotterbeck, Paul K. Adler, Lily Pearl Balloffet, Luis Herrán Avila, Michelle Chase, Aaron Coy Moulton, Dustin Walcher, Jason Colby, Ranaan Rein, Meron Medzini, Gerardo Leibner, Marylin Young, Anne Rubenstein, Anne Garland Mahler, Raphael Folsom, Marco Abram, Jaymie Heilman, Mark Overmyer-Velázquez, Monica Popescu, Vanni Pettinà, Jordana Dym, Raymond Craib, James N. Green, Saeed Ahmed, Jason Chang, Abdalhadi Alijla, Lucinda Grinnell, Russell Cobb, Barry Carr, Humberto Cucchetti, Brad Simpson, Gabriela Aceves, Luis Van Isschot, Kerry Bystrom, Jeremy Adelman, Emmanuel Kahan, Andrés Estefane, Jorge "Kokan" Iturriaga Echeverría, Steve Stern, Liisa North, Stella Krepp, Pablo Policzer, Jaime Pensado, Katherine Zien, Renata Keller, Jeffrey Byrne, Greg Grandin, Lincoln Cushing, and Juan Pablo Scarfi. I am particularly beholden to Jason Parker, Ashley Black, Ariel Nicolaides, Fernando Camacho Padilla, and Maximiliano Jozami for their generous assistance in finding sources. Jason kindly invited me to present at the Decolonization Seminar in Washington, DC, and has been a constant source of good leads as this project has progressed. Ashley and Fernando not only each shared important primary sources but have also been the kind of friends and colleagues that make collaborative projects a true delight. Their good company has made the research of this book an adventure. Special thanks are also due to Joshua Nadel for his timely defense of the em dash.

I extend my most heartfelt thanks to the archivists that took the time to assist me in navigating new collections. In particular, I thank a handful of people who assisted the archival work in thoughtful and important ways. I had the pleasure of spending Nelson Mandela Day, 18 June 2017, in the company of Father Peter-John Pearson at the Archdiocese of Cape Town, and I am eternally grateful for the experiences and insights he shared with me. I am also very thankful to Tonci Cacchioli and Father Frank White for helping me navigate the Archdiocese collections and providing such lovely company. At the South African History Archive in Johannesburg, I would like to thank Kerry-Lee Clark and the Struggles for Justice Programme at Wits University for providing wonderful archival support. I also thank Carol Leadenham at the Hoover Institution Archives and Cindy Abel Morris at the University of New Mexico. I thank Daniel Gutierrez and Amina Sharma for being wonderful hosts while I worked in Los Angeles. In Mexico, I am grateful to the helpful staff at the Archivo General de la Nación. I wish to acknowledge and thank the Central Zionist Archives in Jerusalem, the Jabotinzky Institute in Tel Aviv, and the University of Tel Aviv's Latin American Studies program for hosting me at various talks that provided opportunities to travel and critical feedback. Without the help of Raanan Rein, I would not have been able to connect with as wide a network of scholars working on the Middle East as helped facilitate this research. I am extremely grateful to Horacio Tarcus at the Centro de Documentación e Investigación de la Cultura de Izquierdas in Buenos Aires for many hours of conversation and assistance with the archive. I am indebted to him for introducing me to his colleagues and students, and for being supportive of my work over these many years.

This project follows on the heels of copublished work that contributed significantly to the arguments I make here about South-South solidarity. I am very grateful to the many other scholars with whom these earlier works were published, especially Maria del Carmen Suescun Pozas, with whom I spent many years discussing these ideas and working through various thoughts. Molly Todd has been a close companion over the past years in thinking about solidarity history and activism in Latin America. Her work has been an inspiration to me, and I appreciate the time she has taken to critique various iterations of this project. I would also like to thank dear friends who gave feedback on early versions of chapters, listened to rambling thoughts over meals, or asked great questions at workshops. These include Kevin Coleman, Camilo Trumper, Dalia Muller, Matt Karush, Jess Pearson, Geneviève Dorais, Catherine Higgs, Anne Murphy, and Ashley Black. Bonar Buffam and Mike Evans each provided kindly worded but direct advice that likely will have saved me tremendous discomfort down the road.

Several grants and invitations to present were very useful in providing opportunities for feedback. I thank Barbara Potthast for inviting me to present at the University of Cologne, Amelia Kiddle for inviting me to present at the University of Calgary, Luis Van Isschot for inviting me to present at the

University of Connecticut, and Kevin Coleman for inviting me to the University of Toronto. Nicole Salzman encouraged this project from early on and provided excellent questions over coffee in Vancouver. I count myself fortunate to have been able to participate in the "International Solidarity and World Literature" Workshop as part of the American Comparative Literature Association in Los Angeles in 2018, organized by Anna Bernard. Since then, several workshop members have continued to be a stimulating source of community and wonderful companions in thinking through internationalism and solidarity. I also thank the many folks who showed up early on a Sunday morning to attend a "Transnational Mexico" panel at the American Historical Association/Conference on Latin American History meeting in 2017. The questions and comments that Mexican history specialists offered to help strengthen the first chapter of this book were incredibly welcome. I am also grateful to a Social Science and Humanities Research Council Insight Grant and to the Irving K. Barber School of Arts and Sciences for support in funding this research.

Since 2018, I have benefited from the construction of a research community in the International Solidarity Action and Research Network (ISARN). Anna Bernard and Tony Alessandrini have been the kind of trusted colleagues and tireless collaborators who make this kind of work not only possible but worthwhile. I am grateful to the City University of New York Graduate Center and the University of Toronto for providing ISARN with meeting spaces and to the participants in the ISARN meeting in Beirut for providing wonderful dialogue on the possibilities and limitations of South-South solidarity. The invaluable conversations at these meetings have had a significant influence on the writing of this book. In particular, I am grateful to the constructive insights of Alys Moody, Nadje Al-Ali, Libby Garland, Tara Ried, Dina El-Sharnouby, Sophie Chamas, Gary Wilder, Dyala Hamzah, Melissa Forbis, Natalie Kouri-Towe, Alexandre Raymond-Desjardins, Jacey Anderson, Amer Younes, and Anup Grewal. I have never felt more heartened as a scholar than when Kazembe Balagun remarked of my research for this book, "that was dope." I feel grateful to have had the opportunity to observe how incredible the support of a community of people coming together around ideas and shared commitments can be.

I am also grateful to work at the University of British Columbia (UBC), Okanagan, on traditional Syilx land, where I am surrounded by tremendous collegial support. I am so grateful to the friends and colleagues with whom I have been able to share my life here: Tara and Thomas Heilke, Mike Evans, Michelle Smith, James and Ruth Rochlin, Luis Aguiar, Patricia Tomic, Ricardo Trumper, Alwyn Spies, Rory O'Neill, Monica Good, Ben Nilson, Ruth Frost,

John Klironomos, Miranda Hart, Gord Binsted, Taylor Wilson, Anna Alexander, Ryan Alexander, Christopher Craig, Peter Urmetzer, Ann MacKinnon, Francisco Peña, Carolina Restrepo, James Hull, Todd Campbell, Julien Vernet, Tim Paulson, Brigitte le Normand, Ted Sandstra, Shaghayegh Tajvidi, Mike Thompson, Bonar Buffam, Meghan Toal, Evan and Lawrence Berg, Brianna Wells, Vern Nelson, Chris Schneider, Ilya Parkins, Anderson Araujo, Claude Desmarais, Amanda Snyder, Sean and Karine Lawrence, Heather Latimer, Karis Shearer, Christine Schreyer, Ryan Klassen, and Fiona and Pat McDonald. Jodey Castricano has been indispensable in making this place feel like home, cheering me on over the course of writing this manuscript and finding ways to enjoy life outside of work. I am not sure how I would have made it through to the end of this project without her good company next door.

I am also grateful for the wonderful students that I've had the pleasure of teaching at UBC, many of whom have asked questions, contributed thoughts, or have reminded me of why this research is valuable. I especially thank Ariel Nicolaides, Dylan Draper, Dominica Patterson, Stephanie Tissot, Wendy Rajotte, Jake Sherman, Jesse Carter, Douglas Younger, Shao Yuan Chong, Darby Milner, Elise Hahn, Lindsay Balfour, Natalia Gallo, Bethany Wade, Mir Rifat Salaheen, Ange-Aimee Quesnel, and Rachel Losier for their time and thoughts. I am deeply grateful to Christian Helm as well, who spent a semester here as a postdoctoral fellow, introducing my students to the importance of sociological theory to the history of social movements and providing many hours of delightful conversation.

This support at my home institution is magnified by the many wonderful colleagues who have supported my career and research through the Canadian Association of Latin American and Caribbean Studies. I am grateful for the companionship and intellectual community of this association, and in particular the individual members with whom I've worked closely over the years. I specifically thank Amie Kiddle, Julián Durazo Herrmann, Jorge Nallím, Gillian McGillivray, Roberta Rice, Alejandro Hernandez, Daniel Tubb, Carlota McAllister, Michael Kirkpatrick, Amitava Chowdhury, Tyler Shipley, Cristina Rojas, John Carlaw, and David Sheinin for their friendship, advice, and camaraderie.

In the Okanagan, I am blessed with friends outside of the academic community who have provided care and cheered me on, sometimes even helping me with child care or solving seemingly insurmountable problems. I give special thanks to Ash Allen, Astri Jack, Ainsley Kling, David Duncan, Roylene Nichols, Max Mueller, Marcia Maia Santos, Israel and Mila Shapiro, Hannah Krumbein, and Richard Amante. I cannot thank them enough for the thoughtfulness and love they have provided my family over the years. I am thankful for the love and support of Luke Rogers, Rodrigo Cañete, Tori Luna Petite, Travis Millard, and Jason Runyan. They have kept me afloat and been a reminder of what is most important in my life. For the profound joy and optimism that they bring me, from the bottom of my heart I thank Paloma, Julian, Reubin, Oskar, Westley, Maya, Luna, Julieta, Bia, Bruno, Jameson, Sam, Shaelyn, Liel, Rafa, Freya, Kabir, and Cam.

I acknowledge and thank the *Anuario—Jahrbuch für Geschichte Latein-amerikas* for allowing us to reprint sections of the chapter on Cuba and the *Journal of Iberian and Latin American Research* for allowing the reprinting of material from the chapter on the Southern Cone. Thank you to Gwen Walker for encouraging this project at the University of Wisconsin Press and to the two reviewers, Marc Becker and Tanya Harmer, whose comments on the manuscript were absolutely essential. I am particularly grateful that they were able to take time during a global pandemic, when schedules and lives have been turned upside down, to spend time thinking through my arguments and providing such valuable critiques.

I am truly grateful for the unwavering support of Christine Hatzky and Margaret Power, who have been fearless trailblazers and trusted companions over the years. They provided guidance to the writing and organization of the arguments in this book, critical feedback, and productive advice. I thank Christine for inviting me to be a visiting fellow at the Leibniz Universität in Hannover and for being my long-standing teammate in South-South solidarity research. I also thank her for the time she spends helping me navigate the complexities of academic life and for her friendship. Similarly, I thank Margaret for always turning up at my panels, making time to chat on the phone, sending long thoughtful letters, and keeping me connected to the histories and lives of a generation of activists that I greatly admire. Her comradeship has been a great blessing in my life.

There are a handful of people who have been intellectual anchors to me over the years as this project has developed. Not only have they spent long hours in conversation about the project, they have provided the kind of emotional support that is truly sustaining. Their sense of humor and willingness to listen has been a treasure. Jana Lipman's sharp mind and incredible ability to see connections has been a source of remarkable assistance. Martin Nesvig makes me laugh until my sides hurt. His generosity, reassurance, and thoughtful advice has improved my progress and lifted my spirits. I am grateful to Rohan D'Souza for keeping me aware of the meaning of history to the present and emboldening me to work harder by offering his confidence in my abilities. I thank Alison Bruey for her friendship and her excellent recommendations and thoughts on liberation theology and solidarity with Chile. I am grateful to Ernesto Capello, with whom I have shared so many adventures and thoughts over the years, and whose creativity and brilliance have been a constant source of stimulation. I'm grateful for his help in thinking through my arguments on visual history and on Cuba in the 1970s.

In spring 2002, I took the train down from New Haven to hear Mark Healey give a paper at the New York Latin American History Workshop. It was the first time I had been invited to attend anything as an historian-in-training. After the talk, a smaller group headed off to a restaurant. I didn't know it at the time, but this meeting was the beginning of something that profoundly shaped my life. Mark later kept me company in a hospital in Buenos Aires, sent references for my grant applications, and offered sage professional advice when I landed my first academic job, for all of which I am exceptionally grateful. But at the 2002 gathering, I also met Brenda Elsey, whose memory of the evening is much better than mine. From that first Friday evening, Brenda became a mainstay in my life. Over the years, she has asked the kind of questions that made me want to keep digging deeper and has offered the kind of analytical insights that have helped me find clarity. Beyond this, she is the person I most want to talk to every day, the person whose ideas and thoughts most delight me, and the person I trust with all of my uncertainties and doubts. I am in awe of her compassion, reflected in the many ways she shares her time and tremendous capability with others. She has read every chapter of this book, some more than once, and sat through dozens of presentations of its contents. I am humbled by her many labors of love for me.

I am deeply grateful to my family. They have supported me in every way. My maternal grandparents set aside savings so that my siblings and I could go to university, and my paternal grandparents inspired in us a love of history, a rebellious spirit, and a deep appreciation of the art of storytelling. I feel incredibly fortunate that my parents continually provide me with their own perspectives on the past and are willing to indulge me in long debates. My brother Barry has been my rock since childhood; no one could ask for a more steadfast friend.

Last, I wish to thank, in order of appearance, Eyal, Yuval, Ethan, Naomi, and Billy. They have given me plenty of reasons to think about what it is I choose to do for a living. Their attention to and awareness of the world around them inspires me, and getting to be a part of their lives is the most precious gift.

Abbreviations

AAPSO	Afro-Asian Peoples' Solidarity Organization
ANC	African National Congress
APRA	Alianza Popular Revolucionaria Americana (American Popular Revolutionary Alliance, Peru)
CCJP	Catholic Commission for Justice and Peace
CELAM	Consejo Episcopal Latinoamericano (Episcopal Bishops' Conference of Latin America)
COBEM	Comitê dos Brasileiros Exilados no México (Committee of Brazilian Exiles in Mexico)
DFS	Dirección Federal de Seguridad (Federal Security Directorate, Mexico)
DGIPS-AGN	Dirección General de Investigaciones Políticas y Sociales, Archivo General de la Nación (General Directorate of Political and Social Investigations, General Archive of the Nation)
ERP	Ejército Revolucionario del Pueblo (People's Revolutionary Army, Argentina)
FORA	Federación Obrera Regional Argentina (Argentine Regional Workers' Federation)

FRELIMO	Frente de Libertação de Moçambique (Mozambique Liberation Front)
FSLN	Frente Sandinista de Liberación Nacional (Sandinista National Liberation Front, Nicaragua)
GANEFO	Games of the New Emerging Forces
ICAIC	Instituto Cubano del Arte e Industria Cinematográficos (Cuban Institute of Cinematographic Art and Industry)
ICT	Institute of Contextual Theology (South Africa)
IIJ-UNAM	Instituto de Investigaciones Jurídicas, Universidad Nacional Autónoma de México (Institute of Legal Research, National Autonomous University of Mexico)
IMBISA	Inter-Regional Meeting of the Bishops of Southern Africa
MAS	Movimiento al Socialismo (Movement for Socialism, Argentina)
NAM	Non-Aligned Movement
OAS	Organization of American States
OLAS	Organización Latinoamericana de Solidaridad (Latin American Solidarity Organization)
OSPAAAL	Organización de Solidaridad con los Pueblos de Asia, África y América Latina (Organization of Solidarity with the Peoples of Africa, Asia, and Latin America)
PCA	Partido Comunista Argentina (Communist Party of Argentina)
PLO	Palestinian Liberation Organization
PO	Partido Obrero (Workers' Party, Argentina)
PRI	Partido Revolucionario Institucional (Institutional Revolutionary Party, Mexico)

PRM	Partido de la Revolución Mexicana (Mexican Revolutionary Party)
PRN	Partido Revolucionario Nacional (National Revolutionary Party, Mexico)
PRT	Partido Revolucionario de los Trabajadores (Workers' Revolutionary Party, Argentina)
PS	Partido Socialista (Socialist Party, Argentina)
SACBC	South African Catholic Bishop's Conference
SACC	South African Council of Churches
SRE	Secretaría de Relaciones Exteriores (Secretary of External Relations, Mexico)
UCM	University Christian Movement (South Africa)
UNAM	Universidad Nacional Autónoma de México (National Autonomous University of Mexico)
UNHCR	United Nations High Commissioner for Refugees
WCC	World Council of Churches

South-South Solidarity and the Latin American Left

Introduction

How We Think about Solidarity

You and I are separated by
a heap of contradictions
which come together,
galvanizing all my being.
Sweat starts from my brow,
now I am building you.

Miguel Barnet, "Revolución"

In describing the experience of revolution, Cuban ethnographer and poet Miguel Ángel Barnet alludes to the role of solidarity in bringing together those marked by difference and separated by distance in building a foundation for change.[1] Broadly defined, solidarity links the notion of collective responsibility with that of cooperation in pursuit of shared political goals. Acting in solidarity, articulated as a political position, can allow distant parties to orient themselves in larger struggles and align against powerful forces and actors. The term "solidarity" is also used to reflect the calculated relationships in which one group might engage to defend against the exploitation of or injustices committed against another. Welfare states, social movements, labor organizations, civil rights advocates, and activist organizations have used the concept to imply a set of duties ethically owed to others, but historians have begun to demand a more tangible notion of solidarity.

Writing the history of such an expansive pursuit is not a simple task. The first matter at hand is to situate solidarity in the lived experiences of its protagonists, and the second is to examine its relationship to moments of historical change. Latin American solidarity movements have been associated with many transnational revolutionary projects, particularly those of the internationalist left. Some such undertakings, like the Cuban Revolution, were successful, creating lasting ties of solidarity and providing meaningful support to distant parties. Others faced overwhelming obstacles, including violent suppression. The experience of solidarity has often been studied through the lens of social movements, as strategies of resistance and protest. Latin American solidarity movements have been examined primarily "on the ground," as equivalent to the organizing events of which they have formed part. The testimonies of participants, however, reveal this reading to be inadequate in describing the sprawling nature of solidarity politics and the impact such events can have on political views, agendas, and lives. Barnet's image of diverse bodies laboring, sweating, enduring, and ultimately creating change in struggle speaks to the necessity of a greater conceptualization of solidarity. This book introduces a set of challenges to our historical understanding of the experience of transnational solidarity movements and how they provoke change.

Solidarity movements are a vital part of Latin America's contemporary political reality. Those originating in Latin America, however, have been largely overlooked. These movements, prolific in the 1960s and 1970s, brought together participants from the Global South whose relationships were often considered far too peripheral to merit serious attention. South-South solidarity movements were often evaluated and dismissed according to certain forms of measurable success, such as the ability to recruit wider participation, secure a change in government, or forge long-term strategic alliances. Understanding the achievements of the South-South solidarity movements of these decades depends on the ability to turn our attention to their particularities and analyze them from more nuanced frames of reference. Beyond their immediate and material ends, South-South solidarity movements mobilized a consciousness among the Latin American left and provided an identifiable transnational space for critique and debate. These movements also provided a permanent site of resistance—visible not only in the historical record and collective memory but also in material traces and politicized spaces they left behind.

Individual participants have many kinds of encounters and entanglements with solidarity movements. They move both within and outside solidarity actions. They observe change from the center to the edges of movements and witness their own agency shift over time. Determining the usefulness of solidarity to the formation of political subjecthoods means dealing with long-lived experiences, various stirrings and beginnings, and refinings of consciousness. Participants experience geographies of belonging and dislocation—being compelled or challenged to find the correct distance from which to manage their experience of being "with" distant others and defining their own positionality.[2] In enacting solidarity, they also become a site through which an understanding of distant struggle is fashioned and exemplified, from which accurate translations of events and positions might be made. Those who act in solidarity enter an ever-evolving relationship with the movements themselves; the accomplishment of solidarity can thus be seen as a long, sometimes invisible process.

The success of a solidarity movement implies another set of concerns from the perspective of the lived experience. The cultural expression of solidarity, in a tremendous multiplicity of form, can shape both subjectivities and orientations. They may even determine the lens through which objectivity will be framed. As the cultural production of a movement influences the lives and bodies of their producers, it can also shape those of its audiences. These modes of production can challenge and disrupt, or, conversely, can nourish and provide collective grounding. They reproduce plural forms of awareness, thereby opening a path for contention and exploration, narratives and counternarratives. Moreover, the many cultural lives of a movement can help situate identities and provide a channel of interpretation across divides of space and time. As forms of critique, these same experiences can offer strategies of containment. The boundaries they produce might help mark the edges and limitations of mobilization.

In previous research, I grappled with some of the paradoxes of solidarity movements by focusing on the distinctions to be found between North-South and South-South solidarity movements, trying to isolate the factors that distinguished actions between highly unequal parties from those occurring in more reciprocal relationships of exchange.[3] In doing so, I found a need to challenge the conceptual categories that were used to dismiss the importance of South-South transnational political ties. Historians and social scientists of solidarity movements generally judge a movement's importance by whether it achieves its explicit objectives, and many movements of the Global South, with bold goals like ending imperialism or overturning a regime, frankly, failed. Determining the cause and nature of failure yields insight, but in this project, I propose a reassessment of how we evaluate solidarity movements. This book offers a different conceptual model of solidarity, one that takes a South-South perspective and privileges the complex workings of solidarity actions over a movement's stated aims.

For instance, I distinguish between the movement's origin and the impact of its cultural production, participation in actions that extend beyond the initial moment of protest. Such a strategy is necessary because solidarity actions are neither coterminous nor coextensive with the consciousness formation, affective ties, and political awakenings they inspire. Taking a South-South perspective calls for a reading of solidarity movements that actively seeks to recover the significance and irreducibility of this work. It considers more expansive solidarity contexts within which participants define their commitments. Considering solidarity as an iterative and generative process allows us to examine how political subjectivities form and shift over time. It also allows us to conceptualize how competing meanings of struggle are expressed and debated and how realignments and new courses of action can be set.[4]

Solidarity as Historical Feature of the Twentieth Century

As technologies of international travel and communication expanded in the twentieth century, organizing across borders began to flourish. Historians have noted that events like the October Revolution of 1917 precipitated a greater sense of the interconnectedness of class struggle across hemispheres and oceans, which in Latin America erupted in a wave of strikes culminating in 1919.[5] The movement of migrant populations through the empires of the nineteenth and twentieth centuries helped increase awareness of the conditions held in common by oppressed and marginalized peoples separated by great geographic distances.[6] Modes of transnational solidarity in the first half of the century often involved petition and letter-writing campaigns, fundraising, and sometimes volunteering for military service. International communism and labor movements were inherently oriented toward creating bridges of solidarity between workers through revolutionary industrial unionism that could transcend the nation-state, using mechanisms like the May Day International Workers' Day. Many early movements benefited from the efforts of enlightened writers and political leaders in positions of relative power and influence who circulated between the Americas and across the Atlantic. In the aftermath of the international war on communism and during periods of political repression, exile also created communities that served as important networks of political organizing outside and across the region.

Early historical traces of what we might consider the modern transnational solidarity movement can be seen in the strategies of such political organizations as the Communist International, which was committed to a broad and ambitious effort to push back capitalist and imperialist forces. The inclusion of colonized peoples and national liberation struggles in the Second and Third International broadened international solidarity by conceptually extending it more fully to the working classes.[7] Similarly, abolition movements that extended from metropolitan centers to colonial milieus provided a model of a networked solidarity—one that mobilized the work of collectives of intellectuals united around a cause.[8] Movements like these often relied on the intricate ties between preexisting social networks, including connections to powerful families, institutions, publications, political parties, and philanthropic societies.[9] Similarly, the success of independence movements, such as that of Haiti, the United States, and Mexico, provided ready examples of transborder resource mobilization and the usefulness of intellectual labor in laying critical ground work.[10] The earliest pan-American movements forged ties through independence struggles, often fostered in environments such as that of literary movements, sports competitions, scientific exchanges, and international forums that brought together Latin American delegations representing the interests of the region.[11] Transnational mobilization of labor solidarity, such as anarcho-syndicalism and mutualism, not only circulated through intellectual communities but also directly engaged workers' associations and communities of migrant laborers and ultimately worked through unions themselves.[12] All of these strategies can be seen as precursors to and influences on the solidarity movements that followed. In some cases, multiple strategies reinforced each other. Consider, for example, the organization of support for the Spanish Civil War in Argentina, built on preexisting anti-Yrigoyen networks and then mobilized through the anarchist labor organization of the Federación Obrera Regional Argentina (FORA, Argentine Regional Workers' Federation).[13] Combining these strategies enabled organizers to establish clear links between antifascism in Europe and local causes in the labor movement.

By the middle of the twentieth century, however, the precipitous collapse of the British and French empires, along with the rise to power of the United States and the Soviet Union, created a new dynamic that influenced the shaping of transnational solidarity movements. Correspondingly, most movements between 1950 and 1989, and to a large extent afterward, have been historically interpreted through the Orwellian framework of the Cold War.[14] Certainly, many movements have been concerned with the competition between superpowers. As the United States and Soviet Union vied to create imperial relationships with countries of the Global South, many responded to threats of war by proxy and global nuclear holocaust or confronted the ideological battles between capitalism and communism. Local leaders and regimes were often drawn into the Cold War fray to form useful alliances, seeking or resisting intervention, and finding justification to repress dissent. By 1968, large-scale demonstrations increased, and as media technologies facilitated the ability of such activities to reach a wide audience, such events brought together international support as one force in an effective coalition of protest.[15] It was also a period of increasing militancy, as various protagonists of the left sought radical social and political change.[16]

The historiographic debates that have emerged in the literature on solidarity during the Cold War offer a variety of insights. This is perhaps most evident in the case of Latin American history. Studies of the subject in the region attest to the scale and frequency of solidarity movements and present assessments of the historical significance they may have had. Most historical studies of Latin American solidarity approach the subject through a set of key debates: (1) how globalization influenced emergent forms of political citizenship, (2) the challenge posed by an international human rights movement, (3) the nature of East-West conflict during the Cold War, and (4) the history of rights and political representation. These debates provide nuanced perspectives on Latin America's history of international movements of solidarity after 1950. Taken together, they help reveal why, more broadly, this region is of particular interest to the study of solidarity.

In considering solidarity movements through the prism of globalization, some scholars have argued that solidarity movements provided a workshop of sorts, allowing new forms of political citizenship to be formulated and expressed. Not just reflecting new transnational dimensions, solidarity movements might, in this sense, be capable of expanding the range of political imaginaries and demands on the local and national levels. For example, Aldo Marchesi argues that transnational connections between militants in major capital cities of the Southern Cone provided a site for deep regional dialogue, which resulted in a common set of priorities, a new "repertoire of contention," among revolutionary projects, challenging previous histories of the period that failed to account for the importance of these encounters to the history of the Latin American left.[17] In another example, Cuba's internationalist educational missions in Angola yielded tremendous insights about racial solidarity across Afro-Latinx and African communities and became a sort of laboratory that increased awareness of colonialism and race relations within and outside of Cuba.[18] Latin American Catholic activism, influenced by a long history of social outreach, in connecting activists with support from religious networks around the globe, encouraged religious communities to reconsider their commitments to anticapitalist political struggles at home and abroad.[19] Similarly, Sandra McGee Deutsch, examining an earlier period, has credited the solidarity work of the Liga Argentina por los Derechos del Hombre (Argentine League for Human Rights), an offshoot of the Communist Party, with asserting and demanding women's citizenship from a framework of antifascism, revolutionary motherhood, and social embeddedness in community.[20] Whereas communist internationalism provided a vehicle for transnational solidarity, many of the more intriguing challenges to models of citizenship posed by these movements happened on the periphery of political parties and sometimes as a response to their limitations. During the Cold War, as parties of the political left were widely devastated by global antilabor and anticommunist campaigns, solidarity movements became the only organizing space for frustrated projects of and demands for new forms of political citizenship.

Histories of transnational solidarity in and with the region have helped explain the advance of an international human rights movement by the end of the century. In many cases, movements of national solidarity with Latin America helped in collectivizing and lending international support for resistance against military dictatorships in the region. Some scholars have argued that the elevation of these Latin American causes in Europe and the United States put pressure on authoritarian regimes via international diplomacy, and that in doing so, they facilitated the communication and preservation of the lived experiences of struggle and violence that galvanized support for human rights organizations and initiatives in international agencies.[21] For example, Alison Brysk's groundbreaking study of social movements in Argentina and their impact on international institutions was followed by several other studies that confirmed the broad influence of these movements.[22] More recently, Elizabeth Jelin has captured the institutional dimensions of many of the challenges presented by such movements against dictatorship in the region and the demands for social and collective rights that emerged under democratically elected leaders.[23] Scholars like Kathryn Sikkink have looked at the role played by trials of military juntas in articulating and demonstrating the confines of these movements in the region.[24] James Brennan and Greg Grandin, along with other scholars, have criticized rights-based solidarity movements working on behalf of Latin America for prioritizing the rights of the individual over collective interests, thus producing greater inequalities despite supporting demands for democracy.[25] International support for Latin America unequivocally opened up space for local human rights movements despite these tendencies.

Scholars have also argued that solidarity movements present meaningful insights into the East-West context of the Cold War and the prolific neoimperialist activities of the United States and the Soviet Union in the region. Some international relations scholars have concentrated on the movement of military resources and guerilla operations across the area, while others have considered the contest of competing ideologies and how solidarity movements played into larger national and international conflicts. Odd Arne Westad contends that it is impossible to appreciate the decision making of Washington or Moscow without a thorough understanding of the process of decolonization and experiments with socialism in the Third World.[26] This argument is echoed by other scholars, like Van Gosse, who asserted that the rise of the new international left was heavily influenced by solidarity with revolutionary Cuba and

Vietnam.[27] Gosse argues that solidarity in places like Central America could be readily organized to resist U.S. imperialism and protest U.S. support for military dictatorships. This provided a political project narrow enough to channel the energies of a wide variety of organizations and groups, but the pluralism it expressed may have ultimately foreclosed the ability to propose new models of socialist reform.[28] The Nicaraguan Revolution offers a particularly striking example. By allowing "brigades" of activists from around the world to come together and participate in their revolution, the Sandinista government was capable of creating a highly sophisticated interpersonal network of solidarity activism that presented a significant challenge to the counterrevolutionary project of the United States.[29]

Other scholarship has considered the circulation of important figures of Latin America's revolutionary left in the capitals of Eastern and Western Europe, Africa, and Asia, where they found encouragement, financial support, and ideological inspiration. These scholars examine the participation of these traveling revolutionary actors in generating support for national liberation movements and shaping ideas of solidarity among sympathetic groups.[30] A few authors have examined the influence of Latin American solidarity movements on movements in Western Europe, the Soviet Union, and countries in the Eastern Bloc.[31] Some of these histories, building on recently declassified documents, uncover elements of solidarity in armed struggles that had merely been rumored. For example, Miguel Angel Reyes explores the collaboration between guerrilla movements that formed a coalition between Ecuador and Colombia facilitated through training and clandestine resource transfers in Libya. This form of solidarity, resource exchange, and cooperation between militants, Reyes argues, created a shared trans-Andean revolutionary project, which revived the idealism of previous Bolivarian movements and leveled effective critiques against partisan tendencies in each national context.[32]

One of the most productive areas of solidarity research on Latin America can be found in the extensive histories of movements generated in the United States. Margaret Power and Julie Charlip argue that U.S.-based solidarity movements with Latin America are dissimilar from workers' solidarity movements in that they "stem from and respond to more similar realities and experiences." They maintain that these movements often speak more to the revolutionary aspirations held by participants for their own futures.[33] Regarding U.S. solidarity with Chile, Power further argues that solidarity activists found a way to express their frustration with the corruption of the U.S. government and the involvement of corporations in violent intervention, while raising consciousness via North American media outlets about the human rights violations and torture suffered in Chile under Pinochet.[34] These activities, led by organizations like Non-Intervention in Chile, included circulating newsletters and bulletins on political prisoners and highlighting the conditions of workers. Heidi Tinsman reports that the activities of more than one hundred groups organized across the United States against the military regime in Chile led to the greater use of the consumer boycotts that had significant and lasting effects on farm workers' movements across the hemisphere.[35] By contrast, in examining labor solidarity between U.S. and Central American activists, scholars like Rebecca Johns and Jeffrey Gould have critiqued some strategies as accommodationist. Such exchanges can be inadequate, they argue, when failing to challenge the allocative mechanisms of capitalism and the privileging of workers in the United States over those in and from the region, making their impact limited, if not destructive.[36]

Many scholars consider the most meaningful results of solidarity mobilizations to be in shaping the way U.S. power operates in Latin America.[37] Aviva Chomsky and Steve Striffler assert that in the 1980s and 1990s, globalization and solidarity with Central American labor movements against the policies of Ronald Reagan finally shifted this balance beyond the ideological strictures of the Cold War.[38] However, Striffler notes that human rights organizing ultimately may have crowded out other forms of solidarity. Despite putting important pressure on the United States and increasing the visibility of labor struggles, solidarity with the Latin American left eventually faced challenges of discontinuity and conflicts of purpose. Internationalist solidarity, he asserts, lacked a common vision for restructuring the world and its economic and political power relations. Striffler concludes that "this was solidarity without politics."[39] Contrariwise, Teishan Latner and Cynthia Young argue that solidarity with the Cuban Revolution challenged the U.S. left from the mid-1960s onward and maintained pressure on it to push demands for racial justice, socialist economic reforms, and internationalism. Latner notes that although this influence contracted by the 1970s, the connections made with political parties like the Black Panthers and the Young Lords left an important legacy, which the U.S. left was forced to continually revisit.[40] Clearly the offer of solidarity from groups like these was welcomed by the Cuban revolutionary state; what remains less clear is whether expressions of solidarity materialized into meaningful exchange.

A final major historiographic debate relates to the importance of the support of transnational solidarity movements for civil and minority rights struggles in Latin America. For instance, some scholars have noted how critically important the regional left was in organizing support for indigenous Mayans in the aftermath of the Guatemalan Civil War.[41] Martha Vanessa Saldívar similarly argues that student and exile activism on behalf of Palestine in Mexico has assisted in creating "communities-in-relation" that not only facilitated the articulation of critiques of problematic political constructs, such as national security, but also intimately linked local struggles around border walls, policing, and minority representation.[42] Furthermore, a number of scholars argue that Latin American solidarity movements provided spaces for battles over representation, particularly with respect to women's rights, queer politics, and, in a few cases, the struggle of peoples of color.[43] The transnational solidarity of the 1960s provided gestational spaces for a handful of minority rights movements that emerged in the mid-1970s and thereafter. However, a considerable amount of work remains to be done to further our understanding of the mechanics through which transnational solidarity relates to gender, sexuality, and race and to indigenous and minority politics and movements.

These important historiographic debates contribute to our understanding of the location of solidarity movements in larger geopolitical events and present an important contextualization of some of the primary concerns of the Latin American left during this period. However, this volume moves this conversation forward to consider what might be learned from centering Latin America's own projects of solidarity. Aldo Marchesi argues that although many studies contribute important insights into national-level experiences of imperialism and resistance, they still exhibit "historical vacuums related to transnational spaces of horizontal circulation of ideas and actors within the region."[44] In turning our historical attention to South-South solidarity, I do not argue that these movements operated completely outside of the work of North-to-South movements and international relations, nor do I ignore the constant pressures applied by U.S. intervention on Latin America's left. As I hope to make clear, focusing on South-South solidarity movements reveals the uniqueness of how Latin American movements envisioned solidarity and what they hoped to achieve. Repositioning our gaze onto South-South solidarity foregrounds ideas and strategies of transnational solidarity rooted in regional experiences and reveals Latin American agency in solidarity with the Global South.

Solidarity in Social Movement Theory

Solidarity is a critical component of organizing on the left and is foundational to the claims of progressivism of all kinds.[45] Social scientists and theorists have approached the study of solidarity largely through the framework of social movements. Although many of the early questions driving the study of solidarity concerned the relationship of class interests, labor and capital, social welfare demands, and the role of positive moral duties, events such as the collapse of the international labor movement and the crisis of the Communist International led social theorists to reflect on and reevaluate how solidarity operates.[46] Theorists like Jürgen Habermas turned their attention to solidarity and social movements in light of these setbacks.[47] Moral and political philosophers explored questions of how to understand and define solidarity, returning to queries posed by Émile Durkheim about the nature of solidarity. Durkheim argued that solidarities were most likely to emerge between groups that saw themselves as having common causes or with a relationship that could be expressed as an interdependency.[48] Social theorists who followed this tradition analyzed the conditions that favored an individual's participation in relationships of solidarity in terms of questions of moral behavior and rational choice.[49] Some theorists argued that the motivation for particular acts on behalf of distant others was functionally similar to other acts of altruism. This was a move away from economic models based on class or labor, pointing to humanitarian resource transfers as a clear measure of commitment to and appreciation of the common good.[50]

International human rights movements, as humanitarian projects that took aim at the state, reinforced global governance. As a result, theorists of social movements were challenged to address questions posed by the rising prominence of nongovernmental organizations and transnational legal institutions, which provided opportunities for solidarity activities to gain momentum.[51] Sally Scholz's groundbreaking work on political solidarity argues that movements opposing oppression or injustice have the power to assert or strengthen notions of justice, thereby unifying those participating in solidarity actions.[52] Her work has been used to help frame international solidarity in the Americas during the Cold War, alongside that of Kurt Weyland, who offered a model of diffusion to help explain the spread of policies of repression and the responses and calls for reform they engendered.[53] Political solidarities understood in light of the human rights movement have been measured against their promises to enact change. They have been critiqued for merely expressing a symbolic solidarity and failing to stimulate structural change. As such, they have the potential to reinforce hegemonic forces, particularly when inattentive to the consequences of solidarity actions for the most vulnerable.[54] Expressions of solidarity offer a means by which one group might offer mutual recognition or suggest belonging in a moral community that encompasses groups that are considered outsiders, but challenging power structures as instruments of exclusion and inclusion did not always follow acts of solidarity. Social movement theorists thus understood such political expressions to be successful only when able to demonstrate a more direct confrontation with class hierarchies, national borders, gender roles, or other structures of power.[55] The work of Juliet Hooker, for instance, has been influential in situating questions of race and minority rights in political solidarity, questioning how antiracism solidarity truly attends to the needs of racial minorities.[56]

Hooker's work points to one of the central considerations brought to bear by social scientists and historians on social movement theorists' frameworks for understanding transnational solidarity: the premise that any expression of solidarity might be a relatively uniform business. She sets theorists the task of accounting for and distinguishing between the nuances of movements based on their particular historical circumstances. For instance, an international movement in solidarity with African American civil rights should present dimensions in terms of its response to questions of what solidarity means and to questions of motivation that are different from the dimensions the same movement would present when acting in solidarity with a national liberation movement in Africa. However, most social movement theory presents solidarity actions as being largely undifferentiated, monolithic political activities, rather than the multifarious network of relationships and activities that actually form these movements in history. For this reason, important questions remain about social movements that have yet to be fully developed in relationship with solidarity movements, and, as one might expect, very little work has been done on "peripheries" considered at the margins of grand narratives of history.[57] Postcolonial and transnational feminist scholars have challenged these premises, providing the inspiration for this work.[58]

Theorists of feminist transnational social movements who have taken up the challenge of understanding solidarity in its historical complexities have been particularly productive around questions of mobilizing identities, alterity, and representations of the subaltern. These lines of inquiry have led to the mapping of individuals and networks active in solidarity movements in efforts to deepen our understanding of their social history and backgrounds.[59] It has equally motivated studies on the nuances of experiences between different groups in a national solidarity context.[60] Feminist theorists of transnational social movements have also presented a valuable new set of critiques related to structural movement constraints.[61] The work of postcolonial theorists has drawn attention to some of the means by which they might reproduce colonial discourses. As Gayatri Spivak argues, "In the production of knowledge and the new narrativization of that older script it has to be treated with some caution; Third World peoples in the First World claiming that title has [sic] to be treated with some caution. Perhaps even because, in the very locus of their struggle, they have an interest in dominant global capitalism."[62] Scholars like Spivak have pointed to "distant issue" movements and those organized by diasporic populations as building on difference, suggesting that they might ultimately be used to justify clientelism in foreign policy. Scholz describes a similar kind of phenomenon as "parasitic solidarity," and much of this scholarship has found that North-South solidarities have often resulted in increasing political and economic inequities between these regions of the world.[63] These critiques reflect a greater theoretical focus on transnational solidarity movements as mobilizations of resources and on calculating their impact in terms of influence on diplomatic relationships.

During this period in Latin America, the reemergence of the left and the rise of social movements that followed the return to democracy in many countries prompted new studies that employed theories of social movements to map the advance of these actions. Social movement theories were used to examine the role such movements may play in advancing progressive social reforms and in preventing the region from falling back into authoritarianism.[64] Latin American theorists noted the absence of cross-class or class-based alliances in many of the new social movements emerging in the 1980s and 1990s.[65] Maristella Svampa refers to this as a "crisis of paradigms" in terms of the study of collective action, one acutely problematic in countenancing the rising influence of a global neoliberal elite.[66] Considering the effect of social movements on democratization, Ruth Cardoso argues that international political identities and negotiating strategies exhibited troubling tendencies, reinforcing patterns of clientelism and undermining the autonomy of local participants.[67] For instance, Eduardo Viola looks critically at the kind of solidarity offered by environmental movements and conservationists, arguing that it underscores the failures of new forms of transnational organizing by undermining local projects aiming to protect indigenous rights.[68] Many scholars of Latin American solidarity movements have looked at indigenous social movements that have crossed borders, such as the pan-Maya movement of Central America and southern Mexico, solidarity movements along the U.S.-Mexico and U.S.-Canada borders, and the solidarity between the National Liberation Zapatista Army in Mexico or with the Mapuche following the murder of Camilo Catrillanca as illustrating problems of governance and limitations of access to citizenship rights.[69]

Scholars of international solidarity movements have powerfully critiqued the transnational framework of organizing as indirectly reinforcing the nation-state as primary in defining political subjecthood. Verónica de la Torre highlights that the focus of many international solidarity movements is to enact change via the state, thus empowering the state as the primary agent of expressions of collective action.[70] In various ways, these studies uncover some of the problems with theorizing about solidarity without disentangling modes of social solidarity on the national or local levels. New forms of international solidarity emerging from Latin America should not be conflated with those of the North-to-South human rights movement. It would be fair to say that theorists in Latin America were less enthusiastic about the promise of the international solidarity movements of the 1980s and 1990s. New cosmopolitan constructions of political identity did not seem to provide meaningful means of combating economic inequality, injustice, and other social ills in the region. For instance, the human rights movement shifted agency away from local social movements to international nongovernmental organizations. As such, meaningful participation in an imagined global democracy became even less accessible to those most marginalized by the nation-states through which these organizations were ultimately forced to operate.[71]

In the 2000s, the study of transnational solidarity has expanded and begun to reflect a new set of questions, driven by a new focus on the injustices created by global neoliberalism. Social movement theorists have begun to ask questions regarding sharing of risk and the mechanisms by which collective action might lead to governance institutions better able to protect the global commons, as well as about how solidarity movements on behalf of the displaced victims of wars and environmental crisis might redefine notions of political community.[72] Theorists working to understand solidarity movements have tended to sharpen their focus on social networks and media infrastructures.[73] They have begun to fill in some of the gaps left by other theoretical models by taking into greater account the affective politics of social movements and by proposing a model of solidarity as care work.[74] Going beyond asking questions about why a movement might come together, what elements favor success or failure, and what challenges they present to political identities and subjecthood, social theorists have brought previous understandings of solidarity into dialogue with debates on and provocations of contemporary movements.

Historians have much to offer to this new set of theoretical debates by acting as guides to the many ways the past has informed the present. This book's view of transnational solidarity is embedded in a sociocultural historical approach to understanding the construction of political subjects. It focuses on the spaces where participants are offered a voice and are able to engage. Rather than centering analysis on how a movement might consolidate its position on a global stage—a stage that might have as the principal concern maintaining the state and a particular form of international order—it asks how individuals experience the ability to transform their own realities on the ground.

Latin American Solidarity with the Global South

The history of South-South relations has not always figured prominently in the grand narratives of the twentieth century for various reasons. Being subordinate to the history of great powers, European wars, the construction and maintenance of empires, and other themes, countries that have not been geopolitically empowered in the same manner have usually been considered somehow less significant. This perspective is changing rapidly, however. The point of departure for this study follows on the heels of a recent spate of publications that have shed new light on the intricate ways the countries that identify themselves as being part of the Global South have established meaningful connections. A recognition of common cause across regions of the Global South has mobilized tremendous political strength through transregional cooperation and solidarity movements since the 1950s. This project examines the transnational solidarity organizing that emerged during the late 1960s and early 1970s from Latin America and the Caribbean, at the height of the period of mobilizing activities that historians defined as the long "global sixties."[75] It addresses key moments that influenced the political relationships between solidarity efforts in Latin America and emerging transnational ideational "communities." Specifically, it looks at transnational solidarity as a global project of the Latin American left, one naturally fragmented across decades, changing regimes, tumultuous revolutionary projects, and national borders, but nonetheless with significant and lasting influence.[76]

I have elsewhere argued that Latin American solidarity movements were high-visibility moments during the Cold War, capturing attention from around the globe and mobilizing critical consciousness around distant causes outside of the region and those taking place in domestic spheres.[77] This research builds on those findings by asking how South-South movements of solidarity influenced or contributed to long-range struggles. My central argument is that the efforts of the Latin American left mattered and are worthy of a central place in narratives of internationalism in the twentieth century. This study examines the multiple ways movements originating in Latin America participated in constituting, maintaining, and advancing a distinctive framework of South-South solidarity. It challenges the view that Latin Americans have operated at a remove from other anti-imperialism and antiracism solidarity projects given their displacement from the narratives of imperial experiences in French- and English-speaking parts of the world.[78] The many ways Latin America offered solidarity across and beyond the region present new horizons for theorizing transnational social movements, which is the crux of the argument of this book.

The chapters are organized around four primary agents of solidarity that can mobilize change by and on behalf of movements: the state, international institutions, political parties, and social networks. These collective spaces and organizations provide traditional vehicles through which political resources are assembled and put into action. I identify four case studies, each of which can be taken as an example of the strength of a particular mode of South-South solidarity organizing. Although each chapter is presented from a particular national context, the movements were certainly not contained within national boundaries. I chose events that were of a global significance broad enough to allow them to be recognized as important successes, if not universally then certainly in the context of conversations across the international left. Unpacking the dynamic tensions between the historical events, social structures, prominent actors, and ideological challenges of widely recognized movements allows Latin American efforts to be historically reframed. It also presents an opportunity to advance a particular set of ideas about South-South transnational solidarity and political possibility.

The case studies illustrate a variety of methodological approaches to present unique aspects of the interpretative framework advocated in this volume. In each chapter, I argue for conceptualizing South-South solidarity in a specific way to assess its various successes, failures, accomplishments, and limitations. Each case study is meant to deepen my argument by paying attention to its practices. This approach foregrounds a particular way of expanding our understanding of the work of solidarity, intended to demonstrate some of the nuanced mechanisms that the Latin American left used to advance causes on behalf of distant others. The specific mechanisms underscored in each chapter can be understood as overlapping, multiple, and intimately interconnected with those presented in the others. By centering the multifaceted interplay between the transnational dimensions of these movements and their national contexts, this research hopes to address Hooker's challenge and offer insight into the uniqueness of Latin America's experience of the global sixties.

Expanding Conceptualizations of Solidarity

One of the principal goals of this book is to examine what South-South solidarity meant to the Latin American left, to those that offered and organized solidarity. A starting point for thinking about what is different about what took place within and beyond the region during this period has to do with the revolutionary state. Understanding and interpreting the role of the revolutionary state in Latin America in mobilizing consequential transnational solidarity actions demands an expansion of thinking about solidarity movements to include actors who were able to mobilize from within public institutions. Solidarity movements are certainly aimed at altering structures of power, but we often neglect to consider just how long it takes to effect changes from within the confines of legal environments and bureaucracies. To push back against powerful forces or to make room to devote resources to those that exist outside of the state's official mandate requires constancy and dedication. The notion of a revolutionary state in Latin America provided a powerful source of legitimacy to the left in arguing for legal mechanisms that might be used to effect solidarity. Revolutionary governments were poised to allow solidarity movements influence over the priorities of reformers in institutions, policy makers, and those holding public office. The first chapter considers the case of long-standing legal debates on political asylum in Mexico and the state's willingness to receive exiles as a tool of solidarity.

The second chapter considers the case of Cuba's revolutionary state and its commitment to internationalism. It expands on a set of practices of solidarity—which I refer to as rendering—as a mode of mobilizing a kind of historical agency embedded in cultural form, visual objects, and texts that are produced as acts of solidarity. Building on the conceptual argument that transnational social movements "in the work of framing social discourses, present visual and performative pathway-spaces through which subjectivities can be crafted and realigned," rendering solidarity is perhaps one of the most expedient tools of transnational solidarity movements.[79] The choice of the word "rendering" relates to its several meanings. "To render" can mean to provide or to give, such as to "render service," and can be used to describe the means by which knowledge of some form is submitted for consideration or otherwise delivered. For instance, the phrase "render judgment" is used to indicate a process of submitting a verdict or opinion, implying that deliberation or the application of some sort of ethical framework to an idea or an act has informed its conveyance. The notion of rendering solidarity points to the many ways cultural practices and forms can communicate judgment, suggest ethical considerations, describe the particularity of events, and frame narratives in the service of political consciousness. Perhaps most critically, "to render" also means to bring into being. The power of the cultural production of solidarity to generate new political imaginaries allows us to see beyond the specific moments during which movements operate. Examining Cuba's production and circulation of cultural renderings in solidarity, this chapter explores how the Cuban revolutionary state's commitment to internationalism established far-reaching political influence.

To fully measure the importance of Latin American South-South solidarity, however, it is necessary to consider what effects it had on participants. The cultural forms and practices of solidarity certainly affected the politics of representation of the left. Expanding our conceptualization of solidarity to consider how it can intersect with internal representational politics illuminates another important way that transnational solidarity mattered. The argument of this book follows this line to explore representational solidarity as a form of multiple intersecting political consciousnesses—recognizing alterity and difference but also attending to the necessity of self-representation. To publicly act in solidarity, to identify oneself or one's cause with those of another, means to participate in representational strategies of interconnection. Such strategies can combine causes that might even be in conflict. They can respond to the experience of a particular cause without diminishing the weight or tension of another. Often representational solidarity uses this tension—and sometimes historical or geographical distance—to produce fruitful comparisons or connections. For instance, representational solidarity might be useful when a particular local cause lacks an adequate constituency to be advanced or suffers from a lack of determinacy, wherein the meaning of a cause could be easily misconstrued or co-opted. This form of solidarity also offers the ability to deal with internal conflict through the pluralization of political consciousness, creating spaces from which to articulate points of debate or new meanings. Signaling a synchronicity between two disparate events, representational solidarity can provide a clearer sense of meaning and generate a larger base of support in a complicated context. The third chapter of this book examines just such a case: Argentine solidarity with Palestinian nationalism. It argues that during moments of political crisis, this solidarity offered parties of the left a way of finding and expressing unity while articulating their ideological identities and pursuing their own, often conflictive agendas.

Latin American solidarity with the Global South, beyond its effect on participants, has had important consequences and aftereffects for those on the receiving end. Some of these were certainly direct, but others were the result of practices that created lasting influence and facilitated strong transnational sites of resistance. I argue that to recognize the longer reach of the Latin American left's solidarity, solidarity must also be understood as complex. Solidarity can be used to describe the multiple, compound forms of agency over extended periods of time provided by complex organizational structures. Solidarity movements are often seen as networks of social agency, but I argue that solidarity must also be seen as networked social actors requiring access to sites of agency. Strategic maneuvers are not just advanced through interpersonal relationships; they necessitate opportune moments and serviceable mechanisms of exchange. Such solidarity occurs when a set of actors has access to connected but distinct organizational locations and multifaceted institutional connections from which to leverage action. Like a complex of facilities, individual elements (such as institutions or networks) in a successful complex of solidarity are interconnected in such a way as to constantly reinforce and necessitate each other. Together, they maintain a stability capable of countenancing threats to any individual part. In essence, multilayered and entangled opportunity structures allow for networked individual actors to have influence in multiple interconnected arenas, making it more difficult for such interventions to be thwarted or dismissed. Knotty, multisited connections can advance a cause directly and indirectly, subtly or brazenly, as openings appear from manifold directions. Solidarity through complex structures can provide a sophisticated means by which essential architecture is constructed and maintained. Its principal achievement is that it has the ability to outlast individual leaders, can resist the bureaucratic pressures of containment in institutions, and can sustain the fluctuations—including legal challenges—of political parties and open demonstrations. To illustrate this concept, the last case study examines the influence of the transnational Latin American left on the struggle against apartheid in South Africa. It presents the circulation of ideas and practices of Latin American liberation theology as they were incorporated into ongoing antiapartheid struggles and as they inspired anti-imperialist activism among Catholic activists in Southern Africa. This case provides an example of solidarity in a complex form and shows how this form of political agency is able to create opportunity for solidarity actions to create change beyond their own temporal reach.

Sources and Contents

As a work of transnational history, this volume is the result of a decade of archival research in multiple sites. Each chapter relies on archival records related to the case study in question. Chapter 1 considers the case of Mexico's solidarity with Chilean political asylum seekers in the aftermath of the 1973 military coup, a movement recognized for its capacity to facilitate the organizing of a broad international effort. Research in Mexico was conducted at the Archivo General de la Nación (AGN, National Archive), the Ministry of External Relations, and the Archive of the Instituto de Investigaciones Jurídicas at the Universidad Nacional Autónoma de México (IIJ-UNAM, Institute of Legal Research, National Autonomous University of Mexico), all in Mexico City, where I was able to access documents produced by legal scholars and activist reformers and various offices of the Mexican state, including newly released police investigation records and diplomatic correspondence. I was able to consider how the Mexican news media interpreted various reforms, perceived the reception of Chilean and other political asylum seekers, and reported on solidarity activities. The papers of the Department of the Interior housed at the AGN provided clues to the many ways important communities, including university students, youth and labor organizations, and political parties, were able to respond to and incorporate Chileans into activism on the ground.

Chapter 2 examines the unprecedented influence of Cuba's Organización de Solidaridad con los Pueblos de Asia, África y América Latina (OSPAAAL, Organization of Solidarity with the Peoples of Africa, Asia, and Latin America) in promoting Tricontinentalist solidarity through widely distributed print media and visual artifacts. Research relied on OSPAAAL's archive in Havana, now permanently closed; the poster collection at the Sam Slick Collection at the University of New Mexico; and reports on the Tricontinental meetings archived in the AGN in Mexico. This chapter explores solidarity from a visual and cultural history perspective, analyzing the evolution of Cuba's self-presentation and the documentation of its political relationships in solidarity movements launched in North Africa, Southern Africa, and the Middle East. I consulted the United Nations archive in New York City, where I was able to access meeting notes, correspondence, working group agendas, annotated speeches, and other documents that could attest to the concerns of the Afro-Asian solidarity bloc and Cuba's involvement in resolutions and debates in this space. The chapter examines the interplay between the image-based work of Cuban solidarity organizations and the strategies of solidarity they reinforced for targeted audiences at the United Nations and in the Non-Aligned Movement (NAM).

Chapter 3 offers the case of solidarity among Argentine leftist groups with the cause of Palestinian national liberation in the wake of increasing conflict in the Middle East. For this chapter, records were consulted in the Centro de Documentación e Investigación de la Cultura de Izquierdas and the archives of leftist political parties in Buenos Aires, alongside the John and Janet Wallach Papers at Princeton University's Firestone Library. This chapter offers a sociocultural interpretation of political organizing on behalf of Palestine in Argentina, reflecting how Argentine leftists mobilized their own identification with the Palestinian Liberation Organization (PLO). It also examines how Argentine leftists contemplated pan-Arabism and Nasserism as political movements. The chapter takes into consideration the activities of the Arab League and the Organization of Arab States in Argentina, which included the movement of key figures between continents, using records from the Central Zionist Archives in Jerusalem and the National Security Archive in Washington, DC. I consulted the archive of the Jabotinsky Institute in Tel Aviv, which included important anti- and pro-Zionist Argentine pamphlets, educational materials, and correspondence. These documents revealed strategies related to youth organizing, reactions to the creation of the state of Israel, Soviet interaction with Palestine, and the wars of the Israel-Palestine conflict. I traveled to the Library of Congress and the National Archives in the United States and to the Ibero-American Institute in Berlin to track down rare publications produced by various Argentine intellectual and political figures of the left not available elsewhere.

Finally, chapter 4 considers the influence of Latin American liberation theology and the intricate networks of Catholic solidarity organizing in the struggle against apartheid in South Africa. This chapter examines public speeches, political essays, correspondence, library collections, media coverage, minutes of organizing meetings, resolution advocacy at congresses, Catholic publications, and political pamphlets held at the Archive of the Archdiocese of Cape Town. This archive holds one of the richest collections of materials related to religious solidarity organizing in the country, partly because many of the headquarters of other major organizations, such as that of the South African Bishops' Council, were frequently threatened by the apartheid state, and two were destroyed by arson. I also consulted the South African History Archive in Johannesburg, which houses a collection of political documents related to the international antiapartheid movement and the related struggle against South African imperialism in the region. The findings from these archives are complemented by sources found in special collections at Stanford University's Hoover Institute and in digital archives hosted by Michigan State University, the University of Witwatersrand, and the National Archives and Records Service of South Africa.

I should note that the research for this volume was by no means exhaustive, and in each case study, there remain many details to uncover and additional archives that could be usefully consulted. This is particularly true concerning limited access to the fragmented and dispersed archives of the PLO, which have been elusive to many scholars. The current state of archival collections of materials related to the Latin American left has much improved, but given the precarity of the left's activities during much of this vital period, far more remains to be unearthed, collected, and preserved. By offering insight into moments of heightened tension or activity, historians can point to noticeable absences in archives. One of the advantages of transnational historical research is that it can sometimes locate external archives that speak to silences and omissions in a particular national historical record. In a way, it is also in the act of documenting the past that social movements have found power. Solidarity narratives can cross multiple generations and navigate vast geographies. Solidarity movements, through archival traces, transcend temporal limitations and provide alternative locations of memory, keeping record of past injustices and becoming living repositories of organized resistance. This study focuses on Latin American South-South movements of the 1960s and 1970s. As each new iteration of this solidarity history emerges, it is continually being reheard, revisited, and remapped onto the continuing struggles of the present.

1

The Revolutionary
Latin American State

On 5 February 1917 in Santiago de Querétaro—a city that came to the attention of the international public in 1867 as the site of the execution of Emperor Maximiliano—Mexico's revolutionary forces convoked a constitutional congress. This momentous occasion in the long and tumultuous path of the Mexican Revolution marked a signal event for the Latin American left. The resulting document would be the first modern constitution to include social rights.[1] Mexico's 1917 constitution not only provided a foundation for leftists and reformers to argue for the validity of a revolutionary state but also offered an early hint of one of the pivotal ways that states could provide a mechanism for solidarity action. News of the sweeping nature of the new constitutional provisions spread quickly, providing inspiration to proponents of the October Revolution in Russia and laying a blueprint of demands that would take hold across the region. Articles 3 (on public education), 27 (on land reform), and 123 (on labor rights) are perhaps its most well known, but the congressional congress also adopted Articles 11 and 15, which related to individuals defined as "foreigners," or *extranjeros*. These articles protected foreigners' rights to enter, exit, and travel through Mexico. They also guaranteed them freedom from extradition treaties meant to enforce laws that contravened the interpretation of rights in Mexico. Although the new constitution limited the political activities and property rights of foreigners, these laws were intended to reiterate Mexico's resistance to the dictates of its aggressive northern neighbor.

The establishment of Mexico's cultural status as a safe haven from political violence elsewhere can be traced to its refusal to sign on to fugitive slave treaties. In 1824, after defeating Spanish colonial rule, the Mexican state prohibited the slave trade, formally abolishing it in 1829. Between 1836 and 1845, thousands of enslaved people sought refuge in Mexico, and fugitives were formally included in the 1857 constitution under Title I, Section I, Article 2, which states, "Slaves that set foot upon the national territory shall recover, by this act alone, their freedom and enjoy the protection of the law"; this clause is reproduced verbatim in the 1917 document.[2] Article 22 of the 1857 constitution further underscores the humanitarian nature of these provisions by prohibiting punishment by mutilation, branding, flogging, or torture of any kind, unambiguously naming and thus emphasizing the specific forms of humiliation and violence perpetuated against enslaved people in the United States.[3] Article 15 of both constitutions provided that no treaty would be upheld that extradited political offenders, of which enslaved people were seen as one class, when the offense, such as escape from slavery, contradicted the rights of man enshrined in the constitution.

Mexico's constitutional protections against the encroachment of the U.S. protected its legal autonomy. The lack of extradition treaties between the two countries encouraged many runaway slaves to head to the border and became the subject of widespread folklore, inspiring several notable outlaws and vulnerable political figures to escape across the border. Despite the large number of economic and political activities that crossed the border in the second half of the nineteenth century, public opinion steadily prevented the Mexican government from cooperating with the United States on enforcement of its criminal investigations and from entering into any agreements until 1882, when "savage Indian raids" were finally declared sufficient cause for U.S. law enforcement officers to cross the border without express permission. This was the only significant concession Mexico made to the United States around extradition law until well into the 1930s, when common ground was finally found between the postrevolutionary Mexican state and the United States on the subject of organized crime and illicit trade, which had escalated between the two world wars.[4]

The 1917 Mexican constitution announced a revolutionary state in Latin America. This concept emerged in part from ongoing independence struggles and movements of resistance to U.S. encroachment beyond its hemispheric boundaries and began to take shape fully as Mexico's postrevolutionary ruling party realized the power of revolutionary rhetoric in consolidating its power. According to David Armstrong, "a revolutionary state is one whose relations with other states are revolutionary because it stands, in some sense, for fundamental change in the principles on the basis of which states conduct their relations with one another."[5] Although a revolutionary state can also be defined as one in the midst of or the product of revolutionary change, a revolutionary posture is a unique form of agency in both state formation and diplomatic spheres. Examining Mexico as a revolutionary state also speaks to a refusal to abandon the projects of the revolution and the ongoing role assigned to the state to serve as an agent of revolutionary change. In essence, to see the Latin American state from the vantage point of how people experienced the changes brought by the revolution, true revolutionaries would be those that enforced the revolutionary constitution.[6] In declaring itself to be a revolutionary state in the 1920s, Mexico illustrated a model for change that was embraced across the region and served as an example to Cuba and Nicaragua, open to emulation or critique in equal measure, where the overthrow of dictatorships supported by the United States resulted in calls for an even bolder approach to revolutionary state-making.

Intraregional Solidarity and Asylum Law

This chapter traces the transnational solidarity made possible by the revolutionary propositions embedded in the 1917 constitution. Specifically, it examines solidarity with political asylum seekers as an embodiment of Mexico's commitment to self-determination and anti-imperialism in the region. This chapter discusses the deliberate and methodical ways Mexico interpreted the constitution to create conditions for meaningful South-South support. The revolutionary state as a permanent state in Mexico not only impacted flows of solidarity resources but was also a generative source of political orientation for the Latin American left. Revolutionary actors across the Americas idealized the Mexican revolutionary constitution and frequently demanded that the state live up to its revolutionary promises. Many more Latin American states adopted versions of Article 123 into their labor codes. This chapter argues that the foundational means by which the revolutionary state in Mexico would situate the country's place in regional affairs also played a crucial role in shaping transnational social movements, particularly in the local aftermath of the 1968 massacre and the tenuous afterglow of the "radical" global sixties.[7] This chapter considers the ability of social movements to mobilize solidarity from within the state and through state-level involvement in intraregional governing bodies.

Mexico's advocacy on behalf of asylum seekers in the inter-American treaty system provided a context for its government to assume the revolutionary posture that gave it legitimacy. The larger challenge that solidarity presented to the revolutionary state in Latin America was an opportunity to perform and enact ideals but also brought to the fore unresolved challenges to each state's identification with and claim to a revolutionary heritage. This chapter examines the political institutions, policies, and attitudes that set the stage for these openings and asks how certain revolutionary ideals were operationalized and implemented. It focuses on Mexico for two reasons. The first involves Mexico's role as the center and vanguard of revolutionary state formation. This focus highlights the rich history of relationships of solidarity across the Americas that Mexico's history of political asylum law both draws on and informs. Second, it reframes the most notable example of transnational solidarity within the region, Mexico's role in the Chile solidarity movement. Expanding the framework of analysis to incorporate solidarity as its agency expands beyond social movements to actors and institutions of the state, this case study reveals how a revolutionary state can be poised to offer political resources to solidarity actions.

Political asylum laws in Mexico were continuously evaluated and reformed from 1917 through to the 1950s and 1960s. The work of movements to push for reform eventually resulted in providing a legal foundation for Mexico to receive Chilean and other South American exiles during some of the worst episodes of state-sponsored violence in the 1970s. The activism of several generations leading up to the fall of the Salvador Allende government in 1973 positioned the state to respond to this international crisis in a way that enabled Mexico to serve as a safe haven for political refugees and exiles and as a hub of organizing activity for the transnational movement that became one of the most influential of the twentieth century.[8] As transnational subjects pursuing antimilitarism in Chile after Allende's fall, Mexican citizens were able to demand the implementation of the revolutionary state's commitment to the *extranjero* seeking civil rights protections on its soil. What was unique about Chilean exiles' experience in Mexico was that they were met with a sympathetic government that facilitated the establishment of an exile community. The Mexican state allowed this community to maintain a politicized presence and take part in transnational solidarity organizing, despite the formal prohibition against foreigners' participation in Mexican politics.[9]

The movement raised consciousness and generated international pressure on Augusto Pinochet's authoritarian regime. However, this did not mean that the movement succeeded in removing Pinochet from office nor that exiled radicals in Mexico necessarily received the support they wanted from the Mexican government. Most Chileans seeking asylum were not on the initial list that granted automatic admission and status. This list prioritized high-profile figures from Allende's government, and the majority of those fleeing Chile had to wait for the second and third lists to be developed, which meant that they did not benefit from an expedited process and sometimes waited several years to be admitted. In addition, most were expected to be in the country for only six months, so many asylum grantees spent much of their time looking for possible third countries to which they would be allowed to immigrate or considering possible return. Despite this limitation, the commitment of Mexico to solidarity with political asylum seekers raised timely challenges. Solidarity with Chile highlighted the tensions in Mexico created between the revolutionary state, sovereignty in international courts, and increasing calls for democratic change. Frequent demonstrations forced the state to address the contrast that emerged between the hosting of radical exiles and the state's policing of its local activists.[10] But, perhaps most meaningfully, this solidarity challenged the international justice system and pushed back on its use as an instrument of imperialism.

Mexico as a Site of Refuge

As many historians of the nineteenth century have illustrated, state-building activities across the Americas involved entanglement. Active collaboration and conflict confounded the impulse to draw neat boundaries between the priorities of emerging independent states. Bolivarian anti-imperialism, anti-U.S. sentiment, and several varieties of pan-Americanism contributed to alliance building across the Americas; in some cases, political imagining projects also saw Latin American self-determination as a regional project rather than something that concerned individual leaders and national movements alone. In the case of solidarity with Chile in Mexico, there is evidence of clear continuity with earlier pan-American efforts. The movement stood in opposition to a U.S.-backed military coup that ousted a democratically elected government and the denial of the socialist platform of Allende's government, echoing the anti-imperiaism, anti-interventionism, and anti-capitalism of earlier moments of solidarity.

Mexico's effectiveness as a site of refuge is tied to its historical process of revolutionary state formation. The revolution itself, following the rule of Porfirio Díaz from 1876 to 1911, brought together several different threads of leftist thought in demanding change. Mexico had undergone a period of intense modernization, urbanization, and social stratification. The state's power under Díaz was centralized through structural transformations that reinforced the authority of the executive and courted foreign investment. Demands for reform came from urban and rural sectors impacted by the advance of foreign capital and frustrated by increasing inequality. When revolutionary armies finally forced the removal of Díaz from power, it was unclear if the state would be able to manage the widespread social upheaval and ongoing (often armed) challenges to the state that followed. Establishing the legitimacy of the Mexican state meant embracing the spirit of the revolution and uniting the various social groups that led the struggle to construct a new government. It also meant reinforcing Mexico's autonomy and bolstering its independence from foreign powers.

Lázaro Cárdenas, who served as Mexico's president from 1934 to 1940, crafted his political rhetoric around fulfilling the revolutionary ambitions of the 1917 constitution. The Partido Revolucionario Nacional (PRN, National Revolutionary Party)—created in part to bring together competing revolutionary factions—changed its name to the Partido de la Revolución Mexicana (PRM, Mexican Revolutionary Party), underscoring the commitment of the party to the nationalist project. Cárdenas announced the PRM's intention to fulfill the goals of the revolution by establishing social rights and enacting broad redistributive economic reforms. He extended a foreign policy of friendship to the Americas, emphasizing nonintervention, and lent his support to causes such as land reform, democratic education, and pan-Americanism. He appointed foreign services officers who were "united by their understanding of the Mexican Revolution and its potential applicability to the rest of the region," making Mexico "El Faro de América," the lighthouse of the Americas, for those seeking socialist reform.[11]

From the 1940s to 1968, the state consolidated power. It articulated a formidable one-party system led by the successor to the PRM, the Partido Revolucionario Institucional (PRI, Institutional Revolutionary Party), which would in theory make it impossible for the revolution's gains to be reversed. In many ways, the PRI created what Peruvian novelist Mario Vargas Llosa referred to as a "perfect dictatorship," as the party maintained the appearance of democracy while increasing control over political organization and repressing dissent.[12] However, while seeking to balance socioeconomic reform and policing the opposition, the PRI constantly had to negotiate different priorities.[13] Mexico's general economic prosperity from the 1940s to the 1960s provided a means by which to dismiss popular protest, but the events of the following decade brought a serious challenge to the party's ability to maintain control. Particularly after the Cuban Revolution, political protest in Mexico grew steadily against the corruption of the party and a number of other ills, including social inequality, authoritarianism, and corruption. Civil unrest came to a head in 1968, when the state massacred at least three hundred student protesters in a peaceful demonstration at the Plaza de las Tres Culturas in Tlatelolco in the center of Mexico City. After this event, the distinction between Mexico's ruling party and the military dictatorships on the rise across the region became strikingly unclear.

The PRI had to make major concessions to emerging social groups like those represented by the students. Interior Secretary Luis Echeverría Álvarez, considered one of the principal figures responsible for the massacre, maintained a hostile position toward the student movement. However, when he later became president, serving from 1970 to 1976, he spent considerable energy in refashioning himself as the inheritor of Cárdenas's legacy. In addition, although the Mexican state cautiously avoided supporting the Tricontinental conferences or the revolutionary activities undertaken by Cuba abroad, Echeverría adopted a more "Third Worldist" position, emphasizing national liberation and revolutionary anticolonialism. Allying himself with other countries that had chosen not to ally with the United States or the Soviet Union, Echeverría praised Cárdenas's nationalization of Mexico's oil industry and held it up as a successful model of economic nationalism and as a tested means of resisting U.S. imperialism. The Mexican state maintained an official position against the United States' intervention in "dirty wars" in Bolivia, Chile, and Argentina.[14] Echeverría looked to the international arena to realign the image of the party and bolster confidence in its ability to adhere to its revolutionary founding principles.

Enforcing the right to asylum allowed the state to reposition itself in the revolutionary spirit of its founders and respond to public calls for action.[15] This constitutional provision paved the way for Mexico's participation in and leadership of important multilateral *convenios* on political asylum. Held in Havana in 1928, Montevideo in 1933 and 1939, and in Caracas in 1954, these meetings were where Latin American states (Mexico often first among them) articulated and signed binding international agreements.[16] By the 1970s, these agreements, alongside Mexico's status as one of the region's most active asylum-granting states, could be invoked as a symbol of Mexico's regional leadership. It was clearly in Echeverría's interest to remind the public of Mexico's "protector" status in the face of charges of complicity with U.S. Cold War aims.[17] Mexico's participation in these *convenciones* on asylum laid the groundwork for an important moment of intraregional solidarity. By committing to a strong position in these agreements, Mexico established the legal framework that facilitated the welcome of asylum seekers from Chile in 1973.

Legal Reform, Political Asylum, and the Haya de la Torre Case

The *convenciones* allowed for cross-regional dialogue and the harmonization of asylum policy. These meetings also created a space for policy makers to identify issues and plan together strategically. For Mexico, participation in these events provided a means for confronting potential threats to the ideals of the revolutionary government and negotiate complicated cases, such as that of providing a safe haven for notable political exiles. These exchanges brought into focus the application of legal reforms and their tremendous variation, offering functionaries—as representatives—space to consider the practices, norms, and sensibilities of their counterparts elsewhere and establish personal ties that would facilitate enforcement.[18] One such figure was Antonio Carrillo Flores, a brilliant legal scholar who had been involved in constitutional amendments related to nationalizing the oil industry in 1938 under Cárdenas and went on to hold several prominent government posts.[19] The case that laid the groundwork for the arrival of Chilean asylum seekers in 1973 was one that vexed legal scholars and policy makers at the *convenciones* and reformers like Carrillo Flores in Mexico City.

The debate that captured the attention of Carrillo Flores involved an influential decision made by the International Court of Justice in November 1950, which had left a chilling impression on many Latin American states. This decision involved the Peruvian leader of the Alianza Popular Revolucionaria Americana (APRA, American Popular Revolutionary Alliance), Víctor Raúl Haya de la Torre, who sought refuge in Colombia after having led an unsuccessful rebellion against the increasingly authoritarian Peruvian state. Haya de la Torre wrote to the Colombian ambassador in Lima requesting diplomatic asylum, and his case was eventually forwarded to the highest international court for determination. The ruling upheld the 1928 Havana Convention on Asylum and the 1933 and 1939 Montevideo conventions, as well as the Bolivarian Agreement on Extradition of 1922, but noted that Peru had not signed the Montevideo conventions. By noting that Peru was not a signatory, the court ruled that Colombia did not have the right to accept Haya de la Torre or request that Peru grant him safe passage, "with due regard to the inviolability of his person." The court also denied Colombia the right to "qualify the offence for the purpose of said asylum."[20] Haya de la Torres spent five years confined to the Colombian embassy while the case was being considered.

Haya de la Torre had made strong connections in Mexico during a previous trip, including with powerful members of the Mexican Communist Party.[21] Peruvian exiles who had come to Mexico by the 1930s and had been organizing on behalf of the APRA were not only acutely aware of the Haya de la Torre case but also provided a vocal source of interpretation to a Mexican audience of what the refusal of his exile represented.[22] The notoriety of the repression faced by the APRA in Peru meant that many leftists across the Americas were aware of this case. Peruvians abroad also engaged in consciousness-raising activities, and, as a result, the APRA became an important early case of transnational solidarity organizing.[23] Haya de la Torre was seen as a strong supporter of Mexico's revolutionary experiment, offering to host demonstrations in favor of Mexico during its 1938 goodwill mission to Lima.[24] The chief lesson of the Haya de la Torre case was that the problem of asylum seeking would be compounded by delays to mobility or prolonged periods during which asylum seekers were unable to leave their home country.[25] It became clear that the international judicial system would most likely be used to maintain the sovereignty of governments, privileging the legitimacy of the charges made by the issuing country over enforcing the priorities espoused by the inter-American treaty process to allow asylum-recipient countries to determine criminality according to their own legal mandates.[26] Throughout the 1950s and 1960s, legal reformers focused on the degree to which adjudication through the international court system could backfire, undermining Mexico's autonomy and the spirit of its revolutionary protection of asylum seekers like Haya de la Torre.

Mexican representatives to the *convenciones* emphasized the purposes of protecting against violent regime change and ensuring the right to protest or postulate an ideology that might not be popular. Mexico incorporated the political asylum category into the Ley General de Población in 1947 to address concerns regarding the judicial recognition of individuals in the country. These were particularly necessary for those seeking what would be called "territorial asylum," or asylum granted to those already on Mexican soil, a category available only to those coming from the Americas, so they could be governed as legal entities under Mexican civil and penal law.[27] Mexican legal scholars, such as José Augustín Martínez Viademonte and Carlos Augusto Fernandes, argued for establishing stronger protections for asylum seekers. Fernandes argued that the Tratado de Derecho Penal Internacional, signed in 1889 in Montevideo, enshrined the principle of the right to asylum in the penal codes of all of its Latin American signatories.[28]

Distrustful of bodies such as the United Nations, these legal scholars were well aware of how international laws and treaties on migration and refuge echoed imperialist priorities. Their writings and thoughts attended to developments such as the Universal Declaration of Human Rights, adopted in 1948 by the UN General Assembly as Resolution 217. These legal scholars criticized the orientation of the UN and the limitations of such declarations in protecting migrants, asylum seekers, and non-citizens. Resolution 217 included the provision of the right to seek asylum against politically motivated persecution, but the enforcement and oversight of this measure was formally placed under a new office, the UN High Commissioner for Refugees (UNHCR). Created in 1951, the UNHCR responded to the dictates of the most powerful states in the international system and was attuned to their anticommunist positions.[29] The Haya de la Torre case made clear to legal reformers that diplomatic asylum should include more timely and stricter provisions for ensuring safe passage outside of UN oversight.[30] Mexico's advocacy and internal mobilization—particularly around diplomatic asylum—were important in reinforcing the greater protective measures adopted at the Convención de Caracas in 1954, though Mexico ultimately refused to sign.[31]

Carrillo Flores, perhaps the most critical voice on the subject at the time, defended Mexico's refusal to sign the Caracas convention. He argued on the legal grounds that the convention was unconstitutional and that it violated the Ley de Población. The Mexican constitution, he argued, clearly protected the autonomy of Mexico with respect to determining the status of political asylum seekers, and the Ley de Población expressly gave the Secretary of State the sole authority to grant residence to any political asylum seeker, "por el tiempo que la Secretaría de Gobernación juzgue conveniente."[32] In making this legal argument, Carrillo Flores clarified that in Mexico, the principle of national sovereignty would be upheld over international treaties. He had paid close attention to rulings at the International Court of Justice and criticized the ruling on the Haya de La Torre case. The court had determined the case to be that of a common crime and its defense to be representing a common criminal. In ruling that the court was obliged to protect individuals only in cases of political crimes, it had allowed the state of origin rather than the state of refuge to determine the nature of the offence. From this ruling, Carrillo Flores saw the need to advocate for clarifying distinctions between common and political offenses and for the ability of individual states to make such determinations upon reception of asylum cases. He argued that the Mexican legal precedent was one of universal respect for other countries' determinations of what constituted a political crime, noting that Mexico had never rejected another country's decision to grant asylum to a Mexican citizen. Mexico also had a strong record of ensuring safe passage for all asylum seekers regardless of the signatory status of the other countries involved.[33]

In his arguments for legal reform to expand political asylum protections, Carrillo Flores made use of the trials and appeals related to the assassination of Álvaro Obregón on 17 July 1928. Obregón's assassin, José de León Toral, had been given the death penalty, but Toral's defense appealed the decision, claiming the act as a political crime. The Supreme Court had ruled against Toral on the grounds that Obregón had been elected but was not yet a sitting president, determining that the crime was thus not political. The defense, in turn, argued that the assassination could not be viewed as having been motivated by any kind of reasoning other than political. It argued that given the threat that Obregón represented to religious institutions in Mexico, the crime was justified. The court ultimately refused to grant that Toral could have foreseen laws that might have been passed in advance of their appearance. However, Carrillo Flores considered these court arguments to be weak and used the case as a means to illustrate the necessity of external perspectives and independent legal determinations of the criminal acts of asylum seekers.

Luis Ortiz Monasterio, another legal scholar, argued during this same period for the right to asylum as a reciprocal privilege, ad hoc. His argument was that the right to grant asylum existed not only between embassies but also between encampments, boats, and warplanes, making pains to exclude consular offices as places where such transactions should occur. He followed the congressional debate on the new Ley General de Población to determine what kind of scope of validity would be opened up by the law for territorial asylum seekers. Unlike Carrillo Flores, who based much of his argumentation on the centrality of Mexican constitutional law and sovereignty, Ortiz argued that the region was accustomed to violence, and that Mexico occupied a central role in establishing the rights to independence and self-determination in the hemisphere. His arguments against ratifying various international treaties and conventions frequently referred back to the humanitarian considerations of granting asylum and the need to expand its interpretation on practical grounds. He illustrated this point by referring to the gesture made by Manuel Márquez Sterling, Cuban ambassador to Mexico, who offered Francisco Madero asylum just before Madero was killed.[34] Both sets of arguments were crucial to debates in the inter-American system and led to significant changes to Mexico's Código Penal, which was revised in 1970.

Largely through the efforts of Carrillo Flores and other legal reformers aligned with his perspective, legal reform brought additional strength to Mexico's asylum-granting possibilities. The 1970 penal code reform reflected the pressures on the Mexican state to align with its earlier commitment to revolutionary objectives. From 1964 to 1970, Carrillo Flores was Secretary of Foreign Affairs, where he personally oversaw the management of asylum cases, and this position provided him with access to the means of influencing public opinion on high-profile cases of asylum seeking. In 1970, for example, forty-six people accused of communist agitation sought refuge in the Mexican embassy, and one in the ambassador's residence in the Dominican Republic. At stake in this case were the lives of at least two young Dominican men, who were accused of having thrown a hand grenade to kill a professor from the United States, raising fears of violent repercussions for many others. Evidence used to verify the authenticity of the case included evidence of police maltreatment of the two prime suspects and their previous criminal charges, the former implying official harassment and the latter the possibility that these might be "common criminals."[35] Carrillo Flores gave the Mexican ambassador full authority to launch an independent investigation into the nature of the crime and determine eligibility for asylum in Mexico. Within just six months, Mexico also granted asylum to twenty Dominicans accused of kidnapping U.S. Air Force attaché Donald Crowley.[36] The Catholic archbishop of Santo Domingo, Hugo Polanco Brito, accompanied these asylum seekers on their flight to Mexico to serve as a mediator and to give additional assurance of the guarantee of safe passage.[37] During this time, Carrillo Flores took the opportunity to issue statements asserting Mexico's commitment to autonomy in the determination of ideologically and politically motivated cases and to praise the virtues of Articles 15 and 33 of the constitution.[38]

By 1970, the new penal code reflected years of refining. The revision included three categories of crime that could be considered political—rebellion, sedition, and mutiny—all purposefully ambiguous terms. What they had in common was that they could each be considered the result of a shared political goal or collective action. For instance, an assassination could be defined as the political crime of rebellion, as long as its purpose was to "separar por fuerza," or abolish a constitutional system by eliminating its relationship to a high functionary.[39] This definition also helped distinguish between such crimes as terrorism and sabotage, a distinction that proved critical when Brazilians looked to Mexico for asylum in the aftermath of a military coup.[40] Useful in demonstrating the reach of the changes to the code were cases like that of the "dinamiteros," six men accused in 1969 of planting a bomb in Mexico City's Televicentro studio and another in the offices of the newspaper *El Heraldo*. These cases had given courts ample legal and public space to debate the terms of what could be considered an act of sabotage as a form of rebellion versus a common act of violence. The national press closely followed the case, and, through statements issued from his office, Carrillo Flores defended his interpretation of the distinctions.[41] Notably, these liberal interpretations were not often applied in the cases of Mexicans accused of similar acts of terrorism in their processing and trials.[42]

Perhaps the most controversial political asylum case under the new law was that of Antonio Arguedas Mendieta, Bolivia's Minister of the Interior from 1964 to 1969. Arguedas, a member of the communist-leaning Partido de la Izquierda Revolucionaria (Revolutionary Left Movement), sought political asylum in Mexico in 1969. The ministry was accused of having some relationship to the death of Ernesto "Che" Guevara, who was assassinated on Bolivian soil in 1967. Arguedas had been fired on by an unknown shooter in the center of Lima and barely survived multiple gunshot wounds. His case was viewed suspiciously, given the widespread accusation that he had worked with the CIA and had been involved in the war against liberation groups in Bolivia during his term in office. These accusations were underscored by Arugedas's role in returning Guevara's famous diary to Cuba. He claimed in interviews that it been given to him by a CIA agent present at Guevara's murder who preferred the diary be returned to Cuba so as not to provoke another U.S. invasion or risk U.S. tampering with its contents. Arguedas pleaded his case while spending ten months in the Mexican embassy in La Paz and managed to make a breakthrough only when he claimed that he knew and could disclose the whereabouts of Che's severed hands. The hands had been amputated before Guevara's corpse was secretly buried so the CIA could use fingerprint analysis to make a positive identification. However, the hands were stolen before they could be sent to Washington.

The Mexican press chronicled the Arguedas case in great detail. The scandal surrounding his request for asylum included a debate on how he had come into possession of the diary or the information about the missing hands, whether he had been paid by the CIA or other parties, and conjecture about a potential escape he might make to Cuba. His request was ultimately granted, and Arguedas arrived in Mexico City in April 1970, later joined by his wife.[43] Speculation about his involvement with Cuba and the CIA continued in Mexico until his return to Bolivia in 1978. The details of this case tied Mexico directly to intrigue between Cuba and the United States, foregrounding the importance of its role in the protection of the Americas against U.S. imperialism, echoing the popular sentiments of the Cuban revolutionary government, and earning praise from left-leaning intellectuals for Mexico's new legislation. Arguedas served three years in prison after his return to Bolivia for his involvement in the kidnapping of a businessman, and died in 2000, killed by a homemade bomb.[44]

The 1960s and early 1970s in Mexican foreign policy were a period of delicate balance between adhering to postwar agreements made with the United States and confronting regional pressures to defend against co-optation.[45] Solidarity stemming from the state's transnational commitments frequently pushed the state toward reform. Prominent figures within the PRI deliberately courted left-leaning reforms and external positions, including former president Lázaro Cárdenas, who spent time visiting other Latin American countries and positioning himself as an "elder statesman of the left."[46] Cárdenas even hosted a Latin American Peace Conference in Mexico City in 1961, which praised the Cuban Revolution and lauded the struggles of agrarian movements across the region, to distance himself from the heavy baggage of the PRI's failed attempts to deliver social progress to its marginalized rural population.[47] The Haya de la Torre case had threatened the image of Mexico as key to the region's independence. Mexico's revolutionary posture as a haven for those fleeing political persecution included support for those fleeing from the Spanish Civil War, as well as for Leon Trotsky, Fidel Castro, and Iranian shah Reza Pahlavi. This commitment could be called into question if it could not be defended in the international justice system.[48] The Haya de la Torre case not only became a black mark on Mexico's proud legacy and reputation but, according to legal reformers, it also threatened the state's ability to enforce its constitutional provisions.[49]

Peruvian exiles in Mexico City continued to make use of the Peruvian embassy as a space where groundwork could be laid to facilitate safe conduct.[50] Peruvian activists coordinated through the transnational Comité de Solidaridad y Apoyo al Pueblo Peruano, and their allies around the world argued for the urgency of speeding up the processing of applications for political asylum throughout the Americas and for the recognition of the sovereignty of national courts over international bodies of justice. They were able to support the reception of asylum seekers in Mexico and used the committee to launch a demonstration in protest of human rights abuses in Peru.[51] Relocation was necessary before the determination of an enforcement of the law could be contested, and asylum seekers were encouraged to immediately relocate to the grounds of an embassy to issue claims. The Haya de la Torre case was held up as a legal example of the danger of the unequal hierarchy of power in the international system. It provided reformers grounds for articulating an independent Mexican position on asylum granting in the inter-American and international justice systems and catalyzed activism in the exile community.

By the late 1960s, Mexico had had some success, as roughly one hundred Brazilians had come to Mexico between 1964 and 1966 after the military coup against João Goulart. These political asylum seekers, many of whom did not permanently relocate to Mexico, were seen as affluent, skilled, and of a professional class that would benefit Mexico's progress. Members of the PRI continued to defend Mexico's adherence to socialist principles, and by the end of the 1960s and early 1970s, PRI leaders such as Adolfo López Mateos and Echeverría took every opportunity to praise Mexico's approach to economic decolonization and its distance from Washington. Echeverría articulated Mexico's foreign policy approach as a "Third Way," in similar fashion to his counterparts in the Non-Aligned Movement. By this time, the PRI advocated maintaining good relations with revolutionary Cuba and frequently referred to the socialist nature of their party's revolutionary posture in terms that mirrored those of Castro. Complicating matters, however, was the fact that the state had provided only minimal support to Guatemalans fleeing the 1954 coup. Despite the reception of some 318 Guatemalans at the Mexican embassy in Guatemala City, diplomatic efforts were critiqued on the grounds that the PRI did not wish to welcome people they considered socially undesirable (notably indigenous people) to Mexico.[52] Despite the failure to incorporate indigenous groups fully into asylum granting, Mexico's reputation for independent diplomacy advanced.

By the time of the Chilean military coup in 1973, the practice of granting asylum had evolved to make way for the speedy and uncomplicated entry of desirable groups of dissenters. Mexico largely avoided the use of international systems predisposed to reinforce unequal regional power dynamics. Legal reformers in Mexico redesigned asylum-granting policies to benefit primarily those coming from the Americas, turning away from earlier policies that had favored Europeans, as a way of making clear the commitments of the state to pan-American solidarity. Specifically, Mexico refused to sign several new international treaties following the Haya de la Torre case and declined to align itself with any UN policies that would have reduced its autonomy in determining the validity of political asylum cases. In doing so, Mexico retained the right to determine the legitimacy of claims to political asylum, regardless of such determinations in any other judicial body. Even at the expense of UN funding and in the face of harsh critiques from the Organization of American States (OAS), President Gustavo Díaz Ordaz, the United States, and political leaders elsewhere in the region who argued that Mexico's asylum policies had been converted into a tool of guerrillas, Mexico's legal institutions refused to recognize the international court system as the highest court on these issues throughout the 1960s and 1970s.[53]

The tension between the PRI, the presidency, and Carrillo Flores was evident, despite these gains. As Secretary of Foreign Affairs, Carrillo Flores was supported by legal scholars like Jorge Martínez Ríos, who defended Mexico's ability to determine eligibility on a case-by-case basis.[54] In a 1970 interview as the PRI presidential candidate, Echeverría referred to the asylum granted to Dominicans and Brazilians involved in *secuestros*, or political kidnappings. While he spoke of granting asylum as primarily a preventative measure, he avoided taking a direct stand against such actions. Instead, he emphasized the complexity of the issues that led to *secuestros* and promised to work on untangling Mexico's position upon his election.[55] The visibility of Mexico's intransigence in the international legal environment coincided with growing support in the PRI for the socialist government of Salvador Allende in Chile. As a consequence, those fleeing Chile in the aftermath of the coup were aware of Mexico's distaste for military dictatorships and U.S. intervention and its promise to safeguard asylum.[56] The strange contradiction of Mexico's policy of tolerance for radicalism elsewhere but not at home reflected the PRI's position that outsiders posed no real threat to Mexico's internal stability. The image of Mexico as a safe haven for leftists instead highlighted revolutionary values and democratic rights, even if the PRI was determined not to extend such rights equally to all.

Receiving Chileans, 1973

For Chileans in particular, Mexico held special promise as a place of safety and political escape. Within the recent memory of many Chileans during Pinochet's coup was the story of an earlier escape, that of Pablo Neruda in 1949, who had fled over the Andes and eventually made his way with coordinated international assistance to Mexico, where he finished his seminal work, *El Canto General*. This had happened under the presidency of Gabriel González Videla in Chile, who, despite being elected with the support of communists and socialists, eventually bent to far-right and U.S. pressure in 1948 to pass into law the Ley por la Defensa Permanente de la Democracia (Law for the Permanent Defense of Democracy). This law was designed to silence communists and other opposition groups and became known as the "Ley Maldita." Under this law, members of the Chilean Communist Party could be persecuted, but many of the leadership of the party were exiled and fled to various places, many to Argentina and a good number to Mexico. Although Article 33 of the Mexican constitution prohibited arriving Chileans from participating in politics, the members of the Communist Party brought "frenetic" activism and political energy to their temporary home.[57] In the background, awareness was also growing of upcoming changes to the 1951 Geneva Convention, which was influenced by struggles for justice in the process of decolonization.

Support in Mexico in the form of solidarity organizing was also strong in the decades before the coup. Mexican groups ranging from political parties to student associations, labor organizations, and professional associations formed a strong basis of support for the Comité de Solidaridad y Apoyo a Chile.[58] While in Chile, Communist Party leaders acted as interpreters of Chilean politics for local Mexican media and the Mexican state. They frequently gave interviews to the press about the situation in Chile and González Videla's abuses. These Chileans were welcomed in solidarity by the Mexican Communist Party, which participated in advocacy to ensure Neruda's safe passage and freedom through an extensive network that reached from Bolivia to the United States. As members of the exiled party, Chileans also participated in pamphlet distribution, printing and distributing literature throughout 1949 about González Videla across the region and to Europe. When Neruda finally arrived in Mexico in 1950, in the party's spirit of regional solidarity, he organized a formal visit to Juan José Arévalo, the controversial social reformist president of Guatemala who had been the people's choice in the first elections after the revolution. The activism of these exiles was cause for great concern in the Chilean embassy in Mexico, and González Videla demanded that Mexico's Secretaría de Relaciones Exteriores (SRE, Secretary of External Relations) confiscate the passports of the exiles so that they could be easily requested for extradition if needed. The SRE refused, however, and disregarded the pleas of the ambassador to suppress the political activities of the exiles.[59]

After the fall of the Palacio de La Moneda in Santiago in 1973, many of Allende's supporters and others among the left, fearing repression from Pinochet, left for countries such as France, Sweden, Canada, the United Kingdom, and Mexico. Chilean exiles covered a wide geography, and this made a significant difference in terms of the influence of the Chile solidarity movement that followed.[60] These countries of refuge faced challenges from their own legal systems to accept political asylum seekers despite public support.[61] However, Allende's Unidad Popular (Popular Unity) party laid the groundwork for the reception of Chilean political asylum seekers in Mexico. Unidad Popular's challenge to the ruling capitalist logic of the day had been celebrated as a major socialist victory and model for the international left.[62] The party was even embraced by social democrats, who saw Allende's platform as a move away from communist-leaning tendencies on the left. For Echeverría, Chile's nationalization of its copper mines echoed a commitment to the principles enshrined in the 1917 constitution. Beginning in 1974, Chilean exile communities maintained political parties abroad to organize and facilitate relief efforts.[63]

Unidad Popular in Chile had strong support among leftist and left-leaning groups in Mexico as well as in the PRI. Chilean asylum seekers' experience in Mexico was underwritten by a sympathetic government. Mexico was attentive to CIA involvement in Chile, particularly with respect to the telecommunications sector, and noted their concern in the years immediately after the election in 1970.[64] Allende had been warmly received in Mexico on a visit in 1972, and Echeverría enjoyed a visit to Chile in the same year. Linking himself to Allende seemed a strategic but safe way for Echeverría to present himself to the Mexican public as progressive.[65] Despite Mexico's close but fraught ties with the United States and its history of internal repression, Allende's 1973 fall was an event that made a huge impression on Mexican society, as is reflected in Echeverría granting special status to Chilean asylum seekers and the opening of the Casa de Chile, which provided political and social support to exiles.[66] The opening ceremony was a grand event that hosted more than five hundred notable figures from creative and political sectors, together with exiles, including María Esther Zuno de Echeverría, the president's wife.[67]

Media outlets had portrayed Allende's government as relatively progressive, and many left-leaning groups and parties considered it an example of a democratic and peaceful path to socialism. Some saw the Unidad Popular platform as having much in common with Mexico's PRI in terms of resisting North American capital.[68] Mexico's Supreme Court received a lengthy report in 1976 from Enrique Urrutia, auxiliary bishop of the Vicaría de la Solidaridad of the archbishop of Santiago, Chile, providing extensive details on constitutional and other laws broken under military rule. He detailed human rights abuses, disappearances, and irregularities in military tribunals and in the actions of the Chilean intelligence service.[69] This open communication evidences a perceived relationship between the Mexican state, its legal institutions, and any potential future international project of seeking justice and a return to democracy in Chile. As a further gesture on behalf of the state, Echeverría sent his Minister of Foreign Affairs, Emilio Rabasa, to Chile in 1974 to broker the safe passage of seventy-two asylum seekers.[70] Despite Rabasa's success, Mexico broke off diplomatic relations with Pinochet's military regime shortly thereafter and opened a specific path to diplomatic asylum for high-level functionaries in the Unidad Popular government. Diplomatic relations between Mexico and Chile were not restored until 1990. While Mexico was receiving Chilean asylum seekers, they were also welcoming Argentines, Uruguayans, and Peruvians, some of whom were considered more radical than their Chilean counterparts. Mexico's solidarity with leftists from South America, demonstrated through its asylum granting, illustrates the importance of the relationship of the state to its revolutionary constitution. Providing a safe haven for political opposition in the region did not just symbolize a stance against imperialism; it created and protected a space of resistance.

Transnational Agency and Shifting Priorities of Solidarity

One of the results of asylum-granting policies during this period in Mexico was the rise of solidarity organizing in Mexico City. The influx of exiled Chileans in the city, along with other exile communities of different generations, meant that newcomers could enter easily into active spaces of political organization. The two means by which Chileans entered the country—asylum seeking through the embassy or exile after arrest—meant there was very little delay in coming to Mexico. This is an exceptional case for refuge seekers in the twentieth century, particularly large groups. Today, political asylum seekers often face long periods of waiting, occasionally followed by confinement, and regularly face demoralizing restrictions while being processed or awaiting their status to be secured. Police records reveal that although they were under scrutiny, Chilean exiles' political activity was minimally restricted, and exiles often found themselves embraced in local activist communities. In one representative example, the University Section of the Mexican Communist Party organized an event in October 1974 titled "El Frente Antifacista en Chile," which welcomed Chilean activists and provided a venue for their inclusion in other activities of the section.[71]

Chilean refugees as participants and as interlocutors became quickly integrated into the political activism of other groups. As they were organized into local political groups, they simultaneously found support for antimilitarism in Chile that contributed significantly to the international Chile solidarity movement. Particularly in the space in and around the Casa de Chile and the Universidad Nacional Autónoma de México (UNAM), proximity and inclusion created a contact zone where solidarity efforts could flourish. The demands of ongoing local actions were partly met by the enthusiasm of new Chilean recruits, who infused the movements with a sense of urgency. They offered fresh perspectives, new information, and a certain cachet as solidarity activities took on more transnational dimensions and points of contact. The state's role in facilitating this networking effect is not the only factor that led to the increasing agency of participants, but it served in critical ways. Although Chileans were not Mexican citizens, their interests and affiliations were a constant reminder to the state of the purpose of political asylum in protecting those seeking to oppose authoritarianism.

Beyond the policies that were favorable to asylum seekers and expediency in processing, the favorable disposition of the government toward Chilean exiles and what they represented for Mexico allowed for even greater support. Mexican public universities were given the opportunity to recruit and employ Chilean intellectuals. The rector of UNAM, Pablo González Casanova, went to the University of Chile to recruit scholars, and Rodolfo Stavenhagen brought Chilean academics to the Colegio de México in 1973 and later to the Facultad Latinoamericana de Ciencias Sociales in 1975.[72] Students were welcomed to the UNAM, and the Casa de Chile organized scholarships that assisted Chilean students. The Casa de Chile also hosted Chilean activists who advocated for solidarity. Chileans organized a hunger strike in 1977 against the Argentine military dictatorship and another on behalf of Chilean relatives of political prisoners and exiles.[73] Organizing activities were coordinated among at least twelve different groups in solidarity with Chile through these spaces. For instance, the Juventudes Comunistas de Chile (Communist Youth of Chile) organized at the UNAM and participated in numerous cultural and intellectual events of solidarity, including strikes and demonstrations. Chilean former senator Alejandro de la Toro and Hugo Miranda, director of the Casa de Chile, organized an International Day of Voluntary Work, at which at least sixty young Chilean asylum grantees participated, alongside members of the Communist Party of Chile, Juventudes Comunistas de Chile, Movimiento de Acción Popular Unitaria–Obrero/Campesino (Movement of Unified Popular Action–Worker and Peasant), Juventud Radical Revolucionaria (Radical Revolutionary Youth), and Izquierda Cristiana de Chile (Christian Left of Chile). The voluntary work helped restore a school, the Instituto Nacional de Protección a la Infancía (National Institute for the Protection of Children). The event aimed to encourage the Mexican government to increase pressure on Chile to return to democracy. In mobilizing youth, it appealed to the PRI's need to appear relevant to and connected with students.[74]

As intellectual and political spaces opened for organizing solidarity efforts, Chileans interacted with several Mexican institutions and members of the PRI. These interactions shaped the dimensions of the international movement for Chile but also influenced Mexico's presence in international solidarity organizing spaces. Allende was well known for having participated in the creation of the Organización Latinoamericana de Solidaridad (OLAS, Latin American Solidarity Organization) in 1967, which served an important role in transmitting notions of internationalist solidarity to the rest of Latin America. However, in Mexico, Echeverría tried to present himself in this framework as a proponent of development and economic progress as an alternative to Cuba's militancy.[75] Echeverría's alliance with Allende would help secure a more prominent voice and greater influence for Mexico at OLAS and in the Non-Aligned Movement, as he situated Mexico as a model of how countries in the "Third World" could forge strong political and economic relationships independent of pressures from the United States or the Soviet Union.[76] Favorable comparisons between the PRI and the Unidad Popular government in these spaces included note of Chile's role in taking refuge seekers, specifically from Argentina and Brazil. Moreover, although some would criticize Allende's government for allowing "extremism," others looked to Chile as an example of the strength of democratic pluralism.[77] This comparison strengthened Mexico's reputation as an ally against authoritarianism during the Cold War.

In Mexico, previous exile communities, particularly those that had come more recently, played a part in the reception of Chilean exiles and shaping the solidarity actions that followed their arrival. The Comitê dos Brasileiros Exilados no México (COBEM, Committee of Brazilian Exiles in Mexico), for example, had been organizing since the 1964 dictatorship and advocated for exiled communities having a fraternal relationship with the government of

Mexico. COBEM was clear that this did not mean that Mexico would be responsible for making citizens of its exiled guests.[78] Rather, it argued that being exiled did not equate to *apatrida*, or patriated.[79] This meant that taking in asylum seekers underlined a commitment to their rights as citizens elsewhere or beyond their citizenship status. The Mexican Secretary of Foreign Affairs took very seriously the political voice of this group. In internal debates, the ministry followed COBEM's publications closely, eventually deciding that although Mexico had not ratified the most recent regional conventions on asylum, COBEM's arguments were compelling enough to extend greater protections on rights such as free speech and public gatherings.[80]

Mexican leftists were preoccupied with the ability of political asylum seekers to have a recognized political voice. However, they were also aware that the Mexican state did not want increased support to flow to local movements. Public platforms shifted from notions of militant struggle against oppressive forces of imperialism, a narrative that had predominated in the asylum discourse of transnational solidarity movements before 1973, toward a concern for civil protections in these spaces. After 1976, as Argentine asylum seekers entered Mexico in greater numbers, and certainly by 1979, when solidarity with Peru became a rallying cause among many of these same groups, a more conservative form of solidarity, one in which human rights protections took priority, overtook earlier and more revolutionary political visions.[81]

When groups of Chileans arrived in Mexico, their appearance was celebrated in the popular press and by the PRI. Newspapers gave detailed accounts, as they had concerning Dominican and Brazilian asylum seekers earlier, of the physical violence and repression suffered by individuals. Descriptions of the concentration camps in Chile mentioned the poor quality of the food prisoners were served, "hastiados de poroto (frijol), el garbanzo, y la lenteja," the kind of leftover-style meals associated with the rural and urban poor. Articles emphasized exiles' subjection to periods of sensory deprivation, the cold they endured, and their separation from families. On the exiles' arrival in Mexico, these same news sources extolled the reconnection of families and feelings of safety and comfort provided by the state to those who were granted asylum.[82] These stories emphasized the higher-class status of the Chilean exiles. Also emphasized were the individual ties many of the new Chilean migrants had with the Unidad Popular government. The articles tended to underscore their various levels of education and skill and implied a desirability of Chilean immigrants that would distinguish their needs from those of new refuge and asylum seekers from the Caribbean and Central America, whose political formation and professional capacities were perceived as substandard, and who were frequently described as ungrateful and problematically unable to adapt to life in Mexico.[83]

When Echeverría's commitment to political exiles waned, Cuauhtémoc Cárdenas, son of Lázaro Cárdenas, issued a statement reminding the public and the PRI of the role Mexico continued to play in leading hemispheric resistance to the United States. Cárdenas explained that denying asylum seekers would be tantamount to capitulation to dictatorship and imperialism.[84] The new Secretary of Foreign Affairs, Alfonso García Robles, successor of Carrillo Flores and a Nobel Peace Prize laureate, also issued statements to the press regarding Echeverría's evident concern about Argentine asylum seekers' impact on Mexico's internal affairs. Receiving asylum seekers was not a threat to Mexico's internal stability, García Robles argued, but a testament to its robustness.[85] Mario Moya Palencia, Secretary of the Interior with responsibility for claims of territorial asylum, provided multiple public statements regarding the lack of crimes committed in Mexico by those given asylum.[86]

Moya's tone differed from that of previous defenders of Mexico's asylum law. He argued that the right to asylum in Mexico was principally of a humanitarian nature rather than a measure of revolutionary commitment.[87] Journalists and legal reformers challenged Echeverría, Moya, and the PRI on this interpretation and implored them to protect the original intent of Mexico's autonomy in matters of political asylum, which they saw as providing a means for Mexico to assert its support of political freedoms through the direct political action of granting asylum. In doing so, they found support across the region, including from the Federación Latinoamericana de Periodistas (Latin American Federation of Journalists), which called on Echeverría to help maintain juridical independence across the Americas.[88] Nevertheless, as protests against the PRI in Mexico increased, the president moved the state away from its earlier revolutionary position on asylum law. Instead, he increased the surveillance of and conditions placed on new asylum seekers. Legal scholars contested each restriction, drawing attention to the repercussions of each measure and the constitutional principles at stake.[89]

Echeverría Confronts the Legacies of Solidarity with Chile

The success of solidarity with Chile in Mexico comes down to the coordination and community building that took place in Mexico City throughout the 1970s. Reformers inside the state created policies that allowed Mexico to offer safe harbor to Chileans in 1973. Careful coordination of a policy of observing but not interfering allowed for local networks to absorb and accommodate exiles' continued efforts to organize. Asylum grantees were able to integrate into Mexican university, labor, party, and activist communities, creating *lazos* between strong local networks and dispersed exile communities. Many of the solidarity activities undertaken by exiled Chileans, Uruguayans, Bolivians, Peruvians, and others were infiltrated by intelligence agents. These Dirección Federal de Seguridad (DFS, Federal Security Directorate) agents documented the linkages solidarity groups had with Mexican leftists and others. The DFS paid special attention to communist and labor organizations, keeping track of individual members, taking meticulous notes at meetings, and collecting all distributed materials. Beyond providing a wonderful documentary source of information about the activities of these groups in Mexico City, as well as their political orientations, resources, and alliances, it seems somewhat clear that the Mexican state did little to prevent their assembly.[90] Although these records are chilling in the context of information sharing between security and intelligence offices across the region, they attest to the ability of Chileans to mobilize local support, as investigation records demonstrate, by building on the efforts of groups that were already active in support for their cause.[91] The consolidation of a Chile solidarity movement in Mexico speaks to several structural advantages and to a centralization of coordinated transnational struggle that would become a model in many ways. Latin American states in general were well aware of how political asylum cases could be used to foment solidarity, and Mexico provided a model of such mobilization in this time.

This chapter examines how one of the most efficacious transnational solidarity actions between two Latin American nations took place and examines it from the perspective of the state actors and institutions that provided the grounds for its accomplishments. The decision to provide political asylum represents a relationship between the revolutionary state, those that would call on its commitments to principles, and the labor of those working in its institutions. Solidarity with Chile in Mexico was important to the image of the revolutionary state for those who were concerned about the left's challenge to the PRI. Just as Allende's Unidad Popular government had been an important beacon of light for the Latin American left, solidarity with Chile became a cause célèbre across the region. When Mexico hosted International Women's Day in 1975, as Jocelyn Olcott documents, "Mexico's Popular Socialist Party petitioned the Mexican government to reject the credentials of the official Chilean delegation and instead accredit Salvador Allende's widow, Hortensia Bussi de Allende, to lead the Chilean delegation."[92] Mexican trade unions and political parties invited Chilean exiles to participate in meetings and events as a way to raise their profile. Allende's closest circle and family members were greeted with tremendous fanfare when they attended public events and were frequently invited to give speeches in cultural spaces.

The successful reception of Chilean asylum seekers reveals the long-standing efforts of reform-minded legal scholars and policy makers to concretize the 1917 constitution's role in fostering international solidarity. Even if Mexico's diplomatic and police records reveal that Echeverría hoped to deter local groups from seeking militant paths to reform, a unique expression of solidarity can be seen in governance under the sign of a revolutionary state.[93] This chapter hints at the success of Latin American revolutionary states, specifically Mexico and Cuba, in providing each other with counterparts to resist hegemonic forces. South-South solidarity here can be seen in the ability of Mexico, as a revolutionary state, to successfully articulate a position regarding the purpose of political asylum policy and to defend and strengthen it through iterative strategies of reform. That Mexico was poised in 1973 to receive Chileans in a meaningful act of solidarity was not an accident. This mode of solidarity, crafted over time, speaks not only to Mexico's ability to maintain its sovereignty and its regional influence but also to the influence of waves of leftists, reformers, exiles, and others in constantly testing the authenticity of Mexico's commitments. Mexico's revolutionary state created and sustained a mechanism of solidarity that defied the pressures within the international system to conform to a particular world order. This case study affords us a critical way to think about Latin American approaches to South-South solidarity, one that treats institutional and state actors as agents of change with and beyond movements.

Solidarity with Chile, as an international movement, spread rapidly. This is partially due to strong support in Mexico. As the transnational movement expanded from the Global South to the North, where it was eventually championed in France, Sweden, Germany, Canada, and the United States, Mexico's influence could be seen in comparison. However, as the movement expanded, its goals began to gradually shift. Solidarity with Chilean exiles, which began as a movement to oust Pinochet's government, became in these contexts increasingly about human rights. Despite international rebuke, Pinochet stayed in power for more than fifteen years. The Unidad Popular government never returned and the fragmented left that eventually returned to Chile from exile failed to rebuild its former strength. As the movement shifted toward a focus on ending torture and illegal detention, the movement's international stature may have mitigated some of the most atrocious forms of abuse, but the Chilean "economic miracle" ensured that the right would be staying in power even after Pinochet died of natural causes in 2006.

A national plebiscite in 1988, not pressure from the international community, eventually brought the end of Pinochet's rule. In other words, the transnational solidarity movement itself might be judged by a variety of measures to have failed. The solidarity movement did not fail, however, to provide

Mexicans with an opportunity to reconsider what it meant for the state to fulfill its early promises of protecting political freedoms in the Americas. Mexico was able to maneuver its sovereignty to promote a vision of regional solidarity. This solidarity movement smoothed the path for Argentines and Uruguayans who, after 1973, relied on many of the same solidarity partners and means of survival forged by Mexico on behalf of Chilean exiles.

The 1973 fall of Allende made a huge impression on the Mexican left and marked an important high point of transnational solidarity in the region. Allende's government was sympathetically received in the international media—particularly in the Soviet orbit but also by progressive and left-leaning parties in the region—as a democratic path to socialism. After the fanfare of Chile solidarity died down, the PRI became more concerned about internal dissent and radicalism. In 1974, amendments were made to the Ley General de Población to include a provision that shifted the interpretation of the right to asylum to make it a temporary status and to increase the authority of migration officials to deport or revoke asylum seekers' status.[94] By the time Echeverría was succeeded by José López Portillo, winning an unopposed election in 1976, the PRI had taken a definitive shift to the right. Internal party critics and the regional left continued to hold up the model of solidarity with Chile as they critiqued PRI initiatives and new laws. It is perhaps no surprise that the first U.S.-Mexico extradition treaty was signed in 1978.[95] By then Mexico's government had spectacularly departed from the ideals of its revolution in ways that were perhaps irreparable. Despite the fact that state-led initiatives and policies continued to facilitate exchange and resource mobility across various solidarity movements, the state faced an internal crisis. Pressure on the state to police its internal dissent meant that the same movements that were aided by revolutionary rhetoric later complicated the state's relationship to conservative leadership in the party. By the late 1970s, the revolutionary state had the capacity to provide a safe haven for exiles fleeing "dirty wars" in South America but persecuted its own radical left.

By the early 1980s, after a steady flow of Argentines had arrived in Mexico and on the eve of a wave of Central American asylum seekers, Mexico finally signed a treaty with the United Nations under President López Portillo to receive support for refugees.[96] As early as 1982, the numbers of those granted asylum in Mexico reflected an uneven application of political asylum policies. The UNHCR raised the flag of discrimination regarding the rising numbers of deportations of Central Americans, putting pressure on the Mexican government to address the discrepancy.[97] In this same year, the United Nations calculated 140,000 refugees living in Mexico, a statistic that was used by the PRI to present a "refugee crisis" narrative and justify changing its previous policy of independence from international treaties on political asylum.[98] The PRI refocused public debate from celebrating Mexico's role in welcoming political exiles from South America to preparing for an impending disaster. The Comisión Mexicana de Ayuda a Refugiados (Mexican Commission for Aid to Refugees), founded in 1980 under the office of the Secretary of State, soon came to play a central role in responding to incoming requests for asylum and eventually became one of the formal institutions that partnered with the UNHCR to receive funds to deal with Central American migrants, requiring Mexico to formally recognize UN refugee and asylum policies.

As the decade wore on, the PRI also began to rely on mere symbolic acts, such as receiving the remains of Juan José Torres, assassinated president of Bolivia, to represent Mexico's commitment to the past.[99] Despite the state's turn away from the internationalist left, Mexico's solidarity movement with Chile served as a prime impetus for the rise of other transnational solidarity movements. The case of solidarity with Chile provided activists with a blueprint for what kind of legal mechanisms could be invoked and hinted at the usefulness of calling on the state to measure itself against its revolutionary commitments. Partly because of the longevity of Pinochet's regime, solidarity with Chile also provided continuity across movements, connecting an earlier period of internationalist, Marxist solidarity to that of the 1980s human rights era. Mexico benefited in no small way from the outpouring of support it received for its quick response to the coup and for facilitating the political asylum of Chileans in its immediate aftermath.[100] The Chile solidarity movement was able to build a solid foundation from Mexico across the region and around the world. As Mexico's 1974 Day of World Solidarity with Chile announced, solidarity with Chile was destined to be a global event, fostering the spread of organizing practices and principles.[101]

2

 Tricontinental Culture

I f Mexico provides an example of a Latin American revolutionary state in intraregional solidarity, Cuba's state-led solidarity
was internationalist and more radical. Mexico and Cuba integrated and managed commitments to solidarity through the various offices of the state, but
one important difference was that Cuba explicitly hoped to "export revolution" within and beyond the region. Lacking Mexico's economic security and
regional influence, Cuba's 1959 revolution was more at risk. Its leaders mobilized a vision of socialist South-South solidarity to seek external support and
reinforce revolutionary consciousness on the island. Cuba became an unrivaled
inspiration to the left in the Global South, its influence far surpassing what
might have been expected given its size and situation.

Influenced by his experience of exile in Mexico, Fidel Castro found creative ways for Cuba to bring together revolutionary allies. In 1966, Cuba hosted
eighty-two nations at an international congress intended to champion a Latin
American vision of solidarity between the regions of the Global South. Using
a term that had evolved from several important meetings of what eventually
became known as the Non-Aligned Movement, the meeting was dubbed the
"Tricontinental Conference." The use of this new term responded to the failures of previous forms of internationalist political community to respond to
the direction and needs of formerly colonized nations. Castro intended this
movement to focus on Africa, Asia, and Latin America. As a vision of solidarity, Tricontinentalism held central a critique of imperialism and racism and
offered a "deterritorialized conceptualization of imperial power."[1] The Cuban
revolutionary state turned Havana into a hub of leftist exchange. The Tricontinental spirit, in turn, encouraged transformations of the Cuban state. Cuban
tricontinental solidarity demonstrates the influence of South-South solidarity,

particularly through cultural exchange, to create productive relationships between revolutionary projects and ideals.

Founded by the Tricontinental Conference, the Organización de Solidaridad con los Pueblos de Asia, África y América Latina (OSPAAAL) was created to be a conduit of revolutionary ideas. Its mission was to circulate news of national liberation struggles and to coordinate solidarity efforts. Based in Havana, the organization published a monthly newsletter, *Tricontinental Bulletin* (1966–88, 1995–), and a bimonthly magazine, *Tricontinental* (1967–90, 1995–). These publications delivered interviews, news reporting, and speeches of key figures of national liberation struggles to distant parties around the globe. The organization promoted a Cuban interpretation of the Cold War and examined ongoing colonialism to generate transnational support for causes in Latin America, the Middle East, Asia, and Africa. This chapter examines OSPAAAL's publications and their use in promoting revolutionary ties. The images and stories that OSPAAAL circulated among communities of internationalist leftists across the Global South were a crucial strategy of Cuban solidarity. To explain the reach and significance of OSPAAAL's solidarity work, this chapter considers the mode of rendering solidarity as a practice critical to South-South organizing.

In terms of solidarity activism, the work of translating a conflict from one national context to another is not an easy task. Rendering distant struggles knowable in order to mobilize political resources requires a commitment to both abstraction and some version of accuracy. Meaningful representativeness requires the translation of ideas through forms that have the ability to speak and be interpreted.[2] The work of translation in OSPAAAL's poster art went far beyond ideology and foreign policy to convey a clear message regarding the relationship between local and regional struggles and the larger fight against imperialism and global capital. The visual material published by the organization presented a vision that was simple and compelling to non-Cubans but also presented a central role for Cuba in leading and organizing cooperation. This chapter argues that the cultural work of OSPAAAL rendered a vision of anticolonial conflict that facilitated Cuba's internationalism. Its publications reached a broad audience of activists and advocates who, in turn, helped shape the agenda of the United Nations.[3]

Cuban Internationalism and the Non-Aligned Movement

Cuban efforts built upon movements that predated the revolution. When Indonesian president Sukarno hosted the first Afro-Asian

Conference in Bandung in 1955, this event symbolized the beginning of a concerted effort by formerly colonized nations to carve out a space for economic and political independence. The conference also aimed to reinforce the efforts of these countries to maintain neutral relations in the escalating violence of powerful nations, such as Russia, China, and the United States.[4] This conference echoed the aspirations of earlier antiracism and anticolonialism conferences, such as the League of Colored Peoples, founded in Britain in 1931 by Jamaican civil rights leader Harold Moody, and the Communist International–led League against Imperialism, founded in 1927 in Brussels specifically to argue on behalf of containing China's expansion, reducing U.S. intervention in Latin America, and promoting nationalist self-determination in Africa.[5] As a result of this meeting, the Afro-Asian Peoples' Solidarity Organization (AAPSO) was formed, which subsequently organized conferences in Cairo in 1957 and Conakry in 1960 to articulate a collective position against the racism and imperialism faced in these regions.[6] Between these conferences, Cuba's armed revolution in 1959 brought a radical socialist government into power, and the United States mobilized in reaction, including work through the Organization of American States (OAS), to isolate Cuba in the hemisphere.[7]

Beginning in Bandung, the Non-Aligned Movement (NAM) challenged the international hierarchy of power that privileged European and North American interests in international institutions. As the United States attacked Cuba's revolution as a threat to hemispheric stability, Castro looked to parties within and outside the region to help establish his government's legitimacy. It had not gone unnoticed that African and Asian delegations had formed a bloc at the United Nations that limited the ability of France to undermine Algeria's independence movement. The United Nations admitted Algeria and recognized its claim to sovereign statehood, confirming "the UN's role as an arbiter of the new international order."[8] The NAM represented formerly colonized nations that sought to resist imperialism and protect the independence of new states. It coordinated a third bloc against the pressures of global capitalism and that of expansive communism. Although the NAM's primary goal was peaceful coexistence, Cuba hoped it would provide support against U.S. intervention and for revolutionary armed struggle. Cuba's position on armed intervention created heated debates among UN delegations, including those that represented newly independent states. Cuba viewed the NAM as crucial to gaining support at the UN.

When Castro decided to attend his first UN General Assembly meeting in 1960, he was not as warmly received as he had expected to be.[9] Castro was clearly an outsider at the United Nations. However, he chose to make Cuba the first Latin American nation to join the Non-Aligned Movement. In joining the NAM, Cuba signaled the beginning of a more formal alliance of Latin American anti-imperialism and noninterventionism with Asian and African decolonization. In 1961, the NAM, led by heads of states that attended the Cairo and Conakry meetings, convened in Belgrade, Yugoslavia. Castro was not yet well connected in Belgrade, but from roughly 1962 to 1965, he and his advisers persistently sought an entry point for influence in the Afro-Asian bloc at the United Nations through the NAM. Castro considered the United Nations, with its ability to sanction, key to seeking support for the Cuban revolutionary government. Part of Castro's strategy for increasing Cuba's influence in these organizational settings was to ally himself with Algerian leaders who would be able to help articulate the relationship the Americas could have to national liberation struggles in Africa and the Middle East.

During these years, the Algerian Revolution stood as a clear example of national liberation from colonial forces. In the early 1960s, Algiers had become something of an informal headquarters and site of exchange for many groups involved in transnational revolutionary activity. When Algerian President Ahmed Ben Bella visited Cuba in 1962 in the aftermath of the Bay of Pigs invasion, he vowed to assist the small island nation in defending itself against a North American invasion. Castro determined that Algeria and Cuba could form a partnership in fostering revolution.[10] Algeria and Cuba became allies in assisting armed groups in Africa and Latin America, moving arms and humanitarian aid through North Africa. During these years, Castro formed a strong alliance with Ben Bella. Castro's reputation benefited from close connections to high-ranking Algerian revolutionary leaders, as did Cuba's ability to spread information and calls to action. Jorge Masetti, an Argentine in charge of overseeing arms transfers from Cuba to Algeria, was put in charge of founding Cuban news agency Prensa Latina, which disseminated news from Latin America to a global audience.[11]

In 1965, Ben Bella's government was toppled by a military coup, and Cuba was forced to look for another way to maintain its position of influence within the Afro-Asian bloc.[12] In 1964, the NAM met in Cairo, Egypt, where Gamal Abdel Nasser nudged the movement from its earlier commitments to national liberation and socialism and toward more nationalist and alliance-based aims. In Cairo, Nasser steered the movement away from support for military aid and military alliances, despite the fact that weapons and military personnel continued to be moved through Egypt, including from Cuba to Zanzibar and the Republic of the Congo. It became clear to Castro that Nasser, the most prominent and powerful figure of the NAM, hoped to redirect the bloc away from support of national liberation and armed conflict and toward a pan-Arab nationalism, strategically positioning Egypt as the primary regional power in

North Africa. Algeria had been set to host the next Afro-Asian Solidarity Conference, but after Ben Bella's fall, the conference was canceled, opening the door for Havana to host the conference. In this moment, Cuba saw an opportunity to persuade leaders to push beyond the limits of Nasser's vision of anti-imperialist struggle. Castro criticized Nasser's vision of socialism due to its limitations of women's rights and restrained labor reform. Castro pushed for a more far-reaching revolutionary socialism, which saw anticolonialism as deeply intertwined with other social reforms, such as education and health care, and an ongoing commitment to liberation by revolutionary force.

In 1966, Cuba hosted the first Tricontinental Conference, responding to how these other organizations had communicated broader goals to critical audiences such as at the United Nations. OSPAAAL was created out of the conference to increase the presence of Latin American and Caribbean nations in these forums—and specifically to challenge the redirection of what was emerging as the "Third World movement" away from what Castro considered Nasserist compromises. The conference was the result of careful planning and orchestration by many, particularly Ernesto "Che" Guevara and Moroccan leader Mehdi Ben Barka, who intended to create a more central position for Cuba in internationalist organizing. OSPAAAL's mandate closely reflected this purpose.[13] OSPAAAL's early years coincided with the short-lived Organización Latinoamericana de Solidaridad (OLAS), extant from 1966 to 1967, which was founded at the same time by twenty-seven Latin American delegations to the Tricontinental Conference, with the express goal of coordinating resistance to the imperialism of the United States and in response to the recent Sino-Soviet split, articulating the Cuban position as the ideal path to socialism.[14] In principle, the OLAS articulated some of the grander plans Castro had in 1966: to have a new international that would be Cuban-led, driven by revolutionary socialism, and ideologically grounded in the ongoing struggles of Latin America.[15] Under the leadership of Osmany Cienfuegos Gorriarán, the first secretary-general appointed by the Cuban Communist Party (1966–80), OLAS's mission was incorporated into OSPAAAL.

From 1961 through to the late 1980s, Cuba's foreign policy reflected a rising commitment to involvement in African and Middle Eastern liberation causes. By 1976, more than thirty thousand Cubans were actively involved in military, educational, and medical missions in Africa alone.[16] This commitment extended well beyond the 1970s, and, by the 1980s, Cuba played a decisive role in preventing South African colonization of Namibia and supporting independence movements in Angola and Mozambique. Cuba's direct intervention in Africa, later described as "selfless internationalism" by leaders like Nelson Mandela and as revolutionary idealism bordering on the fanatical by the U.S.

Central Intelligence Agency, also exerted influence on the Soviet Union and the United States in other areas of Cuban interest and mobilized public support at home, particularly among Afro-Cubans and other racialized groups.[17] However, sending direct military and humanitarian assistance were not the only means by which Cuba signaled its willingness to advance internationalist revolutionary objectives.

OSPAAAL and Cuban Political Poster Art

Beginning in 1967, OSPAAAL published a magazine, called *Tricontinental*, that at its peak published more than thirty thousand issues in four languages and was distributed to eighty-seven countries. Distribution was most often by diplomatic pouch directly to organizations and leaders allied with Tricontinentalist ideals. OSPAAAL published books and reprinted important speeches, but its widest reach was via its richly illustrated magazine, which included political poster art, stapled as an insert between the centerfold. Although it is always difficult to speak directly to the question of reception, it is notable that archives of leftist political parties and organizations around the world still contain sizable collections of its issues, and references to its articles and reprints of its photographs and images feature prominently in the circulation of the news stories of many leftist news media. OSPAAAL's poster art was the most enduring and effective "international poster distribution system in the world."[18] Part of the success of this endeavor can be traced to state support for printing political posters through OSPAAAL, the Instituto Cubano del Arte e Industria Cinematográficos (ICAIC, Cuban Institute of Cinematographic Art and Industry), and Editora Política, the publishing department of the Cuban Communist Party. Poster art was a critical feature of the Cuban Revolution, flowing naturally as a form of ideological persuasion from other revolutionary artistic traditions like the avant-garde art of the Russian Revolution. Castro commissioned Eladio Rivadulla Martínez to make the first poster art of the revolution, celebrating the victory of the 1959 revolution through *afiches* to be plastered across the island, announcing the new order of the day, designed in a style that paid tribute to the poster art of the Taller de Gráfica Popular, which had served as a vital organ of solidarity in Mexico.[19]

Many of the primary artists who were employed in designing the poster art of OSPAAAL, such as Martínez, Eduardo Muñoz Bachs, Alfredo J. González Rostgaard, and René Mederos Pazos, made their living designing posters for Cuba's film industry. The ICAIC printed poster art for every film it produced and for other international films distributed in Cuba that lacked marketable materials. This prolific production supported artists and provided a space where poster art could refine its new visual languages. In this space, artists were called on to create posters that would speak to revolutionary themes in the language of bold, captivating, vibrant images. Two central artistic characteristics made the production and distribution of OSPAAAL posters unique in this period. The first was their visual uniqueness in public spaces. The noncommercial nature of the images, in striking contrast to the preponderance of "marketing" images in poster advertising across most recipient countries, suggested that these posters "had nothing to sell," no commercial aims.[20] This absence of commercialism visually highlighted the relationship these posters had to the presentation of revolutionary ideas, advertising Cuban socialism as an alternative to free market capitalism as they competed for space on public walls next to advertisements for consumer products or political posters. Second, the posters aesthetically embodied the spirit of the Cuban Revolution and its slogan "Within the revolution, everything; outside the revolution, nothing." This meant that artists were not tethered to any particular style, allowing for a tremendous amount of creative experimentation.[21] Art made by OSPAAAL and the ICAIC was equally at home in the worlds of silkscreened, wearable Pop Art, the psychedelic designs of 1960s album covers, and "take it to the streets" protest culture. Posters might mirror the abstract minimalism of Pablo Neruda's poetry or the loud expressionist painting of urban São Paulo. Cuba's view of revolutionary culture even extended to sport. The state invested tremendous resources in creating a National Institute of Sport, Physical Education, and Recreation, and in exporting a model of socialist, deprofessionalized athletics. Cuba sent athletes and physical educators around the world, where their success in international events like the Olympics stood in defiance of the highly capitalized U.S. model of professional sports. Cuba gave strong support to the Games of the New Emerging Forces (GANEFO) as an alternative to the Olympics. GANEFO was founded following the International Olympic Commission's suspension of Indonesia after the controversial 1962 Asian Games in Jakarta, in which Indonesia had refused entry to Taiwan and Israel.[22]

By investing in the circulation of revolutionary culture and art, Castro hoped to create a revolutionary consciousness that would visualize notions of political solidarity. The Cuban state used cultural forms as a means to exhibit and promote socialist values, "exporting" the revolution. U.S.-based activist Susan Sontag described it as providing a seductive source of ideological motivation to revolutionary causes and ongoing resistance.[23] Cuban posters gave visual form to solidarity work in the context of institutional organizing. Prior to OSPAAAL, from 1959 to the mid-1960s, Cuba had been engaged "with fervor" in training revolutionary guerrilla soldiers and encouraging socialist revolution in places like Panama, Paraguay, Colombia, and Argentina, any-where under significant threat of U.S. intervention.[24] However, by the mid-1960s, it was clear that this strategy was not working. In the wake of increasing criticism of Cuba's alignment with the Soviet Union, Castro decided to pursue a more pragmatic path, allying himself more vigorously with *tercermundismo* and the NAM, inspired to "bring Bandung" to Havana.[25]

As Castro traveled around the region, speaking with trade unionists, stu-dents, rural peasants, and the urban poor, he and his advisers did not find as much sympathy for militarism or guerrilla violence as they had expected. Castro was somewhat surprised to find that the primary concern of many of these groups was increasing the basic standard of living rather than overturn-ing regimes.[26] By 1965, after several years of increasing economic isolation and concerned about the economic future of the island, Castro turned his focus more centrally to the Cuban economy. He shifted his energies to reframing the experience of revolution through decolonization and national liberation struggles. From 1966 to 1968, he used OSPAAAL's poster art to promote a radical-socialist, anti-imperialist version of Tricontinental solidarity that would appeal to the emerging leaders of the NAM. The poster art of *Tricontinental* was directed toward making visible the specific initiatives that were being ad-vanced by Cuba in its solidarity activities and the institutional setting of the UN. The twin goals of cultural production according to the revolution were to promote armed struggle and advance the *guerra popular*. Artists and intellec-tuals were discouraged from creating esoteric art that might not be accessible and were prompted to produce work that could easily communicate with and convince the popular classes. Posters and articles were printed in a variety of languages, including French, Spanish, Portuguese, English, Italian, and Ara-bic, offering the organizations that received copies print literature and art that could easily be shared.

Cuban poster art circulated by *Tricontinental* took on a set of explicit themes that dovetailed with Castro's vision of revolutionary Cuba and reinforced the role he imagined for Cuba in providing leadership to NAM countries in the struggle against imperialism. Artist René Mederos Pazos, best known for his images celebrating the history of the revolution through the lens of Castro's and Guevara's roles in leading armed struggle in the trenches, was sent to Vietnam to document the Viet Cong struggle. The images he produced were circulated in the magazine, juxtaposed against speeches given by Ho Chi Minh and Che Guevara, interpreting the Vietnamese struggle through the framework of internationalism. Mederos Pazos developed a style that com-bined the same iconographic characteristics of his earlier depictions of Cuban combat with shapes and forms that reflected the Vietnamese landscape and folk art, such as local tropical foliage and sweeping paintbrush strokes to mimic Vietnamese lettering. Depictions of the conflict not only emphasized a similar, common enemy in representations of militarized empire but also rendered shared heroes of national liberation in the figure of Minh. They illustrated a naturalness by including local political projects in the scope of Tricontinental internationalism. Mederos Pazos's most iconic images were used on postage stamps (figure 2.1), traveling visual reminders of Cuba's solidarity with the Viet Cong in its struggle against colonialism and the United States.

The poster art of this period showcased the antiracism Castro wanted to emphasize as part of the shared fight against colonialism. Despite a poor record on racial inequality within Cuba, Castro built his platform on long-standing Cuban solidarity with African American suffering in the United States and against the institutionalized racism of colonialism in Africa.[27] Antiracism as identified in Cuban solidarity presented racial equality as an accomplishment of the revolution, although it was not necessarily the case that Afro-Cubans experienced an end to racism on the island.[28] In 1968, *Tricontinental* published a poster in collaboration with a designer affiliated with the Black Panthers to commemorate the Watts riots, a civil rebellion that followed police violence in Los Angeles in 1965.[29] Castro highlighted the connections between forms of racism "in the belly of the beast" and ongoing colonialism. San Francisco–based artist Jane Norling came to Cuba in 1972 on exchange from the People's Press to bring into focus the connections between racial struggles in the United States and the Caribbean. Norling's later work demonstrates the influence of national liberation poster art on interpreting U.S. race relations, particularly in drawing attention to the exploitation of women and people of color working in poorly paid industries such as health care and domestic service.[30] Reminding viewers of the place of subaltern subjects in the capitalist imperial project—specifically that of Puerto Rico in the context of ongoing colonialism—these images suggested that challenging the hegemonic narrative of global capital first meant rejecting the exploitative racist and sexist ideologies on which it was based.

Castro embraced the struggle of Black solidarity and Black power movements in the United States. Antiracism in these images spoke to his critique of Nasserism and the centrality of labor and women's rights to internationalist revolutionary struggle. As a point of contrast, in January 1968, when Cuba hosted the Congreso Cultural de la Habana, bringing artists together from more than seventy countries to reinforce the role of cultural production in anti-imperialist struggle, the Cuban government expressly forbade Afro-Cubans from speaking publicly about race relations on the island. Instead, artists and intellectuals of African descent suspected of participating in what

Figure 2.1. René Mederos Pazos, Vietnam series of Cuban postage stamps, 1969. Courtesy of Lincoln Cushing / Docs Populi.

Castro characterized as divisive ethnic politics were expressly prohibited from participating; some were put under house arrest and others imprisoned for the duration of the event under the accusation that they had conspired to publish a "manifesto negro."[31]

Cuba's revolutionary internationalist poster art was aimed at a local audience of Cubans and at an audience abroad. The art illustrated a connection between Cubans whose participation in internationalist solidarity often required significant material sacrifices and their counterparts among the growing membership of NAM countries. Castro wanted to declare the ideals of Cuba's revolutionary government and suggest that Cuba's interest in the affairs of Africa, Asia, and the Middle East were aligned with long-standing Cuban ideals of anticolonialism, antiapartheid, and antiracism. However, these posters circulated for another purpose as well, in that they drew attention to the ongoing imperialist violence of the United States. The publications' bold criticism of the U.S. reinforced the necessity of maintaining armed struggle and the permanence of Cuba's revolutionary regime. OSPAAAL's poster art visually explained the connections between these goals, using imagery of armed struggle and graphic representations of the intellectual underpinnings of anticolonialism.

Third World Solidarity at the United Nations

At the United Nations, the Afro-Asian Peoples' Solidarity Organization (AAPSO) organized a platform, formalized in 1960, from which to advance the goals of national liberation in Africa and Asia.[32] The AAPSO was founded in Cairo in 1957 at a solidarity conference held by representatives of a variety of different national liberation movements in Africa and Asia. Its purpose was to uphold the principles of anticolonialism. Much of its energy was directed to garnering international support for newly independent states and the fight against ongoing colonialism. Its regular conferences were aimed at deepening understandings of apartheid and recruiting representative delegates from key international organizations who would help widen the reach of their actions.[33] They pushed for recognition of the principles of Bandung in the United Nations charter, which included nonintervention, self-determination, and upholding national sovereignty by means of the national control of resources and unfettered socioeconomic development.[34] The AAPSO's voice at the United Nations was the strongest source of support for these priorities, and its members determined whether and how related resolutions would succeed in the General Assembly. By the late 1960s, Cuba's international priorities had aligned with that of the AAPSO, particularly in the struggle against the

South African apartheid state.[35] Castro's internationalist foreign policy called for humanitarian and military intervention in Africa, particularly in the Congo and Angola, and he required the support of the AASPO's African leadership for these efforts.[36] During this period, Cuba struggled with shifts in the Soviet position not only on Latin America but also on its expansionist designs in the Middle East and sub-Saharan Africa. Cuba's position in Angola (and later Mozambique and Namibia) became points of tension with the Soviet Union, particularly during the years of nuclear treaty negotiation with the United States.[37] At the UN General Assembly, many countries outside the AAPSO bloc questioned the logic of coupling political and economic independence and challenged the national liberation position as a viable approach to international security.

The Middle East presented a particular challenge for all parties concerned at the United Nations. Modern states in the Middle East had only recently become independent from British and French colonialism, the League of Nations mandate system, and occupations predicated on strategic military interests during World War II. Most countries in the region continued to experience high levels of conflict throughout the 1960s and early 1970s around borders established by the UN and the fate of displaced populations, such as "stateless" Kurdish and Palestinian refugees. In addition, external intervention in pursuit of access to natural resources and strategic military locations continued to add pressure on independent national governments. The Arab-Israeli War (1948), followed by the Six-Day War (1967), the War of Attrition (1970), and the Yom Kippur War (1973), illustrated the ongoing commitment on behalf of Israel's allies (notably the United Kingdom and the United States) to forcefully promote Zionist colonialism in the region. Most Arab states were concerned that the UN would deprive the peoples of Arabic descent in Israel's borders of a meaningful form of citizenship, much less a path of return to Palestine for those who had fled to nearby countries.

From the perspective of the OSPAAAL, the policies of the Israeli state to use legal, military, economic, and other tactics to expel Palestinians and deprive them of territory represented a renewed commitment by internationally empowered capitalist governments to colonialism.[38] With Egyptian leadership, countries within the NAM mobilized by concern around the Arab-Israeli conflict turned their attention to Israeli territorial occupation and aggression. This shift created an opportunity for Castro to speak to the question of Palestine in a nuanced way in these spaces and advocate for the armed struggle of Palestinian nationalists in the Middle East as akin to the ongoing need for armed struggle elsewhere. From the late 1960s through the early 1970s at the United Nations, the AAPSO primarily focused on the liberation of African peoples, with Angola's independence movement, finally achieved in 1975, as a central rallying point. Angola's independence, although not the watershed in terms of national liberation struggles that Ghana might have represented, helped tie together a notion of the Black Atlantic, not only connecting Black solidarities but also serving as an important point of reflection for future Black intellectuals.[39] This perspectival shift to thinking about Cuba's role in Angola, particularly as it moved through intellectual and political spaces, increased Castro's influence among the AAPSO bloc at the United Nations, which served Cuba well, particularly among representatives less interested in directly taking on the powerful interests of expansionist states like Israel and South Africa.

Castro hoped to advance a prorevolutionary platform at the United Nations by crafting a majority position around which NAM countries would organize themselves. Associating his national and regional goals with the cause of national liberation in the Middle East and Africa, Castro was able to increase the visibility of Cuba's leadership and advocate for its interests in these spaces. Rallying support around the common ills of racism and apartheid, OSPAAAL publications would echo this strategy. In 1968, the United Nations organized a special commission to investigate Israel's treatment of Palestinians, following several resolutions made by the General Assembly, the Security Council, and the UN High Commissioner for Human Rights. Pressure from AAPSO at the UN forced these bodies to address the plight of Palestinian refugees and acknowledge the occupation of Palestinian territories.[40] From 1968 to 1974, the United Nations passed many resolutions to deal with the fate of the Palestinian peoples, largely aimed at mobilizing humanitarian assistance through the United Nations Relief and Works Agency for Palestine Refugees in the Near East and establishing some form of recognition of a right to return. This advance at the UN could be largely attributed to the work of Cuba and Afro-Asian solidarity bloc organizing, which garnered support among European and Arab states similarly concerned with neocolonialism or more generally interested in seeking support for stateless peoples and refugees. Castro's involvement fostered additional support for resolutions from other Latin American nations.

On 14 October 1974, the United Nations heard and passed a resolution (no. 3210) that finally gave the Palestinian people a voice by inviting the Palestinian Liberation Organization (PLO) to deliberations on Palestine in the General Assembly. This provided a superficial endpoint of sorts to Castro's influence, in that the PLO's agenda shifted the dynamics of debate at the UN significantly. The PLO opened a consulate in Havana the same year. Before 1974, solidarity with the Palestinian cause provided an anchor for establishing the credibility of Castro's claims to support nonaligned, anti-imperialist struggles, allowing him to move beyond challenges of his position with respect to the Soviet Union. The lasting influence of this support can still be seen in Palestine. Guevara had been one of the first visitors to Gaza, and his image remains emblazoned across various walls in Gaza City. Cuba offered citizenship to displaced Palestinians and invited Palestinian students to Cuban universities.[41] According to Santiago Rony Feliú, the director of the magazine, the increasing and constant visibility of Cuba's Tricontinental's coverage of the Middle East over these years contributed to shaping perspectives on the Arab world.[42] OSPAAAL's reporting welcomed the Latin American left to envision its commitment to revolution as inclusive of positions on the Middle East, Zionism, and Palestinian nationalism.

Rendering Cuban Solidarity in Africa and the Middle East

OSPAAAL artists contributed significantly to the circulation of ideas about armed struggle as a mode of solidarity in transnational political spaces of the Latin American left. The rendering work of visual connections underscored principles of solidarity that allowed a particular hierarchy of struggle to take precedence over others in these contexts. Artists depicted African and Middle Eastern liberation struggles with strong visual references to Cuban and Latin American revolutionary iconography, building on the argument made by African American militants that Black art could be used as a weapon to transform culture and thought. Using bold colors—particularly yellows, oranges, and reds—against thick black lines, artists abstracted images of struggle and portraits of revolutionary heroes, as intellectuals and combatants. The posters created a symbolic visual language that was immediately accessible to audiences receiving *Tricontinental* publications. Poster art was accompanied by essays written by figures such as Minh and Guevara, interviews with Yasser Arafat, pronouncements by Luis Cabral, and calls for specific acts and days of solidarity with various causes. The use of minimalism and an aesthetic that mirrored highly reproducible, cinematic poster art (figures 2.2–2.4) visually suggested that the struggle for liberation had made its way into the idiom of the times.[43] OSPAAAL's poster art iconographically connected the ideological struggles of Latin American revolution with those of Vietnam, Palestine, the Congo, Yemen, and elsewhere, suggesting that individual causes should be seen as interconnected and transregional. The posters also visually framed Castro's desire for solidarity action to move away from Nasserism. Castro saw Nasser as a gatekeeper, limiting Latin American internationalist approaches to solidarity

Figure 2.2. René Mederos Pazos, "Rocinante," 1971. Stamped on back "Taller de Divulgación." Printed by Comisión de Orientación Revolucionaria del CC del PCC. Folder no. 25, "Mederos," pictorial number SS674-469, Sam L. Slick Collection of Latin American Political Posters, Center for Southwest Research, University Libraries, University of New Mexico.

Figure 2.3. René Mederos Pazos, "La historia me absolvera—1953," 1973. Printed by Departamento de Orientación Revolucionaria. Folder no. 25, "Mederos," pictorial number SS674-471, Sam L. Slick Collection of Latin American Political Posters, Center for Southwest Research, University Libraries, University of New Mexico.

Figure 2.4. Antonio Pérez Gonzàlez, "Semana de solidaridad con América Latina," 1968. Folder no. 6, pictorial number SS674-100, Sam L. Slick Collection of Latin American Political Posters, Center for Southwest Research, University Libraries, University of New Mexico.

action in international institutions. He viewed Nasserist nationalism and interest in regional influence as a potential threat to liberation movements. Appealing to the Afro-Asian bloc, the poster art used symbolic and visual connections to not only identify but also demonstrate a more thorough rendering of these struggles and different possibilities for resistance.

Images circulated by OSPAAAL also highlighted the central relationship between racism and colonialism. Featured images were frequently meant to highlight the role of formerly excluded peoples in armed struggle, such as women, peasants, and Black intellectual leaders. Although Cuba's commitment to resolving issues of racial inequality on the island was sometimes unclear, the magazine reproduced numerous images of Amílcar Cabral and Patrice Lumumba as revolutionary leaders, depicted in ways similar to images of U.S. civil rights activist Malcolm X, Cuban poet and independence hero José Martí, and Nicaraguan revolutionary Augusto César Sandino. Major figures in the U.S. civil rights movement visited Cuba in the early 1960s, such as Robert Williams, Assata Shakur, Harry Belafonte, Amiri Baraka (LeRoi Jones), Angela Davis, George Jackson, and Stokely Carmichael. These exchanges offered an international perspective on the place of African Americans in the wider history of imperialism.[44] Out of respect for the cultural practice of avoiding figurative representation, OSPAAAL posters used the basic shapes, bold colors, contrast, and minimalist presentation to present a direct comparison with Middle Eastern causes (figures 2.5–2.13). This poster art circulated in such a manner as to define these causes as part of a larger project of resistance to colonialism. It rendered specific struggles legible through a common visual framework, making visible the work of the AAPSO in privileging national liberation struggle as a common one against colonialism, racism, apartheid, and intervention to their memberships and the broader public.

Tricontinental Photojournalism

Beyond its poster art, other successful tools of rendering solidarity that OSPAAAL used were its documentary and experimental photography work. Due to global interest in Cuba's revolution, the early 1960s was a boom period for Havana-based photojournalists. Opportunities ranged from local and national newspapers to international publications. The number of photographic images printed in the major Cuban newspapers reached its peak in 1965 and remained relatively high until 1973, declining only when print media began to compete more directly with televised news reporting.[45] Photojournalists realized that having their work published depended on an intimate

Figure 2.5. Artist unknown, "For an Independent South Yemen," 1969. Courtesy of Lincoln Cushing / Docs Populi.

Figure 2.6. Faustino Pérez, "Day of Solidarity with the People of Palestine," 1968. Courtesy of Lincoln Cushing / Docs Populi.

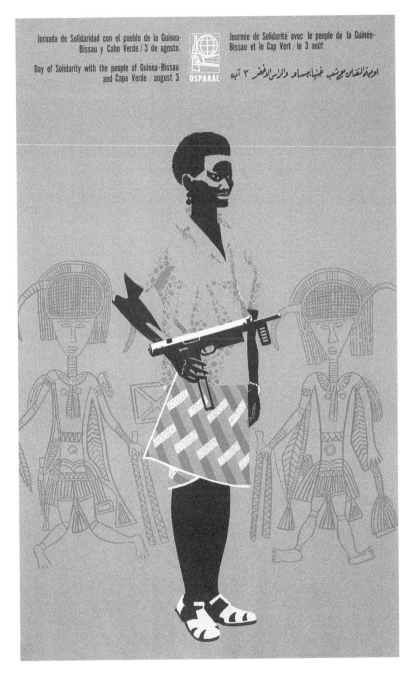

Jornada de Solidaridad con el pueblo de la Guinea-Bissau y Cabo Verde / 3 de agosto.

Day of Solidarity with the people of Guinea-Bissau and Cape Verde / august 3

OSPAAAL

Journée de Solidarité avec le peuple de la Guinée-Bissau et le Cap Vert / le 3 août

يوم التضامن مع شعب غينيا بيساو والرأس الأخضر ٣ آب

Figure 2.7. Berta Abelénda, "Day of Solidarity with the People of Guinea-Bissau and Cape Verde," 1968. Courtesy of Lincoln Cushing / Docs Populi.

Figure 2.8. Berta Abelénda, "Day of Solidarity with Palestine," 1968. Courtesy of Lincoln Cushing / Docs Populi.

Figure 2.9. Lázaro Abreu, "International Day of Solidarity with the Arab Peoples of Syria," 1970. Courtesy of Lincoln Cushing / Docs Populi.

Figure 2.10. Lázaro Abreu and Emory Douglas, "Solidarity with the African American People," 1968. Courtesy of Lincoln Cushing / Docs Populi.

Figure 2.11. Bert Abelénda, "Day of Solidarity with the People of South Africa," 1968.
Courtesy of Lincoln Cushing / Docs Populi.

Figure 2.12. Rafael Enríquez, "Lumumba 20° Aniversario," 1981. OSPAAAL, Folder no. 6, pictorial number 674-95, Sam L. Slick Collection of Latin American Political Posters, Center for Southwest Research, University Libraries, University of New Mexico.

Figure 2.13. José Papiol Torrent, "80 Primaveras del Tío Ho," 1970. Stamped on back "Taller de divulgación, Comisión de orientación revolucionaria del CC." Folder no. 30, "Jornada del 23 de abril al 19 de mayo pre-CJC," pictorial number SS674-563, Sam L. Slick Collection of Latin American Political Posters, Center for Southwest Research, University Libraries, University of New Mexico.

knowledge of how to identify moments worthy of capture. They needed to be fluent in ascertaining which people were important enough to be included in a frame and to be able to read a gathering to ferret out its broader social or political implications. They also needed to be expert in conveying ideas and stories through careful composition. Students of photojournalism were aware that their work might be called on as a matter of public record to confirm the factual basis of a historical event or to attest to its significance. In the 1950s, most photojournalists got their training in advertising or fashion photography and made their living working for traditional portrait studios. Professional photographers might participate in the activities of the Club Fotográfico de Cuba, whose distinguished members had frequent access to international visitors and notable guests. Amateur military photographers worked alongside brigades to capture images of combatants and events during the revolution, and the island also boasted a rich tradition of art photography.[46] Even prior to the revolution, Havana boasted a vibrant experimental photography scene, including many artists who circulated in the world of revolutionary Cuban intellectuals and rubbed elbows with artists across Latin America and other key centers of experimentalist art like Prague, Paris, and Moscow.[47]

One of the major subjects of Cuban photojournalism that interested newspapers in the early 1960s was the image of soldiers. Photographs of these soldiers, smartly dressed in casual uniforms, moving freely about in public spaces, engaging in community action, or being honored in public ceremonies, sold well. Cuban photographic images of the early 1960s were "a central medium for not only defending the present day but also 'offensively' defining the future on its own, hyper-real terms."[48] Photographs published in Cuban newspapers accompanied stories that documented the celebration of soldiers, the "new men" of socialist Cuba. Dignified and handsome, these soldiers reflected a reverence for the sacrifices of the men and women who served during the revolution and pointed toward the correct stance on ongoing armed struggle as a means of combating imperialism. These were not images of a postrevolutionary military regime, with combatants evolving into police or security forces. Instead, they were public servants, requiring no reintegration, as they had never been truly separated from meaningful social roles and civic life. These images resonated in the countryside and urban areas in Cuba alike, as they affirmed the direction of the revolutionary leadership and simultaneously participated in crafting a collective memory of combatants as being one with the people and, as such, of the people as primary agents of historical change.

In the ambitious political era of the early 1960s, an urgency to document socialist political reforms and economic experiments fueled an increase in the output and professionalization of photojournalists. Foreign press agencies were interested in sending their photographers to capture the changes brought on by the new government, adding layers of professional exchange and competition to the local scene.[49] Projects of urban renewal headed by the Ministry of Construction employed bold architects to erect monuments to the revolution, and many prominent cultural figures who had moved away returned to take their place in the artistic undertakings, imagined as part of the revolution's vision for the future.[50] Photojournalists had plenty of opportunities to stay busy documenting the progress of new buildings and cultural productions. The revolution of the 1960s prioritized the revitalization of cultural pursuits and building new National Art Schools of Plastic Arts, Music, Drama, and Ballet with fanciful modernist flair. Many architects of these schools tried to incorporate elements of Afro-Cuban form into their design, complementing the antiracism of other state art.[51] Although they were not universally lauded in this pursuit, their determination attests to the attachment of both the state and artists to a revolutionary revision of cultural form.

Photojournalists were also influenced by a new generation of documentary filmmakers that emerged in the 1960s and were interested in social realism and experimentation with form.[52] The genre of the film essay paralleled the work of photojournalists in providing a narrative and visual presentation through which audiences could reflect on arguments made by the revolution and consider critical points of view. Supported by the new film institute, the ICAIC, Santiago Álvarez, one of Cuba's most innovative filmmakers, used montage-style documentaries to make political arguments in a format that mimicked traditional newsreel films shown before feature films. Filmmakers around the world who were inspired by the Cuban Revolution or were seeking refuge—like Miguel Littín, Fernando Solanas, Fernando Birri, and Joris Ivens—participated in a cinematic movement aimed at revolutionizing the documentary form and were welcomed as guests of the ICAIC to participate in projects of instruction for local film students.[53] The ebullience of the film scene, certainly by the mid-1960s to the late 1970s, was appreciated by Cuban photographers and photojournalists, many of whom led conversations and reflection about how aesthetics and practice might participate in the art of a more revolutionary political and social commentary in Latin America.

Giving Visual Expression to Conflict

Photojournalism in OSPAAAL publications rendered visible the solidarity activities, intellectual figures, and key actors that shaped the discourse of Cuban alignment with various projects of anticolonialism. Part of the publication's strategy was to position it in important spaces of anticolonial intellectual conversation. The first issue of *Tricontinental*, printed in summer 1967, was distributed through OSPAAAL with the assistance of two publishing houses in Europe, Éditions Maspero in Paris and Editore Feltrinelli in Milan. It featured on its cover a high-contrast reproduction of a photograph of Congolese guerrilla soldier Pierre Mulele armed with a machine gun pointing jauntily toward the bottom corner of the frame. The image of Mulele set against a large yellow circle on a bright red background was modernist and bold, while referencing conflict on the front lines. The magazine announced its intention—to speak to an educated and well-established internationalist left, using the networks of prominent, established figures in publishing.

Giangiacomo Feltrinelli had become internationally renowned when he published *Doctor Zhivago*, smuggled out of the Soviet Union in 1956, and later when he participated in left-wing radicalism during Italy's Years of Lead civil conflict. Feltrinelli established a close friendship with Cuban photographer Alberto Korda, and later he was personally responsible for printing and circulating the famous image of Che Guevara widely considered to be the most iconic representation of the Latin American left. Feltrinelli's press was involved in publishing materials for a European audience related to various interests of the international left in the Middle East, Southeast Asia, and Latin America, and his family was known to have sent funds and developed personal ties of support to several notable figures. François Maspero in Paris was involved in publishing the work of Frantz Fanon and Régis Debray and a variety of important pieces on the independence movement in Algeria. He published new editions of the writings of Jean-Paul Sartre, Rosa Luxemburg, and, later, Che Guevara.[54] Son of a professor and a Holocaust survivor, he translated John Reed's *Ten Days That Shook the World* into French and won awards as a journalist. He opened his press in 1959, and his reputation as a publisher of leftist intellectual texts grew as he faced censorship, lawsuits, and even a bomb threat over publishing texts critical of the French in Algeria and promoting decolonization in Africa.[55]

The image of Mulele on the cover of the first *Tricontinental* (figure 2.14) echoed the location of the magazine in a particular ecology of leftist publication. The editor's preface was followed by letters of support and editorials written by Ho Chi Minh, Nguyen Huu Tho, Stokely Carmichael, Kim Jong-il, and Frantz Fanon. Fanon's contribution to the first issue was a lengthy analysis of the situation in the Congo, the death of Patrice Lumumba, and the failures of the United Nations to adequately assist in the struggle against colonialism.[56] The images that accompany these pieces include photos depicting racially motivated police violence in the United States. These photographs

Figure 2.14. Photo of Pierre Mulele, *Tricontinental* 1 (1967): cover. Courtesy of Cuban Heritage Collection, University of Miami Libraries.

were experimental in form—a repeated image, without explanatory text or byline. In the middle of an extensive analysis of U.S. race politics, three portraits of Stokely Carmichael, dressed in a white, collared shirt and wearing dark sunglasses, appear, occupying full-page spreads. Two of these are identical likenesses of Carmichael reflectively looking upward while pinching his throat just above the neck of his dress shirt (figure 2.15). They sit just above a larger portrait of him, in a profile shot, with the dark shape of his head occupying the majority of the frame. Carmichael's mouth is open in this image, and he appears to be speaking. Again, without captions, these images reflect a presumed readership that would be familiar with the Black Power movement and its key front men. They reflect a modernist photographic tradition—minimalist, boldly high-contrast—and offer no explanatory defense. The cover feature article, on Pierre Mulele, includes a reprinted letter written by Mulele from the previous summer, accompanied by a full-length portrait. In this image, the Congolese freedom fighter is armed, in a casual khaki uniform, arms at his sides, looking contemplatively into the camera. In a later image, Mulele is seated on a long bench or fallen tree branch alongside villagers and other soldiers, with hands folded in his lap and ankles exposed over his leather shoes. The men seated beside him are barefoot. What follows could be described as a photo essay comprising eleven other photos, some of which exhibit qualities of a photomontage and all of which display a group of armed men of various ages conducting activities inside the close quarters of a temporary dwelling, sometimes displaying weapons—bows and arrows, spears, and firearms (figure 2.16). Photographic images using strong contrasts between dark and light, chiaroscuros, are a central part of the issue's composition, resonant with films made at this time, creating dramatic tension between image and text. Mulele is engaged in the same business as Carmichael; both are versions of the Cuban socialist revolutionary ideal.

Photographers participated in constructing an idealized Cuban revolutionary posture. For instance, regarding resistance to French imperialism in Indochina in 1967, writers for the magazine elaborate the setting as a "surrealist vision," with combatants stationed in hundreds of hillside caves and mountains, enjoying cultural activities, making the best of scarce resources, and engaging in political consciousness raising and self-improvement.[57] To illustrate these points, the images depict not only armed insurgents—troops en route to their posts, crowds seated for a cultural performance or a meeting, displays of firearm technology—but also images of educational sessions, of teachers at a blackboard, surrounded by attentive students, considering the wartime activities in which they will soon participate.[58] Many spreads use a photomontage style, also common in the ICAIC's documentary films and

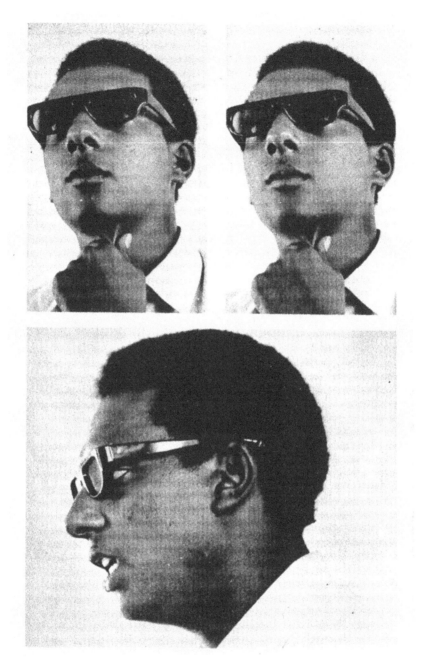

Figure 2.15. Photos of Stokely Carmichael, *Tricontinental* 1 (1967): 16. Courtesy of Cuban Heritage Collection, University of Miami Libraries.

Figure 2.16. Photo of Congolese guerrilla fighters in camp, *Tricontinental* 1 (1967): inside back cover. Courtesy of Cuban Heritage Collection, University of Miami Libraries.

features, with a part of a duplicated photograph cut out and pasted over another, a combatant's face duplicated, a diplopia, two matching images of the same figure, a stare fixed twice into the distance, the same man's arms replicated side by its own side, or a weapon cut into pieces that fail to align.[59] The duplicate portrait, like that of Carmichael, was used with other key figures of the political and intellectual left, such as Luis de la Puente, of Peru's Alianza Popular Revolucionaria Americana and the Movimiento de Izquierda Revolucionaria (Revolutionary Left Movement); Mário de Andrade of the Movimento Popular de Libertação de Angola (Popular Movement for the Liberation of Angola); C. L. R. James, author of *The Black Jacobins*; and many others.[60] Some photographs, such as those accompanying a report by journalist Teófilo Acosta on atrocities committed in Israel against Palestinians since 1948, provide evidence of torture, mistreatment, and forced displacement. None of the photographs used to illustrate Israeli violence include easily identifiable individuals, very few facial features can be determined at a glance, and most of these images frame a medium-sized grouping of five to twenty figures, both victims and perpetrators, providing a measure of the scale of the violence and hinting at a possible public record of such events.[61]

Quotidian scenes in the lives of those engaged in armed struggle were also frequently used to illustrate or complement accounts that positioned various conflicts in broader narratives of the role of revolution in anti-imperialism, antiracism, and other ideological contests. Such images might feature smiling combatants sitting around the communal kitchen of an outdoor encampment, cooking and serving food, washing dishes, fishing, building huts, or attending to the medical needs of the community.[62] They might depict combatants communing with what appear to be locals, sharing conversation and food, or simply inhabiting the same spaces in encampments. Beginning in mid-1969, more images appeared of women in camps and marching in protest movements; by 1970, whole women's demonstrations were featured.[63] These stories might be juxtaposed with editorials or news reports illustrated by photographs of long tables of participants at the United Nations. Mostly images of men, these photographs captured and conveyed the sense that these men represented larger social forces than their governments. Individuals from the NAM, AAPSO, and other UN member countries were pictured listening intently, considering arguments, and making speeches, sometimes looking perplexed or frustrated. They conveyed a reading of the political stances taken by, for example, Israel and the United States during sessions devoted to the Palestinian cause. Several issues feature UN speeches made by Castro or Guevara, most often highlighting the commanding presence of these two revolutionary icons or their reception—being applauded by delegates or famously flaunting the chamber's no-smoking policy with large Cuban cigars.[64] Stories and images from the United Nations might be followed by interpretations or correspondence from participants. Similarly, interpretations of events and photographs of the public activities of influential civil rights leaders such as Martin Luther King Jr. captured a spirit of attentiveness to public audiences.[65]

The Tricontinental spirit, echoed in the creative transformation of the arts in Cuba, embraced this more universalist, simple presentation, relying on the form to communicate a certain relationship between revolutionary projects and ideals. Subsequent issues continued to boast highly stylized photographic content. In 1968, one issue featured a striking image of Carmichael giving a speech. This image is reproduced four times: once under the portraits of two Student Nonviolent Coordinating Committee leaders, H. Rap Brown and James Forman; twice by itself filling a full page with identical versions, one on top of the other; and then twice cropped to highlight features of the speaker, one framing just Carmichael's head and the final image a full-page close-up of the right side of the speaker's mouth and neck, cropped just below the eyeline.[66] This image, zooming in on a medium shot of the speaker, followed by four sets of identical street images of conflict between civil rights demonstrators and the police, uses a coolly modern, cinematic idiom.[67] Photo spreads like these suggested hipness and the distinctiveness of revolutionary leaders and internationalist guerrilla armies, setting them apart from their counterparts in the war stories of previous generations. Socially engaged, modern, informed, and curious, combatants in a national liberation struggle were not interchangeable pawns; despite their combat roles, they did not correspond on any level to soldiers fighting on behalf of an empire.

OSPAAAL's style, seen in its poster art and magazine, emphasized clear ideological leadership. The preference of a central figure, often almost overfilling the frame, was repeated across the magazine. In keeping with this vision, soldiers, politicians, intellectuals, workers, and others were unmissable reflections of Cuba's vision of the centrality of the social to revolutionary economic and political experiments on the island. Presentations of conflict deliberately connected the narratives presented by leading figures of the left to images of armed combatants. Often printed in proximity to images, editorial pieces, or speeches by key political figures, such as graphic and photographic images of Che Guevara, individual national liberation movements were bookended by voices of major figures of African liberation such as Amílcar Cabral, a symmetry between the aims of the intellectual and material struggle between the forces of imperialism and those united with the cause of the Tricontinental.[68]

The visual expression of a conflict created an unequivocal connection between the fields of intellectual analysis of the principles at stake and the physical means by which a liberating resolution might be sought.

Conveying Solidarity in Graphic and Photographic Art

One of the key functions of the magazine, like its poster art, was to highlight the Cuban Revolution and argue for its continued realization. It did this by trying to blend the social and political history of struggle on the island with revolutionary causes elsewhere. For the ten-year anniversary of the revolution, the *Tricontinental* published a series of photographs of Castro and key moments in the celebration of the revolution's success at home.[69] The magazine privileged Cuba's role in supporting causes elsewhere, and connections were often made obliquely rather than directly, with unstated but obvious comparisons evident across the layout and the reporting. The magazine offered itself as a form of Cuban solidarity. It was intended to present a clear analysis of historical and political conditions in relevant liberation struggles and offer a vehicle of support to those seeking change. An example of this can be seen in an article written by Basil Davidson on the ongoing imperialism of the Portuguese in Africa.[70] A lengthy treatment of the history of colonial violence, the piece was illustrated with an experimental series of photographs of dictator António de Oliveira Salazar. The first of these featured a full-page black-and-white reproduction of a cutout of his head, which was repeated in subsequent pages folded in on itself, progressively becoming more distorted, as if the magazine itself were giving couched visual instructions, like an origami manual, on intellectual assessments of Salazar's position and a possible means of resistance.[71] Similarly, a photograph appearing in full color inside the cover of another issue, giving the appearance of an advertisement or a still-life painting, simply presents the ingredients of a Molotov cocktail, as if set up on a bar, under the simple heading "Coctel Libertad," or "liberty cocktail."[72] One issue included easily cut-out postcard images of combatants of the Frente Sandinista de Liberación Nacional (FSLN, Sandinista National Liberation Front) in Nicaragua, very similar to images circulated of Cuban revolutionaries just over a decade earlier, which could be mailed as a gesture of solidarity or as a means of spreading consciousness.[73] One inside cover included an image of Richard Nixon opening the breast of his jacket to reveal a photograph of piles of dead bodies in Vietnam.

The art of the magazine and bulletin proposed ethical considerations and political consciousness frameworks with simple, straightforward, and sometimes humorous image constructs. Covers might include color illustrations, hand-written diary entries, psychedelic cartoons, reproductions of donated fine-art *cuadros*, and line drawings of a fairly wide variety. Accompanying the dual columns of some news stories are graphics interwoven through the text. For instance, one common presentation style used inserted blocks of graphics, proportionately large and partially filling an entire column, similar to comic book panels. One report on the Black Panthers included text interrupted by partial images of a graphic of a panther-like black cat, ending with a story on Black Power illustrated with a full image of the same cat (figure 2.17).[74] Another common motif used by the magazine is the progressive comic story, generally accompanying a related report or editorial but not necessarily, which would occupy panels within the text columns and would reveal a concept over several pages. One such graphic depicted a soldier over several frames, gradually being dressed in increasing layers of uniform and equipment, including a gas mask, until, in one panel, a mysterious hand from above inserts a coin into a slot that appears in the top of the helmet. The following panels depict the soldier firing his weapon and images of a gas explosion, with large text block letters spelling out "GRR" and "BANG" (figure 2.18).[75] Another depicts an American foot-ball player running with a pigskin ball under his arm, speeding progressively forward, functioning as a flipbook thumbed quickly over several pages, on the last of which the player rams his helmet into the chest of an armed police officer with the full weight and speed of his body, knocking the latter off his feet.[76] These graphics play on a shared political sensibility, using dark humor to suggest creative pathways of resistance.

Another common theme across several issues is the appearance of a thought or speech bubble, familiar to cartoon readers, placed over the photograph of a clearly identifiable figure, such as a civil rights or national liberation leader, but instead of containing words, the bubble includes an illustration, such as a panther on the attack, a documentary-style photograph of an event, or a pho-tomontage of an idea, such as a collage of different participants in a demon-stration.[77] For instance, a report by Eduardo Mondlane, founding leader of the Frente de Libertação de Moçambique (FRELIMO, Mozambique Liberation Front), published just before his assassination, is illustrated with a photograph of Mondlane's face, clearly speaking, with speech bubbles above his head con-taining an image of FRELIMO fighters, followed by photojournalistic images of organizing meetings and combatants standing proudly facing the camera for a group portrait.[78] These images emphasize and add weight to the text,

A so-called Permanent Group of Industrial Mobilization is functioning in Brazil, closely tied up with U.S. interests, and especially with the Pentagon, for the mass production at low cost of war equipment which has a high cost in the United States. They will receive orders for materials that will be used in the war on Viet-Nam. A Caribu plane factory has been installed in the state of Ceará; these planes have a special use in anti-guerrilla warfare. A uniform factory was set up in Belo Horizonte. 2,000 small and medium-sized industries went bankrupt in the state of Sao Paulo during the period of 1964-66. The assets of these companies have been absorbed by the U.S. monopolies, or by "Brazilian" outfits operating with foreign capital.

¶ *Tricontinental* confirms the outbreak of guerrilla fighting in Rwanda. The revolutionary forces of the Rhodesian National Union Party, that adopted armed struggle as the only possible means of attaining the independence of Rwanda from the pro-imperialist government of K. Gregoire, assert that armed struggle is in the foremost place and that it shall forge the desired unity. The Rwanda guerrillas enjoy the firm support of certain governments that, in this African zone, must face the Rwanda government and the troops of Mobutu, that violate their frontiers in order to carry out acts of terrorism.

¶ The CIA aids Israel through Hussein. It has been learned that, at present, the intelligence and security services of the monarch are concentrating their efforts on the repression of the Palestinian commandos. Mohammed Rassoul Kailani, Jordanian chief of intelligence, is likewise a liaison agent of the CIA.

Figure 2.17. Drawing of black panther, *Tricontinental* 2 (1967): 178–79. Courtesy of Cuban Heritage Collection, University of Miami Libraries.

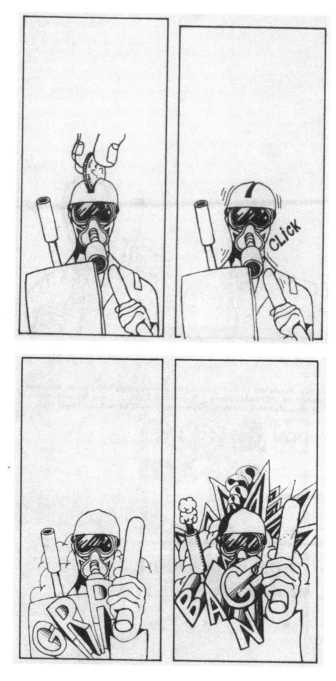

Figure 2.18. Drawing of gas-masked soldier, *Tricontinental* 9 (1968): 116–19. Courtesy of Cuban Heritage Collection, University of Miami Libraries.

connecting the ideological points Mondlane made to the individual combatants and their commitment to the movement.

Full-color graphics printed on the inside of the front and back covers of the magazine often took a jocular tone, seemingly designed to be cut out and used to educate children or simply suggest fanciful play (figures 2.19 and 2.20). Drawn in the style of playing cards, board games, paper dolls, comic books, Russian dolls, jigsaw puzzles, and other children's games, these visual referents made ideological positionings seem whimsical, natural, and even fun (figure 2.21).[79] A "tactic of internationalist political education," these illustrations and graphics made an appeal to emotion that might stimulate a playful affinity with revolutionary politics.[80] Similarly, a number of graphic spreads, mimicking advertisements, subtly critique linkages between political regimes and industry, such as false ads for nonexistent national airlines, boasting of the travel delights of countries with poor records on human rights and pointing to the possible surprises that might await the unschooled tourist of the colonized world.[81]

Cuban photojournalism slowed by early 1971, as did the richness and quality of the photographic and graphic art included in *Tricontinental*. As Castro began to struggle to maintain his reputation abroad, local access for Cuban photojournalists decreased. Many contemporaries began to look skeptically on Castro's increasing centralization of power; this tension was reflected in the pages of the bulletin and magazine, which took a more serious tone by the mid-1970s. Although several new phases of artistic novelty followed, the magazine's creativity never reached the heights of this early period of experimentation. Issues of the magazine suffered from a noticeable decline in image resolution, perhaps as a result of a greater reliance on transmitted and reproduced photographs rather than originals. There was also a decline in the creativity of the magazine's graphic design, possibly the result of a smaller staff or a scarcity of quality printing supplies but also reflecting a turn to more sober themes. In fall 1971, the first traditional newsprint political cartoons began to appear, which were a far cry from the magazine's previous cartooning.[82] Despite these changes, the magazine's poster art continued to be just as strong as before, and its cover art referenced earlier motifs and strategies of communicating ideas. One of the most important graphics that remained unchanged was the OSPAAAL logo; it continued to communicate the mission of the organization, spreading revolutionary ideas, specifically those of armed struggle, to a broad global audience. Comprising a fist raising a tightly held automatic rifle superimposed over the image of a globe, this symbol remained the same until OSPAAAL finally closed its doors in June 2019.[83]

Figure 2.19. Cover, *Tricontinental* 6 (1968). Courtesy of OSPAAAL Archive.

Figure 2.20. "Sabía usted que América Latina . . . ," *Tricontinental* 6 (1968): inside back cover. Courtesy of OSPAAAL Archive.

Figure 2.21. Inside cover, *Tricontinental* 7 (1968). Courtesy of OSPAAAL Archive.

Tercermundismo and Rendering Solidarity at the United Nations

The work of rendering solidarity performed by OSPAAAL was intended for several audiences; chief among them were key intellectuals and political leaders of the NAM and the AAPSO. Circulating the writings of influential figures within both audiences, as a gesture of solidarity and a way to help clarify for a broader audience the historical factors and key issues at play in any given context, gave OSPAAAL a leading role in communicating and defining common goals. Moreover, it mobilized visual objects to offer its audiences practical strategies of ideological resistance. One of the most meaningful connections made by the magazine was between Africa and Afro-diasporic populations in the Americas. Several issues directly tackled the reluctance of African leaders to see the diasporic population as a source of useful alliances. Writers spent time revisiting the history and culture of Africa, tracing its ties to the new world through slavery, and elevating the connection of the political consciousness of Afro-Americans to that of national liberation leaders on the continent. One such article, a lengthy piece written by Cuban historian José Luciano Franco, includes reprinted historical lithographs—one of a bound slave being tossed out to sea and another depicting the sacrifices made by Africans during their participation in early North American settlement.[84] This article highlights how Afro-Latinos were failed many times over, having never been fully assimilated in the colonial Americas, given secondary status in independence wars, and suffering as exploited victims of ongoing state repression. Other issues reproduced iconic images of traditional dances, face masks, spears, and other African symbols. These images accompanied stories of cultural connection between the Americas and Africa and echoed the work of the poster artists who intended to create such associations.[85]

Reprinting the words of leaders of liberation struggles alongside images of training camps was also an irrefutable way of communicating Cuba's support for armed struggle. Images of soldiers receiving weapons and being instructed in how to use them could be interpreted only as references to the role Cuba played or hoped to play in supporting various guerrilla campaigns. Visual and narrative interpretation of these conflicts through the lens of the Cuban Revolution was also a means by which the magazine conveyed a sense of common enemies across these distant armed struggles.[86] In addition, because many of these images had no photo credits, they faintly suggested the presence of Cubans or close contact with combatants on the ground. It was no secret that Castro extended military support to liberation movements in open conflict, but Cuban political and military resources also circulated through clandestine channels. The magazine's success in subtly hinting at these channels without revealing sensitive information was a strong means of communicating support.

By 1979, OSPAAAL's success in rendering Cuban solidarity could not be denied. Cuba was a rising force in the NAM, hosting its annual conference in Havana. OSPAAAL's poster art had helped establish a dialogue useful for advancing the broader goals of not only Castro but the movement. With a visual pathway space for Cuban internationalist solidarity, transnational communication of its goals across the Global South continued long into the 1980s and 1990s as these same parties confronted the apartheid regime in South Africa and U.S. interventionism in Central America and the Caribbean. Wresting the tremendous force of the NAM and the Afro-Asian solidarity bloc at the UN away from the orienting frameworks of Nasserism was no small feat. Posters that reframed Middle Eastern, Asian, and African conflict through a Latin American and internationalist framework visually displayed Cuba's advocacy for Afro-Asian national liberation and the notion of permanent revolution. As a tool of solidarity, OSPAAAL visually articulated Cuba's intention to partner with the aims of the AAPSO at the United Nations and eventually to provide direction. The result of Cuba's ongoing solidarity activity, with its various complementary strategies, allowed the bloc to advance resolutions on the national liberation of African nations and eventually insert Latin American (specifically Cuban) interests into the center of these spaces. By the late 1970s, Castro's interventions provided an intellectual resource to solidarity movements in refusing to conceptualize regional hegemons as a useful alternative to European or U.S. neocolonialism. Framing the struggles of Palestinians, Angolans, Vietnamese, African Americans, and others through a Latin American internationalist frame helped Cuba defend the particular nature of the ongoing Cuban revolutionary position and its foreign policy. It also helped Castro deflect some external criticism of the revolution's domestic failings. Another success of this solidarity can be seen in its legacy for subsequent generations of Cubans in imagining Cuba's role abroad. Cubans in the late 1990s and early 2000s were quick to express pride in Cuba's role in Angola and in fighting against South Africa's attempts to colonize Namibia.[87] In part, this pride in revolutionary internationalism helped fuel Cuba's ongoing commitment to sending medical personnel and technological support abroad. One afterlife of OSPAAAL's efforts can be seen in the assistance Cuba sent to West African nations in the wake of the Ebola pandemic in 2014.

At the 14 September 1976 meeting in Mexico City of the Conference on Economic Co-operation among Developing Countries, UN Secretary-General Kurt Waldheim announced in his opening remarks that "the movement toward economic integration and cooperation among States based on equality, one might say based on collective self-reliance, has deep roots in Latin America, going as far back as 150 years to the visionary ideas of the liberator Simón Bolívar." Waldheim, a former National Socialist and antisemite, was not a well-received public champion of revolution; he was later challenged for his seat by former Mexican president Luis Echeverría, albeit unsuccessfully. In his speech, Waldheim continued, "the movement for third world solidarity may be entering today a new and decisive phase," one to which he attributed the significant influence of the UN framework and its commitment to the values and goals of transregional cooperation.[88] The rest of the statement continued to laud Latin America's revolutionary path to independence. It is notable that the secretary-general framed these goals so squarely in the language of *tercermundismo*— Third Worldist solidarity as a movement, a force of global change, and pointedly as a primary source of restructuring resource mobilization. This articulation of internationalist solidarity rhetorically mirrored the vision of *tercermundismo* advanced by Cuba in the late 1960s, even if in some ways it contradicted the essentially pragmatic approach advanced at the conference. This reshaped narrative about what Latin American countries might contribute from within institutional frameworks to South-South solidarity movements of the early 1970s was in no small part the product of Cuba's work with the NAM and AAPSO at the UN.

As a case study, OSPAAAL's experience and efforts to promote national liberation at the United Nations underscore the increasing importance of visual culture and media in creating a distinct sense of transborder political community. The importance of the work done through the art of the magazine and its editing is clear from the many means by which it reappeared over the next decades. The connections made through culture, in particular, illustrate the ability of art, culture, sport, and narrative to advance solidarity outside the sphere of states, across geographies, and in multiple temporal periods. Rendering solidarity as a mode of South-South organizing does the critical work of providing an argument on behalf of a cause that may be too far away and too unfamiliar. Building layers of connection and directing clear, focused attention, rendering solidarity sharpens the means by which a conflict can be usefully articulated. Useful articulation, a product of such rendering, has the unique advantage of facilitating deconstruction—dismantling through argument. Like Nixon flashing a chest full of fallen victims of imperialism, these connections, once rendered, are difficult to dismiss. The influence of the Cuban Revolution on generations of Black activists in the United States also stands as a testament to the effect of successful cultural exchange.[89] Anne Garland Mahler argues that OSPAAAL during this period was "the primary engine of radical cultural production throughout the world" and the "ideological backbone of current conceptualizations of global subalternity."[90] Although OSPAAAL was not always considered a resounding success in organizing international cooperation, its continuing importance in Latin American and Third Worldist narratives of solidarity efforts presents a strong point of contradiction to the dismissal of these efforts as being predominantly rooted in developmentalist ambitions or being "fundamentally ambivalent in nature."[91]

By 12 October 1979, Castro had become the clear spokesperson of the NAM countries at the United Nations, having been chosen at the Sixth Conference to present the position of the ninety-five constituent countries with respect to disarmament, trade inequities, global poverty, and, without any hesitation, the urgency with which the Cuban Revolution should be shielded against the aggression of the United States.[92] Tricontinentalism provided a coherent revolutionary politics with which to facilitate OSPAAAL's rendering acts of solidarity, allowing a vision of socialist internationalism to be interpreted into local contexts and applied to understandings of distant movements. Cuba's work in advancing this interpretation at the United Nations helped pave the way for different imaginings of global political economy. It resisted criticism of agreements made between socialist countries and undermined neoliberal economic planning initiatives delivered as veiled anticommunist rhetoric. Although the fruits of the labor of the artists and writers of *Tricontinental* could be interpreted as being profoundly about the Cuban Revolution in many ways, they are perhaps one of the most enduring and far-reaching examples of solidarity activism from the South that the twentieth century has to offer.

3

For Palestine in Argentina

I n 2003, a handful of activist groups in Argentina adopted the *keffiyeh* as a symbol of collective identity to distinguish themselves from other groups of demonstrators in antiglobalization marches. This black-and-white checkered scarf, part of traditional Palestinian dress, is a symbol of the Palestinian nationalist cause and radical subaltern resistance across Latin America and in many parts of the world.[1] Demonstrators in the streets of Buenos Aires proclaimed identification with the struggle of Palestinians, "nuestros Palestinos," to be as much a part of a shared struggle against oppression and the forces of global imperialism as their own domestic grievances.[2] Latin American solidarity with Palestine offers a case study for observing the reception of a global solidarity movement and its incorporation into a local context. From protest against the creation of the Israeli state in 1948 to current acts of solidarity with occupied Gaza and medical relief, reflection on Palestine has been an integral part of Argentine leftist politics. This chapter considers the history of making common cause with the fate of Palestinian nationalism in Argentina as an example of South-South political mobilization. Specifically, I examine how political parties of the Argentine left during the 1960s and 1970s encountered and incorporated Palestine into their own platforms, local positions, and strategies of resisting dictatorship.

Solidarity with Palestine has had many variations in the international and Latin American left, not the least of which is direct connection with and support for Palestinian nationalism. Armed insurgent groups such as the Sandinistas in Nicaragua, the Revolutionary Armed Forces of Colombia, and the Montoneros in Argentina had direct contact with Yasser Arafat and leaders of Palestinian movements. Others had more symbolic relationships with Palestinian nationalism. For example, Palestine occupied a central place in the political imaginary of *independentistas* in support of Puerto Rican self-rule, crafting a shared notion of global coloniality and allowing activists to advocate more successfully for particular causes, such as the release of political prisoners. Framing Puerto Rico's independence movement as a call for decolonization and self-determination akin to that of Palestine elevated the local cause to one of international concern.[3] Anarchist punk activism in Mexico, as another example, situates the Palestinian cause within internationalist anarcho-punk sensibilities across the Atlantic, as fundamentally against patriarchal hierarchies and an example of the need for increased nonstate political autonomy.[4] In a similar fashion, Palestinian nationalism offered Argentine leftists a rallying cry with which to critique both distant and local power structures.

In one sense, for leftists in many parts of Latin America, Palestine provides an emblematic struggle by which to reenvision the legacy of imperialism. It provides a critique of citizenship regimes, border politics, and international institutions' roles in failing to provide a safeguard for stateless peoples. In the case of Cuba, one of the first nations to formally recognize the Palestinian Liberation Organization (PLO) in 1964 when it was created in Cairo, solidarity with Palestine went further. A highly synergistic relationship existed between Arafat and Castro, who each stood to gain by being recognized by the other (figure 3.1). Mutual commitments to armed struggle provided opportunities for Castro and Arafat to collaborate materially in national liberation struggles elsewhere. In the Southern Cone, ties to the Middle East manifested in a tradition of solidarity with Palestine evolving from diasporic ties and relationships. As a case study, Argentina provides an excellent example of how a distinct form of South-South solidarity operated in a local context. It would be impossible to reduce solidarity with Palestine in Argentina to a mere function of relationships between leftist groups or transfers of material resources. Political recognition, unlike in Cuba, did not serve as a primary motivation. Where the use of the *keffiyeh* in many parts of the world served a more figural purpose, solidarity organizing in Argentina on behalf of Palestine had a more entangled historical trajectory. This chapter argues that for the Southern Cone—and for Argentina specifically—representational solidarity with Palestine allowed political parties of the left to fashion a critical lifeboat in the wake of dictatorship. This solidarity also helped the Argentine left face a local crisis of indeterminacy and provided a source of unity.

Throughout the twentieth century, transnational solidarities were implicated in the ideological positioning of the Argentine left. From antifascist civic associations and anarcho-syndicalist labor organizing to influential networks of intellectuals and transgressive media activism, a variety of movements oriented themselves toward external causes.[5] The means by which various parties

Figure 3.1. "Esta es la voluntad de nuestros pueblos," *Tricontinental* 85 (1983): 113. Courtesy of OSPAAAL Archive.

and currents of the left used representational solidarity with Palestine as an instrument of change can be seen clearly in the aftermath of its most recent military dictatorship, which lasted from 1976 to 1983, a period that significantly reduced the ranks of the political left through various modes of oppression, including illegal detention, torture, and disappearance. Although pro-Palestine expressions had much deeper roots, South-South solidarity with Palestinian nationalism was more clearly visible in the aftermath of the return to civilian government, due partly to the connections between the radical left and the PLO before and during the dictatorship. This chapter examines solidarity with the PLO proceeding from the human encounters that brought the cause of Palestinian nationalism into the purview of the radical left during the 1960s and 1970s. It traces these ties through the 1990s, when Palestine nationalism provided a means by which the Argentine left could incorporate emerging social movements and rebuild itself. It reads the "Question of Palestine" across fragmented encounters between the Argentine left and the Arab League, the Organization of Arab States, and the Non-Aligned Movement (NAM) and then examines how these relationships provided a representational solidarity field from which the left later drew unifying strength. In addition to outlining these moments of exchange, this chapter is concerned with narrative construction, examining how pro-Palestine strategies have been mobilized beyond concrete connections between the Argentine left and various counterparts in the Middle East.[6] The chapter concludes by offering a contrast between the Argentine experience and that of Chile to consider how a solidarity movement that might seem to be similarly motivated, taking place in a similar context, might produce alternative outcomes.

The Argentine Left Considers the PLO

From 1880 to 1915 and at the fall of the Ottoman empire, Argentina became an important destination for migrants from the Middle East. With its open immigration policies, Argentina welcomed roughly 130,000 migrants from the region, primarily from the Levant, which includes present-day Syria, Lebanon, Palestine, and Jordan. Labeled variously *turcos, Otomanos, sirio-libaneses,* or simply *Árabes,* these migrants organized themselves into associational groups, often with philanthropic groups, cultural clubs, voluntary organizations, or mutual aid societies, such as the Club Sirio Libanés of Buenos Aires, Patronato Sirio-Libanés, Club Sirio Libanés, Club Libanés, Homs Club of Buenos Aires, and the Hospital Sirio Libanés. These associations provided newcomers with vital connections and support. They often served as a means of staying connected with family members living elsewhere in the Americas or those who had not left the Middle East.[7] Over time, the diaspora in Argentina achieved a degree of middle-class stability, published their own periodicals, and, as a predominantly Christian and politically conservative ethnic minority, eventually enjoyed a degree of respectability.[8] By the 1940s, many Sirio-Libanés families had become business owners and entered various professions; the list of politicians of Argentine Arab descent also began to grow, including mayors and governors, and eventually included a president of the republic.

In 1941, Arab immigrants from North and South America convened in Buenos Aires to discuss European colonialism in their homelands and published a declaration denouncing the proposed creation of a Jewish national homeland in Palestine.[9] World War I and the interwar period had offered intellectuals in Argentina opportunities to reflect seriously on imperialism in the Middle East. During the interwar years, the increased circulation of news about events related to the mandate territories and works by important anti-imperialist writers influenced the thinking of many Argentine intellectual figures. This reporting also shifted attention away from negative associations with the Arab world that had characterized Argentine political writing in previous eras.[10] In 1947, when the UN Special Committee on Palestine declared the formal partition of the former British Mandate into two separate nations, one Jewish and one Arab, the Argentine state had already firmly established itself as politically neutral to the two parties involved.[11] This was partly motivated by Argentina's refusal to answer to the dictates of the Allied countries in the aftermath of World War II, but with its long history of Arab and Jewish immigration, the country maintained important political and socioeconomic ties to competing groups in the Middle East.[12] In addition, the Arab League frequently sent delegations to South America to facilitate communication between leaders in the diasporic community and the Middle East and to encourage economic and political support for key diplomatic causes, including that of Palestine.[13] In 1948, Argentina was even proposed as a potential refuge for Palestinians displaced by the creation of the state of Israel, as it had been proposed as a potential refuge for Jews fleeing persecution in Europe decades earlier.[14]

Following the partition, the first pro-Palestine efforts in Argentina came from the civil associations of the sizable Syrian Lebanese community in Buenos Aires.[15] Despite moments of public notoriety, activism among the diaspora in Argentina was limited and was usually a far cry from the anti-imperialist stridency of internationalist leftists. Most members of the diaspora, among the ranks of successful businessmen and the middle class, tended toward conservative policies and had connections to clientelist local governance structures. President Juan Perón, a former army general who led a populist government from 1946 to 1955, extended support for Gamal Abdel Nasser's revolution and subsequent populist regime in Egypt, considering Egypt to be a sister nation with much in common with Argentina. Building on existing ties between Egypt and the diaspora, Perón increased Argentina's diplomatic ties in the region, just as Nasser increased his profile by nationalizing the Suez Canal. When rivalries between Arab states began to intensify in the early 1950s, key political figures in Argentina—particularly communists, socialists, and the increasingly radical syndicalist left—became more skeptical of the Perón administration's intentions with respect to the region, particularly his admiration of and friendship with Nasser, and they began to look to the Palestinian diaspora for answers.[16] As both Egypt and Iraq attempted to "conjure up 'their own' Palestinian entities," the Soviet Union used the Arab-Israeli conflict as an opportunity to negotiate new relationships with Arab states.[17] This move prompted increased international critique, which included skepticism among many leaders attending the Bandung conference, and gave many Argentine leftists pause. They carefully considered the conflict's relationship to broader geostrategic relationships, the alignment of the various local parties, and the motivation of Soviet support for Arab nationalism.[18]

During this time, several outspoken leaders of the Argentine far left expressed suspicion about the anticolonialist claims made by several prominent figures in Third World revolutionary politics, including regionally powerful proponents of pan-Arabism such as Nasser and Castro. *Palabra Obrera*, the media organ of Argentina's Trotskyist revolutionary workers and eventually of the Partido Obrero (PO, Workers' Party), argued as early as 1959 that Castro was pro-imperialist and frequently spoke out against Castro's foreign policy overtures.[19] Describing Nasser, Nehru, Cárdenas, Perón, and Castro alike as Bonapartist, the PO argued that these revolutionary leaders all gave power from one sector of the bourgeoisie to another.[20] The PO critiqued the Israeli left, coining the term "social imperialism" in describing its position with respect to the socialist programs in both Jewish and Palestinian areas.[21] By contrast, the PO supported land occupation and *syndicalismo campesino*, sending militants to Peru, for example, to help with rural land occupations in the Cuzco area. The PO argued for Palestinian resistance to pan-Arabism and other forms of leftist nationalism along similar lines.[22] Through the early 1960s, many leftist parties in Argentina, including the Partido Comunista Argentina (PCA, Communist Party of Argentina) and the Partido Socialista (PS, Socialist Party), also took a public stand against the expansionist impulses of the state of Israel, increasing the validity of their claims to stand against imperialism. This trend came to a head during the Six-Day War, as the Israeli state's aggression in the region became widely reported across news outlets.[23] When the PO joined forces in 1963 with the Frente Revolucionario Indoamericano Popular (Indo-American Popular Revolutionary Front) and later with others to become the Partido Revolucionario de los Trabajadores (PRT, Workers' Revolutionary Party), its position on Palestine signaled a particular form of leftist militancy that enabled it to connect Argentina with wider global struggles. In 1967, the PO called for the destruction of the Israeli state but at the same time was careful to denounce antisemitism and affirm the need for unifying Jewish and Arab workers.[24]

The PRT brought together Marxist leftists, rural insurgents, and indigenist revolutionaries to press for a socialist and trade unionist agenda. From 1965 to 1973, the PRT was at the center of radical resistance to a series of military governments in Argentina and to Peronist nationalism. The PRT responded to the Palestine-Israel conflict largely through Al-Fatah, the organization of Arafat's nationalist diasporic project, which also had deep roots in socialism and trade unionism. Established in 1958 in Kuwait and Qatar, both marginalized states in the Arab Middle East, Al-Fatah could be found across the region by 1962. Al-Fatah circulated its own media organ, *Our Palestine*, and set up an international office in Algiers, capital of the liberated postcolonial world.[25] In January 1964, at the First Summit of the Arab League in Cairo, a swelling of nationalist sentiment among the Palestinian diaspora, particularly in refugee camps, led to the creation of a Palestinian governing entity. The PLO replaced the Arab Higher Committee, which had been responsible for representing the Palestinian cause since the 1947–48 Arab-Israeli War, and theoretically maintained a greater degree of autonomy for Palestinians. Although the League of Arab States carefully managed the new Palestinian entity, this represented an increased visibility for Palestinian refugees and leaders in the conflict. Maoist China extended diplomatic recognition to the PLO, offering military and communications support.[26] Argentine leftist organizations, such as remnants of the PO and the new PRT, refused to fully embrace the PLO until the organization clearly distinguished itself as autonomous from the League of Arab States. This allowed them to demonstrate a nuanced internationalist perspective, which might deflect criticism that the left was unfit to lead because of a lack of credible positions on foreign relations.

The Sino-Soviet split tended to be an important dividing line for many leftists in Argentina. As Nikita Khrushchev announced his plans to de-Stalinize the Soviet Union and Mao became more suspicious of Soviet involvement in conflicts in Asia, the split became a vehicle for articulating the local left's evolving ideological positions on Marxism, imperialism, and foreign affairs. Some factions of the left criticized the ignorance of the Soviet Union about what was happening in a postcolonial Third World, whereas others were suspicious of

China's persistence in seeking a leading role in Third World movements at the Bandung and Cairo meetings that prefigured the NAM.[27] In this wider frame of Cold War leftist politics, the PLO's struggle was rumored to pivot on resistance to Soviet imperialism in the Middle East or, alternatively, suggested a Maoist tendency in pan-Arabism. Matters were somewhat clarified when the PLO Charter of 1964 (amended in 1968) supported national liberation through armed struggle, declared the partition illegal, and urged the establishment of an autonomous Palestinian state. Before joining the PLO, Al-Fatah advocated waging a long guerrilla war against Israel. Al-Fatah was also clear that it aimed to Palestinize the conflict and thus separate the question of Palestine from the regional contest between the United States and the Soviet Union.

In this early period, the genius of Arafat's strategy was apparent to Latin American leaders on the left. Mario Santucho, founder of the PRT, recognized Arafat as a credible representative of the cause, with strong credentials from founding a student movement and leading a transborder labor union among the Palestinian diaspora.[28] Like Guevara, Arafat also represented a "masculine ability to launch armed struggle," a kind of new Revolutionary Man.[29] In addition, the PRT recognized Arafat's movement as a refusal to take part in the imperialist contest of the Cold War. Palestinian self-determination became the primary cause taken up by Argentine communists, including several militant groups, particularly as the Argentine Communist Party felt increasingly distanced from Guevarism.[30] When the Central Organizing Committee of the Argentine Communist Party issued a call in 1967 to repudiate Israel's aggression, it also denounced the increasing influence of oil-producing countries, such as Saudi Arabia, Iraq, and Iran, in the region, which it saw as imperialist.[31] Some internationalist concern was raised regarding the alienation of the Israeli Communist Party when delegates from Arab states objected to their presence at meetings, but the Argentine branch of the party relegated the controversy to a low priority, circulating a translation of the complaint letter from Jerusalem but not taking an active position.[32] Using a representational solidarity with Palestine to encode their positions allowed the Argentine Communist Party to align itself with the increasingly important Third Worldist agenda.

In 1964, the League of Arab States set up an information office in Buenos Aires. This office began publishing a steady stream of informative pamphlets, books, and magazines on the Palestine-Israel conflict, by which Argentine leftists could be better informed about politics in the Middle East.[33] When Al-Fatah finally joined the PLO in 1968, quickly establishing control of the Palestinian National Congress and the PLO Executive Committee, previously conflicting utopian ideals finally united in one cause. The Argentine left could align around the PLO in its call for self-determination and national liberation, without sacrificing support of Al-Fatah's commitment to the diasporic student and labor movements that had made Arafat's organizing so politically successful. In 1969, Arafat was elected chair of the PLO, and communist and socialist periodicals in Argentina began to frequently discuss the political situation of Palestinians, offering solidarity as a matter of ideological principle. Already in 1967, the Executive Council of the Federación Universitaria Argentina had passed a series of resolutions denouncing Israel, which resulted in increasing campus protest and consciousness-raising events across the country.[34] By 1973, a cross-party solidarity movement finally began to take shape. The Partido Comunista passed several resolutions denouncing Zionism, Israel's regional aggression, and the treatment of Palestinians by the Israeli state and defense forces.[35] In this phase, intellectuals and leaders on the left sided (at least ideologically) with Araftat's PLO in its stated goals of self-determination and the right of return.[36] Left-leaning intellectuals, like Jorge Luis Borges, Ricardo Piglia, and Manuel Puig, began to actively celebrate Argentina's Arab immigrant past in their writings.[37] Leftist writers and artists, particularly journalists and filmmakers, participated in transregional cultural activism with their counterparts in Palestine and elsewhere in the Middle East, championing the PLO as an authentic form of leftist resistance to Cold War forces. The notoriety of the films of Fernando Solanas, Octavio Getino, and Fernando Birri, in turn, inspired political filmmakers in the Palestinian diaspora.[38] Beyond ideological support, leftist leaders began expressing open support for Arafat, including establishing connections between political parties.

The Partido Socialista provides an interesting case in the emerging solidarity movement. During the early years of the Arab-Israeli conflict, the PS had been aligned with European socialists in favoring the creation of the state of Israel. During the 1950s, Argentine socialist party leaders offered mostly unflagging support of several prominent socialist leaders in the Zionist movement. Notably, Enrique Dickmann, who had been a party leader until his death in 1955, penned a work on the threat that fascism and German national socialism posed to Argentina.[39] This position reflected not only the party's close connection with the local Jewish community but also its bilateral and multilateral ties with the United Kingdom and the United States, which were considered important to the interests of the party well into the late 1970s.[40] The PS and the PCA did participate in the coalition of leftist interests that formed in the 1960s in resistance to the dictatorship, but not until after 1967 did their increasingly militant members take on more pro-Palestine positions. When the PRT and other more radical factions of leftist political parties gradually recruited militant socialists and communists, former PS and PCA leaders began to take more vocal positions on the ongoing Israeli hostilities. Most prominently, the militant Partido Comunista Revolucionario began to critique the Israeli state as genocidal.[41]

The Peronist Left and Argentine Zionism

While Argentine socialists, communists, and radical leftist groups wrestled with the conflict between anti-imperialist ideals and the transnational dimensions of the Cold War, the Peronist left had different concerns. Peronism, the political movement based on the ideas and policies of Juan Perón, was largely a populist movement strongly tied to a working-class, unionist support base. Peronism, also sometimes called *justicialismo* (after the Partido Justicialista that became Perón's party), emphasized a strong central government and economic nationalism and was to the left of the Socialist Party in the 1950s but later, like many populist parties, shifted direction to reflect new leaders or to match new priorities. Where Perón had always attempted to walk a fine line in foreign policy toward the Middle East, official Peronism had tended to focus more attention on the problem of international capital and the benefits of nationalism. As a result, rumors of Perón being antisemitic began to circulate, particularly in the Jewish Argentine community. Much of this reputation came from Perón's identification and close relationship with Egypt, including his vocal support for the NAM under Nasser's leadership.[42]

More than a decade after Perón's 1955 exile, the Peronist resistance, trying to rehabilitate the populist's former support, tried to revive Perón's anti-imperialist rhetoric by repackaging Peronism as an authentic source of resistance to colonial violence.[43] The Montoneros, a militant political group that emerged from a confluence of Peronist unionists, radical Catholics, and student activist groups in the early 1970s, used urban guerrilla tactics to confront the military, hoping for Perón's return from exile and the restoration of his populist rule. The Montoneros saw in Perón a leftist who could support the revolutionary vanguard in establishing socialism and put an end to authoritarian military rule. Whether this was the case was very much in question. Montonero leaders advertised their own vision of Perón as a counterpart to national liberation leaders found elsewhere and hoped to rehabilitate elements of his legacy that did not square with this image. They invoked Perón's deceased second wife, Eva Perón, or "Evita," as "Santa Evita Montonera," portraying her social Catholicism and compassion for the poor as central to the movement.[44] The Montonero publication *Militancia* began running frequent updates on the Palestinian situation, decrying Zionism as a form of colonialism, while maintaining a critique of the impracticality of pan-Arabism, distancing leftist Peronism from

Nasser's legacy. Reporting by journalists for *Militancia* differed from that of other news magazines in that they frequently situated the Palestinian situation in the context of a longer capitalist and imperial project, beginning under the Turks, the British, and now Cold War rivals. Their reporting also describes U.S. involvement with Middle Eastern oil companies, tying the national liberation struggle to local debates regarding foreign investment, oil interests, and neoimperialism.[45]

In January 1974, *Militancia* introduced descriptions of a phenomenon called "sub-imperialism," criticizing the expansionist impulses of Brazil, Argentina, and other Latin American countries involved in land, resource, and border disputes. Many intellectuals and political groups on Argentina's left, including the Peronist left, came together under the banner of the Frente Antiimperialista y por el Socialismo (Anti-imperialist and Pro-Socialist Front) to protest ongoing colonialism at home and abroad.[46] Later that year, *Militancia* began to report on the PLO's cause as a movement synonymous with a Palestinian revolution, an independence war conducted against Arab imperialism. Reporting turned to focus on Arab states in league with the United States, jointly responsible for the oil crisis that threatened the independence of NAM countries.[47] Using similar rhetoric, student groups, some allied with Peronism, began to issue calls for solidarity against the Vietnam War.[48] In exile, Perón denounced the pro-Palestine and anti-Zionist camps of the Arab League, trying to distance himself from critiques of the intellectual left, of which many prominent figures were Jewish.[49] Anti-Peronist intellectuals critiqued his anti-intellectualism, his authoritarian policies, and his repression of rights, hinting at antisemitism as well.[50] The Peronist left had some success via the return of Perón to Argentina and then to power in 1973 but did not find their efforts rewarded by a leader who supported militancy. Instead, they found themselves increasingly at odds with the Argentine state and began to look to the revolutionary, internationalist left to orient their demands for liberation.

In 1974, the Palestinian National Congress endorsed UN Resolution 242, which set up national authority on any liberated territory. The PLO campaigned actively to win political recognition, and Arafat visited more than one hundred countries to promote the PLO as the sole legitimate representative of the Palestinian people. A crucial moment came in 1975, when the PLO became an official member of the NAM, a year before becoming a full member of the Arab League, and Brazil formally promoted a UN resolution that "Zionism is racism."[51] During this period, from 1975 to 1979, the Latin American contingency in the NAM steadily gained ground, as its aims became more important to some of its members, particularly Fidel Castro. At the sixth NAM conference in 1979, held in Havana, the principal objectives of the movement were declared to be the "elimination of colonialism, neo-colonialism, apartheid, [and] racism, including Zionism," thus foregrounding the question of Palestine as a part of internationalism and Third World solidarity for many leftists.[52]

For their part, Zionist organizations in Buenos Aires contended with the Israel-Palestine conflict and the allegations of complicity with an imperialist project in the Middle East by issuing their own narratives of the conflict. Targeting their constituency of Zionist Jews in Argentina and communicating to a broader audience (specifically youth that might be sympathetic or recruited to the anti-Zionist cause), the Departamento Latinoamericano del Betar issued the magazine *Etgar Desafío* to present an alternative vision of the conflict. Issues of this periodical are a rich source of political debate targeted at left-leaning Jewish youth, particularly those who had ties to the Communist Party and student leftist groups. Although small at the time, in the early 1960s, it was noted that the founding members of the PO, including Jorge Altamira, Roberto Gramar, and Julio Magrio, were not only Jewish but also initially had strong connections to the Zionist left.[53] They illustrate the complicated nature of at least one group's attempt to wrestle with the cultural significance of what this conflict meant in the context of Third World struggle and in terms of antisemitism.[54]

One *Etgar Desafío* piece written by Ada Luchatto, a correspondent in Italy for the well-respected Israeli newspaper *Ma'ariv*, details the experience of families leaving the Soviet Union for Israel because of religious repression. Luchatto had traveled to Moscow to interview representatives of the National Jewish Liberation Movement in the Soviet Union, which she referred to as "la 'familia' combatiente de Moscú" (figures 3.2 and 3.3).[55] In this way, Luchatto framed Zionism for young readers as the answer to the hostilities of the Soviet empire and its antisemitism rather than a form of imperialism itself. The periodical juxtaposes this discussion against two more stories that reframe Palestine as simultaneously a proxy of Arab aggression in the Middle East and victim of a false leftist consciousness. This latter point is emphasized by an accompanying piece in the same issue, a man-on-the-street interview in which an Israeli Palestinian, a self-described statist communist, asserts that the rumors about secret police in the Soviet Union are false, circulated by bribed Jews. This representation of Palestinian political consciousness is punctuated with lines like, "Arabic countries would be better off if Russia were in charge," "Russia helped keep Czechoslovakia from becoming imperialist," and "Arabs believe in Russia and China."[56]

The efforts of *Etgar Desafío* to untangle the ideological complexities of the emerging left for its Jewish audience reflect the seriousness with which groups like these battled for the allegiance of Argentina's youth. Young people were

Figure 3.2. Front and back cover, *Etgar Desafío* 2 (July 1971). Courtesy of the Archive of the Jabotinsky Institute.

the social demographic radicalizing most rapidly during the period. These pieces appeal to a politicized youth wrestling with their involvement in an imperialist cause by pitting them against a more threatening imperialist enemy. Many of the pieces in the magazine were taken directly from the content of seminars hosted by like-minded organizations, addressed to the "inquietudes intelectuales . . . en el campo ideológico, politico y existencial" (intellectual disquietudes . . . in the ideological, political, and existential field) of a community with deep ties to Argentine communist and socialist parties.[57] What Zionists and the Peronist left had in common were projects that tried to find the margins of the radicalizing political landscape of Argentina's political left, to find a place for Zionism or for nationalism, respectively, without ignoring the difficulty of ideological deliberation. The radicalizing left's internationalist solidarity threatened both projects.

Antisemitism and the Pro-Palestinian Left

Zionists in Buenos Aires had good reason to be suspicious of the radicalizing left, as rumors proliferated regarding the complicity of leftist

                    Ada Luchatto, corresponsal en
               Italia del diario "Maariv" tuvo re
               cientemente la oportunidad de visi
               tar Moscú en compañía de un grupo
               de periodistas italianos, y en tal
               ocasión pudo entrevistarse con re-
               presentantes del Movimiento de Li-
               beración Nacional Judío en la URSS.
                    Esta es una crónica de uno de
               aquellos encuentros.

          "Shalom. Puedes felicitarme, he recibido re-
cién el permiso de salida para Israel". Al escuchar estas pala
bras en susurrante voz, en un inglés con acento ruso, pude ver
un par de chispeantes ojos negros y unos labios jóvenes, sonrientes.
          Hora:19,00 - Lugar: Correo Central de Moscú.
          Ahí esperaba encontrar a algunos de los jóve
nes dirigentes del movimiento por ellos apodado orgullosamente:
"Movimiento de Liberación Nacional Judío de la URSS".
          Habíamos convenido como contraseña que yo sos
tendría en mis manos, visiblemente, una guía de turismo italiana.
          Luego de telegrafiar a mi familia en Roma y
después de abonar tres rublos me uní a mi nuevo amigo.
          A pocos pasos de la pesada puerta de madera,
me esperaban otra vez aquellos sonrientes ojos negros. Nuevamen
te susurraron "Shalom" estrechando mi mano con energía. Ya te-
nía otro amigo.
          Los tres juntos salimos penetrando en el tem-
plado aire del anochecer.

                         - 1 -

Figure 3.3. "Con la 'familia' in Moscú," *Etgar Desafío* 2 (July 1971): 1. Courtesy of the Archive of the Jabotinsky Institute.

groups in antisemitic violence. The most infamous of these cases is that of the Movimiento Nacionalista Tacuara (Tacuara Nationalist Movement), a group alleged to have had direct financial support from the Arab League. In 1964, Hussein Triki, an active Nazi sympathizer and collaborator during World War II, was a delegate of the Arab League to South America, with his base of operations in Buenos Aires. Triki was publicly linked to Tacuara and cadres of the federal police suspected of antisemitic attacks.[58] In the same year, the Argentine military circulated a rare strategy document (later obtained by the Central Zionist Organization) that identified ten different strains of political radicalism considered threatening to the nation-state. Of these, two were labeled antisemitic, nationalist with leftist *tendencias*, and were recorded as "Nasserist." Described in the document as *violentamente antisionista*, Nasserism was considered by the military agency that produced the document to be a "tendency toward popular democracy like that of Nasser in the RAU [República Árabe Unida], identified with Pan-Arabism."[59] The document identifies Triki as a known funder of the Tacuara and the Uturuncos, an earlier guerrilla group associated with Peronism.

When Triki was active in South America, the PLO was busy bolstering its revolutionary image by establishing ties with a number of militant underground movements. It aligned itself with groups such as the Dev-Genç in Turkey, the Irani National Front, the Japanese Red Army, the Black Panthers, the National Front for Liberation of Eritrea, the Irish Republican Army, the Moroccan Leftist Underground, the Frolinat in Chad, and the Uruguayan Tupamaros, along with the neo-Nazi National Democratic Party in West Germany and neofascist groups in Italy.[60] In 1972, Cuba severed ties with Israel and gave the Israeli embassy in Havana to the PLO, actively sponsoring Arafat in public forums and inviting PLO fighters to the island to train in revolutionary tactics.[61] As support for the PLO grew among the more radical Latin American left, more moderate and antimilitarist groups became increasingly concerned about pro-Palestine links to violence and antisemitism.[62]

Tacuara, a group with close ties to the Juventud Peronista (Peronist Youth), and with both Marxist and Nasserist ideological tendencies, was frequently charged in the popular press with having strong antisemitic leanings. This group started as a right-wing nationalist group and gradually moved to the left from the mid-1950s to the 1960s; it was one of the principal bases from which leftist guerrilla organizing emerged by the 1970s.[63] Joe Baxter, secretary general of the Tacuara, a proponent of pan-Arabism and outspoken anti-Zionist, was a frequent target of conservative Zionist and right-wing organizations looking to discredit the left. Although Baxter publicly emphasized that he was anti-Zionist and not antisemitic, he was frequently blamed for antisemitic violence by the federal police, despite the lack or disappearance of convicting evidence.[64] Eventually, Baxter helped found the Ejército Revolucionario del Pueblo (ERP, People's Revolutionary Army) with Mario Santucho of the PRT, after spending two years in China and Vietnam from 1965 to 1966. Baxter fought on behalf of the National Liberation Front and returned to Argentina as a decorated soldier of the Viet Cong. He met Santucho in Paris at the IV Trotskyist International, and by 1970, they headed one of the most active militant leftist groups in Argentina, the ERP-PRT.[65] In 1972, Baxter helped kidnap Oberdan Sallustro, the director-general of Italian car manufacturer FIAT. In 1973, suspicious of Héctor Campora's pardon of the ERP and the return of Peronism, he clandestinely migrated to Chile.[66]

Leftist Militancy and Networks of Solidarity

The year 1973 saw increasing fragmentation and divisions among the traditional and radical left in Argentina. Some parties argued that no third position existed between oppressors and guerrillas, whereas others sought a middle ground.[67] From abroad, the eagerness of Cuban revolutionaries to construct an axis of Tricontinentalist countries seemed a logical measure of resistance to increasing state violence and U.S.-sponsored attacks on the Argentine left. As a result, several groups sought to tap into and create networks of cross-regional solidarity centered on a Cuban revolutionary model with Castro at the helm. As early as 1964, Cuba had promised solidarity with Al-Fatah if they engaged in an armed struggle independent of Arab state powers.[68] Reports of PLO fighters being trained in Cuba began circulating as early as 1969, and news of militants from Latin America being trained on PLO bases in Jordan, Lebanon, and Gaza started circulating shortly thereafter.[69] Even rumored connections between the armed left in Argentina and Palestine elevated the status of the left, lending credibility to their claims of revolutionary possibility.

Direct communication and ties with the PLO were actively sought across sectors of the left. Leftist political filmmaker Jorge Giannoni, a member of the ERP, traveled to Algeria in 1973 to represent Argentina in the Third Cinema movement after having directed and produced a feature-length film called *Palestina, otro Vietnam* (1971), which presented the PLO's cause as part of a broader Third World battle against colonialism. Giannoni returned to Buenos Aires and founded the Center for the Study of the Third World and the Middle East at the Universidad de Buenos Aires, which was alleged to have supported the dissemination of information about the cause to various parties, both academic and otherwise. In 1977, Arafat "saluted the Argentine popular resistance, under the guidance of the Movimiento Peronista Montonero, in its struggle for the fulfillment of its programme of peace and liberation."[70] Around this time, Mario Firmenich and Fernando Vaca Narvaja, key Montonero figures, met with Yasser Arafat (figure 3.4) and were promised support from Al-Fatah in return for their vocal support of self-determination.[71] Arafat's support of the Montoneros gave the group a certain standing it had lost when Perón refused to acknowledge the group's militancy. A photograph of this encounter circulated widely, perhaps signaling a Montoneros strategy of presenting themselves as the PLO of Argentina—the national liberation front of a broad leftist Peronism. Alternately, the comparison could have been a strategy of justifying armed struggle abroad, the country having fallen again into military rule after Perón's untimely death in 1974 and the 1976 removal of his third wife and vice president Isabel Perón from office.[72]

The PLO skillfully crafted networks of communication and solidarity with potential allies across Latin America throughout this period. Following Cuba's lead, when the Sandinistas came to power in Nicaragua, one of their first acts was to break off ties with Israel and turn the embassy over to Arafat and the PLO. At least two hundred Sandinistas had received training at PLO–Popular Front for the Liberation of Palestine camps in Jordan and Lebanon, and Castro actively encouraged a relationship, funneling funds to the Frente Sandinista de Liberación Nacional (FSLN) through the PLO as early as the

Figure 3.4. Mario Eduardo Firmenich and Fernando Vaca Narvaja with Yasser Arafat, 1977. Reprinted in *Página 12*, 19 August 2013, https://www.pagina12.com.ar/diario/elpais/1-24312-2003-08-19.html.

late 1960s.[73] The PLO supported antigovernment guerrillas in Argentina, Uruguay, and Peru, even though each country's national government technically supported the PLO in public forums such as the United Nations and the Third World Convocation.[74] During this period of active network building, the Montoneros published a periodical titled *El Descamisado*, which chronicled the group's struggle against military regimes and its engagement with the last Perón presidency. Most issues featured long sections on anti-imperialism, with special sections on the Vietnam War, Palestine, and regional struggles such as the war in Bolivia or socialism under Allende in Chile. One of the most distinctive features was a serialized graphic novel by Héctor Germán Oesterheld, illustrated by Leopoldo Durañona, titled "Latinoamérica y el Imperialismo." It presents another picture of the Argentine left's struggle with its own legacy of complicity in imperialist designs, but from a Peronist perspective.

Having established a readership among leftists in an earlier strip, *El Eternauta*, Oesterheld was a natural fit for *El Descamisado*.[75] Oesterheld undertook the ambitious project of trying to understand imperialism in a more profound way, from Spanish conquistadors to present struggles of marginalized groups in modern Argentina. It revisited Argentine national history, reading figures like Juan Manuel de Rosas as deeply engaged in imperialist ambitions. Oesterheld dedicated issues to "the Negro," "the Border," and "Soldaderas," examining, respectively, the Argentine state's colonization of Afro-Argentines, indigenous groups, and women, subtly describing the many continuities between colonial armies and the current Argentine military. His critique of long-standing forms of imperialism in Argentina provided a means for representing unresolved injustices and highlighting the connection of local inequality to sensibilities forming elsewhere. This vision allowed the Montonero left to fashion itself as a part of the struggle of decolonization and national liberation. Iconography of Evita Perón, occasionally added in the background of a historical scene, suggested that a return to an earlier tradition of socialist welfare reform, one based on Catholic socialist values, might provide a means of liberation for those locked out of the economic advances made under the military regime.

Oesterheld joined the Montonero militancy in 1973, along with his three daughters, and all four went underground after Isabel Perón became president following her husband's death in 1974. In publishing this long series of political comic strips, Oesterheld tied together strands of Montonero thought with larger themes of imperialism, connecting the state of Argentina to a larger imperial project. Within these frames, the experience of British colonialism in Palestine and the Rio de la Plata could be compared and knitted together, carefully bringing into dialogue internationalist solidarity projects such as that of the PLO with the local left's critique of the military state. Oesterheld's work is an example of rendering solidarity as it was situated in the radicalizing Peronist left. Kidnapped and murdered in 1978, Oesterheld did not see the end of the dictatorship, but he witnessed a key moment in Argentina's political history. He saw the radicalizing Argentine left participate in solidarity with a national liberation struggle in the Middle East and Montonero militants photographed beside Arafat as brothers in arms.[76]

Perón's Third Administration to the
End of Military Rule

Juan Perón's return brought a shift in Argentina's foreign policy with the Middle East. In 1972, Kuwait was Argentina's primary oil supplier. After careful negotiations with the Argentine military, Saudi Arabia was providing half of the country's oil by 1973. Upon taking office for the third time, Perón reconfigured Argentina's oil market, recognizing the problems associated with continuing to rely on Kuwait and Saudi Arabia, both considered strongly tied to U.S. interests. By 1974, he had signed agreements to make Libya Argentina's primary supplier. Egyptian pressure on Argentina led to Perón's reluctant declaration of support for the PLO, and Perón was rewarded for Argentina's support of UN Resolution 242 with increased investment from Arab League countries, which rose from $24 million to $215 million annually by 1975. In 1974, it was rumored among diplomatic circles that Argentina had received a loan for $2.3 billion from Arab sources through a Swiss bank account.[77] Rumors circulated that José López Rega, Argentina's Minister of Social Welfare and founder of the clandestine paramilitary Argentine Anti-Communist Alliance, was conducting a close relationship with Muammar Gaddafi. Whether or not this was true, he signed three agreements initiated under Perón's administration.

The three agreements signed under Perón evidenced the influence of the left's position on Argentina's relationship with the region. The first of these was a trade agreement on agricultural and manufactured goods, to be exchanged for three million tons of oil at a fixed rate. The terms included an arrangement by which Argentina would provide agricultural assistance and build Libya an oil refinery and gas bottling plant. The second agreement included a promise that Libyan scientists would be brought to Argentina to be trained in uranium exploration and the production of nuclear materials. Finally, a cultural pact pledged that Argentina would distribute notices of the Arab Revolutionary News Agency in Latin America and that Libya would distribute Télam, the national news agency of Argentina, across the Middle East.[78] In 1976, when the coup against Isabel Perón began Argentina's longest period of military rule (from

1976 to 1983), the military regime took an unambiguous turn in foreign policy away from Perón's flirtation with the Arab League and toward U.S. interests.

The fate of Argentine support for Palestine from 1976 to the transition to civilian rule in 1983 became more a matter of grand strategy. The Falklands War brought the Israel-Palestine conflict into stark relief in Argentine foreign policy circles as a theater of Cold War confrontation and a "great powers proving ground."[79] In this new period, any previous alliances of the Argentine state with Palestine—which centered on Arafat, Al-Fatah, and the PLO—faded into the distance, but so had Perón's courting of Arab states. Fear of Soviet influence in the region and suspicions surrounding the infusion of petrodollars into the Argentine economy were also on the decline. During these years, pro-Palestine solidarity activity was significantly curtailed by the persecution of the left, as the Argentine state engaged in a "dirty war" aimed at stamping out dissidents, left-wing Peronists, communists, socialists, and militant organizations. The military regime took on a variety of neoliberal economic policies that bottomed out many of the gains made by the union movement. In addition, what remained of the internationalist left was confronted with the economic failings of the Soviet Union, which signaled to many a defeat of anticapitalist possibilities. The traditional left that survived the dictatorship was highly fragmented, unanchored in the context of a promised return to democracy.

The left faced a crisis in the aftermath of the dictatorship. Collapsing support for the working classes combined with decades of discrediting and a lack of adequate leadership. The militant left had provided the right-wing military with a bogeyman, and despite the widespread knowledge that militancy had been on the decline before the coup, this circumstance leveraged a degree of acquiescence and even support for repression among conservative political groups. Many Argentines were fearful of both the return of the military and of leftist radicalism. By 1982, however, even before the end of the military regime, the PO had resumed publication of *Prensa Obrera*. Following a smaller, more bulletin-style publication, *Internacionalismo* (1980–83), *Prensa Obrera* eventually became a major vehicle of news distribution for workers from a variety of sectors. It offered a battleground on which debates in different factions of the left could be given voice, particularly those between nontraditional emerging parties, the PO, Izquierda Socialista, and the Partido de los Trabajadores Socialistas (Socialist Workers' Party).[80] On 6 July 1984, a declaration was signed in São Paulo by a variety of organizations across South and Central America and the Caribbean to "concentrate efforts to liberate Palestine by organizing diasporic communities in Latin America."[81] Just a year later, the influential Institute of Palestine Studies began to publish a Spanish translation of its journal with a Latin American editorial staff headquartered in Buenos Aires. These events marked renewed interest in Palestine nationalism in the region, and *Prensa Obrera* noted the engagement of Argentina's left.

These events seemed to go relatively unnoticed by the civilian administration of Raúl Alfonsín. Alfonsín was preoccupied with ensuring the legitimacy of Argentina's return to civilian rule and protecting human rights. The recovering left also seemed little interested in large-scale international solidarity efforts. Human rights became the primary rallying call of the transition period, and the priorities of advancing human rights overshadowed appeals to the socialist ideas the left had espoused before the military coup. Alfonsín's presidency was followed by that of Carlos Menem, a *sirio-libanés* Peronist from the province of La Rioja.[82] Menem was a staunch developmentalist and was responsible for privatizing many of Argentina's public services and developing a special economic relationship with the United States. His presidency reestablished several economic relationships between Argentina and the Middle East that had been dissolved by the military regime and reestablished ties with the United Kingdom that had been severed in the Falklands War. Menem was well known for his pardons of military personnel for human rights abuses during the dictatorship. His incorporation into the Peronist political machine is evidence of the integration of the diaspora into Argentine political life and of the relative political conservatism of the the diaspora's leading public figures. Menem accepted substantial funding from Saudi Arabia to build Latin America's largest mosque in the Palermo neighborhood of Buenos Aires, cementing symbolic ties between neoliberalism, powerful U.S.-allied petroleum producers, and the Argentine state.

Crafting a Symbolic Politics amid Financial Crisis

During this period, while visible solidarity with Palestine seemed to have all but disappeared in Argentina, several opportune events occurred. In 1985, the PLO discreetly founded an office and later a social club in the city of Rosario. By 1989, under Menem, the organization began plans for an embassy of Palestine in downtown Buenos Aires and finally, in 1996, secured a building from the Argentine state to house its operations. The Federación de Entidades Argentino-Palestinas and the Asociación Argentina de Solidaridad con Palestina were founded during this period and began to be more actively supported and recognized by political leaders across the left. Palestine became a *cause célèbre* around the world again in 1987 with the beginning of the Intifada. After 1987, Palestine became a global symbol of resistance to the emerging new world order. By the 1990s, demonstrations against the state of Israel had become common across Europe and North and South America, frequently attached to new social movements and emerging leftist political parties. In Argentina, this globalized struggle was situated in a much more complex historical frame. A modest local interest in the conflict waned after attacks on the Israeli embassy and a Jewish community center in Buenos Aires.[83] Only after several failed trials against the alleged perpetrators of the attacks did Argentine leftists revisit the Palestinian cause, but this time as victims of neoliberalism rather than of imperialism. The ambiguity of the Argentine left on Palestine during this period was characteristic of the uncertainty of its leadership and the limitations of parties that lacked wide public support. However, the era of financial crisis would change these circumstances.

By 2001, the left confronted a crisis. That July, at the Plenario de Militantes del Polo Social de la Capital y la Provincia de Buenos Aires, more than five hundred people met to debate and determine how to approach the upcoming elections. Present at the meeting were activists representing the movement of retirees, communitarian soup kitchens, university student groups, cultural centers, neighborhood assemblies, human rights groups, and a variety of civil associations. Also present were the Casa de la Memoria, the Association of State Workers, the Federation of Land and Housing, and representatives of the official Partido Communista, the Peronism for Liberation party, and the Special Aid Group. The common rhetorical thread of the speeches from members of these groups was an attack on neoliberalism, a repudiation of the state—specifically Menem's neoliberal economic platform—and a call to revisit Guevarist principles. The Plenario decided to meet the demands of these social movements by constructing a Polo Social as a political alliance to stand in the next elections.

This assemblage prefigured the loose coalition that began to march in the streets just a few months later, when measures taken by the Argentine state to corral the financial system created a financial collapse. In the aftermath of the 2001 financial crisis, arguing for a renewed commitment to solidarity, the Polo Social coalition called for alliances between social movements within Argentina and also with oppressed peoples across the Global South. One of the participating organizations, Patria Libre, identified the Palestinian fight against colonialism—together with U.S. imperialism in Iraq, Afghanistan, and Colombia—as a new phase of collusion between neoliberalism and Yankee aggression.[84] These rumblings were not the only evidence of a return of interest in solidarity with Palestine.

The Movimiento al Socialismo (MAS, Movement for Socialism) had also begun to use imagery that suggested its common cause with the peoples of Palestine. An organization created by Nahuel Moreno on the eve of the transition,

MAS was aligned with a more traditional socialist position. The cover of the first issue of its *Socialismo o barbarie* features a young man with his face and head covered, throwing stones in a street confrontation with the police—images nearly identical to those featured prominently in the international media of the Intifada from 1987 to 1991. This issue was dedicated to strategies of financial resistance to the International Monetary Fund, featuring Argentina's connection to other Third World nations in the struggle against global capital. Like earlier Tricontinental interest in the practice of holding congresses, the reporting focused on the importance of participation in international forums such as the World Economic Forum in Seattle.[85] Forums of debate that brought together parties from the Global South protested the encroachment of financial capital into systems of government. This position appealed to the Argentine left as its priorities began to take shape and its base expanded. The image of stone-throwing youth emphasized the unequal power relations between the forces behind state violence and the many groups in Argentina who fell below the poverty line during the crisis.

Later that year, *Socialismo o barbarie* expanded on the connections between Palestinians under occupation and emerging social movements in Argentina. It printed a nine-page spread on the Palestine question, titled "The Just Anger of an Outraged People," whose author aimed to debunk the myth of the "fanatical terrorist" and critique the failures of the peace process and Oslo Accords. Taking on the question of Zionist colonization, the article labels Palestinians the "natives" of the region, claiming that Israeli "colonists, even those that are civilians, possess the right to bear arms . . . and their favorite sport is not football (soccer), but target practice, using Palestinians as marks."[86] The feature story includes an inset chronicle of colonization, beginning with the Balfour Declaration of 1917 and ending with the 1967 Arab-Israeli War. It describes the 1947–49 period as an "ethnic cleansing."[87] These descriptions parallel the language used to describe police violence against demonstrators. Deconstructing the myth of radical fanaticism responded directly to popular media accounts of young men in Argentina who had taken to the streets. Hinting at an earlier era of international economic possibility, the periodical's authors point to the fall of the Soviet Union, which they describe as a literal bankruptcy followed by a spiritual one, suggesting that perhaps the traditional leftist parties in Argentina similarly abandoned useful models of anticapitalism.[88] The long essay asserts that the PLO represents a secular, democratic, and nonracist state, and argues that for this reason the Argentine left should begin to use the flag of the PLO as a symbol.[89]

These emerging leftist parties soon united to organize demonstrations. The MAS and the Movimiento Socialista de los Trabajadores (Workers' Socialist

Movement), in coalition with the Izquierda Unida (United Left), featured a call to solidarity with Palestine in its 10 April 2002 issue of *Alternativa socialista*. The issue called Israel "un estado genocida" and chronicled events from 1948 to 1967 that brought substance to the charge of Western European and Israeli imperialist designs. In this issue and several others, writers compare the tactics used in Israel against the Palestinian people to those of Nazi Germany.[90] The MAS led several demonstrations in front of the Israeli embassy, chanting "Palestinos y argentinos: los mismos enemigos, la misma lucha."[91] The magazine also attacks Israel for its support for the Latin American dictatorships of Somoza, Pinochet, and Videla and its cordial relations with apartheid South Africa.[92] Beside an article on demonstrations in Rabat, Izquierda Unida comments on an earlier demonstration, noting that just the day before the MAS demonstration, the Arab Argentine community had protested in the same space, questioning why the groups do not protest together despite having a common cause. *Socialismo o barbarie* convoked a subsequent demonstration on 15 April led by the Inter-Barrio Assembly to demand that Israel leave the occupied territories. In a longer statement, the Izquierda Unida political platform listed among its demands regarding Israel the creation of a new Palestinian state, the right of return for displaced peoples, the return of confiscated properties, secular democracy, and an end to racism.[93] The use of Palestine to signal an ideological shift among leftist parties emerging from the crisis was soon taken up by more radical groups.

The Movimiento Patriótico Revolucionario Quebracho (Revolutionary Patriotic Movement Quebracho, or simply Quebracho), with strong ties to Hugo Chávez in Venezuela, is likely to have been the first group to begin wearing the *keffiyeh* in public demonstrations. The organization's publication *Quebracho* openly supported the PLO and eventually Hezbollah. In 2001, it argued against all forms of imperialism in the Middle East, labeling the United States and Israel racist states and denouncing their colonialism and violence against the Arab world. Issuing a call to action, it urged supporters to join the Comité de Defensa Contra la Agresión a los Pueblos Arabes (Committee for Defense against Aggression against Arab Peoples), an organization without political, social, or religious ties. This group met in September 2001 in La Plata with high-profile members of the Arab Argentine community, such as Palestinian ambassador Suhail Hani Daher Akel, Horacio Mounir Haddad of the American-Arab Entidades, and secretary of the Arab Federation of Buenos Aires, Juan Gabriel Labaké.[94] Images in *Quebracho* after this meeting regularly featured scarf-wearing men throwing rocks or using slingshots in street demonstrations, an obvious allusion to the emblematic popular resistance of the Palestinian struggle. By 2003, the scarf worn most frequently by all three of these groups of demonstrators was the *keffiyeh*. In 2006, leaders of the Jewish community (Delegación de Asociaciones Israelitas Argentinas and Asociación Mutual Israelita Argentina) and the Israeli Foreign Minister condemned Quebracho, calling the organization a threat to Argentine democracy. Since then, the state also openly began to identify the group as too radical, principally due to its call to abolish private property and its negative depictions of the police.[95]

Closer to the center of the left, the University of Buenos Aires student bulletin *En clave rojo* took up the cause of Palestine nationalism in September 2001, roughly at the same time as the Quebracho demonstrations. Aligned with the workers of occupied factories and committed to unity between the labor and student movements, its authors argued that conflict in the Middle East provided the imperialist bourgeoisie in the United States with justification for military expenditures and antiterrorist propaganda that directly enabled the repression of its working classes. Connecting the ongoing wars in Iraq and Afghanistan with Arafat's political operations and an uprising in Pakistan, the anonymous authors of the editorial argue that the fight against international terrorism, the hallmark of George W. Bush's foreign policy, falsely separates the masses of the semicolonial countries from the struggle of workers in imperialist nations.[96] Identification with the internationalist vision of the left of the 1960s and 1970s gave these new elements on the left, through a form of representational solidarity, a clear way to articulate their concerns. In this way, they could trace their lineage back to the successful national liberation struggles and popular figures of the Tricontinental or the NAM, bypassing some of the more challenging elements of identification with the local radical left of the period preceding the dictatorship. By doing so, these movements and new parties hoped to avoid being identified with earlier discredited leftist parties, while still leveraging their connection to important moments of global connection from that same left's fragmented past.

Representational solidarity with Palestine was a statement about the future of the left in Argentina. Humberto Tumini, secretary-general of Patria Libre, delivered a campaign address in November 2004 from a podium draped in the *keffiyeh* (figure 3.5).[97] An organization founded in 1987 in Córdoba with a strong union following, Patria Libre represented even more established groups aligned with labor that came to identify strongly with the Palestinian cause. A former ERP militant and staunch critic of neoliberalism, Tumini used the occasion of Arafat's failing health to don the podium with the most recognizable symbol of Paletsinian nationalism. Tumini argued that the scarf represented the struggle against "fascism, neoliberalism, and moderate progressivism," which he attributed to the likes of both Néstor Kirchner, president of Argentina at the time, and Elisa Carrió, one of his perennial rivals in coalition building. Tumini called on the Movimiento Barrios de Pie, the Movimiento de Educación Popular, the Red de Mujeres Solidarias, Venceremos, and other allies to resist falling into divisive political camps. Tumini's use of the *keffiyeh* signaled the possibility of unity among the assembled groups that might transcend the divisiveness of competing agendas. He also urged them to reconsider the ideological lines of Arafat, Che Guevara, Evita Perón, and independence hero San Martín.[98]

Likewise, just a few months earlier, *La Verdad Obrera*, organ of the Partido de los Trabajadores Socialistas, issued a scathing critique of Ariel Sharon's visit to Argentina.[99] For Tumini, Palestine represented a symbolic tie to anti-imperialism that resonated across leftist parties, social movements, and generations. For the authors of *La Verdad Obrera*, the case of Argentina's support for Israel offered a critique of foreign policy from the standpoint of a stronger, perhaps more electable left. The coalition that emerged after the financial crisis identified with Palestine as a representation of connection to anti-imperialist struggle that allowed the left to recuperate some of its own past. Drawing on a previous consciousness of the left and calling this representation into a present understanding of relationships of power, Tumini and these organizations were able to consolidate a new social movement. The new left of the early 2000s was able to use representational solidarity with Palestine to emerge from a crisis of indeterminacy and signal its most pressing concerns. Unifying under this common banner helped the left mobilize support and garner votes. Eventually, a limited transnational solidarity with Palestine, mostly symbolic, also followed.

Figure 3.5. Humberto Tumini, secretary-general of Patria Libre, 8 November 2004. "'Nacimos para unir, luchamos para vencer': Hace 30 años nacía Patria Libre," *Libres del sur*, 15 November 2017, https://libresdelsur.org.ar/noticias/nacimos-unir-luchamos-vencer/.

Contrast in the Southern Cone, the Chilean Left, and Palestine

Argentina's representational solidarity with Palestine demonstrates the importance of local context to understanding Latin American internationalism. The place of solidarity in the history and development of Argentina's local left was a determining factor in its advance. Contrasting Argentina's experience with that of Chile, Argentina's Southern Cone neighbor, provides further evidence of the necessity of considering this embeddedness. Chile is home to the largest self-identifying Palestinian diasporic population in South America, today totaling more than 300,000 mostly Christian people, equivalent to roughly 60 percent of all Palestinians that relocated to Latin America during the twentieth century.[100] Beginning in 1905, Palestinians came to account for the largest proportion of Middle Eastern migrants to Chile. They quickly established more than ten Arabic newspapers and a wide variety of civic associations. Already by the 1920s, issues related to people identified as Palestinian were being carefully differentiated in the Chilean press from those from Syria and Lebanon, and activism was emerging on behalf of those displaced and denied rights of citizenship by the British Mandate system. Relative to the press in other countries that received Palestinian migrants, the Chilean Arabic press was far more committed to protesting on behalf of the Palestinian cause.[101]

Despite and perhaps because of discrimination, Chile's diasporic population formed an important support base for new immigrants.[102] Increasing numbers arrived after 1948 and many maintained close ties with Palestinians in the Levant and other parts of South America.[103] As in Argentina, Chile's Palestinian community, having built a number of cultural and civic associations to facilitate cooperation between immigrants and Chileans, was benefiting from upward economic mobility and via appointment to public offices by the 1950s. President Arturo Alessandri assisted the Palestinian Yarur family in increasing their operations in Santiago, "offering him incentives that included no customs duties on imported machine tools, low tariffs on imported supplies, and a loan of more than one million U.S. dollars from the Banco de Chile, the country's largest bank."[104] The increasing influence of the Palestinian diaspora sparked a degree of resentment from other Middle Eastern immigrants, as they became wealthy business owners and courted political support via civic associations and sports clubs.[105] The status of the diaspora by the 1960s was well established, and notable Palestinian Chilean families were seen as wealthy industrial capitalists, favored recipients of government contracts, and beneficiaries of large transfers of wealth from the Arab world.[106]

In 1970, Salvador Allende was elected president of Chile, heading the socialist Unidad Popular coalition government. The Allende government undertook an ambitious agenda, including the nationalization of several industries, agrarian reform, increased and new investment in social welfare programs, and bold economic restructuring that included controversial increases to minimum wages. Allende's reforms were praised by many leftist groups and left-leaning leaders around the world, including Mexico and Cuba, and many saw the Unidad Popular government as enacting a revolutionary socialist agenda.[107] Between 1970 and 1973, as Chile pursued a socialist reorganization of the economy, its foreign policies reflected an increasingly strident anti-imperialist stance as a means of seeking liberation from the forces of capitalism. In reaching out to other governments with similar resolve, Allende's foreign minister began to pursue closer relationships with communist nations, including Cuba, the Soviet Union, and nations affiliated with the NAM.[108] While Allende's and the left's ascension to power might have provided more space for international solidarity movements to form, this was not the case for solidarity with Palestine. After Nasser's passing in 1970, solidarity with Afro-Asian proponents of national liberation and anti-imperialism in Chile took a different shape. The rise of Arafat and the PLO as the only legitimate spokesman of Palestinians in the diaspora after the Six-Day War was not as widely embraced in Chile as it was elsewhere.

Among leftist parties in Chile during the Unidad Popular government, active solidarity organizing on behalf of Vietnam brought together many different groups, including most prominently the Partido Comunista de Chile (Communist Party of Chile) and the Partido Socialista, and included the members of the militant Movimiento de Izquierda Revolucionaria. Chilean *nueva canción* folk singers protested the war in Vietnam, and leftist news outlets published stories of the heroic efforts of Ho Chi Minh and his successors and lauded Chilean leaders who advocated for and sent resources to Vietnam.[109] Organizing on behalf of Palestinian nationalism was far more contained. When the Soviet Union called for solidarity with *los pueblos árabes* at the XXIV Congress of the Communist Party of the Soviet Union, more muted calls for solidarity with Palestine ensued, and despite the continuing spirit of internationalism, stories in the communist press about the fate of Palestine and conflict in the Middle East tended to be more informative and less inflected with calls for solidarity.[110] Other factions of the left looked more skeptically on Soviet involvement in the region. The Palestinian diasporic community in Chile enjoyed a regular radio broadcast, *Palestina por Siempre*, which brought news in Arabic from the Middle East along with music and cultural programming to Chilean listeners between the 1960s and 1970s. The goal of the program was to inspire a feeling of cultural and political connection across the diaspora, revitalize interest in Palestinian roots and ancestry, and promote the Arabic language.[111] The activities of Palestinian militant nationalists did not necessarily complement the cultural outreach mission of the radio show, and news of the guerrilla exploits of Arafat, Al-Fatah, and later the PLO were not met with an outpouring of enthusiasm. Most incidents were reported as brief news items, commented upon with skepticism, as if they constituted dangerous folly.[112]

Chile was home to a small local chapter of Arafat's General Union of Palestinian Students, which tended to view the cause of Palestine as part of a broader resistance to military rule and imperialism.[113] Leftist intellectuals and Palestinian-descended politicians increasingly identified with working-class issues and created a Front for the Liberation of Palestine, but this organization and students confronted a significant challenge in that the most visible face of the local Palestinian community—its prominent business community leadership—was deeply wedded to the politics of neoliberalism on which military rule was premised and promised to defend.[114] Palestinian Chilean reactions in the face of the violence of the dictatorship that displaced Allende played "into wider processes of erasing the violence of the recent Chilean past and, importantly, the violence it continues to inflict on local communities in the neoliberal era of post-dictatorship."[115] Having a sizable Palestinian diaspora that could not embrace the PLO hindered Chile's ability in democracy and in its aftermath—a period of prolonged military dictatorship from 1973 to 1991—to generate solidarity organizing. The largely Christian diaspora in Chile might have benefited from a heightened status as a refugee community in this time, but it was not aligned with the left and did not see itself reflected in the aims of pan-Arabism or the PLO. It was easier for the PLO to gain support in Argentina, which never had a significant Palestinian population relative to other Arabic-speaking immigrants and never boasted civic associations with the same profile and vibrancy. Until a Chilean-born Palestinian immigrant to Argentina established the Federación de Entidades Argentino-Palestinas in 1993, most associations remained relatively small in membership and local in their activities. The contrast between Chile and Argentina in identification with Palestine among the left demonstrates the importance of the historical context within which solidarity projects were transmitted. With Unidad Popular offering a socialist, internationalist government in power in the early 1970s, the Chilean left might also not have experienced the same need to create counterpoints and comparisons outside the national context. The PLO did not find the same reception in Chile as it did in Cuba and Argentina, where connections to Palestinian nationalism were pivotal to the strategies of leaders on the left. South-South solidarity movements were successful when they spoke to local contexts in meaningful ways, and although the Chilean left did extend solidarity to Palestine, it experienced less integration of these ties in the formation of the left's strategies of self-representation.

Complicity and Continuity

Recent studies of the PLO's international networking have illuminated key modalities in the global left's identification with the Palestinian cause. The case of Argentina might be suitably considered within and against this global frame. The PLO courted support by transmitting meanings of political struggle that enabled it to form strategic alliances across the Third World. The Palestinian Authority, with the Israeli-U.S. alliance as its powerful neocolonial enemy, significantly contributed to the prevalence of solidarity movements around the world. Many of the connections made by solidarity with Palestine illustrate "differentiated experiences of oppression and struggle against universalizing systems of domination like imperialism and capitalism."[116] In Palestinian nationalism, distant others find an unfinished struggle against apartheid, colonialism, and state violence that foregrounds the issues denied in other debates, such as that of the Chicano people and Native communities living on the border in the United States. Representational solidarity with the Palestinian struggle can thus be seen as clarifying. It can present a notion of unequal citizenship, such as the denial of rights of property, movement, or settlement, which creates a disenfranchised and subaltern working class.[117] It can illustrate the failures of the left to propose alternatives to capitalism or to combat colonialism. Or it can highlight connections between parties that might otherwise be seen as divergent, as in the case of the emerging left of the early 2000s in Argentina.

The Argentine left's use of the question of Palestine over time speaks to entangled historical connections between the 1960s and the postcrisis left. Palestine as a symbol, while sometimes contested, was shared most often by Argentine leftists to position themselves within a national context and against a landscape of international affairs. The Palestinian cause came to occupy an important symbolic space in connecting various historical claims of the political left to anti-imperialism and in dispelling complicity in the denial of full citizenship rights to marginalized and impoverished groups at home after the crisis. Images and narrative schemes constructed to mobilize support for Palestine, as representational solidarity, were manifestations of critical reflections on Argentine political realities and the left's shifting priorities. Despite rhetorical claims that framed the call to action as solidarity with the Palestinian cause, they were often overshadowed by persistent preoccupations with Argentina's relationship to colonization, Zionism, and imperialism and—to a slightly lesser extent—with the dangers of exclusive varieties of nationalism that denied many the benefits of the state. Palestinian nationalists' conflict with the Israeli state served as a kind of mirror for the left, a reflection of their struggle that could overcome the nontrivial fragmentation of local leftist parties after the dictatorship.

Solidarity actions often provide a political resource of hope for the left, particularly in encountering an enemy as unyielding and powerful as imperialism or global capital. Argentine solidarity with the PLO adds to a more nuanced understanding of South-South solidarity as such a resource and as a tool of broad cultural resistance to imperialism and neoliberalism. On 31 May 2010, the orthodox Argentine left—the Communist Party and Socialist Party—led support for the Turkish flotilla to Gaza in its confrontation with the Israeli armed forces, clearly hoping to garner support with the many competing social movements and coalitions of Argentina's emergent New Left. This move imitates the way Montoneros tried to reframe Perón's legacy by attaching him to the Palestinian nationalist cause. As an issue that the Latin American left rendered visible and knowable for local audiences, Palestine provided space for reflection on the local left's own goals and self-representation. As a narrative of subaltern resistance to neoimperialism, solidarity with Palestine provided the Argentine left with a useful frame that could overcome challenges to its legitimacy. In offering determinacy, this solidarity united competing visions of a way forward for the emerging left. Representational solidarity allowed Palestine to be a cause that brought together social movement actors, new and old political parties, and leaders of the emerging left to meaningfully challenge the policies of neoliberal strands of Peronism. Its effect can certainly be seen in the turn of Nestór Kirchner's postcrisis bid for office as a Peronist tied to the social movements of the new left.

In the Southern Cone, as elsewhere, solidarity is a central practice of the left, "indispensable to the activity of radical social and political movements."[118] Following multiple periods of authoritarianism, the Argentine left sought to craft an identity that was politically viable in the face of internal crisis and external repression. Situating local political experiences in the context of national liberation struggles, the Argentine left found a way to revisit and reposition its history of anti-imperialist thought. Latin American revolutionaries "inscribed their own histories" into their readings of national liberation struggles in the Arab world, claiming a "unique revolutionary partnership," but alliances forged between political parties alone do not fully account for the commitment of solidarity with Palestine experienced in the Southern Cone.[119]

This chapter argues that the left's representational solidarity with the Palestinian cause provided a pathway through which political strategies could be mapped onto expressions of political reasoning and self-representation. This practice of solidarity allowed for a greater sense of determinacy while holding space for unresolved internal conflict. Argentines recognized the alterity and difference of the Palestinian struggle while finding ways for Palestinian nationalism to be a useful source of self-representation. Their solidarity with Palestine did not result in elaborate exchanges of personnel or transfers of resources, nor did it attempt to reduce the tension of the Israel-Palestine conflict. Instead, it mobilized understandings of the complexity of Palestinian nationalism to advocate for a form of principled solidarity with internationalist and local dimensions. Although Argentina's left did not send tremendous resources to Palestine as did Cuba, solidarity with Palestine was still an important site of consideration and orientation. The South-South solidarity forged with the Palestinian cause in Argentina highlights the way that ties of solidarity can be implicated in broader political projects, informing and extending their directions.

4

Liberation Theology
and Apartheid

The Latin American left's South-South solidarity moved far beyond the region to advance liberation in Southern Africa. The centrality of national liberation struggles to the left's internationalism during the 1960s and 1970s mobilized action not only through international organizations like the United Nations and the Non-Aligned Movement but also through powerful institutions like the Catholic Church. The internationalist left's solidarity provided a vital resource to Catholic activism and helped forge networks through which Latin Americans could support struggles outside Latin America. Across the region, leftists criticized the Church's involvement in colonialism, its exploitation of indigenous peoples, and the role it played in perpetuating class hierarchies. Revolutionary states in Mexico and Cuba both pursued forceful anticlerical reforms in seeking liberation from colonial structures of power. In Mexico, anti-Catholic reforms resulted in the Cristero War, and Castro's success in 1959 nearly brought a total shutdown of the Church in Cuba. Some progressive Latin American Catholics acknowledged these criticisms and an increasing number engaged with the social and political causes of the left through the Church. Liberation theology emerged from this exchange as a religious movement that hoped to reorient the Church toward addressing the "sins" of socioeconomic injustice. It conveyed ideas from the Marxist left and emerging transnational movements into the center of Latin American Catholic activism.

Liberation theology quickly spread from Latin America to other parts of the Global South. It took hold in many Catholic communities that served marginalized groups. The keystone event of the theological movement took place in 1968, when the Latin American Bishops' Conference met in Medellín, Colombia, and signed a statement on the rights of the poor, condemning capitalist elites who profited at their expense. The movement caused a major fracture within the Church, whose hierarchy perceived the challenge as undermining their credibility and authority. Leaders within the movement, like Brazilian Fransiscan bishop Dom Hélder Câmara, even took on the anticommunism of the Vatican, formally decreed by the Sacred Congregation of the Holy Office in 1949, and directly attacked specific activities of several prominent figures, including Pope Pius XII. Gaining strength in the 1970s, liberation theology was eventually seen as a radical threat in Central America and to military regimes in countries like Argentina, Brazil, and Chile. It met with pushback from both the Vatican and conservative elements within local branches of the Church. This became increasingly the case as some parishes sheltered militants and prominent bishops sought information on behalf of the families of the disappeared. The theological movement was eventually persecuted by many of these regimes and repudiated by the papacy, but despite these defeats, it left an important legacy of solidarity.

This chapter broadens the book's argument for the importance of South-South solidarity to Latin American history during this period by exploring how it works its way through complex institutional structures. It argues that the transnational solidarity movements of the Latin American left advanced their political agency by gaining access to connected but distinct organizational locations and institutional relationships. This chapter focuses on how Latin American internationalist solidarity mobilized Catholic activists through such intertwined structures to lend strength to antiapartheid and anti-imperialist movements in Southern Africa. Liberation theologians during the 1960s and 1970s forged sophisticated social and professional networks, infiltrated international organizations, inspired debate, and perhaps most importantly, created opportunities for activism in deeply grounded religious institutions, such as bishops' councils and Catholic civic associations. Latin America's role in helping establish networked sites of agency, where dynamic transfers of ideas could take place between distant regions, helped transmit Latin American ideas of national liberation and resistance that had enduring aftereffects in Southern Africa. This chapter illustrates how Latin American liberation theology proponents constituted and maintained the discursive framing of the movement from one context to another and highlights the lasting influence the movement had by examining its impact on a specific site of reception.

This case study focuses on nonstate actors—activists organizing through communities of faith. During the apartheid period, religious organizations in South Africa were among the most prominent sources of resistance to the state due to severe restrictions on other political organizing. As in Latin America, churches sometimes provided spaces through which militants and activists could interact clandestinely; they also offered important spaces for minority-led and women's activism. Religious institutions have historically been vital in sustaining social movements, partly because of the uniqueness of their ability to harness and transfer resources. The Catholic Church boasts efficient hierarchical organizational structures and often diverse membership, regularly facilitating transmissions of knowledge between distantly connected social groups through educational programs and charitable works.[1] Liberation theology can be described in many ways, but understanding it in part as an extension and cultural outgrowth of internationalist leftism recognizes the social and political history of radical Catholics in Latin America who used a theological movement as a vehicle of transnational solidarity.[2] Latin American liberation theology provides a window onto the means by which South-South political agency can be marshaled across transnational contexts through complexly entangled organizations even when the associations and institutions involved might be fundamentally conservative in nature. This example provides a possible explanation for how some movements persist over long periods of persecution.

Latin American Liberation Theology

The story of liberation theology as a set of ideas and imperatives begins with what is known as Vatican II, or the Second Vatican Council. Vatican II was a momentous opening that provided a platform for many Catholics to revisit the relationship of the Church to the nation-state and to the laypeople who made up congregations in areas where Catholicism was sometimes challenged by or implicated in state operations. The impetus for the Vatican Council was somewhat unusual—a call from Pope John XXIII, which surprised high Church officials because such meetings had been exceptionally rare over the past centuries. Those invited were asked to consider the Church's engagement with modern society and democratic governance. To insiders in Rome, its urgency derived from a need to break the stranglehold on decision-making exercised by a core group of conservative leaders in the Roman Curia. When the pope issued a call for proposals to be considered at the council, it was clear that those invited to present more radical ideas would be faced with procedural and governance matters. Curial maneuvers behind the scenes would otherwise have prevented or overridden decisions in favor of change.[3] Once an agenda had been agreed on, the Second Vatican Council convened in a series of meetings from 1962 to 1965.

In Latin America, the Vatican's ties to Christian-Democratic political parties and Catholic officeholders were at stake. The outcome of Vatican II would be critical in the lead-up to the 1968 meeting of bishops in Medellín with respect to how the Church responded to human rights abuses at the hands of military dictatorships and Catholic nationalists. Ethical challenges faced Catholic leaders head on: two world wars, the rise of fascism, and workers' struggles in rapidly industrializing cities. Several priests, like Gustavo Gutiérrez in Peru and Juan Luis Segundo in Uruguay, had begun to question the Church's complicity in national political agendas. Theologians like Ernesto Cardenal in Nicaragua argued that U.S. military intervention and economic interests in the region were a form of imperialism and even advocated support for revolutionary armed struggle. They viewed the Church's complicity with oppressive states and U.S. imperialism as contradicting deeply held Catholic theological principles. Various high-profile bishops were called out for their support of the anticommunist persecution that followed in the wake of World War II. Notably Hélder Câmara accused Archbishop Geraldo de Proença Sigaud of Brazil not only of working in collaboration with Brazil's anti-communist persecution but also of being a fascist and an antisemite. Catholic laypeople supported these positions and public remonstrations surfaced from all kinds of Catholic organizations, including universities and youth organizations, mutual aid societies, and theological seminaries.[4]

Tensions between Rome and progressive Catholics in Latin America had begun several decades earlier. Catholic Action, for instance, began as a lay Catholic movement in Europe. It emerged in Latin America and Africa as a support to workers' movements in the 1930s and represented important connections between Catholic civic organizations and trade unionism. It frequently critiqued the relationship of the Church hierarchy with powerful business leaders in countries like Argentina and Brazil. It followed the lead of local leftist intellectuals to call for university reform and rural literacy campaigns. By the 1950s, Catholic outreach included a diverse range of youth and popular educational groups in the region, many of which were in dialogue with Marxist student groups and created connections between Catholic youth and university political movements.[5] From the point of departure of the Scriptures, many Catholic Action activists argued that the Church had a duty to alleviate the suffering of the poor and eradicate all forms of oppression.

The Consejo Episcopal Latinoamericano (CELAM, Episcopal Bishops' Conference of Latin America) had its first meeting in Rio de Janeiro in 1955. CELAM brought together representatives from across Latin America and the Caribbean to consider popular critiques of the role of the Church in the region's history, debate reform to Church structures, and reflect on the function of Catholicism in civil society.[6] CELAM's conversations largely reflected the dialogues that had emerged in organizations like Catholic Action. The political ideas of the Latin American left, specifically Marxist critiques of capital and imperialism, shared through lay organizations, shaped the central focus of debate when meetings were held in the lead-up to Vatican II. At the 1968 Medellín meeting, which took place on the heels of several regional military coups—Brazil and Bolivia in 1964 and Argentina in 1962 and 1966—Latin American Catholic bishops censured the traditional conservatism of the Church and its alliances with authoritarian states and powerful elite families. The meeting called out the questionable relationship of the Church to economic injustice, violence, and military repression in the region. Catholic youth and university students, influenced by Paulo Freire's notion of *concentização*, shaped CELAM debates on social issues.[7] Freire echoed the concerns of social movements in Europe and the United States that took a stand against imperialism, and considered its cultural reproduction in racism, sexism, and restrictions on civil liberties.[8]

As Latin American bishops hosted and attended events such as the Latin American Study Week, organized in 1967 in Medellín, they began to demand that the Church actively support the work of national liberation movements. Bishops like Gutiérrez argued that a simplified, democratized Church was necessary to relieve socioeconomic injustice and entrenched poverty in formerly colonized nations. Solidarity with national liberation movements became a central part of the articulation of Latin American liberation theology in the course of these meetings. Catholic activists were in conversation with the writings of the Latin American left, speeches by Castro and Guevara, and the thought of figures like Peruvian socialist José Mariátegui. This dialogue began to reflect a sustained focus on decolonization and calls for solidarity with Afro-Asian independence struggles. In February 1968, for instance, Berlin hosted a World Assembly for Peace organized around the themes of conflict in Vietnam and the Middle East, anticolonialism, national liberation, and disarmament. The conference brought together the Afro-Asian Peoples' Solidarity Organization and twenty additional organizations. It included a large number of delegates from Christian international organizations, including many Catholic activists. The importance of connections made possible by such an event are hard to understate, and its impact was felt far beyond the meeting itself. Even though Catholic clergy were not allowed to attend,[9] in Argentina alone, fourteen Catholic priests from the various provinces signed a petition in support of the assembly's statements of solidarity. Their signatures, alongside public figures, lawyers, former senators, Communist and Socialist Party leaders, highranking union members, university professors, a folklorist, actors, a photographer, and even a ballerina, signaled a willingness to stand up to not only the Church but also the Argentine state.[10]

Despite persecution, between the early 1950s and 1979, many progressive Latin American Catholic organizations, congregations, activists, and leaders expanded their political participation with the left.[11] Although this new direction was neither evenly nor widely embraced throughout the region, the culmination of these complex realignments provided the basis for what is known today as Latin American liberation theology. Those involved in the movement sometimes organized what became known as Christian base communities to educate and encourage political participation among communities of the rural and urban poor; some offered asylum to groups actively confronting dictatorship; some taught liberation theology and Marxist class analysis in seminaries; and many spoke out against human rights abuses, such as torture and illegal detention. The writing of Gustavo Gutiérrez, with its insistence on liberation though economic equality, captures the spirit of connection between socialist economic principles and support for national liberation that influenced these exchanges.

By 1979, at the Latin American Bishops' Conference in Puebla, Mexico, more radical Catholic organizations such as the Conference of Brazilian Bishops started to question and challenge the legitimacy of the state and pushed for a more dynamic role for the Church in elevating tension to provoke change.[12] Liberation theology proponents like the Movement of Priests for the Third World in Argentina, closely tied to left-wing Peronists, spoke out against the military dictatorship's persecution of workers and U.S. intervention. In 1979, CELAM issued a statement condemning economic injustice as "social sinfulness."[13] The Puebla meeting became an important site of interaction for bishops to consider and engage with the question of social justice as it related to the Church. Leftist political parties also circulated reports of violence through priests and their interlocutors at the meeting, hoping to prompt advocacy. Several high-profile liberation theology activists faced repression or exile during these years. Archbishop of San Salvador Óscar Romero, for example, spoke out about human rights abuses and paramilitary violence, unsuccessfully seeking support from the Vatican to censure the Salvadoran state. His assassination in 1980 became the most visible representation of the movement for an international audience and drew attention to Catholic activism against repressive states.[14]

Liberation theology was a threat to the institutionalized Church. It emerged in Latin America at a crucial juncture at which individual bishops claimed the right to interpret Scripture in ways that might be at odds with papal authority.[15] Latin American bishops proclaimed a "preferential option for the poor," over calls from the pope to unify the Church and denounce Marxism.[16] Prominent liberation theologians, such as Leonardo Boff in Brazil,

Gustavo Gutiérrez in Peru, Renato Poblete and Pablo Richard in Chile, Jon Sobrino and Ignacio Ellacuría in El Salvador, José Míguez Bonino in Argentina, Otto Maduro in Venezuela, and Juan Luis Segundo in Uruguay, argued forcefully for a new direction for the Church in securing better conditions for the marginalized. Argentine-born theologian and Marxist philosopher Enrique Dussel called on the Church to direct its energy toward addressing social issues such as racial discrimination and poverty, which he clearly identified as interconnected with class struggle. Brazilian seminaries in the south and northeast of the country began to prioritize students from poor and working-class backgrounds and for the first time actively recruited nonwhites.

As Vatican II–influenced priests participated more actively in the organizational life of the Church, some advocated on behalf of nonwhite groups. In Brazil, Afro-Brazilians seeking an end to discrimination led critical theological debates centered on race.[17] At the 1979 meeting in Puebla, bishops of color identified with the emerging *movimento negro* in Brazil. These bishops criticized the discrimination they faced in the seminary, formally proposing that the National Conference of Brazilian Bishops start sponsoring meetings for Catholic Afro-Brazilians. They also pushed for a stronger commitment from the Church to oppose racial discrimination in Brazil and abroad.[18] Interest in the fate of Southern Africa within the *movimento negro* spread through seminaries, along with support for decolonization and solidarity with independence movements in former Portuguese colonies. Familiar with internationalist reporting on Africa from Cuba, they were most concerned with Angola and Mozambique, where South Africa threatened military and security interventions. Many saw Africa as a mirror of the fragility of Brazil's independence and became actively involved in supporting the economic future of liberation governments, encouraging Brazilian investment in Angola.[19]

Throughout this period, the Catholic Church became a conduit for reflection on race. Even though Church leadership in Rome was unsupportive, outspoken theologians and organizers in the Church in Brazil challenged racial discrimination. Seminaries and parish churches provided gathering spaces and networks through which the antiracism ideas of Cuban internationalism and the Brazilian left could be articulated and mobilized as part of popular protest.[20] Although the Latin American Church did not necessarily become a source of radical activism everywhere in the region, the ideological frameworks presented by liberation theologians clearly had a profound influence on politics and helped in constructing a Third Worldist Catholicism.[21] This influence quickly reached Southern Africa, where it would be adapted to the antiapartheid movement.[22]

Beyond theological positioning, one of the most important outgrowths of Latin American participation in Vatican II was the establishment of the

Pontifical Council for Justice and Peace. This council, modeled on social movements in Latin America, was designed to deepen the social commitment of the Church, particularly to labor and the working classes. The council would be responsible for assembling an international team to organize the collection and exchange of reports related to antilabor violence and state aggression. It would also authorize individual justice and peace commissions to be local task offices for Catholic activism. These commissions would organize local activities, such as reporting or coordinating actions, and the council would provide a mechanism for local teams to solicit international organizational support. One of the first Justice and Peace commissions would be set up to monitor the apartheid state in South Africa.

South African Social Catholicism

In South Africa, Catholic activism was influenced by Latin American liberation theology to take on neocolonialism and apartheid. South Africa's apartheid state, formally initiated in 1948, and reinforced by the 1950 Suppression of Communism Act, was a key target of Latin American internationalist solidarity organizing. South African anticommunism was part of the same internationally coordinated effort felt in the region. External support provided tremendous new power to the postcolonial state by which to repress dissent, justify discrimination, and target antiapartheid opposition leaders. Section 10 of the act brought into force house arrest and "banning orders," which could be used broadly by the Minister of Justice to isolate presumed communists simply on suspicion. It provided the office the power to detain political prisoners indefinitely despite an absence of evidence.[23] One way that members of the Catholic Church became active in interpreting and debating apartheid early on was by circulating pamphlets that explained these laws. Pamphlets could be easily distributed among clergy and used as guides to assist their congregation members in understanding their rights.

In 1957, for instance, the South African Institute of Race Relations produced a pamphlet interpreting the Native Laws Amendment Bill, with special attention to its effects on religious freedoms, freedom of expression, and rights of association. The pamphlet included a piece by Anglican Bishop Ambrose Reeves, based in Johannesburg, who wrote a scathing indictment of the state's interference in religious organizational life, particularly in predominantly Black African urban areas, though it did not take on racial discrimination directly.[24] Reeves also traveled to the United States to raise funds to fight apartheid legislation, which was reinforced and elaborated in amendments to the Native

Lands Act Group Areas Act, the Prohibition of Mixed Marriages Act, the Population Registration Act, the Immorality Amendment Act, the Native Building Workers Act, the Native Laws Amendment Act of 1952 (later known as the Bantu Laws Amendment Act), and the Reservation of Separate Amenities Act, all enacted and amended between 1949 and 1953.[25] The first official conference setting out principles for Catholic Action in South Africa was held in 1959, when a local office was founded in Johannesburg. Its foundational documents suggest that the most important priority of the local branch was to extend social services to the African population of the country as a means of increasing charitable social responsibility and fostering unity in the Church.[26]

The Catholic Church serves roughly 10 percent of South Africa's population. Among those South Africans who identified as Catholic between 1960 and 1980, more than 80 percent were Black, making it a majority Black-serving church, as were most Protestant churches.[27] It was certainly not the largest Christian denomination relative to the Anglican and Dutch Reform Churches, and it remained fairly minor in terms of influence among the Afrikaner population, except insofar as the South African Catholic Church broadly represented all South African Catholics in international spaces. However, as a predominantly Black church, the Catholic Church in South Africa could hardly ignore challenges to think critically about the role of the Church in confronting apartheid legislation. When the National Party came to power in South Africa in 1948, the Church had already been organizing resistance to the increasingly repressive laws imposed by the state. At this time, a few bishops—notably Franziskus Hennemann, followed by Owen McCann—were becoming known for speaking out against segregation, facing conservative backlash from the hierarchy of the Church and its white-minority congregants. In the Western Cape, the region that includes Cape Town, a more sizable population of Blacks fostered a push in the Church to engage in issues related to the lower-class status of Black laborers.[28]

In 1952, the South African Catholic Bishops' Conference, established only a year earlier, issued its first joint statement regarding racial segregation and announced its opposition to institutionalized racism of this form. Although operating through a conservative and hierarchal institution, some Catholic leaders were becoming increasingly concerned about the worsening conditions of their congregants, responding to regular reports of violence and discrimination, particularly in areas with more open hostility. Increasingly discriminatory legislation passed throughout the 1950s as "security legislation" targeted Black protest groups. Extending the work of earlier laws, such as the Riotous Assemblies Act of 1930, the Unlawful Organizations Act of 1950, and the Public Safety Act of 1953, new security laws set a precedent that allowed for the disruption of the activities of Black political leaders, including those in religious associations and among clergy, and eventually threatened the leadership of the African National Congress (ANC). Legislative measures for repressing the political activity of Blacks were further elaborated in the 1960s and 1970s, as additional laws were passed that framed resistance to segregation and protest related to Blacks' loss of citizenship rights as an official form of terrorism.[29]

One of the Church's earliest efforts against the apartheid system in the 1950s was its active stance against the Bantu education laws. Mandatory racial segregation was passed into law in 1953 via the Bantu Education Act, moving the administration of schools for "natives" to the Ministry of Native Affairs and thus taking control from a variety of provinces or other organizations that served these communities. This placed them under the control of the federal agency most preoccupied with elaborating the apartheid regime.[30] The Catholic Church, largely in an effort to save Catholic schools, refused to accept the premise that Black people should be relegated to a separate educational system, adding that the physical condition of many of these schools was inadequate. Bishops and other Catholic leaders began to take action, issuing statements and actively protesting the reforms. This proved somewhat effective in intensifying antiapartheid attitudes in the Church, particularly due to the Church's long-standing role in providing education. The work of social action facilitated by Catholic schools—particularly the work of sisters who taught in Catholic schools together with laypeople in social programs associated with these schools—created a meaningful display of resistance. As 15 percent of schools that were designated to fall under the act were Catholic, their protest was not insignificant. When the Church refused to follow the provisions of the Bantu Education Act, they lost considerable funding, as a large share of state subsidies was withheld. Even with local community efforts to raise funds to supplement teachers' salaries and provide basic building maintenance, the Church had to close more than half of their schools.[31]

Resistance in Catholic institutions to the segregation of schools in many ways mirrored the Defiance Campaign of the ANC. The Defiance Campaign encouraged mass actions organized through a national volunteer corps, including strikes, sit-ins, and other forms of civil disobedience in defiance of unjust laws. The dialogue between social Catholicism in South Africa and the ANC extended to the use of churches as secret meeting places to allow for political organizing. Churches were acknowledged as one of the few places where even those accused of being communists were still allowed to gather freely, and the ANC later encouraged the use of churches as safe spaces.[32] Despite these efforts, Sister Margaret Kelly later noted, "no one could accuse the bishops in the fifties of being revolutionary."[33] Until the late 1950s, most bishops in South Africa tended to take a conciliatory approach to the apartheid state and rarely commented on events beyond the scope of Catholic institutions.

Justice and Peace Commissions in South Africa

Despite conservative elements among the hierarchy of the Church in Africa, a handful of politically active archbishops were beginning to gain a reputation in Rome. While archbishops in Cape Town and Durban gained some recognition for standing up against the South African government's repressive segregationist policies in schools, their counterparts in Congo, Algeria, and Egypt challenged the Church's silence on the political violence of imperialism and its lack of attention to the needs of marginalized populations and minorities.[34] By the time Vatican II was called, Denis Hurley, archbishop of Durban, was modestly aware of the tendencies of other national branches of the Church toward the political. Either by luck or by unknown intervention, he was invited to participate in the organizing conferences for Vatican II, where he quickly became an outspoken proponent of governance reform. His first and likely most significant mediation was questioning the procedural matters of the meetings, which over time broke up some of the control of the conservative Curia. The Curia was somewhat unprepared as this forthright critic from South Africa undermined its stranglehold on the agenda. By insisting on minor changes to the format of meetings and rules around discussion, Hurley created important openings for exchange.

Before and during the council, Hurley frequently called on the Church to turn its attention to the "rights of man."[35] His reputation among his colleagues grew in 1966 when he addressed the banning of a speech by Martin Luther King Jr. by the South African state. An Anglican minister had convinced a recording label to press and distribute a recording of the speech, which spread widely across the bigger cities, where many Black South Africans were inspired by King's words. In response to the banning, Hurley insisted: "If there is anything subversive or unchristian in Dr. King's address, we challenge the authorities to make it known. Otherwise we, and most of the 10,000 people who have heard the record, must conclude that the Government has been frightened by the effectiveness and eloquence with which Dr. King calls on the church to examine its attitude to the racial question."[36] Hurley was not considered an especially radical thinker and did not approve of Latin American liberation theology, but his reputation as a critic of racism and the challenge to discriminatory positions of the South African Catholic Church made him stand out as something of a firebrand in South Africa and Rome.[37]

Pope Paul VI decided to write an Apostolic Letter, the *Octogesima Adveniens*, announcing a shift in the position of the Vatican to form an alliance with the poor. Facing the reverberations of the Medellín meetings, the papacy sought to provide a conciliatory platform. This proved to be a critical turning point for the Church in South Africa. Vatican II's influence, however, went further. On 6 January 1967, the Pontifical Council for Justice and Peace inaugurated a formalized program of communication that began between national Churches and Rome on matters related to social responsibility. Its role was to maintain links between Catholic organizations, religious movements, lay associations, and institutes, including those that were interdenominational. To further elucidate these directions, in 1971, the Synod of Bishops issued a statement from Rome titled *Justice in the World*, which issued what could only be described as a paradigm shift in Catholic social thought.[38] The Justice and Peace commissions, made possible by the activities of the liberation theology movement in Latin America, provided a ready-made space for Catholic activists to find support. Each bishop's conference had its own commission, and each diocese was meant to have one branch of Justice and Peace, eventually extending to every parish. The papacy saw these commissions as a mechanism to gain support from the working classes, but Latin American liberation theologists saw them as a tool of transferring information and resources across borders. Hurley founded the first Catholic Commission for Justice and Peace (CCJP) in South Africa in Durban in 1968.

Over time, the CCJP subtly moved South African religious councils toward an antiapartheid position. The commission reported to the South African Catholic Bishop's Conference (SACBC), but between 1968 and the mid-1970s, it also forged strong ties to the Protestant South African Council of Churches (SACC).[39] Despite the social activism of many Catholics in South Africa in the 1960s, it was not until the galvanizing events of 1976 and 1977 that the CCJP took on a more active engagement with Latin American liberation theology. In 1976, an uprising began in Soweto that would have important consequences for the Church. Following the controversial decision to make Afrikaans and English mandatory as languages of instruction, students began organizing. Through the South African Students Movement's Action Committee, they eventually organized a protest march, supported by leaders in the Black consciousness movement and the Young African Religious Movement, which was used as a cover for the banned Pan Africanist Congress to connect with students for consciousness-raising.[40] When thousands marched on 16 June 1974 to the Orlando Stadium for a rally, heavily armed South African police threw teargas into the crowd and opened fire on the peaceful student protesters. The deaths of between twenty-three and two hundred students led to several other demonstrations and increased support for the ANC and other militarized groups. Armed clashes between the police and guerrillas affiliated with the ANC broke out in several parts of the country; in the following police raids, a number of activists were arrested and detained. Many of these activists were charged under the Terrorism Act, accused of conspiring to overthrow the government. In October 1977, six hundred teachers resigned their posts to protest the detention and deaths of their students.[41] Catholic sisters in Soweto pushed for the Church to respond. Following their lead, the SACBC issued a "Declaration of Commitment." The declaration called for support to oppose the racist system under which Black South Africans were silenced and oppressed.[42]

Women played a significant role in galvanizing solidarity through local Justice and Peace commissions. As the Soweto Uprising and its aftermath unfolded, nuns and lay women organized through the commissions to collect files on political prisoners and detainees. They collected photographs and profiles in order to track individual cases and provide direct support to families.[43] The organizing secretary of the Cape Town commission, Imelda Davidson, who later directed Catholic Relief Services in Johannesburg, urged a broader mandate, including active investigation. These women broadened the activity of the commissions, initiating investigations of social injustices and racial discrimination, gaining influence as they spoke out about public figures. The commissions also introduced outreach to "needy regions," which later included missions to other parts of Southern Africa and for migrant laborers in South Africa.[44] The establishment of these missions as channels also soon connected the exiled ANC with Catholic activists.

Women in the Cape Town commission provided leadership in turning the CCJPs into transnational networking sites. In 1975, the Cape Town commission was only four years old, but it was chaired by Margaret Malherbe, and of its fourteen members, four members of the leadership were women. The only full-time employee of this branch, Sister Brigid Rose Tiernan, served as secretary and recordkeeper. Sister Tiernan's responsibility was to author outgoing correspondence, and hers were the letters that connected the Cape Town CCJP to archbishops, Rome, and Catholic organizations abroad.[45] In Durban, "Louise" Loek Goemans, a member of the Catholic feminist Grail theological community, served in this capacity, and the secretary of Pretoria's SACBC headquarters took on similar duties.[46] Justice and Peace Commissions often incorporated lay activists, many of which were women, providing connections to other social organizations through women's leadership on the ground.[47]

Nuns like Tiernan and Malherbe possessed special reporting activities, often on the most sensitive issues, such as race relations. Reporting activities included sending letters and reports on forced relocations, poor labor conditions, state oppression, bannings and detentions, and violence against women and girls, which were then relayed to internal councils and bishops. The women provided materials for advocacy through official channels, such as the International Commission for Justice and Peace in Rome, and the Inter-Regional Meeting of the Bishops of Southern Africa (IMBISA; also known as the African Synod), which was the convention mandated to deal with interregional conflict and violence. They also helped circulate clandestine publications, such as accounts of politically motivated violence and international news media censored by the state.[48] Publications were made available to activists from other organizations on the ground and South African reports were circulated outside the country via women's organizational channels.[49]

Catholic sisters and lay women played an important role in managing support within communities. In some cases, these women traveled to give lectures outside South Africa or supported traveling bishops. Malherbe took a trip to Australia in 1976 to raise support for the antiapartheid cause. They were able to communicate through Catholic newspapers such as the *Southern Cross*, where calls could be made for general solidarity with bishops' statements.[50] On the one hand, Catholic sisters were very visible when taking part in protests dressed in their habits; on the other hand, they facilitated the more guarded initiatives of the CCJPs and often became custodians of commission activities, providing security and concealment. They used their positions to elaborate a system of antiapartheid education that worked its way through parishes, instructing congregations in tactics of peaceful resistance and reinforcing the value of the struggle. Laywomen and Catholic nuns brought their own ideas to the fore, such as advocacy for the labor rights of domestic and migrant workers.[51] By the mid-1970s, the work of Catholic women had not only strengthened the antiapartheid effort but had also broadened it.

The Cape Town commission printed a short-run magazine, *Pax*, which raised consciousness on issues central to the antiapartheid organizing efforts of the Church. Because open opposition was not possible, the magazine used anonymized authors, most likely the commission secretary. One such issue covered aspects of forced removals, explaining key concepts and positions, including appeals to conscience and Scriptures to grasp the injustice presented by such state actions. The magazine also explained the effects on labor issues and land distribution, social connections, and physical security for those affected by forced removal.[52] Justice and Peace activities also mobilized information about support for those affected by apartheid through other circuits in close contact with the Catholic nuns involved in the commissions. In addition to schools, the commission relied on other groups, such as the Citizens' Advice Bureau, Women's Movement for Peace, the Anglican Board of Social Responsibility, Young Christian Women, the Black Sash, the Christian Institute, and the Catholic Welfare Bureau.[53] Most of these were coordinated if not entirely led by women activists.

Under the leadership of Margaret Malherbe, the Western Cape Justice and Peace Commission created strong ties to local communities. Malherbe was in charge of the commission responsible for Langa and Nyanga, two of the oldest areas designated for Black Africans. She circulated documents at local parishes, mobilizing through women's organizations to provide assistance in the aftermath of violence in Black townships and refuge centers for Blacks living in predominantly white parishes.[54] This branch of the CCJP worked closely with the Black Sash, an antiapartheid women's organization that was critical in giving legal advice, writing a bill of rights for Blacks in the Western Cape, and organizing community resources in areas affected by forced resettlement.[55] Malherbe also gave an interview to the *New York Times* as chair of the Cape Town Justice and Peace Commission, calling Catholic leadership out for having failed to act more forcefully against apartheid. The interview indicated her conviction that the youth of the Church were not satisfied with the lack of action by the Church on political matters. This opinion was echoed by Catholic scholars concerned with losing ground among new generations, who were interested in an antiapartheid position and a prosocial role for the Church.[56]

Catholic women leaders were a crucial channel of information exchange between Latin America and Southern Africa. Malherbe documented in her letters to Archbishop Owen McCann the influence of Austrian-born Hildegard Goss-Mayr. Beginning in 1962, Goss-Mayr, along with her husband, Jean, had spent many years in Latin America working with grassroots Catholic communities. She provided Malherbe with nonviolent political resistance strategies developed by Catholic leftists including those produced by trade unionists, student groups, and local priests allied with groups like the Catholic Peronist left in Argentina. Goss-Mayr also held workshops on nonviolent resistance in the 1970s for bishops in Bogotá, during which, at the request of the president of the Conference of Latin American Bishops, many of the proposals for the 1979 Puebla conference were drafted. Goss-Mayr and her husband traveled for long periods between Latin America and Southern Africa, working at the end of the colonial period in Angola and Mozambique and, by the early 1980s, in Zimbabwe, South Africa, Lebanon, and Israel.[57] As part of the International Fellowship of Reconciliation based in the Netherlands, Goss-Mayr and counterparts from thirty other countries were successful in acquiring consultative status with the UN Economic and Social Council, a platform through which economic sanctions against South Africa could be formally proposed. According to Malherbe's letters, Goss-Mayr was a source of tremendous inspiration and support for local activism.

In 1981, following the Puebla conference, Sister Thora Pérez, Malherbe's successor, led a successful investigation on behalf of Justice and Peace Cape Town into evictions in the Western Cape, particularly Nyanga and Langa, where roughly fifteen hundred people were evicted from the Single Quarters. She revealed that the forced evictions of predominantly single women and children imposed by the South African state were designed to make room for barracks for private companies' employees. Pérez worked closely with local parishes to accommodate the displaced and, with the Black Sash, offered legal advice and coordinated with local community organizations to secure food, bail money, and other supplies, which became critical because the displaced were at risk of being accused of illegal squatting.[58] Information like this could be quickly circulated through networks from local parishes all the way to the United Nations, where it would reach organizational efforts set in place by Goss-Mayr.

Internationalizing South African Antiapartheid

The Justice and Peace commissions made solidarity with national liberation movements a central part of antiapartheid Catholic activism. CCJP officials were sent from South Africa to places like Zimbabwe and Namibia to report on imperialist conflict, attesting to violence committed by South African troops and local governments. This provided a means for Catholic activists to interact with national liberation groups abroad and in exile, organize social events, and promote antiracist positions. When traveling, many Justice and Peace representatives faced deportation or were refused reentry to South Africa. While in these commissions the beginnings of an internationalism akin to that of the Latin American left could be seen, it is important to recognize that the Church was still a largely conservative organization in South Africa. A political counterpoint to the radical nature of CCJP activity can be seen in the contemporaneous rise of Catholic South African nationalist organizations like the Catholic Defence League and Tradition, Family, and Property. Neither group had official standing with the Church, but both were vociferous public critics of leftism in Catholic associations and clergy, charging that the

Church could easily be overtaken over by communists. Many Catholics during this period demanded a reinforcement of conservative Catholic leadership and an end to political activities within the Church.[59]

Pope John Paul VI made a concerted effort to close down the activities of the more radicalized organizations in the Church. However, the complex networks that this movement produced, which extended through youth and women's organizations to political parties and across networks of international activists, continued to be a sustaining resource for many Catholic clergy and laity involved in ongoing struggles in Southern Africa. The harassment many faced challenged laypeople in the Church to examine the actions of the state. During this time, major conferences were held in Dar es Salaam in 1976 and Accra in 1977, organized by the Ecumenical Association of Third World Theologians.[60] The South African Catholic Church's support of the commissions and their ongoing missions was noted at these meetings. These meetings reported that the Justice and Peace goal was to support the implementation of social teachings by means of clear actions in communities and to provide spaces for Church leaders to exchange views and expand on ideas of liberation theology.[61]

Another activity central to the business of Justice and Peace commissions that later bore significant fruit was the organization of protest around international transfers of funds to the South African government. As early as 1973, the commissions began to collect information from the banking sector that demonstrated the support of large financial institutions, both direct and indirect, for the increased military and security expenditures of the apartheid state.[62] South African Catholic activists followed a strategy that had been successful in Chile, wherein banks had been called out by the Church for supporting the military regime of Augusto Pinochet, whose record of human rights abuses were well known to the international community. U.S.-based Catholic leaders worked in concert with the Christian Institute, an antiapartheid Christian think-tank founded in 1963 by Afrikaner theologian Beyers Naudé, funded by the World Council of Churches, and banned in 1973.[63] Together they mobilized information sharing and circulated critiques of international institutions' economic agendas.

The Christian Institute, with its complex of partners in solidarity, sent out an international call to cut off military and financial support to South Africa. It advocated for the withdrawal of invested funds from any South African business or branch of government that could be implicated in South Africa's actions in Rhodesia and Portuguese Angola or in its policies of racial discrimination.[64] Through an interchurch Taskforce on Corporate Responsibility, the group traced significant loans, such as from Canadian banks including the Bank of Montreal, the Toronto-Dominion Bank, the Royal Bank, the Canadian Imperial Bank of Commerce, and the Bank of Nova Scotia, to support for the South African military. These funds were designated to provide liquid capital to the South African government to continue efforts in "problem areas," continue to produce military armaments, and free up public sector capital in other areas. The report demonstrated that from 1971 to 1978, investors indirectly allowed increased public funds to be redirected to an expanding security budget to enforce apartheid.[65] The taskforce encouraged Christian communities and organizations to move their Canadian funds to credit unions in Canada, whose policies prevented the kind of loans of the size and low transparency made by other Canadian banks. It claimed that the public withdrawal of funds, already in practice by organizations like Cuso International and Oxfam, could have a tremendous effect on South Africa's ability to continue on its current course.

This strategy eventually led to a wider church divestment movement. The Protestant South African Council of Churches followed this lead in 1985, resolving at their national congress to encourage economic sanctions against South Africa.[66] However, Catholic bishops were not unanimous in their support for the movement. White bishops, particularly in wealthier areas in the Western Cape, were concerned with property and financial matters, and along with prominent conservative clergy, they railed against the activities of the CCJPs. However, the Justice and Peace commissions created a labyrinth of institutional and social networks through which advocacy could find manifold support. This vehicle of transnational solidarity even survived the Church's later turn toward conservative counterparts, such as the Prelature of the Holy Cross and Opus Dei, which were rumored to support Pinochet's dictatorship.

Pope John Paul II took a stand against liberation theology, including defrocking and making a televised demand of Nicaraguan priest Ernesto Cardenal to distance himself from the Marxist revolutionary Sandinista government.[67] The pope's public rebuke was a lesson intended to be shared with Catholic activists everywhere. Liberation theology priests and nuns were tortured and disappeared across Latin America in the following years. Colombian priest Iván Betancourt in Honduras in 1975 was brutally tortured and murdered. Three Pallottine priests and two seminarians were beaten and killed by unidentified gunmen in Argentina in 1976. The discovery of the bodies of four Maryknoll nuns, Ita Ford, Dorothy Kazel, Jean Donovan, and Maura Clarke, in 1980 in El Salvador, sent a strong message on behalf of right-wing military dictatorships. They understood that the Church would not defend leftist liberation theologists.

Black Consciousness, Liberation Theology, and Racial Representation

Beyond the Justice and Peace activities, Latin American liberation theology fueled the Black theology movement in South Africa. Black theology's embrace of Latin American liberation theology shaped the movement's political orientation. This influence emerged in a variety of settings, chief among them the work of activist theologians who participated in seminars led by the University Christian Movement (UCM) and the Black Theology Project. Founded in 1967, the UCM quickly grew to include thirty branches at seminaries and universities, then mostly de facto segregated and white. Eventually the UCM became a large, ecumenical religious movement with Black-majority membership.[68] The other key foundational moment for the movement, the Black Theology Project, was started by the Wilgespruit Fellowship Centre in Johannesburg under the direction of Sabelo Ntwasa. In attendance at these early meetings were Manas Buthelezi, Alpheus and Lawrence Zulu, Clive McBride, and Basil Moore—all well-established figures in theological debates in South Africa.

Ideas were translated from American contexts through Black theology spaces. Reading texts and debating Black consciousness and theological approaches to race relations, the movement included the pivotal writings of James Cone on Black theology in the United States.[69] The South African Students' Organisation established a study group to conduct research on Black theology, which gave additional space for considering the influence of Black African religious, anticolonialist, and pan-Africanist thinkers like Amílcar Cabral, W. E. B. Du Bois, Marcus Garvey, and Frantz Fanon, as well as the work of early Christian missionaries who, along with African independent churches from the late nineteenth century, looked at religion as a possible force for liberation.[70] The underlying goal of Black theology, which resonated with liberation theology, was the notion that true freedom required transcending the material and spiritual alienation produced by racist institutions.[71]

Anglicans, Lutherans, and other Protestants of the Black theology movement eventually attracted interest from Catholic theologians. While South African Catholics joined the ranks of liberation theology only later, Black theology groups were already circulating reports and interviews published in English and circulated in Africa by Cuban and Brazilian solidarity organizations, notably OSPAAAL and the Comité Brasileiro de Solidariedade aos Povos da África do Sul e Namíbia. They offered analysis in English of national liberation struggles in Portuguese-speaking Africa and brought many debates around decolonization and racism into the center of their discourse. These groups included Catholic thinkers who circulated the sociological texts of Latin American liberation theologians like Gustavo Gutiérrez and Enrique Dussel, which contributed to the conversations around class struggle, antiracism, and anti-imperialism in the South African context.[72] Many of these texts offered revolutionary perspectives, imagery of armed struggle (figure 4.1), and exchanges that openly questioned the validity of the South African apartheid state.

By the 1970s, the Catholic Church counted on more Black bishops and had even established a Permanent Black Priest Solidarity Group, which was well connected to the ecumenical Black theology movement.[73] In 1974, Catholic bishop P. F. J. Butelezi issued a statement on Black consciousness that was recommended to the Bishops' Plenary Sessions that year.[74] This statement argued that rather than finding inspiration from Irish and German expatriates, the national Church should begin to rely on the voices of Black South Africans, whose ability to understand social injustice from a local perspective exceeded that of outsiders.[75] In a pamphlet titled "Call to Workers and Employers" issued by the Young Christian Workers' National Secretariat, the relationship between Black liberation struggles and the trade union movement was made clear. The text enumerated a list of recommendations on a range of issues, including working conditions, professional training, migratory labor, and responsible action that identified these as race issues.[76]

In 1977, as the Catholic Church started to increase its formal commitment to appointing Black bishops and priests and advancing Blacks employed by the Church in areas that served white communities, there was an increase in Black adherents. Black congregations grew by a remarkable 76 percent during the last years of the decade.[77] In 1977, when all Black organizations were banned in South Africa, the church was an exception, and within its purview the Black Bishops Solidarity Group formed to formally protest the exclusion of Black South Africans from political life. They were later charged under the Riotous Assemblies Act for carrying Bibles in John Vorster Square in Johannesburg.[78] By the 1980s, the clergy was measurably more radicalized, and Latin American liberation theology had become integrated into the theological debates of Black Catholic organizations. Black townships were by then facing military invasion, and this increased the urgency of incorporating racial equality into the hierarchy of the Church.[79]

Key theologians in university and seminary settings were consuming works produced by radical Christian thinkers. The UCM reflected the development of new vocabularies of resistance and new forms of conceptual analysis. It also presented an African face to the movement in publications that featured photographs of its leadership (figure 4.2). The "contextual theology" approach, in dialogue with the Black consciousness movement, held Blackness as the most

Figure 4.1. Cover, *ICT News* 2, no. 1 (March 1984). File ZA HPRA AG2843-E-E1, Institute for Contextual Theology Records, Historical Papers Research Archive, University of the Witwatersrand, South Africa.

immediate framework of political affirmation but did not publicly embrace connections to national liberation struggles, hoping to avoid interference from the South African state. Contextual theology, as a movement, was aimed at providing a response to the problems related to inequalities of power, using the church as a grassroots source of resistance to political and economic injustice.[80] It incorporated teachings from African theology, feminist theology, liberation theology, and Black theology into a set of workshops, courses, and critical studies, publishing findings and reaching out to an international network from its base in Johannesburg at the Institute of Contextual Theology (ICT).

The ICT published a newsletter beginning in 1983 that circulated advice for setting up Christian base communities modeled on those in Latin America. The newsletter highlighted the work of independent Black churches in advancing liberation theology. The ICT circulated notices of violence against Christian activists by the South African state and made announcements for conferences and other events to bring together different constituencies, such as academic congresses and women's organizations. It printed images on the

Figure 4.2. Seminarians from St. Joseph's Scholasticate, Cedara, with Natal University Students, South African Bishops' Conference. "Standing for the Truth," *Internos* 2 (September/October 1989): 23. File ZA HPRA AG3375-M-M11-M11.4, Young Christian Students South Africa, Historical Papers Research Archive, University of the Witwatersrand, South Africa.

newsletter cover that reflected the themes and aesthetics of Tricontinentalist publications, including the use of high-contrast portraits of intellectual leaders, the iconography of the armed guerrilla soldier, and photographs of African communities embracing revolutionary visitors. At such meetings, articles such as South African Catholic liberation theologian Mike Deeb's "Pastoral Planning: Lessons from Latin America" would be circulated. Participants might be asked to consider the implications of the models provided in places like Nicaragua, Brazil, and Chile for South Africa. One of the most commonly circulated texts at these meetings was Gustavo Gutiérrez's 1971 *A Theology of Liberation*. Analytical and theological treatises were not the only texts that circulated. These events often included materials developed in Latin America for teaching liberation theology to youth and children.[81]

Transnational Networks of Activism and Resistance

Catholic activism expanded its reach through participation in transregional and ecumenical church organizations. As meetings of the African Synod, IMBISA, became more frequent in the late 1970s, communicating ideas and information through these channels across Southern Africa became easier. This was partly due to pressure from below, paired with what was perceived as official sanction. Vatican II and the CCJPs gave Catholic bishops in South Africa a renewed sense of purpose and validated the work they were already doing, if perhaps haphazardly. Increasing protest movements against apartheid gave them further motivation to integrate their efforts into more comprehensive international strategies to confront the state. This had the effect of correcting previous efforts that fell short of addressing apartheid directly.

The Church had not been unanimous in its support of efforts to address racial discrimination and political repression. This was particularly true in areas like Bloemfontein, where the concerns of wealthy white business and property owners preempted much of the discussion about addressing racial inequalities. These tensions help illustrate how complex forms of solidarity manage to survive institutional pressures and changes in leadership. When Pope John Paul II came to power in 1978, the Catholic Church was already suspicious of revolutionary movements. The papacy took a serious turn back toward support for the state and began a rollback of Vatican II initiatives. Nevertheless, the variety of interconnected institutions carrying on the vision of liberation theology were able to continue building in Southern Africa. Challenges presented by communities like Bloemfontein were met with a delicate shifting of more radical activities away from bishops, who might be tied more closely to the Vatican, and into organizations at the grassroots, in missions and inter-regional meetings, in charitable and educational institutions led by women, and other bases of support farther away from the center.

The Christian Institute was set up in 1963 by mostly white ministers of different denominations with the intention of theologizing around resistance to apartheid. Over time, it became more tied to the politics and theology of liberation. The institute originally took an approach centered on education and calls to conscience directed toward the white population. As the influence of Latin American liberation theology grew in the mid-1970s, the institute gradually moved to this approach. This shift reflected engagement with the Black consciousness movement and the writings of proponents of national liberation in the Americas and North Africa that called for structural changes to combat racism and apartheid. In dialogue with the Christian Institute, the Catholic Bishops' synods in Africa compared approaches of the Catholic Church in different regions. Reports were frequently offered on the state of the Church and its operations in Latin America and, to a lesser extent, other parts of the world like Asia and the United States. Reports prepared by South African bishops considered Latin America to be the region most comparable to Africa. They remarked on the distinct advantage of Latin America as a site of activism because of its far greater percentage of Catholics. Lengthy studies of "basic communities," decolonization efforts, "underdevelopment," and lib-eration theology in Latin America circulated via speeches and informal reports given at meetings from the late 1960s to well into the 1980s.[82]

By 1976, the Christian Institute had become a hotbed of radical thinking, and its publication *Pro Veritate* circulated ideas of liberation and antiracism to a wider audience, which gradually included Black Catholics and Catholic activists. This meant that it also became the target of state repression. Theo Kotze was a Methodist minister who was banned, along with the institute and many of its partner organizations, which were also banned in 1977, following the Soweto crisis. Banning meant that these leaders were not allowed to gather with more than one other person and had to report to the police every day. Under a form of house arrest, they were barred from writing for a public audi-ence, public speaking, and political organizing of any kind. They were not allowed to speak to anyone while traveling and would be immediately arrested if they met other banned individuals. In addition, they could be employed only under certain conditions, where their actions could be closely monitored.

In 1971, Franciscan priest Father Cosmas Desmond, British-born but liv-ing in South Africa, wrote *Discarded People*, a controversial book on apartheid laws. As a result, Desmond was placed under house arrest.[83] Following his arrest, Jeremy Hurley, nephew of Archbishop Denis Hurley, led a student demonstration at the University of Natal in protest.[84] Desmond's situation was fairly typical of Catholics who came to South Africa from elsewhere to serve and work. Foreign Catholics could have their work permits canceled and be deported. Such was the case of several Irish Catholics who continued to participate in the antiapartheid struggle from Ireland after they had been forced to leave South Africa.

Foreign and exiled Catholics could be found in bordering nations such as Zimbabwe, working to support others in similar conditions and share information. For example, exiled priest Dick O'Riordan spent time in and out of Zimbabwe, later becoming active in the antiapartheid struggle in collaboration with other exiled activists. The Church would sometimes support them financially or make token appeals for their cases to be dismissed. However, these exiles were influential in terms of helping shape the movement, particularly as they often occupied the same spaces the ANC leadership used outside the country. Their views, often benefiting from the circulation of information through the Christian Institute, IMBISA, and associated networks, communicated larger issues from metropoles in Europe back and forth to Africa. They also carried messages between exiled and banned priests and helped inform those who were still in South Africa.[85]

In 1972, when the Church issued the papal "Call to Conscience," Vatican II ideas emanating from the Global South had clearly found a place in more mainstream social Catholicism. The call recommended that the Catholic Church support trade unions, redistributive taxation, and protections for the poor. In South Africa, it was interpreted to indicate support for those who had been banned, detained, and oppressed on the grounds of race and for those who suffered discrimination under unjust legal regimes, the numbers of whom increased significantly after the Soweto uprising in 1976.[86] Catholics who were part of specific orders or groups could travel to Rome, where they could have personal contact with leading figures, including the pope. The Young Christian Workers and the Young Christian Students, for example, had access to overseas meetings and later were key to the circulation of ideas back to South Africa upon their return.

The bishops' council also tried to use the Theological Exchange Program to allow students to travel between South Africa, Brazil, and Cuba. Although this program was not as successful as was hoped, it demonstrated a commitment to connection with Latin America. Gustavo Gutiérrez met with South African bishops at several conferences from the late 1970s through the 1980s. His work was never banned in South Africa and did not appear to be of much interest to local censors, so his publications circulated widely—perhaps accounting for why they were so frequently included in the reading material at various meetings. This was not the case for other prominent advocates of liberation theology. Brazilian liberation theologian Leonardo Boff was reprimanded after he criticized the Church hierarchy and the new pope for failing to attend to the needs of the poor. The Church took measures to keep him from actively participating in any Church affairs in the subsequent decades. When Cardinal Paulo Evaristo Arns of Brazil was not allowed a visa to visit South Africa, it became clear to many Catholics how the South African state perceived the threat of international networks of liberation theology Catholics.[87]

In 1974, Black Catholic Bishop Peter Fanyana John Butelezi made strong declarations of support for Black consciousness in Johannesburg and became a key figure in broadening the influence of liberation theology beyond South Africa's borders.[88] He was among the bishops most active following the 1976 Soweto uprising in increasing Catholic attention to the political. After 1976, many bishops began issuing pastoral letters in response to new initiatives, such as the detention of political figures, South African intervention in Namibia, and forced removals. The Christian Institute published a report on the detention of more than sixty-nine activists in Namibia, publishing details of their treatment, including the allegation of one detainee that she was hung from the ceiling for ten hours while under interrogation.[89]

Perhaps one of the most obvious ways the lasting influence of Latin American internationalist solidarity can be seen during this period is in how church institutions mobilized support directly to national liberation movements. The World Council of Churches (WCC), for instance, invested in financial support for groups in various Southern African conflicts, sending funds to national liberation parties such as South West African People's Organization, the Movimento Popular de Libertação de Angola, the Revolutionary Government of Angola in Exile, and the Mozambique Institute of the Frente de Libertação de Moçambique (FRELIMO).[90] An ecumenical Protestant organization, the WCC was vocal about the nature of South African aggression in Namibia's independence struggle. South Africa invaded Namibia after Germany's defeat in World War I and occupied it until 1990. During those seventy-five years, thousands of South Africans settled in Namibia, imposing apartheid laws, as if Namibia were a province rather than an occupied territory. The WCC's Commission on the Programme to Combat Racism issued a scathing critique of South Africa's involvement in the region in 1975. Citing documentation on South Africa's designs to unite the region into a commonwealth under the government of Pretoria, the WCC called the project neocolonial and one of "white supremacy."

The role of Catholic Justice and Peace reporting proved indispensable to spreading awareness of South Africa's neocolonial agenda. Informed by South

African CCJP reports, the WCC argued that the main driver of South Africa's intervention in neighboring countries was the intent to recruit foreign laborers for South African mines and create new markets for its consumer goods, noting Namibia's dependent economic status as an importer of South African electricity and coal.[91] In 1978, the WCC created a Namibian branch, which included members of the Justice and Peace commissions of the Catholic Church, even though the Church was not formally a member of the WCC. The Namibian commission was given the task of investigating the "repressive South African machinery."[92] Bringing liberation theology to bear on national liberation and anti-imperial struggles in the region put the WCC and Catholic activists directly at odds with the South African state's foreign policy, but allied them with Cuba's anti-imperialist missions in Africa.[93]

Solidarity with National Liberation in Southern Africa

In 1978, the nationalist, conservative Catholic Defence League in Pretoria republished an interview with Sister Janice McLaughlin, former press secretary for the Commission for Justice and Peace in Rhodesia (Zimbabwe). The interview had been printed in the *Zimbabwe News*, a news outlet of the Patriotic Front. The Patriotic Front was one of the minority white political parties involved in organizing terror campaigns against groups involved in the struggle for Black majority rights and national liberation. In the interview, the Irish-born nun gives her account of the role of Catholic missionaries in providing a main source of reports on the atrocities perpetuated against civilians and those fighting for independence (figure 4.3). The periodical goes on to warn that if South African Catholics are not vigilant, these same elements would soon dominate the local Church structure. The increasing influence of Catholic activism in solidarity with national liberation clearly threatened white nationalist interests within the South African state.

The same *Zimbabwe News* story included an excoriating description of South African Catholic liberation theologian Albert Nolan's interpretation of the place of Marxism in Christian teaching.[94] It criticizes Nolan, then serving as the national chaplain of the National Federation of Catholic Students, for placing radical action at the center of his interpretation of Christ's teachings. It also asserts that Young Christian Workers were brainwashing the youth. Photos of two children killed in the struggle, one Black girl shot in her sleep and one white girl killed in a bombing incident, were printed just above the articles, side by side. With a caption meant to indict all parties involved, the

Figure 4.3. Drawing accompanying the article "Sister Janice McLaughlin Still on the Way to Hell," *Candidus*, June–August 1978, 1. File ZA HPRA A1654-H-Ha-5, Namibia Records, Historical Papers Research Archive, University of the Witwatersrand, South Africa.

piece suggested that perhaps it would be more pacific for Rhodesia to be incorporated into South Africa.[95] The apartheid state made significant efforts to destabilize neighboring states like Zimbabwe that gave refuge to exiles from South Africa, including attacking Catholic transnational activists.

In 1981, the Bishops' Conference took a strong stand against South African actions in Namibia. It made several official statements and sent a six-person delegation to report on the condition of Black Namibians and their experience under South Africa's occupation. This led to a National Day of Prayer in November 1982. As a result, the South African government declared that the Catholic Church's political activity bordered on treason.[96] In 1982, the Western Cape's Justice and Peace Commission released a *Report on Namibia,* a booklet most likely written by Mike Pothia and Lois Law but certainly at the behest of Archbishop Hurley. Hurley, whose intervention during Vatican II paved the way for liberation theology, became the face of the Catholic critique of South Africa's occupation of Namibia. His outspoken critiques of the illegitimacy of South Africa's involvement eventually led to his arrest and a high-profile trial in 1985. Issuing statements about the abuses of the South African Defence Force in Namibia landed the Church in a major court case. Among the state's critique was that the Catholic Church in Namibia provided illegal shelter for displaced peoples during and after the conflict. Key among the functions of the Justice and Peace commissions in Namibia had been to keep baptismal and burial records. After South Africa withdrew from Namibia, the commissions served as an objective registrar of key populations to establish voting counts. Commissions monitored the first democratic elections, registering and double-checking voter rosters in an area with limited infrastructure.[97] Further, the Church had hosted a provocative Day of Prayer in South Africa for free and fair Namibian elections.[98]

Oblate priest Heinz Hunke of Windhoek, Namibia, sent letters to Cape Town to implore the SACBC to stand behind its position. He urged the bishops to continue to defend the conscientious objection status that protected the many conscripted Catholic South African youth who refused to serve in Namibia. The Church published literature out of its London office to increase awareness of South Africa's aggression and publicize its End Conscription Campaign. Hunke also wrote to Rome to make them aware of a resolution passed by a congress of bishops at Windhoek. He asked the Vatican Council to revisit its caution against militant violence in light of the brutality of the South African forces in Namibia.[99] The Bishops' Council of England and Wales offered its support for independence and self-determination in Namibia, which signaled that the conflict was reaching an important international audience of religious activists.[100] The vicar general of the Diocese of Windhoek documented and circulated information regarding the torture of Namibians by the Koevoet Unit of the South African Security Police, later renamed the Counter Insurgency Unit. His report noted that the South African Minister of Police and administrator-general had agreed to pay R150 000,00 for damages that included detaining schoolteachers and others without trial and torturing detainees with beatings and electric shocks.[101]

Over the course of the 1980s, outspoken South African Catholics urged the Church to take an "understanding" position on armed struggle.[102] Debates among theological communities heated up over questions of "scientific socialism" and "Christian Marxism." They discussed the merits of Castro's government in Cuba and considered revolutionary state models to determine the best way forward in Zambia, Angola, and Namibia.[103] Treatises on the appropriate role of the Church with respect to capitalism, the workers' struggle, and national liberation were debated at critical meetings from Equatorial Guinea to Mozambique.[104] In 1987, the Western Province Council of Churches began to print a publication called *Crisis News*, which covered essential information about various conflicts in Southern Africa and began incorporating commentary on open confrontation of the state by leading religious figures from its members. The periodical printed images and stories from Latin American liberation theologians such as Camilo Torres, Colombian priest and guerrilla soldier, on the value of and need for revolution (figure 4.4), quoting passages such as "every sincere revolutionary must realize that armed struggle is all that remains."[105] It also published personal testimonies of ANC combatants, articulating their thoughts on violence versus nonviolence, alongside similar stories of Latin American figures like Néstor Paz, a Catholic revolutionary from Bolivia who died of starvation at age twenty-five while fighting with the Ejercito de Liberación Nacional.[106] The South African religious community closely followed developments at the United Nations on Resolution 435 for Namibian independence and the efforts of Cuba in Angola, including the Lusaka Accord. Ministers from Brazil and Angola actively supported the resolution. These publications, protest encounters, and discussions point to the influence of Latin American theology well beyond the formal institutions created through the Church.

Archbishop Hurley had taken a strong stance against the intervention of the South African Defence Force in Namibia. Facing trial for having illegally reported on atrocities committed by the Koevoet in Namibia under the Police Act, he had to defend the activities of the Justice and Peace commissions.[107] He supported the right of South African citizens to conscientiously object to being drafted to fight what the SACBC called an "unjust war." Despite the public attention he received during the trial, he was not a central protagonist of activism on the ground.[108] Although he is credited with adopting a stance on nonviolence in the Synod of Bishops meetings in 1971, his most important act was penning the SACBC declaration of 1974 on the right of conscientious objection. He argued that the Church was bound by conscience to disobey any laws that violated the principles of Catholic ethics. The closest connection he had to liberation theology was in 1977, when he elaborated a more detailed statement on the subject, citing Vatican II. Specifically, he noted that the council had declared: "Those that are pledged to the service of their country as members of its armed forces, should regard themselves as agents of security and freedom on behalf of their people."[109] His biggest failure came when he assisted Zwelakhe Sisulu in assembling a news team for the *New Nation*, an

Figure 4.4. End Conscription Campaign (ECC) demonstration for International Namibia Day, 1988. Photo by Billy Paddock / Reflex. Included in the pamphlet "Country and Conscience: South African Conscientious Objectors" (London: Catholic Institute for International Relations, 1988), 12. File ZA HPRA A3261-D-D5-D5.2, Noel Stott Papers, Historical Papers Research Archive, University of the Witwatersrand, South Africa.

antiapartheid periodical published by the SACBC, which relied primarily on Black South African journalists. The *New Nation* was short lived, accused of being a vehicle of international communism. It landed many Catholic writers, mostly Black, on the list of suspected terrorists. Among the critiques launched against the *New Nation* were charges such as that it provided a Cuba-like handbook for guerrillas, failed to report on the Soviet influence in Southern Africa, and incited Black populations to violence.[110] The failure of *New Nation* reflected Hurley's lack of serious consideration of the risks of taking a more revolutionary political stance.

Catholic Activism and the End of Apartheid

Liberation theology–inspired Catholic activism did not topple the apartheid state in South Africa. Under tremendous pressure to take a critical stance against South Africa's intervention in Namibia, Bishop of Johannesburg Reginald Orsmond issued a joint letter in 1988 on behalf of the leadership of the South African Catholic Church. Bolstered by a visit to Rome at which Pope John Paul II issued formal support for the SACBC's cause, this letter condemned the Orderly Internal Politics Bill then moving through Parliament.[111] It presented the position of the Church and spoke to the question of the seventeen organizations and various individuals who were affected most significantly by the proposed legislation, arguing that such a measure would amount to a totalitarian state.[112] The same year, the Church's Standing for Truth action was launched, with the aim of opposing unjust laws, standing in solidarity with victims of apartheid, and advancing a nonviolent defiance of the South African government's discriminatory policies.[113] While these measures were important, they were not the determining events that forced change to the South African state.

A wave of bombings in 1988 brought pressure on the many Church organizations that were aligning against apartheid. The home of Anglican theologian and activist cleric Desmond Tutu was raided, and the Minister of Home Affairs threatened the SACC. The ministry issued charges against Catholic political publications like the *New Nation* for failing to pass through the censors, and litigation was threatened against many Church leaders, including Hurley. The Johannesburg headquarters of the SACC, the Khotso "Peace" House, was bombed in August, and the SACBC headquarters in Pretoria was set alight in October. No arrests for these crimes were made, suggesting that they were conducted by agents of the state.[114] However, the bombings communicated the urgency of the situation quickly to the wider international community. By 1990, under the pressure of economic sanctions, President F. W. de Klerk began negotiations to end the apartheid state. Nelson Mandela was released from prison, taking up an important role in reconstituting the ANC, and, following instruction from the UN Security Council, South Africa began its withdrawal from Namibia.

Catholic activists were not major figures in the postapartheid negotiations. Michael Lapsley spent fifteen years in exile, mostly in Zimbabwe, beginning in 1979, facing death threats from the South African government and receiving a letter bomb as late as 1990 because of his outspoken political advocacy for the ANC. When he finally returned to South Africa in 1994, Lapsley issued a call for truth and reconciliation and against general amnesty for the outgoing regime.[115] When amnesty was first proposed, the South African state suggested giving blanket immunity to security personnel accused of war crimes and human rights abuses. It was unclear what would befall members of the ANC who were still imprisoned for political reasons and those who had taken part in the Umkhonto we sizwe, the armed wing of the ANC created in 1961.[116] Lapsley and members of the Black Sash organization criticized amnesty, citing the Chilean Amnesty Law of 1978 and President Carlos Menem of Argentina's

1990 pardon of senior military officers. They pointed to the means by which such amnesty policies in Latin America had presented obstacles to justice.[117] Their objections went largely unheeded.

International religious institutions continued to be interested in the fate of South Africa. In October 1991, in the early period after the unbanning of liberation organizations in South Africa, Emilio Castro, Methodist minister and general secretary of the WCC, was invited to a Cape Town consultation held by the SACC. His visit was followed by a meeting in Johannesburg and another in Broederstroom the following year, during which attention turned toward the impact of international economic sanctions. These meetings produced the organizations' first Code of Ethical Investments. The culmination of this organizing was a strong response to the South African government's call to churches to withdraw from the political sphere. Refusing this call, the meetings set out a spiritual mandate to advocate for social welfare.[118] The SACC renewed its commitment to speak for the poor and voiceless and to bear witness to the process of postapartheid truth seeking.[119] They also endorsed a WCC declaration that accused the South African counterinsurgency police, the Koevoet, of detaining more than forty-five church and community leaders.[120]

One of the few clear outcomes of Latin American liberation theology's influence on the end of apartheid was a strong statement from the Church on the question of exiles. In May 1990, the SACBC and the SACC convened a conference to bring representatives from all South African political parties together to consider the most pressing questions they would soon face in the return to full participation in elections. The first of these—in order of priority—was the matter of the return of exiles. Presenting the example of the Namibian experience of returning exiles, the conference articulated a coordinated program to receive South African exiles who chose to return, one that would include housing, employment, health care, education, and reintegration services. During this conference, the Black consciousness movement delegation, represented by the Azanian People's Organisation, still based in Harare, raised the concern that the preparations for the returnees might overshadow or complicate ongoing negotiations.[121] This concern reflected the embeddedness of Church support for the exiled members of militant organizations and continuing fears about cooperation with the South African state. The fate of exiles was closely observed in Latin American contexts, notably the coordination of activities between intelligence agencies in North and South America. Increased information sharing, the delegations feared, might run the risk of exposing clandestine networks of support to state scrutiny.

Latin America's participation in Vatican II had a lasting effect on Catholic activism, social teaching, and support for lay political organizing in South

Africa. This chapter highlights how activists used the transnational spaces created by the international institutions of the Church to organize. The political activity of churches in Africa and Latin America advanced progressive changes from within complexly connected religious organizations.[122] Religious institutions in South Africa during the apartheid era, perhaps because they were viewed by the state as fundamentally conservative, were able to launch critiques and transnational campaigns against the state. However, it is important to note that reactionary forces in these same organizations limited institutional support for social movements on the ground. Despite this apparent contradiction, the Church provided an opening for religious-led protest in South Africa to find support. Multisited connections of Catholic activism between Latin America and Southern Africa provided an ongoing resource of resistance to the apartheid state and facilitated a rendering of South African struggles to promote solidarity across the globe.

Solidarity, Reactions, and Afterlives

Most Catholic families in South Africa had links to someone who was in jail or in exile during the apartheid era. Many white Catholic families were also affected by South Africa's regional wars and conscription. Pope John Paul II announced in 1987 that he refused to set foot in South Africa during his planned 1988 African tour, against the wishes of the SACBC.[123] The pope's antiapartheid protest failed to give support to figures in the Church who were actively being persecuted, denied passports, detained, and otherwise harassed. This gesture frustrated Southern African regional religious associations to which the national Catholic Churches belonged. Although apartheid was eventually condemned and South Africa held its first general elections, extending voting rights to its Black majority in 1994, the postapartheid era did not guarantee structural support for solidarity.

After the general elections and with the promise of a new democracy in South Africa, Justice and Peace commissions began to be co-opted by the language of anticrime.[124] Critically, when high-profile gang member Rashied Staggie, leader of the Hard Livings gang, announced his conversion to Christianity, South African police and the SACC issued letters and statements of skepticism, and the council sent formal requests to affiliated churches that they refuse to bury known gang members.[125] The coming of democracy to South Africa in 1994 and the end of South African attempts to colonize Southern Africa marked a turning point in the envisioned role of the progressive church. Before these events, churches had roles in communities and informal ties with people who were members of militant political groups. If some within the Catholic Church might have given audience to armed struggle or in support of antipolicing movements, this was no longer a cause taken up by the Justice and Peace commissions. Although violence was never formally condoned by the institutional Church, leaders on the ground had been prominently linked to the ANC and had suffered at the hands of the South African government as coreligionists of its militancy. In the democratic era, this position seemed unnecessary, and new generations of Catholics did not feel compelled by liberation theology politics to support these causes.

As ecumenical organizations looked to the future, they emphasized national unity. South African Catholics emphasized governance by the rule of law and patient progress toward economic development. Meetings held by the Catholic provincial councils and the SACC urged a turn away from condemning past violence and discrimination and toward confronting problems of international scope, such as global poverty and South Africa's role as an exporter of arms. These calls emphasized that in a "non-racial, non-sexist, democratic" South Africa, the faithful would turn their attention away from the past and toward the future.[126] This future orientation partly reflected a response to calls from the WCC to take seriously the power of the Church's antiapartheid work to expand opportunities—particularly to women and to neighboring African nations affected by ongoing conflict.

Liberation theology was a moment of creative dynamism for the Catholic Church and theologians working in Church structures. Catholics during this period hoped to find concrete solutions to problems of political and structural violence. Liberation theology moved from Latin America to Africa, Asia, and the United States, and its language was adopted as a way to characterize the leftist politics of a small number of Church leaders.[127] Importantly, where loose networks of social movements might otherwise have failed to concretize change, formal mechanisms, like Justice and Peace commissions with wide connections, provided possibilities for transnational solidarity.[128] The remarkable way solidarities can operate through complexes of formal institutions can be seen in how Catholic activists mobilized ideas, research, political support, and advocacy between Latin America and South Africa.

Ironically, sending Catholic clerics from one region to another, intended by Pope Pius XII in 1949 to stem the rising tide of communism, inadvertently created the very connections through which South-South solidarity could present its revolutionary challenges. Of the position papers, commissions reports, and documents that were circulated through CELAM's meetings in the 1970s, observers estimate that more than 25 percent were penned by uninvited guests, Latin American leftists and social scientists working closely with theologians like Gustavo Gutiérrez to introduce whatever modest changes they could.[129] Many observed that the changes were so subtly framed that key documents, lengthy and dense, could easily be overlooked by a casual observer or critic. Subtle word choices and interpretations of Scripture offered pivotal openings. Leftist discursive framings presented liberation as a goal of the Church and suggested the practical mechanisms through which such an aim could be achieved. Latin American liberation theology's influence in South Africa extended far beyond the Catholic Church. It provided critical intellectual and material support to the successful international boycott of South African apartheid and in opening up possibilities for non-Catholic antiapartheid leaders, such as Desmond Tutu, the first black general secretary of the SACC. Latin American liberation theologians were able to foster a complex solidarity, allowing South African activists on the ground to cultivate powerful transnational alliances. They also created a set of institutional mechanisms for crucial support to be channeled to internationalist resistance efforts against South African apartheid and imperialism in the region.

Conclusion

Solidarity at a Crossroads

This work complements studies that have begun to revisit Latin America's political ties with the Global South. It revives a history of internationalist solidarity of the Latin American left previously obscured by a focus on the Cold War. Each of the four case studies provide a different kind of consolidating vision around which the left could unite. These cases also historicize the radical interventions of the 1960s and 1970s and what they accomplished. Attention to South-South solidarity is important now, because this history suggests alternative ways forward for the left in the present. The South-South partnerships created by the Latin American left during these years were dynamic and expansive. They provided essential leadership and inspiration, upon which subsequent generations of solidarity activists continue to draw strength.

What we gain from shifting our historical focus from the Cold War to South-South solidarity is a better understanding of the global left. This provides us with valuable correctives. For instance, previous historical accounts were constrained by the presumption that the left was far too weak to succeed against the structural forces aligned against it, that ultimately the power contest between imperialist powers made all the determinant moves. Caricatures of a fist-shaking Fidel Castro at the United Nations, for instance, denied the strength of Cuban internationalist institutions. Similarly, critics of Mexican solidarity with Chile failed to recognize the long game of Mexico in shaping international legal environments and conditions. Reevaluating Latin American solidarity movements reveals overlooked and underestimated priorities of the left. Shifting focus toward the way Latin Americans offered solidarity outward recognizes crucial target audiences and distinctions of solidarity practice.

Latin America's solidarity in the Global South during these decades tell us much about the history of the region. Previously, these movements were considered through the framework of Third Worldism as a global phenomenon emanating from Europe.[1] By examining these movements instead as a product of the Latin American left and a vital part of its history, we can understand how critical moments of solidarity were a part of the evolution of these lefts. In 1964, the threat of the Cuban Revolution's ongoing commitment to armed struggle made leaders in the Non-Aligned Movement suspicious of including Latin American viewpoints and delegations. Thinking about this moment as a product of Third Worldism would suggest that they were more oriented toward centers and peripheries, East-West splits, which was far from the case. NAM leaders were concerned about local contexts, about maintaining alliances and useful partnerships. In contrast, reading these challenges and moments of solidarity as part of long-standing revolutionary agendas, embedded in lefts that might rise and fall from power, broadens our ability to see how they have shaped the past. The way these movements refuse to neatly map onto Cold War or Third Worldists narratives offers an opening for new readings and reinterpretations of the period.

Yassin al-Haj Saleh issued a critique of the study of solidarity in the wake of the Syrian civil war, arguing that scholars had failed to understand the role of the Global South as an agent of change, as a protagonist in the flow of history. He argues that the failure to understand these movements is based in the failure to understand solidarity inherently as a partnership. Partnership, he continued, "has no center; works in multiple directions rather than one; is based on equality rather than power; and is at odds with mutual competition, and the polarization that follows therefrom."[2] Latin American projects of solidarity with Africa, the Middle East, and other Latin Americans can be understood as solidarities aspiring for partnership. They differ considerably from experiences of solidarity movements with Latin America originating in Europe, Canada, and the United States, even when they include some of the same actors. They also differ in how they can be interpreted and by whom. They force us to reconsider our means of evaluation, to push the boundaries of our theoretical approaches to transnational social movements.

Latin American solidarity directed toward the Global South operated in a political milieu legible in different ways to the partners with whom they collaborated. These movements maintained distinct fields of action and contained their own relational valences. The ideological projects of the internationalist left in the Global South were suspended across alternative spaces of historical possibility that spoke their own languages. Its unique utopian ideals resonated in contexts far removed from the locations where historical analysis of internationalism was taking place. What has governed our thinking about such projects, and our theoretical premises, must therefore be revisited. Social scientists interested in the metrics of movements—measuring outcomes such as resource mobilization, recruitment, and demographics of identity—often miss features that are crucial to what gives a movement lasting power beyond its stated goals or numbers.[3] This work makes the case that by examining solidarity movements originating in Latin America in the 1960s and 1970s, alongside the sites of their reception, scholars might open up vibrant new debates regarding collective empowerment.

In such a conversation, several initial questions naturally arise. The first concerns where to begin and whether to consider the "global sixties" as a turning point in periodization. A longer timeframe might be required to fully understand solidarity across the region—one that perhaps begins in the 1790s and continues to the present—to connect independence movements and the Haitian revolution to solidarity movements of the twentieth and twenty-first centuries.[4] One might begin with the formal introduction of internationalism to the political organization on the left as a meaningful way to think about extending the frame of reference.[5] A narrower periodization, one that begins roughly in the 1940s with decolonization in Asia and might end with the independence of South Sudan, would put an emphasis on anticolonialism. The 1955 Bandung Conference or the 1961 Belgrade meeting of the Non-Aligned Movement may also provide a crucial starting point for an imagined political community of the Global South. An economic history periodization might begin roughly from this point and extend to the shift in the usage of the phrase "South-South cooperation," as earlier notions of political liberation and economic strategies of resistance gave way to notions of South-South cooperation as strategic management of migration, trade, and technocratic assistance. This periodization would recognize the co-optation of such early efforts by the economic expansion of capital, which became the dominant lending paradigm after 1991.[6] Optimistically, I would argue that the Arab Spring and the Black Lives Matter movement should give us pause when thinking of an endpoint. Expanding our understanding of the history of Latin American internationalist solidarity to include new forms of measure breaks with simple periodization.

The failure or success of decolonization and independence movements has usually been tied to the emergence of modern nation-states. New states are considered successful when they establish stable governments, exhibit rising GDP, and grow an urban industrial sector capable of contributing to global markets. Many solidarity movements in support of national liberation and independence have been considered failures when these new states fail to flourish in these particular measures or when the challenge of indebtedness undermines real independence.[7] In his study of Africa during this period, Jeffrey Byrne argues that in the case of many of these movements, the practices adopted by states were eventually those of developmentalist, free market capitalism, far from revolutionary leftist goals.[8] After the liberalization of the Soviet Union's economy in 1986, many critics of the left argued that the hegemon of global capitalism had sealed off any possibility of its replacement, implying a final defeat of the projects of the solidarity movements of previous generations. However, the global economic crises of 2008 and 2020 suggest that this might have been an overly hasty burial of socialist alternatives. In fact, if we do not presume to measure the success of a movement purely in market terms or the stability of a regime in power, the availability of past and ongoing movements to speak productively in new moments of crisis makes the opposite case.

To measure South-South solidarity in an alternative fashion, by its afterlives and legacies, we can see the profound influence they had. An illustrative example can be seen in what might otherwise be judged a failure of solidarity. I offer the example of a bilateral antihijacking treaty signed between the United States and Cuba.[9] The first accord signed between the two nations since 1959, this treaty described the history of airline hijacking, or "air piracy," as a problem of international diplomacy. Highlighting that U.S. citizens were in fact the most prodigious hijackers of this period, making more than ninety attempts to reach Havana between 1968 and 1973, it also targeted racialized groups of leftists in the U.S. who sought refuge during a particularly intense period of repression.[10] At the time, diplomats argued that U.S. citizens simply viewed Cuba as a lawless state and a place of easy escape. However, a closer reading reveals that hijackers imagined themselves welcome in the context of the Cuban Revolution and viewed Havana's commitment to revolutionary internationalism as an opening to have their own political demands taken seriously. I draw on this example to speak to the intergenerational legacy of Latin American South-South solidarity movements. Despite the signing of this treaty, which effectively ended Havana's reception of fugitive leftists from the U.S., the solidarity gesture it meant to close off became the source of inspiration decades later. As a symbol of struggle and a rendering of solidarity, Cuba's solidarity with such fugitives had a powerful afterlife.

In 2019, African American film director Melina Matsoukas released her first feature film, *Queen and Slim*. The film tells the story of a couple who meet on a first date. Their fates are sealed when they are pulled over by a racist white police officer and violence ensues. As the couple try to escape what eventually becomes a long-distance manhunt across the U.S., they visually connect important locations and sources of Afro-American resistance. The couple arrives finally in Florida to try to make their getaway via a small private plane to

Cuba. The promises of this bond of solidarity between African Americans and revolutionary Cuba underlines a historical understanding of the struggle the couple faces against racism in the U.S. It also frames the struggle as revolutionary. The couple trying to escape a racist legal system in the United States by aircraft hints at the boldness of the previous era. It voices a historical memory of international validation, Cuba's militant solidarity with those who face violent oppression, and recognition of the connection between racism and imperialism. Hijacked planes headed to Cuba were an embarrassment to U.S. law enforcement and diplomacy. Airplanes were an emblem of industrial progress, freedom, and leisure. As a symbol that could be appropriated by the revolutionary left, the legacy of this gesture also challenged the premises of capitalist expansion.

Flying to Havana, the means of travel by which so many revolutionary figures circulated and found networks of support, was a physical manifestation of the transportation of revolutionary demands. Hijacking was at its height in the 1960s and 1970s, when the United States and the Soviet Union conducted horrific experiments on pilots in an attempt to conquer each other and master "space," leaving the specter of nuclear bombs to terrorize generations to come.[11] *Queen and Slim* may offer a nostalgic vision, but it is a powerful reminder that the United States was forced to negotiate with Cuba, even while at war with each other and facing the hottest of Cold War dangers. The film signals something important that historians have overlooked about transnational solidarity during this time—that the connections and exchanges that happened despite the Cold War context and under the radar of international diplomacy were in fact often the point. Disentangling what these connections meant, how they challenged hierarchies of power, and what they hoped to achieve reveals a project that is unfinished and ongoing. Matsoukas's film is just one example that prompts us to reconsider why Latin America is so important for understanding how internationalist solidarity shaped the twentieth century and how it continues to inform the present.

South-South Latin American transnational solidarity movements, which flourished in the 1960s and early 1970s, entered a new phase in the mid-1970s. They evolved and began to take on modes and strategies that were more multifaceted. Beyond symbolic goals, they were able to build on a broad set of institutional gains to make inroads through complex embeddedness. These movements may not have defeated their enemies in countenancing neoimperialism, in ending racial discrimination and violence, or in promoting equality among nations, but they produced a useful common language of solidarity that could be easily picked up and put to use by later generations. They stood as a permanent site of reflection and resistance. Engaging with this history helps us move away from frameworks, captured in terms such as "Cold War" and "Third World," that tend to obscure important debates taking place in these sites and between groups whose priorities did not entirely rely on these narrative superstructures. It challenges myopic views of the Global South in their international relations as being merely clients of superpowers or as failing economic experiments in a global market competition. The historical record and collective memory of these South-South connections have left important traces, many of which are still waiting to be found and recovered.

Beyond prompting historians of Latin America and the Global South to reconsider the significance of these movements, this history presents a challenge to social movement theorists. In the late 1980s and early 1990s, many theorists were posing questions along the lines of rational choice theory. Such scholars found it difficult to understand why average citizens would participate in "rebellious collective action," arguing that "they have nothing to gain . . ., but much to lose."[12] This study asks historians and other theorists to reconsider their own frustrations with the kind of knowledge such questions produce, and the recent rise in interest in the history of solidarity should indicate that many are willing to reopen these debates.

Intersectional feminist historians and theorists have already begun to push theoretical boundaries. Lara Putnam, for instance, provokes theorists to be attentive to "people on the move," beyond thinking about racialized peoples as simply part of a migrating diaspora or imperial subjects.[13] Her work asks us to consider transnational social movements led by figures joined together and moved by ideas. Betina Parry, in theorizing strategies of resistance, identified a need for historians to better understand what specific factors move a group in solidarity to change from a passive position, or one of complacency, to suddenly act on their commitments.[14] This attention to the shifting and flexible nature of activism might open up debates around a movement's historical agency and how it can bridge multiple political subjectivities and identities. Further, the challenges posed to individualism as a political strategy of the right by collective self-hoods also open new questions. Anarchist theorists, for example, have begun to revisit understandings of property relations proposed by the international left and how various projects of socialism might have fared under different circumstances. They have begun to examine dispossession as a possible form of empowerment. Historical examples of refusals of power and individual ownership could be productively reexamined to understand how collectivity can recuperate the strength of numbers.

Another set of questions that are opened by centering Latin American South-South solidarity in our understanding of the international left during this period relates to the experience of specific movements. For instance, historians like Tanya Harmer have reconsidered the critical importance of the Chile solidarity movement, which was not considered entirely successful in Mexico but became a reference point in the post-Helsinki international governance debates of human rights protections and political asylum.[15] As in the case of asylum law, Mexico also sought to influence the rules governing international economic relationships through institutional settings in ways that would favorably redistribute wealth to the Global South. Revisiting these histories from the perspective of changing institutions may offer a means of not only recovering but reinvigorating historical agency.

Striffler observes that solidarity movements, "relying on crisis as fuel," are ill-equipped to deal with long-term problems or develop durable strategies of resistance. However, the South-South modes of solidarity examined in this set of case studies expand our knowledge of the long-term strategies that afford such movements greater staying power.[16] For instance, the economic cooperation strategies proposed by Latin Americans at the United Nations were modeled on Cuban cooperation with the Eastern European bloc countries of the Commission for Mutual Economic Assistance, which also borrowed heavily from cooperation experiments in the Middle East. The notion of solidarity as "building each other" in this context meant building a resource base, untethered to empire or apartheid. Understanding how the left proposed to reform international trade and intervene in the movement of capital and goods might also provide greater insight into local strategies of representation and poverty relief. Examining movements precisely at the moments when such projects were undermined by "developmentalism" or co-opted by other interests could hint at key strategies for future movements. Similarly, looking through the framework of solidarity as rendering might help parse the different elements of the proposals of the left and how they were situated in broader projects of promoting social equality. These renderings might help explain how these ideas were communicated to wider audiences, illuminating important questions of reception, allyship, and debate. This book attempts to suggest new ways to read and interpret transnational collective actions that might be useful in overcoming challenges to transnational solidarity. South-South modes of solidarity offer alternative practical approaches and new ideological formulations. Reframing solidarity as partnership, with benefits extending in both directions, might allow us to make better sense of the way solidarity works and the reasons it is often sustained.

There are many reasons to think that the historical memory of Latin America's South-South solidarity is lasting and that it mattered. References to Cuban internationalist solidarity abound in the movements of the Arab Spring, the international women's movement, and Black Lives Matter. Ongoing solidarity in Latin America with Palestine, for instance, is a lightning rod for communities in the Middle East. The lessons and hauntings of Pinochet's regime in Chile and of Argentina's 2001 financial crisis have resonated with protesters in Lebanon's constitutional crisis and the union-driven movements of Tunisia and Algeria. Cuban medical and educational solidarity certainly did not end in the Special Period, and Cuba continues to be the most prominent source of medical personnel and resources to combat Ebola and COVID-19 in Africa. This model of socialist humanitarianism can be seen as an extension and evolution of the South-South solidarity movements of the 1960s and 1970s, even if it can also be critiqued as a solidarity partially in service to creating new markets. Argentine-born Pope Francis, whose papal authority marks a shift in the Church away from older hierarchies of power, signals a future for social Catholicism. The Catholic Church in South Africa maintains an active relationship with Palestine. On one level, this relationship is justified by Church authorities as an important part of maintaining links with Christians in Palestine. However, a small cadre of South African Catholics have followed the Vatican's controversial invitation to Yasser Arafat to meet the Pope in 1982 and continue to look on the relationship between Rome and Palestine as part of a longer project of anti-imperialism and antiapartheid.[17]

New visions of possibility continue to be proposed by the Latin American internationalist left. With challenges to democracy increasingly dire, our understandings of the movements of the 1960s and 1970s to which subsequent waves of solidarity organizing are so indebted is even more essential. In this present moment, Robin D. G. Kelley and Fred Moten point to the work of Manolo Callahan with the Zapatista movement in Chiapas, Mexico, for example, as a source of new formulations and salient propositions for the left, "research grounded in that community in the interest of the preservation and survival of that community," and activism aimed at "renewing our habits of assembly . . . [and doing] a better job with regard to the theory and practice of getting together, being together."[18] Emerging movements in the region continue to help us better understand the importance of alliances and inclusion in the success of movements, as new considerations of transnationalism as a category of historical analysis have helped us reimagine what constitutes a political subject.[19] The history of Latin American solidarity is vitally important to this present.

As Cuban poet Miguel Barnet articulates in his poem on the meaning of revolutionary struggle, solidarity is built on contradictions, on sweat, and on supplications from our shared past.

Notes

Introduction

1. The epigraph by Barnet was reprinted in the newsletter of the Tricontinental: Institute of Social Research upon the closing of the Organisation of Solidarity with the Peoples of Africa, Asia, and Latin America (OSPAAAL), August 2019, https://thetri continental.org/newsletterissue/homage-to-ospaaal-the-organisation-of-solidarity-for -the-peoples-of-asia-africa-and-latin-america-newsletter-thirty-one-2019/.

2. Anthony Alessandrini, "Fanon Now: Singularity and Solidarity," *Journal of Pan-African Studies* 4, no. 7 (2011): 63.

3. Jessica Stites Mor, "Introduction: Situating Transnational Solidarity within Human Rights Studies of Cold War Latin America," in *Human Rights and Transnational Solidarity in Cold War Latin America*, ed. Jessica Stites Mor (Madison: University of Wisconsin Press, 2013), 3–18; Christine Hatzky and Jessica Stites Mor, "Solidarity in Latin America: Contexts and Research Paradigms," *Journal of Iberian and Latin American Research* 20, no. 2 (2014): 127–40.

4. Jessica Stites Mor and Maria del Carmen Suescun Pozas, "Transnational Pathways of Empathy in the Americas," in *The Art of Solidarity: Visual and Performative Politics in Cold War Latin America*, ed. Jessica Stites Mor and Maria del Carmen Suescun Pozas (Austin: University of Texas Press, 2018), 5.

5. Walter LeFeber, *Inevitable Revolutions: The United States in Central America*, 2nd ed. (New York: Norton, 1993), 60; Jeffrey Gould, "Solidarity under Siege: The Latin American Left, 1968," *American Historical Review* 114, no. 2 (2009): 348.

6. This is especially true of African diasporic peoples, about whom there are many excellent studies, notably Lara Putnam, *Radical Moves: Caribbean Migrants and the Politics of Race in the Jazz Age* (Chapel Hill: University of North Carolina Press, 2013); Shana L. Redmond, *Anthem: Social Movements and the Sound of Solidarity in the African Diaspora* (New York: New York University Press, 2014); Robin D. G. Kelley, *Freedom Dreams: The Black Radical Imagination* (Boston: Beacon, 2002).

7. Julien Archer, *The First International in France, 1864–1872: Its Origins, Theories and Impact* (Lanham, MD: University Press of America, 1997).

8. Ana Lucia Araujo, *Shadows of the Slave Past: Memory, Heritage, and Slavery* (New York: Routledge, 2014), 5. See also Jack Shuler, *Calling Out Liberty: The Stono Slave Rebellion and the Universal Struggle for Human Rights* (Jackson: University Press of Mississippi, 2009); Robin Blackburn, *The American Crucible: Slavery, Emancipation and Human Rights* (London: Verso, 2011); Gelien Matthews, *Caribbean Slave Revolts and the British Abolitionist Movement* (Baton Rouge: Louisiana State University Press, 2006).

9. See Jorge Nállim, "Antifascismo, revolución y Guerra Fría en México: La revista *América*, 1940–1960," *Latinoamérica: Revista de Estudios Latinoamericanos* 70 (2019): 93–123; Ricardo Figueiredo de Castro, "A Frente Única Antifascists e o antifascism no Brasil, 1933–1934," *Topoi* 3, no. 5 (2002): 354–88; Rogelio de la Mora Valencia, "Intelectuales guatemaltecos en México: Del movimiento Claridad al antifascismo, 1921–1939," *Signos históricos* 14, no. 27 (2012): 104–37; Pietro Rinaldo Fanesi, "El exilio antifascista en América Latina: El caso mexicano," *Estudios interdisciplinarios de América Latina y el Caribe* 3, no. 2 (2015); Fredrik Petersson, "Hub of the Anti-Imperialist Movement: The League against Imperialism and Berlin, 1927–1933," *Interventions: International Journal of Postcolonial Studies* 16, no. 1 (2014): 49–71; Ricardo Melgar Bao, "The Anti-Imperialist League of the Americas between the East and Latin America," *Latin American Perspectives* 35, no. 2 (2008): 9–24.

10. Jeremy Adelman, *Sovereignty and Revolution in the Iberian Atlantic* (Princeton, NJ: Princeton University Press, 2006), 390. See also David P. Geggus, *The Impact of the Haitian Revolution in the Atlantic World* (Columbia: University of South Carolina Press, 2001).

11. Claire Fox, *Making Art Panamerican: Cultural Policy and the Cold War* (Minneapolis: University of Minnesota Press, 2015), xv; Russell Cobb, "The Politics of Literary Prestige: Promoting the Latin American 'Boom' in the Pages of *Mundo Nuevo*," *A Contra Corriente: A Journal on Social History and Literature in Latin America* 5, no. 3 (2008): 75–94; Dalia Muller, *Cuban Émigrés and Independence in the Nineteenth-Century Gulf World* (Chapel Hill: University of North Carolina Press, 2017); Brenda Elsey, "Cultural Ambassadorship and the Pan-American Games of the 1950s," *International Journal of the History of Sport* 33, nos. 1–2 (2016): 109; Cesar R. Torres and Bruce Kidd, "Introduction: The History and Relevance of the Pan-American Games," *International Journal of the History of Sport* 33, nos. 1–2 (2016): 1–5; Michael Gordon Wellen, "Pan-American Dreams: Art, Politics, and Museum-Making at the OAS, 1948–1976" (PhD diss., University of Texas at Austin, 2012); Karin Rosemblatt, *The Science and Politics of Race in Mexico and the United States, 1910–1950* (Chapel Hill: University of North Carolina Press, 2018).

12. For more on the spread of transnational solidarity through anarchist and labor networks in Latin America, see Julie Greene, *The Canal Builders: Making America's Empire at the Panama Canal* (New York: Penguin, 2009); Geoffroy de Laforcade and Kirwin Shaffer, eds., *In Defiance of Boundaries: Anarchism in Latin American History* (Gainesville: University of Florida Press, 2015); Rafael Borges Deminicis and Daniel Aarão Filho, eds., *História do anarquismo no Brasil* (Rio de Janeiro: EdUFF, 2006);

Paulo Drinot, *The Allure of Labor: Workers, Race, and the Making of the Peruvian State* (Durham, NC: Duke University Press, 2011); Juan Suriano, *Anarquistas: Cultura y política libertaria en Buenos Aires, 1880–1910* (Buenos Aires: Ediciones Manantial, 2001); Boris Marañón, ed., *Solidaridad económica y potencialidades de transformación en América Latina* (Buenos Aires: CLACSO, 2012); Anabel Rieiro, ed., *Gestión Obrera: Del fragmento a la acción colectiva* (Montevideo: Nordan, 2010); Salvador Hernández Padilla, *El magonismo: Historia de una passión libertaria, 1900–1922* (Mexico City: Ediciones Era, 1988); Barry Carr, "Pioneering Transnational Solidarity in the Americas: The Movement in Support of Augusto C. Sandino 1927–1934," *Journal of Iberian and Latin American Research* 20, no. 2 (2014): 141–52; Steven Hirsch and Lucien van der Walt, eds., *Anarchism and Syndicalism in the Colonial and Post-Colonial World, 1870–1940* (Leiden: Brill, 2010); Pierre Coutaz, "Regards sur le Movement Syndical International," *Recherches internationales* 112 (2018): 81–85; Anton Rosenthal, "Radical Border Crossers: The Industrial Workers of the World and their Press in Latin America," *Estudios Interdisciplinarios de América Latina y el Caribe* 22, no. 2 (2011): 39–70.

13. James A. Baer, *Anarchist Immigrants in Spain and Argentina* (Urbana: University of Illinois Press, 2015), 118.

14. This use of this term to describe the post-1945 relationship between global powers engaged in hostilities just short of open warfare except by proxy has been attributed to George Orwell's essay titled "You and the Atom Bomb," *Tribune*, 19 October 1945, https://www.orwellfoundation.com/the-orwell-foundation/orwell/essays-and-other-works/you-and-the-atom-bomb/.

15. Kristin Ross, *May '68 and Its Afterlives* (Chicago: University of Chicago Press, 2002), 106.

16. Greg Grandin, "Living in Revolutionary Time: Coming to Terms with the Violence of Latin America's Long Cold War," in *A Century of Revolution: Insurgent and Counterinsurgent Violence in Latin America's Long Cold War*, ed. Greg Grandin and Gilbert M. Joseph (Durham, NC: Duke University Press, 2011), 1–44.

17. Aldo Marchesi, "Southern Cone Cities as Political Laboratories of the Global Sixties: Montevideo (1962–1968); Santiago de Chile (1969–1973); Buenos Aires (1973–1976)," *Estudios interdisciplinarios de América Latina y el Caribe* 28, no. 2 (2017): 54–79.

18. Christine Hatzky, *Cubans in Angola: South-South Cooperation and Transfer of Knowledge, 1976–1991* (Madison: University of Wisconsin Press, 2014).

19. Alison Bruey, *Bread and Justice: Grassroots Activism and Human Rights in Pinochet's Chile* (Madison: University of Wisconsin Press, 2018).

20. Sandra McGee Deutsch, "The New School Lecture 'An Army of Women': Communist-Linked Solidarity Movements, Maternalism, and Political Consciousness in 1930s and 1940s Argentina," *The Americas* 75, no. 1 (2018): 95–125. For more on the influence of international women's movements in fostering solidarity ties, see Jocelyn Olcott, *International Women's Year: The Greatest Consciousness-Raising Event in History* (London: Oxford University Press, 2017); Jadwiga Pieper Mooney, "Forging Feminisms under Dictatorship: Women's International Ties and National Feminist Empowerment in Chile, 1973–1990," *Women's History Review* 19, no. 4 (2010): 613–30.

21. Samuel Moyn, *Human Rights and the Uses of History* (London: Verso Books, 2014). See also key studies, such as Alison Brysk, *The Politics of Human Rights in Argentina: Protest, Change, and Democratization* (Stanford, CA: Stanford University Press, 1994); James N. Green, *We Cannot Remain Silent: Opposition to the Brazilian Military Dictatorship* (Durham, NC: Duke University Press, 2008); Margaret E. Keck and Kathryn Sikkink, *Activists beyond Borders: Advocacy Networks in International Politics* (Ithaca, NY: Cornell University Press, 1998); Vania Markarian, *Left in Transformation: Uruguayan Exiles and the Latin American Human Rights Networks, 1967–1984* (New York: Routledge, 2005); Vera Carnovale, "El PRT-ERP en el exilio: Armas, comunismo y derechos humanos," *Revista de Historia* 15 (2014): 1–28; Patrick William Kelly, "The 1973 Chilean Coup and the Origins of Transnational Human Rights Activism," *Journal of Global History* 8, no. 1 (2013): 165–86; Margaret Power, "The U.S. Movement in Solidarity with Chile in the 1970s," *Latin American Perspectives* 36, no. 6 (2009): 46–66; Christian Smith, *Resisting Reagan: The U.S. Central America Peace Movement* (Chicago: University of Chicago Press, 1996).

22. Alison Brysk, "From Above and Below: Social Movements, the International System, and Human Rights in Argentina," *Comparative Political Studies* 26, no. 3 (1993): 259–85.

23. Elizabeth Jelin, *Constructing Democracy: Human Rights, Citizenship, and Society in Latin America* (New York: Routledge, 2019).

24. Kathryn Sikkink, *The Justice Cascade: How Human Rights Prosecutions are Changing World Politics* (New York: Norton, 2011); Kathryn Sikkink and Carrie Booth Walling, "The Impact of Human Rights Trials in Latin America," *Journal of Peace Research* 44, no. 4 (2007): 427–45.

25. James P. Brennan, *Argentina's Missing Bones: Revisiting the History of the Dirty War* (Oakland: University of California Press, 2018), 106; Greg Grandin, "Human Rights and Empire's Embrace," in *Human Rights and Revolutions*, 2nd ed., ed. Jeffrey N. Wasserstrom, Lynn Hunt, Marilyn B. Young, and Gregory Grandin (New York: Rowman and Littlefield, 2007), 205.

26. Odd Arne Westad, *The Global Cold War: Third World Interventions and the Making of Our Times* (Cambridge: Cambridge University Press, 2007), 5.

27. Van Gosse, *Rethinking the New Left: An Interpretative History* (New York: Palgrave Macmillan, 2005), 59.

28. Van Gosse, "Active Engagement: The Legacy of Central American Solidarity," *North American Conference on Latin America Report* 28, no. 5 (1995): 23.

29. Paula Daniela Fernández, "Fora o imperialismo da América Central, el caso de la solidaridad brasileña con la revolución sandinista," *Revista de la Red de Intercátedras de Historia de América Latina Contemporánea* 2, no. 2 (2015): 109. See also Héctor Perla Jr., "La revolución nicaragüense y la solidaridad internacional," in *Nicaragua y el FSLN (1979–2009): ¿Qué queda de la revolución?*, ed. Salvador Martí i Puig and David Close (Barcelona: Edicions Bellaterra, 2009): 117–36; Fernando Harto de Vera, "La URSS y la revolución sandinista: Los estrechos límites de la solidaridad soviética," *Cuadernos África América Latina* 7 (1992): 87–93; Irma Antognazzi and María Felisa Lemos, *Nicaragua,*

el ojo del huracán revolucionario (Buenos Aires: Nuestra América, 2006); Víctor Estra-det, *Memorias del Negro Pedro: Tupamaros en la revolución Sandinista* (Montevideo: Fin de Siglo, 2013); Eudald Cortina Orero, "Internacionalismo y revolución sandinidta: Proyecciones militantes y reformulaciones orgánicas en la izquierda revolucionaria argentina," *Estudios interdisciplinarios de América Latina y el Caribe* 28, no. 2 (2017): 80–103; Jan Hansen, Christian Helm, and Frank Reichherzer, eds., *Making Sense of the Americas: How Protest Related to America in the 1980s and Beyond* (Chicago: Campus Verlag, 2015).

30. Alberto Martín Álvarez and Eduardo Rey Tristán, "La oleada revolucionaria latinoamericana contemporánea, 1959–1996," *Naveg@mérica: Revista electrónica editada por la Asociación Española de Americanistas* 9 (2012): 1–36. See also Alberto Martín Álvarez and Eduardo Rey Tristán, eds., *Revolutionary Violence and the New Left: A Transnational Perspective* (New York: Routledge, 2017); Daniel Pereyra, *Del Moncada a Chiapas: Historia de la lucha armada en América Latina* (Madrid: Libros de la Catarata, 1994).

31. See, for example, Quinn Slobodian, *Foreign Front: Third World Politics in the Sixties West Germany* (Durham, NC: Duke University Press, 2012); Tobias Rupprecht, *Soviet Internationalism after Stalin: Interaction and Exchange between the USSR and Latin America during the Cold War* (Cambridge: Cambridge University Press, 2015); Monica Kalt, *Tiersmondismus in der Schweiz der 1960er und 1970er Jahre. Von der Barmherzigkeit zur Solidarität* (Bern: Lang, 2010); Christian Helm, "'The Sons of Marx Greet the Sons of Sandino': West German Solidarity Visitors to Nicaragua Sandinista," *Journal of Iberian and Latin American Research* 20, no. 2 (2014): 153–70; Olga Ulianova, "La Unidad Popular y el golpe militar en Chile: Percepciones y análisis soviéticos," *Estudios públicos* 79 (2000): 83–171; Michal Zourek, "Czechoslovak Policy towards Chile in the 1970s and 1980s," *Canadian Journal of Latin American and Caribbean Studies* 39, no. 2 (2014): 211–28; Matyáš Pelant, "Czechoslovakia and Brazil 1945–1989," *Central European Journal of International & Security Studies* 7, no. 3 (2013): 96–117; Michelle Denise Reeves, "Extracting the Eagle's Talons: The Soviet Union in Cold War Latin America" (PhD diss., University of Texas at Austin, 2014).

32. Miguel Angel Reyes, "La cultura de la revolución en los Andes: Aproximación a las relaciones transnacionales entre el M-19 y AVC en la década de 1980," *Estudios interdisciplinarios de América Latina y el Caribe* 28, no. 2 (2017): 104–28.

33. Margaret Power and Julie A. Charlip, "On Solidarity," *Latin American Perspectives* 36, no. 6 (2009): 4.

34. Power, "The US Movement in Solidarity with Chile," 63.

35. Heidi Tinsman, *Buying into the Regime: Grapes and Consumption in Cold War Chile and the United States* (Durham, NC: Duke University Press, 2014), 179–80.

36. Rebecca A. Johns, "Bridging the Gap between Class and Space: U.S. Worker Solidarity with Guatemala," *Economic Geography* 74, no. 3 (1998): 269; Jeffrey Gould, *Solidarity under Siege: The Salvadoran Labor Movement, 1970–1990* (Cambridge: Cambridge University Press, 2019). Such arguments are echoed by Molly Todd and Hector Perla Jr. in their studies of U.S. solidarity movements with El Salvador and Nicaragua,

respectively. In both cases, collaboration between exile communities and activists in the region put pressure on the United States to reconsider its foreign policy but did little to diminish the abuse of local workers. James N. Green, in contrast, cites the experiences of U.S. activists in Brazil, working with their counterparts on the ground and witnessing firsthand the implications of U.S. foreign policy. Green asserts that participation in solidarity movements led many activists to sharpen their critiques of neoimperialism and demand change at home. Katherine Borland contends that grassroots organizing against U.S. military violence in the region has also contributed to anti–police violence actions in major urban centers in the United States, including Black Lives Matter in Washington, DC. Molly Todd, "'We Were Part of the Revolutionary Movement There': Wisconsin Peace Progressives and Solidarity with El Salvador in the Reagan Era," *Journal of Civil and Human Rights* 3, no. 1 (2017): 1–56; Molly Todd, *Beyond Displacement: Campesinos, Refugees, and Collective Action in the Salvadoran Civil War* (Madison: University of Wisconsin Press, 2010); Héctor Perla Jr., "Si Nicaragua Venció, El Salvador Vencerá: Central American Agency in the Creation of the U.S.–Central American Peace and Solidarity Movement," *Latin American Research Review* 43, no. 2 (2008): 136–58; James N. Green, "Clerics, Exiles, and Academics: Opposition to the Brazilian Military Dictatorship in the United States, 1969–1974," *Latin American Politics and Society* 45, no. 1 (2003): 93; Katherine Borland, "Traditions of Resistance, Expressions of Solidarity, and the Honduran Coup," in *The Art of Solidarity: Visual and Performative Politics in Cold War Latin America*, ed. Jessica Stites Mor and Maria del Carmen Suescun Pozas (Austin: University of Texas Press, 2018), 53.

37. Steve Striffler, *Solidarity: Latin America and the US Left in the Era of Human Rights* (London: Pluto, 2019), 6. See also Green, *We Cannot Remain Silent*, 300.

38. Aviva Chomsky and Steve Striffler, "Reply: Solidarity Latin America Solidarity: The Colombian Coal Campaign," *Dialectical Anthropology* 32 (2008): 191.

39. Striffler, *Solidarity*, 110. See also Steve Striffler, "Latin American Solidarity: Human Rights and the Politics of the US Left," in *Palgrave Encyclopedia of Imperialism and Anti-Imperialism*, ed. Immanuel Ness and Zak Cope (London: Palgrave Macmillan, 2015), 865.

40. Teishan A. Latner, *Cuban Revolution in America: Havana and the Making of a United States Left, 1968–1992* (Chapel Hill: University of North Carolina Press, 2018), 268–69; Cynthia A. Young, *Soul Power: Culture, Radicalism, and the Making of a U.S. Third World Left* (Durham, NC: Duke University Press, 2006), 184.

41. Mario Vázquez Olivera and Fabián Campos Hernández, "Solidaridad transnacional y conspiración revolucionaria: Cuba, México y el Ejército Guerrillero de los Pobres de Guatemala, 1967–1976," *Estudios interdisciplinarios de América Latina y el Caribe* 30, no. 1 (2019): 72–95. In addition, scholars like Vania Markarian have argued that the clout of growing student movements around the world raised the visibility of various political parties and intellectual projects. Vania Markarian, *Uruguay, 1968: Student Activism from Global Counterculture to Molotov Cocktails* (Oakland: University of California Press, 2016).

42. Martha Vanessa Saldívar, "From Mexico to Palestine: An Occupation of Knowledge, a Mestizaje of Methods," *American Quarterly* 62, no. 4 (2010): 823.

43. Emily Hobson, *Lavender and Red: Liberation and Solidarity in the Gay and Lesbian Left* (Oakland: University of California Press, 2016); James N. Green, "The Emergence of the Brazilian Gay Liberation Movement, 1977–1981," *Latin American Perspectives* 21, no. 1 (1994): 38–55; Gabriela Aceves Sepúlveda, *Women Made Visible: Feminist Art and Media in Post-1968 Mexico City* (Lincoln: University of Nebraska Press, 2019); Sonia Alvarez, "Translating the Global: Effects of Transnational Organizing on Local Feminist Discourses and Practices in Latin America," *Meridians* 1, no. 1 (2000): 29–67; Brenda Elsey, "'As the World Is My Witness': Popular Culture and the Chilean Solidarity Movement, 1974–1987," in *Human Rights and Transnational Solidarity in Cold War Latin America*, ed. Jessica Stites Mor (Madison: University of Wisconsin Press, 2013), 177–208. For instance, Melissa Forbis and Thomas Oleson have illustrated how later forms of solidarity influenced the evolution of the Zapatista movement through the use of the internet and international media. Thomas Olesen, *International Zapatismo: The Construction of Solidarity in the Age of Globalization* (London: Zed Books, 2005); Melissa Forbis, "After Autonomy: The Zapatistas, Insurgent Indigeneity, and Decolonization," *Settler Colonial Studies* 6, no. 4 (2016): 365–38.

44. Aldo Marchesi, "Writing the Latin American Cold War: Between the 'Local' South and the 'Global' North," *Estudos Históricos* 30, no. 60 (2017): 187.

45. David Featherstone, *Solidarity: Hidden Histories and Geographies of Internationalism* (London: Zed Books, 2012), 5.

46. Krzystof Jasiewicz, "Problems of Postcommunism: From Solidarity to Fragmentation," *Journal of Democracy* 3, no. 2 (1992): 55–69.

47. Jürgen Habermas, "Justice and Solidarity: On the Discussion Concerning Stage 6," *Philosophical Forum* 21, no. 12 (1989): 32–52.

48. Émile Durkheim, *The Division of Labor in Society*, trans. W. D. Halls (1893; repr., New York: Free Press, 2014).

49. See, for example, Michael Hechter, *Principles of Group Solidarity* (Berkeley: University of California Press, 1987). This line of reasoning found expression in works such as Aafke Elisabeth Komter, "The Disguised Rationality of Solidarity: Gift Giving in Informal Relations," *Journal of Mathematical Sociology* 25, no. 4 (2001): 385–401.

50. Richard Rorty, *Contingency, Irony, and Solidarity* (Cambridge: Cambridge University Press, 1989).

51. Carol C. Gould, "Transnational Solidarities," *Journal of Social Philosophy* 38, no. 1 (2007): 148–64.

52. Sally Scholz, *Political Solidarity* (University Park: Pennsylvania State University Press, 2008).

53. Kurt Weyland, *Bounded Rationality and Policy Diffusion: Social Sector Reform in Latin America* (Princeton, NJ: Princeton University Press, 2009).

54. Kurt Bayertz, "Four Uses of 'Solidarity,'" in *Solidarity: Philosophical Studies in Contemporary Culture*, ed. Kurt Bayertz (London: Kluwer, 1999), 3–28.

55. Arto Laitinen, "From Recognition to Solidarity: Universal Respect, Mutual Support, and Social Unity," in *Solidarity: Theory and Practice*, ed. Arto Laitinen and Anne Birgitta Pessi (Lanham, MD: Lexington Books, 2014), 126–54.

56. Juliet Hooker, *Race and the Politics of Solidarity* (London: Oxford University Press, 2009).

57. The challenge of addressing this gap has been posed increasingly frequently since the mid-1990s and is elegantly articulated by Nelly Richard, "Cultural Peripheries: Latin America and Postmodernist De-Centering," *boundary 2* 20, no. 3 (1993): 156–61.

58. Chandra Mohanty, *Feminism without Borders: Decolonizing Theory, Practicing Solidarity* (Durham, NC: Duke University Press, 2000); Sara Ahmed, *Strange Encounters: Embodied Others in Post-coloniality* (New York: Routledge, 2000); Sara Salem, "On Transnational Feminist Solidarity: The Case of Angela Davis in Egypt," *Signs: Journal of Women in Culture and Society* 43, no. 2 (2018): 245–67; Kwame Appiah, *Cosmopolitanism: Ethics in a World of Strangers* (New York: Norton, 2007); Sandra Bartky, *"On Solidarity and Sympathy" and Other Essays* (Lanham, MD: Rowman and Littlefield, 2002); Amrita Basu, "Globalization of the Local / Localization of the Global: Mapping Transnational Women's Movements," in *Feminist Theory Reader*, ed. Carole McCann Carole and Kim Seung-Kyung (New York: Routledge, 2003), 68–77; Leela Gandhi, *Affective Communities: Anti-colonial Thought, Fin-de-Siècle Radicalism, and the Politics of Friendship* (Durham, NC: Duke University Press, 2006).

59. This theoretical approach has opened up important avenues of research, such as the differences in Catholic solidarity organizing experiences in various geographical locations, such as Mexico versus Canada. See Maurice Demers, *Connected Struggles: Catholics, Nationalists, and Transnational Relations between Mexico and Quebec, 1917–1945* (Montreal: McGill-Queen's University Press, 2014).

60. See, for instance, Pablo Yankelevich and María Luisa Tarres, *En México, entre exilios: Una experiencia de sudamericanos* (Mexico City: Plaza y Valdés, 1998), writing on the experiences of different exile communities in Mexico in organizing against torture and disappearances in South America.

61. Mark S. Anner, *Solidarity Transformed: Labor Responses to Globalization and Crisis in Latin America* (Ithaca, NY: Cornell University Press, 2011), 2.

62. Gayatri Spivak, "Bonding in Difference, Interview with Alfred Arteaga (1993–1994)," in *The Spivak Reader*, ed. Donna Landry and Gerald MacLean (New York: Routledge, 1996), 27.

63. Scholz, *Political Solidarity*, 5; Stites Mor, "Introduction," 4.

64. Scott Mainwaring, Eduardo Viola, and Rosa Cusminsky, "Los nuevos movimientos sociales, las culturas políticas y la democracia: Brasil y Argentina en la década de los ochenta," *Revista Mexicana de Sociología* 47, no. 4 (1985): 35–84.

65. Fernando Stratta and Marcelo Barrera, "¿Movimientos sin clases o clases sin movimiento? Notas sobre la recepción de la teoría de los Movimientos Sociales en la Argentina," *Conflicto social* 2, no. 1 (2009): 118–34; Martín Retamozo, "Movimientos sociales, política y hegemonía en Argentina," *Polis: Revista Latinoamericana* 28 (2011), http://journals.openedition.org/polis/1249.

66. Maristella Svampa, "Protesta, movimientos sociales y dimensiones de la acción colectiva en América Latina," lecture presented in the "Jornadas de Homenaje a Charles Tilly," Universidad Complutense de Madrid-Fundación Carolina, 7–9 May 2009. These concerns appear in an earlier work by Fernando Calderón and Elizabeth Jelin, *Clases y movimientos sociales en América Latina: Perspectivas y realidades* (Buenos Aires: Centro de Estudios de Estado y Sociedad, 1987), 36.

67. Ruth Cardoso, "Popular Movements in the Context of the Consolidation of Democracy," Working Paper Series, Helen Kellogg Institute for International Studies, 120 (March 1989).

68. James W. Nickel and Eduardo Viola, "Integrating Environmentalism and Human Rights," *Environmental Ethics* 16, no. 3 (1994): 265–73.

69. "Mexico's EZLN Expresses Solidarity with Chile Mapuche Struggle," *Telesur*, 30 November 2018, https://www.telesurenglish.net/news/Mexicos-EZLN-Expresses-Soli darity-With-Chile-Mapuche-Struggle-20181130-0018.html.

70. Verónica de la Torre, "La acción colectiva transnacional en las acción colectiva de los movimientos sociales y de las Relaciones Internacionales," *CONfines de relacio nes internacionales y ciencia política* 7, no. 14 (2011): 45–72.

71. Stites Mor, "Introduction," 17.

72. Kees Schuyt, "The Sharing of Risks and the Risks of Sharing: Solidarity and Social Justice in the Welfare State," *Ethical Theory and Moral Practice* 1 (1998): 297–311; Elinor Ostrom, *Governing the Commons: The Evolution of Institutions for Collective Action* (Cambridge: Cambridge University Press, 1990); Donatella della Porta, ed., *Solidarity Mobilizations in the "Refugee Crisis"* (New York: Palgrave Macmillan, 2018).

73. See, for example, Dale W. Wimberley, "Setting the Stage for Cross-Border Solidarity," *Labor Studies Journal* 34, no. 3 (2009): 318–38; Jeffrey C. Goldfarb, "Media Events, Solidarity, and the Rise and Fall of the Public Sphere," *Media, Culture, and Society* 40, no. 1 (2018): 118–21.

74. For example, see Verónica Montes and María Dolores Paris Pombo, "Ethics of Care, Emotional Work, and Collective Action of Solidarity: The Patronas in Mexico," *Gender, Place and Culture* 26, no. 4 (2019): 559–80.

75. Eric Zolov, "Introduction: Latin America in the Global Sixties," *The Americas* 70, no. 3 (2014): 350. See also Tamara Chaplin and Jadwiga Pieper Mooney, eds., *The Global 1960s: Convention, Contest, and Counterculture* (New York: Routledge, 2018).

76. Solidarity was not just practiced by the left. There have been some interesting new works on right-wing and anticommunist international organizing that suggest solidarity (if not necessarily framed in these terms) was practiced by a range of differ ent groups. It is important to note that right-wing discourse about the right's singular ability to speak for and defend the nation's interests against foreign influences finds many contradictions in such projects.

77. Jessica Stites Mor, ed., *Solidarity and Human Rights in Cold War Latin America* (Madison: University of Wisconsin Press, 2013); Stites Mor and Suescun Pozas, "Trans national Pathways of Empathy," 1–22; Lily Balloffet, Fernando Camacho Padilla, and Jessica Stites Mor, "Pushing Boundaries: New Directions in Contemporary Latin

America–Middle East History," *Jahrbuch für Geschichte Lateinamerikas—Anuario De Historia De América Latina* 56 (2019): 1–14; Jessica Stites Mor, "Circum-Caribbean Development and Transnational Solidarity: Perspectives from a Post-Development Research Paradigm," *Canadian Journal of Latin American and Caribbean Studies* 38, no. 2 (2013): 279–81.

78. Thea Pitman and Andy Stafford, "Introduction: Transatlanticism and Tricontinentalism," *Journal of Transatlantic Studies* 7, no. 3 (2009): 198.

79. Stites Mor and Suescun Pozas, "Transnational Pathways of Empathy," 5.

Chapter 1. The Revolutionary Latin American State

1. Beyond the guarantee of civil rights, social rights include the right to social welfare, such as education and poverty reduction, and other measures by which citizens would be able to participate in and share in the benefits of community that could be made available by the state. For more on social rights, see T. H. Marshall and Tom Bottomore, *Citizenship and Social Class* (London: Pluto, 1987).

2. Translation by H. N. Branch for the *Annals of the American Academy of Political and Social Science* (vol. 71) in 1917 as a side-by-side comparison and republished in 2013 by JSTOR as part of their Early Journal Content project, https://archive.org/stream/jstor-1013370/1013370_djvu.txt.

3. Bruce Zagaris and Julia Padierna Peratta, "Mexico–United States Extradition and Alternatives: From Fugitive Slaves to Drug Traffickers—150 Years and Beyond the Rio Grande's Winding Courses," *American University International Law Review* 12, no. 4 (1997): 523–25. Zagaris and Padierna Peratta argue that despite the humanitarian nature of these provisions, there was another political side effect of their enforcement, which was that it undermined some of the settlement efforts of Texas cattle ranchers, who relied on slave labor and head counts of enslaved people for their claims, and later led to resistance against Texas's declaration of independence on the grounds that it would sanction the institution of slavery in a modern state. See also Ronnie C. Tyler, "Fugitive Slaves in Mexico," *Journal of Negro History* 57, no. 1 (1972): 1–12; Sean Kelley, "'Mexico in His Head': Slavery and the Texas–Mexico Border, 1810–1860," *Journal of Social History* 37, no. 3 (2004): 709–23; Sarah E. Cornell, "Citizens of Nowhere: Fugitive Slaves and Free African Americans in Mexico, 1833–1857," *Journal of American History* 100, no. 2 (2013): 351–74.

4. Zagaris and Padierna Peralta, "Mexico–United States Extradition and Alternatives," 526.

5. David Armstrong, *Revolution and World Order: The Revolutionary State in World Order* (Oxford: Oxford University Press, 1993), 3.

6. Raymond Craib, *Cartographic Mexico: A History of State Fixations and Fugitive Landscapes* (Durham, NC: Duke University Press, 2004), 226.

7. For an excellent review of the literature on the crisis of government in Mexico during this period, see Mary Kay Vaughan, "Mexico, 1940–1968 and Beyond: Perfect

Dictatorship? Dictablanda? or PRI State Hegemony?," *Latin American Research Review* 53, no. 1 (2018): 167–76.

8. Rebecca M. Schreiber, *Cold War Exiles in Mexico: U.S. Dissidents and the Culture of Critical Resistance* (Minneapolis: University of Minnesota Press, 2008), xix.

9. There are some notable parallels with the Spanish Republican case, in that Mexico's response to asylum seekers in both cases occurred under populist, internationalist presidents. Both cases were implicated in shoring up domestic support for the ruling party in Mexico. However, the Chilean case relied on commitments to the region and was a significant gesture toward a revolutionary left. It signaled to the rest of the region Mexico's opposition to U.S. imperialism and its many accomplices in foreign industry and military regimes.

10. Renata Keller, *Mexico's Cold War: Cuba, the United States, and the Legacy of the Mexican Revolution* (Cambridge: Cambridge University Press, 2015), 43. For more on state violence and the left, see Gladys McCormick, "The Last Door: Political Prisoners and the Use of Torture in Mexico's Dirty War," *The Americas* 74, no. 1 (2017): 57–81.

11. Amelia Kiddle, *Mexico's Relations with Latin America during the Cárdenas Era* (Albuquerque: University of New Mexico Press, 2016), 14, 22, 199. See also Amelia Kiddle, "Between Two Revolutions: Cultural Relations between Mexico and Cuba," *Jahrbuch für Geschichte Lateinamerikas—Anuario de Historia de América Latina* 54 (2017): 108–28. Cárdenas was also well known for having supported the cause of the Spanish Republicans, prominently leading the region's response to the civil war and even offering Spanish intellectuals the "facilities and income necessary for the continuation of their work," which later became El Colegio de México. Clara Lida, "La España perdida que México ganó," *Letras libres* (May 2003): 32. See also Clara Lida, *Inmigración y exilio: Reflexiones sobre el caso español* (Mexico City: Siglo Veintiuno Editores, 1997); Mario Sznajder and Luis Roniger, *The Politics of Exile in Latin America* (Cambridge: Cambridge University Press, 2009), 122.

12. Jürgen Buchenau and Gilbert M. Joseph, *Mexico's Once and Future Revolution: Social Upheaval and the Challenge of Rule since the Late Nineteenth Century* (Durham, NC: Duke University Press, 2013).

13. For a more detailed discussion of this, see Paul Gillingham and Benjamin T. Smith, "Paradoxes of Revolution," in *Dictablanda: Politics, War, and Culture in Mexico, 1938–1968*, ed. Paul Gillingham and Benjamin T. Smith (Durham, NC: Duke University Press, 2014), 1–44.

14. Felipe Sánchez Barría, "'En la lucha contra el imperialismo, México y Chile de Pie,' Salvador Allende en la política tercermundicsta de Luis Echeverría en la guerra fría interamericana," *Foro Internacional* 54, no. 4 (2014): 966. See also Hans Wollny, "México y el reto del asilo: Una visión desde afuera," *Verfassung und Recht in Übersee/ Law and Politics in Africa, Asia and Latin America* 23, no. 4 (1990): 384.

15. Claudia Fedora Rojas Mira, "El exilio político chileno: La Casa de Chile en México, 1973–1993, una experiencia singular" (PhD diss., Universidad de Santiago de Chile, 2013), 66.

16. See "Inter-American Treaties," OAS, accessed 21 June 2021, http://www.oas .org/en/sla/dil/inter_american_treaties_signatories.asp.

17. See Guillmero Rodríguez de Ita, "Tres asilos otorgados por México a un mismo antitrujillista," *Tzintzun: Revista de Estudios Históricos*, no. 52 (2010): 104.

18. Ibid., 103.

19. Carrillo Flores was the son of composer and violinist Julián Carrillo Trujillo, famous for developing a theory of music based on microtones he dubbed "Sonido 13," or "Thirteenth Sound," referring to the tones in between the twelve-note octave. By the 1950s, Flores had established a reputation as a leading legal mind by evincing the same kind of imitate attention to detail his father had given to sound.

20. "Communiqué 51/24 (Unofficial)," International Court of Justice, Colombia v. Peru, 1950/51 (decision 278, 288), http://www.worldcourts.com/icj/eng/decisions/ 1950.11.20_asylum.htm. See also Rubén Ruíz Guerra, *Mas allá de la diplomacia: Relaciones de México con Bolivia, Ecuador y Perú* (Mexico City: SRE, 2007); Ashley Black, "The Politics of Asylum: Stability, Sovereignty, and Mexican Foreign Policy in the Caribbean Basin, 1945–1959" (PhD diss., Stony Brook University, 2018), 127–30.

21. Geneviève Dorais, "Indo-America and the Politics of APRA Exile, 1918–1945" (PhD diss., University of Wisconsin, 2014), 115–16.

22. Pablo Yankelevich, *México, país refugio: La experiencia de los exilios en el siglo XX* (Mexico City: Plaza y Valdés, 2002) 15. See also Ricardo Melgar Bao, *Redes e imaginario del exilio en México y América Latina, 1934–1940* (Buenos Aires: Ediciones Libros en Red, 2003), 22.

23. Dorais, "Indo-America and the Politics," 157. See also Iñigo Garcia-Bryce, "Transnational Activist: Magda Mortal and the American Popular Revolutionary Alliance (APRA), 1926–1950," *The Americas* 70, no. 4 (2014): 677–706.

24. Kiddle, *Mexico's Relations with Latin America*, 187.

25. "Communiqué 50/48 (Unofficial)" and "Section C.—Request for the Interpretation of the Judgment of November 20th, 1950," International Court of Justice, Colombia v. Peru, 1950/51 (decision 278, 288) http://www.worldcourts.com/icj/eng/ decisions/1950.11.20_asylum.htm.

26. Ernesto Dijigo, "Statement of the Cuban Government," 15 February 1951, "Section C. Declaration of Intervention by the Government of Cuba," 13 March 1951; "Haya de la Torre Case, Judgement of 13 June 1951," International Court of Justice, Colombia v. Peru, 1950/51 (decision 278, 288), http://www.worldcourts.com/icj/eng/ decisions/1950.11.20_asylum.htm.

27. Sznajder and Roniger, *Politics of Exile in Latin America*, 124; Manuel Ángel Castillo, "El dilema del retorno o la permanencia de los refugiados guatemaltecos en México: Una reflexión veinte años después," in *El retorno: Migración económica y exilio político en América Latina y España*, ed. Alicia Gil Lázaro, Aurelio Martín Nójera, and Pedro Pérez Herrero (Madrid: Cátedra del Exilio, Institutio de Estudios Latinoamericanos, 2013), 75–76. See also Manuel Ángel Castillo and Fabienne Venet, "Migraciones internacionales," in *Los grandes problemas de México*, vol. 3 (Mexico City: Colegio de México, 2010), 195–226.

28. José Augustín Martínez Viademonte, *El derecho de asilo y el regimen internacional de refugiados* (Mexico City: Ediciones Botas, 1961), 44–41, Archive of the Instituto de Investigaciones Jurídicas, Universidad Autónoma de México, Mexico City (IIJ-UNAM).

29. Fernando Serrano Migallón, *El asilio político en México* (Mexico: Editorial Porrúa, 1998), 37–38.

30. Anonymous, "El derecho de asilo en la América Latina: Antecedentes y fallo en el caso de Haya de la Torre," *Boletín de las Naciones Unidas* 9, no. 12 (December 1950): 848 (IIJ-UNAM). See also Ana María Pastorino and M. Raquel Ippoliti, "A propósito del Asilo Diplomático," *Revista de la Facultad de Derecho* 47 (2010): 1–37.

31. Manuel Adolfo Vieira, *Derecho al asilo diplomatico* (Montevideo: Facultad de Derecho de la Universidad de la Republica, 1961), 120–31 (IIJ-UNAM).

32. Antonio Carrillo Flores, "Al asilo político en México," *Memoria de el Colegio Nacional* 9, no. 1 (April 1978): 40–41 (IIJ-UNAM).

33. Ibid., 45–46.

34. Luis Ortiz Monasterio, "El asilo político," *Pensamiento Político* 14, no. 54 (October 1973): 203–8 (IIJ-UNAM); "Ante estudiantes, Cruz González habló sobre el derecho al asilo," *El Excélsior*, 13 February 1971, 11, Dirección General de Investigaciones Políticas y Sociales, Archivo General de México, Mexico City (DGIPS-AGN), Caja 1757B, ex. 8.

35. "Asila México a dos dominicanos," *La Prensa*, 26 August 1970, 34, DGIPS-AGN, Caja 1341B, ex. 4.

36. "México acepta el asilo político de los dominicanos," *El Heraldo*, 26 March 1970, DGIPS-AGN, Caja 1341B, ex. 4.

37. Joaquín Bueno, "Llegaron encabezados por el Arzobispo de Santo Domingo," *Ovaciones*, 27 March 1970, DGIPS-AGN, Caja 1341B, ex. 4.

38. "No limitará nuestro país la protección de asilados," *Novedades*, 15 June 1970, and Lorenzo Yañez "Angustiosa situación de dieciocho asilados políticos," *Ultimas Noticias*, 23 June 1070, 10–11, DGIPS-AGN), Caja 1341B, ex. 4; "México negó la extradición de A. Arguedas," *Avance*, 19 June 1970, DGIPS-AGN, Caja 1341B, ex. 4.

39. Carrillo Flores, "Al asilo político en México," 46.

40. "Gestionan rescate del Embajador de EEUU secuestrado," *Prensa Latina*, no. 3328 (6 September 1969): 9–10, DGIPS-AGN, Caja 923, ex. 1, 1969; Leon Roberto García, "Temerosos y agradecidos a México legaron a asilados," *El Heraldo de México*, 16 March 1970, 1, 14A; Juan de Dios Garza García, "Llegaron presos brasileños y el cónsul Nipón fue liberado," DGIPS-AGN, Caja 1341B, ex. 4.

41. "Sus propias declaraciones hunden a los dinamiteros," *El Universal*, 16 February 1970, 1, 7, DGIPS-AGN, Caja 1341B, ex. 4; "Escogen a México los asilados porque el nuestro es un país en el que se respetan los derechos humanos," *El Día*, 2 April 1971, DGIPS-AGN, Caja 1341B, ex. 4. For more on "los dinamiteros," see Jacinto Rodríguez Munguía, *La otra guerra secreta: Los archivos prohibidos de la prensa y el poder* (Mexico City: Random House, 2007).

42. Such as in the case of Salvador Aguilar, news of which appeared on the heels of the Brazilians' arrival and news releases of their mistreatment by police in Brazil.

"Condena al terrorismo," *La Prensa*, 26 March 1970; "Otra terrorista fue consignado," *El Sol de México*, 20 March 1970, DGIPS-AGN, Caja 1341B, ex. 4.

43. "Llegó el Asilado Antonio Arguedas," *El Universal*, 24 April 1970, 1, 8, DGIPS-AGN, Caja 1341A, ex. 1.

44. "Antonio Arguedas," *The Guardian*, 29 February 2000.

45. Sara Katherine Sanders, "The Mexican Student Movement: National Protest Movements in International and Transnational Contexts," in *Human Rights and Transnational Solidarity in Cold War Latin America*, ed. Jessica Stites Mor (Madison: University of Wisconsin Press, 2013), 75.

46. Eric Zolov, *The Last Good Neighbor: Mexico in the Global Sixties* (Durham, NC: Duke University Press, 2020), 21.

47. Keller, *Mexico's Cold War*, 87, 96.

48. See Abdón Mateos, *La batalla de México: Final de la guerra civil y ayuda a los refugiados, 1939–1945* (Madrid: Alianza, 2009). The shah was never a political asylum seeker, however, and he remained on a tourist visa during his stay in Mexico. See also Fernando Camacho Padilla, "Las relaciones entre Latinoamérica e Irán durante la última década de la dinastía Pahleví," *Jahrbuch für Geschichte Lateinamerikas—Anuario De Historia De América Latina* 56 (2019): 66–96.

49. Pablo Yankelevich's excellent anthology, *México, país refugio*, brings together the histories of various notorious moments in Mexico's relationship with political refugees, Leon Trotsky, and Spanish Republicans fleeing Franco, among others. He argues that over the course of the twentieth century, the Mexican state, despite its authoritarian tendencies, benefited from its reputation as a welcoming refuge for critics of governments elsewhere.

50. "Investigación, 14 septiembre 1971," DGIPS-AGN, Caja 1145 B, ex. 3, and "Investigación 14 julio 1978," DGIPS-AGN, Caja 1755C, ex. 10.

51. "Investigación, 8 septiembre 1979"; "Investigación, 14 septiembre 1979"; "Investigación, 19 noviembre 1979"; "Investigación, 23 noviembre 1974," DGIPS-AGN, Caja 1755C, ex. 10.

52. Black, "Politics of Asylum," 7n16, 178. Anti-indigenous sentiment was shared by others, as one author expressed in this editorial piece: "Las noticias recibidas en México indican que nuestra Embajada, como las representaciones diplomáticas de muchos otros países, se encuentran llenas de personalidades del Gobierno derrocado que han pedido asilo, y que pretenden internarse en nuestro país en calidad de refugiados políticos. Se dice que altos jefes policíacos, que consumaron numerosos crímenes, ya se han puesto a salvo cruzando la línea divisoria, y que muchos más quizá también la hayan pasado en lugares intrincados, donde no se ejerce vigilancia, elementos que fácilmente se confundirán con los mexicanos de Chiapas o que pronto se internarán a los distintos de Estados del país que puedan absorberlos" (The news received in Mexico indicate that our Embassy, like the diplomatic representatives of many other countries, finds itself full of individuals from the overthrown regime seeking asylum, and that hope to find refuge in our country as political refugees. It is rumored that senior police chiefs, who committed numerous crimes, have already made themselves safe by

crossing the border, and that many more may also have crossed the border in vulerable places, where surveillance is not exercised, elements that could easily be confused with Mexicans from Chiapas and be absorbed in other Mexican states). "Refugiados y Delinquentes," *El Universal*, 4 July 1954, 3.

53. José Manuel Jurado, "Debe respetarse y también cuidarse," *Excélsior*, 2 April 1970; "No se podrá negar el derecho de asilo para impeder los secuestros," *El Heraldo*, 3 April 1970; "Asilo política, tema de México y EE.UU.," *La Prensa*, 14 April 1970; "Discurso del Lic. Carrillo Flores en la OEA," *El Sol de México*, 15 April 1970; "Urge una reunión continental que modifique el Tratado de Asilo," *El Heraldo*, 3 April 1970, DGIPS-AGN, Caja 1341B, ex. 4; R. Torres Barrón, "Dura prueba al dereco del asilo," *Excélsior*, 31 March 1970, DGIPS-AGN, Caja 1341B, ex. 4.

54. Mario Godoy, "Diplomáticos y juristas se solidarizan con la postura Mexicana en lo del asilo," *Novedades*, 18 April 1970, DGIPS-AGN, Caja 1341B, ex. 4.

55. Moises Martínez, "Asilo a secuestradores para salvar plagiados," *La Prensa*, 16 April 1970; Julio Zetina, "El Gobierno nos está llenando de extranjeros indeseables," *El Heraldo*, 2 May 1982, DGIPS-AGN, Caja 1341B, ex. 4.

56. Yankelevich, *México, país refugio*, 10–11. See also Dalia Muller, *Cuban Émigrés and Independence in the Nineteenth-Century Gulf World* (Chapel Hill: University of North Carolina Press, 2017), 44.

57. Sebastián Rivera Mir, "El otro exilio Chileno en México y Guatemala, 1948–1951; Militancia transnacional en los orígenes de la Guerra Fría," *Historia* 50, no. 1 (2017): 212.

58. This committee included the Partido Socialista de Trabajadores, Partido Popular Socialista Movimiento Revolucionario Magisterio, Sindicato de Trabajadores y Empleados de la UNAM, Partido Obrero Revolucionario Trotskista, Movimiento Revolucionario Estudiantil, Movimiento Estudiantil por el Socialismo, UPTYSIM-PEMEX, Frente Sindical Independiente, Confederación de Jóvenes Mexicanos, Juventud Popular Socialista, Comisión Ejecutiva de al Escuela Superior de Medicina, Confederación Campesina Independiente, the national Federación de Estudiantes de México, and federations of students from several provinces, among others. "Comité Nacional de Solidaridad y Apoyo a Chile, El Pueblo de México," *Excélsior*, 4 September 1974, SRE, III-6010-1, 6a.

59. Rivera Mir, "El otro exilio Chileno," 217, 227. For more detail, see Tanya Harmer and Alfredo Riquelme Segovia, eds., *Chile y la Guerra Fría global* (Santiago: RIL Editores, 2014); Edmundo Olivaries, *Pablo Neruda: Los caminos de América; Tras las huellas del poeta itinerante III (1940–1950)* (Santiago: LOM Ediciones, 2014); Departamento Diplomático, Sección de Archivo General, Secretaría de Relaciones Exteriores, Mexico City, Mexico (SRE).

60. Rojas Mira, "El exilio político chileno," 3.

61. France and Canada, for instance, faced tremendous pressure from leftist, socialist, religious, and humanitarian groups to admit refugees; Canada eventually took in an estimated seven thousand Chilean refugees and France took in fifteen thousand only after each made modifications to their policies for handling such cases. Eva Salinas,

"How the Chilean Coup Forever Changed Canada's Refugee Policies," *Globe and Mail*, 6 September 2013; "1973 Chile Coup Was Defining Moment for French Left," *France 24*, 11 September 2013, http://www.france24.com/en/20130911-1973-chile-1973 -coup-defining-moment-france-left-communist-socialist-party.

62. "Voto para llegar el socialismo," *Excélsior*, 4 September 1974, SRE, III-6010-1, 6a.

63. Fernando Camacho Padilla, "The Swedish Chilean Society: Fascist Solidarity with Pinochet's Chile in Sweden," in *Making Sense of the Americas: How Protest Related to America in the 1980s and Beyond*, ed. Jan Hansen, Christian Helm, and Frank Reichherzer (Chicago: Campus Verlag, 2015), 131–50, 131, 134, 149. See also Joaquin Fermandois, *Chile y el mundo, 1973–1975* (Santiago: Ediciones Universidad Católica de Chile, 1985).

64. "Resumen cable grafico," *Volumen editorial*, 23 September 1971, DGIPS-AGN, Caja 1310B, ex. 4, 15–30; "Servicio Político de Información Confidencial," September 1971, Archivo General de la Nación, Mexico City.

65. Sánchez Barría, "'En la lucha contra el imperialismo,'" 956.

66. Jaime Pensado argues that by the end of the 1960s and into the early 1970s, student movements in Mexico moved away from more revolutionary aims, being threatened and also somewhat co-opted by the state, and deliberately moved away from cultural dimensions seen as militant or rebellious. Jaime Pensado, *Rebel Mexico: Student Unrest and Authoritarian Political Culture during the Long Sixties* (Palo Alto, CA: Stanford University Press, 2015), 239. See also Alexander Aviña, "An Archive of Counterinsurgency: State Anxieties and Peasant Guerrillas in Cold War Mexico," *Journal of Iberian and Latin American Research* 19, no. 1 (2013): 41–51; Jaime Pensado and Enrique Ochoa, eds., *Mexico beyond 1968: Revolutionaries, Radicals, and Repression during the Global Sixties and Subversive Seventies* (Tucson: University of Arizona Press, 2018).

67. Patrick William Kelly, "The 1973 Chilean Coup and the Origins of Transnational Human Rights Activism," *Journal of Global History* 8, no. 1 (2013): 183.

68. Rojas Mira, "El exilio político chileno," 41–43.

69. "Vicaría de la Solidaridad, presentación al presidente de la Corte Suprema," March 1976, SRE, III-6010-1, 6a.

70. Antonio Navarro Zarazúa, "Es una gestión tipo humanitaria: Echeverría," *El Heraldo de México*, 31 May 1974, DGIPS-AGN, Caja 1757B, ex. 8.

71. "Investigación, 30 septiembre 1974," DGIPS-AGN, Caja 1159, ex 2.

72. Rojas Mira, "El exilio político chileno," 85–86.

73. "Investigación, 24 junio 1977"; "Investigación, 27 mayo 1978," DGIPS-AGN, Caja 1757B, ex. 5.

74. "Pidió ex senador chileno H. Miranda 'fortalecer la resistencia en su país,'" *El Excélsior*, 31 May 1976, DGIPS-AGN, Caja 1757B, ex. 8.

75. See Eugenio Anguniano, "México y el Tercer Mundo: Racionalización de una posición," in *Foro Internacional: Antología de estudios de política y relaciones internacionales*, ed. Elodie Brun and Humberto Garza Eliozondo (Mexico City: El Colegio de México, 2019), 4:15–158; Mario Ojeda Gómez, "México ante los Estados Unidos en la

coyuntura actual," in *Foro Internacional: Antología de estudios de política y relaciones internacionales*, ed. Elodie Brun and Humberto Garza Eliozondo (Mexico City: El Colegio de México, 2019), 4:159–90.

76. Vanni Pettinà, "Global Horizons: Mexico, the Third World, and the Non-Aligned Movement at the Time of the 1961 Belgrade Conference," *International History Review* 38, no. 4 (2016): 759.

77. Tanya Harmer, *Allende's Chile and the Inter-American Cold War* (Chapel Hill: University of North Carolina Press, 2011), 17.

78. For more on Brazilians in Mexico during this period, see Daniela Morales Muñoz, *El exilio brasileño en México durante la dictadura militar, 1964–1979* (Mexico City: SRE, 2018).

79. Comité de Brasileños Exilados en México, "Llegamos al clímax de la opresión," *Siglo Veinte*, February 1966, 14–15, DGIPS-AGN, Caja 821, ex. 5.

80. Internal document, relating to circulation of "Boletín Informativo de COBEM, July 1965," and confidential letter written by Gabino Fraga, 21 October 1965," SRE, III-2904-8, 162.

81. "Investigación, 9 septiembre 1979," DGIPS-AGN, Caja 1755C, ex. 10. A much more elaborate discussion of the impact of Allende's fall across the region can be found in Barry Carr and Steve Ellner, eds., *The Latin American Left: From Allende to Perestroika* (Boulder, CO: Westview, 1993).

82. "Ayer llegaron 52 asilados políticos chilenos," *El Día*, 19 May 1975, DGIPS-AGN, Caja 1757B, ex. 8.

83. This perspective changed later, when developmentalist plans for southern Mexico began to see harboring Guatemalans and other refugees as an opportunity to provide cheap labor for the expansion of various industries in states like Chiapas and Quintana Roo. María Cristina García, *Seeking Refuge: Central American Migration to Mexico, the United States, and Canada* (Berkeley: University of California Press, 2006), 45, 57.

84. "Defiende C. Cárdenas el derecho de asilo," *La Prensa*, 4 June 1976, DGIPS-AGN, Caja 1757B, ex. 8.

85. "1,585 Asilados de diferentes nacionalidades ha recibido México," *Ultimas Noticias*, 15 July 1976, and Jorge Aviles Randolph, "No son peligrosos los mil asilados políticos," *El Universal*, 23 June 1976, DGIPS-AGN, Caja 1757B, ex. 8. In 1972, Carrillo Flores accepted a position at El Colegio de México, where he remained until his death in 1987. A fitting tribute to the role of political asylum granting in reinforcing Mexico's revolutionary stance, this appointment hearkened back to a proud legacy of receiving those persecuted in the Spanish Civil War.

86. Augusto Cabrera M., "Que se portan bien en México los asilados," *Prensa*, 28 September 1976, and Víctor Sanchez Baños, "1,600 Asilados políticos y se portan bien," *Ovaciones*, 27 September 1976, DGIPS-AGN, Caja 1757B, ex. 8.

87. "México mantendrá el derecho al asilo," *Heraldo de México*, 27 September 1976, DGIPS-AGN, Caja 1757B, ex. 8.

88. "México a la defensa del derecho al asilo," *Prensa*, 18 September 1976, DGIPS-AGN, Caja 1757B, ex. 8.

89. Letters such as those sent by Jesús Rodriguez Gómez, Javier Gaxiola, and Guillermo Gallardo Vasquez defended against measures such as limitations to the rights of asylum seekers to attend university in Mexico. "Letter from Gaxiola y Gaxiola, Jr" and "Letter from the Illustre y Nacional Colegio de Abogados," DGIPS-AGN, Caja 1757B, ex. 8.

90. This pattern is consistent throughout the decade. "Investigación, 19 septiembre 1971," DGIPS-AGN, Caja 1145B, ex. 3; "Investigación, 30 septiembre 1974," DGIPS-AGN, Caja 1159, ex. 2; "Investigación, 2 febrero 1978," DGIPS-AGN, Caja 1656B, ex. 8. One fascinating report includes notes on the mantras of student protesters, including the times each set was rotated during a march on behalf of disappeared educators. "Investigación, 9 septiembre 1979," DGIPS-AGN, Caja 1755C, ex. 10.

91. For more comprehensive coverage of these DFS reports, see Pablo Yankelevich, "Los rostros de Jano: Vigilancia y control de los exiliados latinoamericanos en México (1960–1980)," *Estudios Interdisciplinarios de América Latina y el Caribe* 30, no. 1 (2019): 125–57. For more on DFS activities in Mexico City, see Louise Walker, "Spying at the Drycleaners: Mexico City," *Journal of Iberian and Latin American Research* 19, no. 1 (2013): 52–61. On a personal note, I was surprised to find in one DFS report that my own graduate advisor, when a student, was recorded as being in attendance at a UNAM rally and had signed a petition on behalf of Argentine exiles.

92. Jocelyn Olcott, *International Women's Year: The Greatest Consciousness-Raising Event in History* (New York: Oxford University Press, 2017), 148.

93. Renata Keller, for instance, argues that Mexico provided an important counterpoint to Cuban Tricontinentalism. Keller, *Mexico's Cold War*, 189–90.

94. Julio Pomar, "En el ejercicio del asilo político, nuestro país confirma su lucha por el derecho y la democracia," *El Día*, 22 April 1974, DGIPS-AGN, Caja 1757B, ex. 8. See also Cecilia Imaz, *La práctica del asilo y de refugio en México* (Mexico City: Potrerillos Editores, 1995).

95. "Protocol to the Extradition Treaty between the United States of America and the United Mexican States of May 4, 1978," published in the *Treaties and Other International Acts Series*, 12897, U.S. Department of State, Washington, DC, 1997.

96. "México y la ONU firman un convenio para ayudar a refugiados políticos," *Excélsior*, 4 March 1981, DGIPS-AGN, Caja 1757B, ex. 8.

97. Ricardo del Muro, David Siller, and Miguel Angel Velázquez, "El total de asilados en México es de 2 mil 203," *Uno más uno*, 28 July 1982, DGIPS-AGN, Caja 1757B, ex. 8.

98. "Calcula la ONU que hay en México 140,000 refugiados," *Excélsior*, 21 October 1981, DGIPS-AGN, Caja 1757B, ex. 8.

99. "Llegaron ayer los restos de Juan José Torres," *El Universal*, 8 June 1976, and "México, país refugio de perseguidos del fascismo," *Prensa*, 9 June 1976, DGIPS-AGN, Caja 1779B, ex. 5; "Investigación, 9 septiembre 1975" and "Comité de exiliados bolivianos en México," *El Día*, 8 June 1976, DGIPS-AGN, Caja 1770B, ex. 5. Mexican

solidarity organizing with Bolivia had included a large number of participants from Chile and Peru, who, together with a committee organized by Bolivian exiles, were accompanied by many of the Mexican youth and labor organizations with which they had been organizing.

100. Diplomatic correspondence attests to the warm reception of Mexico's actions and ongoing support for Chileans from across the region and Europe, in particular. SRE, III-6010-1, 6a.

101. "Comité de Solidaridad y Apoyo a Chile, Pueblo de México," *Excélsior*, 4 September 1974, SRE III-6010-1, 6a.

Chapter 2. Tricontinental Culture

1. Charisse Burden-Stelly, "Reclaiming the Tricontinental: Transnational Solidarity and Contemporary Struggles," *Black Perspectives* (9 November 2018), https://www.aaihs.org/reclaiming-the-tricontinental-transnational-solidarity-and-contemporary-struggles/.

2. This notion of solidarity is articulated well by Julie-Françoise Tolliver in describing the work of poet Aimé Césaire in recuperating the image of Patrice Lumumba as an agent of anticolonial solidarity. Julie-Françoise Tolliver, "Césaire/Lumumba: A Season of Solidarity," *Journal of Postcolonial Writing* 50, no. 4 (2014): 398–409. See also Kristine Khouri and Rasha Salti, eds., *Past Disquiet: Artists, International Solidarity and Museums in Exile* (Warsaw: Museum of Modern Art in Warsaw, 2019).

3. Scholars interested in OSPAAAL's poster art as creative works should consult the excellent catalog work by French historian and curator Olivier Hadouchi in preparation for the exhibition "La Tricontinental: Cinema, Utopia and Internationalism," Museo Nacional Centro de Arte Reina Sofia, Madrid, Spain, 19 April–10 June 2017, and Beth Tamar Rosenblum's work on the aesthetics of OSPAAAL's poster art, "OSPAAAL Posters and the Cuban Vanguard Aesthetic" (master's thesis, University of California at Los Angeles, 2005).

4. Bradley Simpson, "Southeast Asia in the Cold War," in *The Cold War in the Third World*, ed. Robert J. McMahon (New York: Oxford University Press, 2013), 58.

5. Fredrik Petersson, "Hub of the Anti-Imperialist Movement: The League against Imperialism and Berlin, 1927–1933," *Interventions: International Journal of Postcolonial Studies* 16, no. 1 (2013): 50.

6. See Vijay Prashad, *The Darker Nations: A People's History of the Third World* (New York: New Press, 2007), 52.

7. All Latin American states (except Mexico) broke ties with Cuba by 1964. See Keller, *Mexico's Cold War*, 133. See also Vanni Pettinà, "Global Horizons: Mexico, the Third World, and the Non-Aligned Movement at the Time of the 1961 Belgrade Conference," *International History Review* 38, no. 4 (2016): 741–64.

8. Jeffrey Byrne, *Mecca of Revolution: Algeria, Decolonization, and the Third World Order* (London: Oxford University Press, 2016), 114.

9. Complaining of poor treatment at the upscale accommodation arranged for him in Manhattan, Castro eventually decided to relocate the Cuban delegation to the

Hotel Theresa in Harlem, a move that stirred up coverage in the press, resulting in the visit of several high-profile leaders in the African American community, including Malcolm X, to the hotel and partly inspiring a longer connection between Cuba and the African American civil rights movement in the United States. See Anne Garland Mahler, *From the Tricontinental to the Global South: Race, Radicalism, and Transnational Solidarity* (Durham, NC: Duke University Press, 2018), 80–81. For more on Cuba's complicated foreign policy landscape during this period, see also Margaret Randall, *Exporting Revolution: Cuba's Global Solidarity* (Durham, NC: Duke University Press, 2017), esp. chap. 5, which deals with Cuban solidarity with Africa, and Benedetta Calandra and Marina Franco, *La guerra fría cultural en América Latina* (Buenos Aires: Biblos, 2012). See also Damián J. Fernández's excellent review essay, "Fiction and Nonfiction: Problems in the Study of Cuban Foreign Policy," *Latin American Research Review* 25, no. 3 (1990): 237–47.

10. Federico Vélez, *Latin American Revolutionaries and the Arab World: From the Suez Canal to the Arab Spring* (London: Ashgate, 2016), 69. For a more engaged and longer discussion of the Latin American left's engagement with intellectual ideas from the Middle East written from the Argentine perspective, see Martín Bergel, *El oriente desplazado: Los intelectuales y los orígenes del tercermundismo en la Argentina* (Quilmes: Editorial de la Universidad de Quilmes, 2015).

11. Vélez, *Latin American Revolutionaries*, 78. Argentina signed a formal agreement in 1976 to distribute notices of the Arab Revolutionary News Agency in exchange for the greater circulation of Télam in the Middle East. Jessica Stites Mor, "The Question of Palestine in the Argentine Political Imaginary: Anti-Imperialist Thought from Cold War to Neoliberal Order," *Journal of Latin American and Iberian Research* 20, no. 2 (2014): 191. See also Conchita Dumois and Gabriel Molina, *Jorge Ricardo Masetti, el Comandante Segundo* (Havana: Editorial Capitán San Luis, 2012).

12. Vélez, *Latin American Revolutionaries*, 90.

13. Roger Faligot, *Tricontinentale: Quand Che Guevara, Ben Barka, Cabral, Castro et Hô Chi Minh préparaient la révolution mondiale (1964–1968)* (Paris: La Découverte, 2013).

14. For more on this topic, see José C. Canton Navarro and Arnaldo Silva León, *Historia de Cuba 1959–1999: Liberación nacional y socialismo* (Havana: Editorial Pueblo y Educación, 2009).

15. Patricia Calvo González, "La Organización Latinomamericana de Solidaridad (OLAS) a través del boletín de información de su comité organizador (1966–1967)," *Revista de Historia Social y de las Mentalidades* 22, no. 1 (2018). On OLAS, see Aldo Marchesi, "Revolution beyond the Sierra Maestra: The Tupamaros and the Development of a Repertoire of Dissent in the Southern Cone," *The Americas* 70, no. 3 (2014): 523–53.

16. Piero Gleijeses, *Conflicting Missions: Havana, Washington, and Africa, 1959–1976* (Chapel Hill: University of North Carolina Press, 2002), 9. See also Christine Hatzky, *Cubans in Angola: South-South Cooperation and Transfer of Knowledge, 1976–1991* (Madison: University of Wisconsin Press, 2015). For Cuban accounts, see Roger

Ricardo Luis, *Prepárense a vivir: Crónicas de Cuito Cuanavale* (Havana: Editora Política, 1989); César Gómez Chacón, *Cuito Cuanavale: Viaje al centro de los heroes* (Havana: Editorial Letras Cubanas, 1989).

17. Nelson Mandela, "Speech by President Nelson Mandela at the Banquet in Honour of President Castro of Cuba Paarl, South Africa, 4 September 1998," Robben Island, South African History Archive, 4 September 1998, https://www.sahistory.org .za/archive/speech-president-nelson-mandela-banquet-honour-president-castro-cuba -paarl-4-september-1998; Piero Gliejeses, *Visions of Freedom: Havana, Washington, Pretoria, and the Struggle for Southern Africa* (Chapel Hill: University of North Carolina Press, 2013), 25; Christine Hatzky, "Cuba's Concept of 'Internationalist Solidarity': Political Discourse, South-South Cooperation with Angola, and the Molding of Transnational Identities," in *Human Rights and Transnational Solidarity in Cold War Latin America*, ed. Jessica Stites Mor (Madison: University of Wisconsin Press, 2013), 174.

18. Lincoln Cushing, "Revolucion! Cuban Poster Art," Lahabana.com, 2011, accessed 8 April 2018, http://www.lahabana.com/content/revolucion-cuban-poster-art/. For more on Cuba's use of art in creating revolutionary consciousness, see David Craven, *Art and Revolution in Latin America, 1910–1990* (New Haven, CT: Yale University Press, 2002), 75–116. See also Lincoln Cushing, *¡Revolución! Cuban Poster Art* (San Francisco: Chronicle, 2003), and Lincoln Cushing, "Republic of Cuba, 1959," in *Communist Posters*, ed. Mary Ginsburg (London: Reaktion Books, 2020), 321–67.

19. See Melanie Herzog, "'My Art Speaks for Both My Peoples:' Elizabeth Catlett in Mexico," in *Art of Solidarity: Visual and Performative Politics in Cold War Latin America*, ed. Jessica Stites Mor and Maria del Carmen Suescun Pozas (Austin: University of Texas Press, 2018), 28.

20. David Craven, "Latin American Posters: Public Aesthetics and Mass Politics," in *Latin American Posters: Public Aesthetics and Mass Politics*, ed. Russ Davidson (Santa Fe: Museum of New Mexico Press, 2006), 16.

21. Teresa Eckmann, "The Latin American Poster: Image, Message, and Means," in *Latin American Posters: Public Aesthetics and Mass Politics*, ed. Russ Davidson (Santa Fe: Museum of New Mexico Press, 2006), 47.

22. For more on GANEFO, see Rusli Lutan and Fan Hong, "The Politics of Sport: GANEFO—A Case Study," *Sport in Society* 8, no. 3 (2011): 425–39; Terry Vaois Gitersos, "The Sport Scramble for Africa: GANEFO, the IOC, and the 1964 Africa Games," *Sport in Society* 14, no. 5 (2011): 645–59.

23. Dugald Stermer and Susan Sontag, *The Art of Revolution: 96 Posters from Cuba* (London: Pall Mall, 1970).

24. Dirk Kruijt, "Cuba and the Latin American Left: 1959–Present," *Estudios Interdisciplinarios de América Latina y el Caribe* 28, no. 2 (2017): 46.

25. Eric Zolov, "¡Cuba sí, Yanquis no! The Sacking of the Instituto Cultural México-Norteamericano in Morelia, Michoacán, 1961," in *In from the Cold: Latin America's New Encounter with the Cold War*, ed. Gilbert M. Joseph and Daniela Spenser (Durham, NC: Duke University Press, 2008), 223.

26. Hal Brands, *Latin America's Cold War* (Cambridge, MA: Harvard University Press, 2010), 25.

27. On African American suffering in the United States, see Frances Peace Sullivan, "'For the Liberty of the Nine Boys in Scottsboro and Against Yankee Imperialist Domination in Latin America': Cuba's Scottsboro Defense Campaign," *Canadian Journal of Latin American and Caribbean Studies* 38, no. 2 (2013): 282–92; Teishan A. Latner, "'Assata Shakur Is Welcome Here': Havana, Black Freedom Struggle, and U.S.-Cuba Relations," *Souls* 19, no. 4 (2017): 455–77. On colonialism in Africa, see Stephen Henighan, "The Cuban Fulcrum and the Search for a Transatlantic Revolutionary Culture in Angola, Mozambique and Chile, 1965–2008," *Journal of Transatlantic Studies* 7, no. 3 (2009): 234.

28. Carlos Moore, "Afro-Cubans Push Back," *Journal of Pan African Studies* 4, no. 2 (2010): 457–61.

29. David Kunzle, "Public Graphics in Cuba: A Very Cuban Form of Internationalist Art," *Latin American Perspectives*, 2, no. 4 (1975): 89–109.

30. For more on Norling, see Lincoln Cushing, ed., *Visions of Peace and Justice*, vol. 1, *San Francisco Bay Area, 1974–2007* (Berkeley: Inkworks Press, 2007).

31. Sílvia Cezar Miskulin, "O ano de 1968 em Cuba: Mudanças na política internacional e na política cultural," *Esboços* 15, no. 20 (2008): 47–66. See also Carlos Moore, *Castro, the Blacks, and Africa* (Los Angeles: University of California Press, 1988); Frank Guidry, *Forging Diaspora: Afro-Cubans and African Americans in a World of Empire and Jim Crow* (Chapel Hill: University of North Carolina Press, 2010).

32. Letter, Youssef El-Sebai, 12 July 1975, United Nations Archive, New York, "United Nations Representation and Participation in Meetings of the Afro-Asian Peoples' Solidarity Organization," Folder 433 (2-855), pt. 1, 2.

33. Letter, Youssef El-Sebai, Secretary General, AAPSO, United Nations Archive, New York, "United Nations Representation and Participation in Meetings of the Afro-Asian Peoples' Solidarity Organization," Folder 433 (2-855), pt. 1, Document no. 58/2/77, 3.

34. AAPSO International Meeting on Bandung and the Afro-Asian Solidarity in Commemoration of the 20th Anniversary of the Historic Bandung Conference, 13–14 April 1975, Cairo, Egypt, United Nations Archive, New York, "United Nations Representation and Participation in Meetings of the Afro-Asian Peoples' Solidarity Organization," Folder 433 (2-855), pt. 1.

35. Nicole Sarmiento, "Cuba and the South African Anti-Apartheid Struggle," *Links: International Journal of Socialist Renewal* (21 January 2010): 1–6, http://links.org.au/node/1485.

36. Edward George, *The Cuban Intervention in Africa, 1965–1991: From Che Guevara to Cuito Cuanavale* (London: Routledge, 2005), 21–22. See also Isaac Saney, "African Stalingrad: The Cuban Revolution, Internationalism, and the end of Apartheid," *Latin American Perspectives* 33, no. 5 (2006): 81–117; Hedelberto López Blanch, *Cuba: Pequeño gigante contra el apartheid* (Buenos Aires: Acercándonos Editorial, 2015).

37. Gleijeses, *Conflicting Missions*, 28.

38. Omar Jabary Salamanca, Mezna Qato, Kareem Rabie, and Sobhi Samour, "Past Is Present: Settler Colonialism in Palestine," *Settler Colonial Studies* 2, no. 1 (2012): 5.

39. Monica Popescu, "On the Margins of the Black Atlantic: Angola, the Eastern Bloc, and the Cold War," *Research in African Literatures* 45, no. 3 (2014): 93.

40. See Official Records of the Economic and Social Council, Forty-fourth Session, Supplement No. 4 (E/4475), chap. 18.

41. Salman Abu Sitta, "Che Guevara in Gaza: Palestine Becomes a Global Cause," *Middle East Monitor* (20 July 2015): 3–11. For more, see Carlos Fernando López de la Torre, "Encuentros solidarios en épocas revolucionarias: La Revolución Cubana y el Frente Sandinista de Liberación Nacional ante la causa Palestina," *Crítica y Emancipación* 7, no. 14 (2015): 45–106.

42. Fernando Camacho Padilla and Eugenia Palieraki, "*Hasta Siempre*, OSPAAAL!," *North American Congress on Latin America Report on the Americas* 51, no. 4 (2019): 415.

43. Craven, "Latin American Posters," 15.

44. Beth Hinderliter, "An International Alliance of 'Colored Humanity': Robert Williams in Asia," *Journal of Postcolonial Writing* 50, no. 4 (2014): 438. See also Lisa Brock, "Back to the Future: African-Americans and Cuba in the Time(s) of Race," *Contributions in Black Studies: A Journal of African and Afro-American Studies* 12, no. 1 (1994): 1–24; Lisa M. Corrigan, "Cross-Pollinating the Revolution: From Havana to Oakland and Back Again," *Journal of Postcolonial Writing* 50, no. 4 (2014): 452–65; Ruth Reitan, *The Rise and Decline of an Alliance: Cuba and African American Leaders in the 1960s* (East Lansing: Michigan State University Press, 1999).

45. Darío Gabriel Sánchez García, Iraida María Calzadilla Rodríguez, and Ramón Cabrales Rosabal, "Anatomía del Fotoperiodismo Cubano," *Alcance: Revista Cubana de Información y Comunicación* 8, no. 20 (2019): 104–17.

46. Randall, *Exporting Revolution*, 33.

47. Grethel Morell Otero, "Absolut Revolution: Revisitando la imagen cubana de los años 60 (1959–1969)," *Discursos fotográficos* 5, no. 7 (2009): 64.

48. Lillian Guerra, *Visions of Power in Cuba: Revolution, Redemption and Resistance, 1959–1971* (Chapel Hill: University of North Carolina Press, 2012), 318.

49. Otero, "Absolut Revolution," 70.

50. John A. Loomis, *Revolution of Forms: Cuba's Forgotten Art Schools*, 2nd ed. (Princeton, NJ: Princeton Architectural Press, 2011), 14.

51. Roberto Segre, *Diez años de arquitectura revolucionaria en Cuba* (Havana: Ediciones Union, 1969), 87.

52. For more on the film movements that inspired many Cuban filmmakers in the early 1960s, see Masha Salazkina, "Moscow-Rome-Havana: A Film-Theory Road Map," *October* 139 (2011): 97–116.

53. For a wonderful discussion of the documentary movement in Cuba during the 1960s, see Michael Chanan, *Cuban Cinema* (Minneapolis: University of Minnesota Press, 2004), 218–46; for more on Latin American filmmakers in Havana and their involvement in the ICAIC, see Julianne Burton, "Film and Revolution in Cuba: The First Twenty-Five Years," in *New Latin American Cinema*, vol. 2, *Studies of National*

Cinemas, ed. Michael T. Martin (Detroit: Wayne State University Press, 1997), 123–42; for more on the evolution of political filmmaking in the region, specifically on the role of figures like Birri and Solanas, see Jessica Stites Mor, *Transition Cinema: Political Filmmaking and the Argentine Left since 1968* (Pittsburgh: University of Pittsburgh Press, 2012).

54. For more, see Roberta Cesana, *"Libri necessary": Le edizioni letterarie Feltrinelli (1955–1965)* (Milan: Edizioni Unicopli, 2010); Gabriela Torregrosa, "François Maspero, retrato de un editor," *Trama and Texturas* 28 (2015): 113–22.

55. See Ekchardt Breitinger, "Lamentations Patriotiques: Writers, Censors, and Politics in Cameroon," *African Affairs* 92 (1993): 557–75; Phillis Taoua, "The Anti-Colonial Archive: France and Africa's Unfinished Business," *SubStance* 32 (2003): 146–64.

56. *Tricontinental* 1 (1967): cover, 1–28, Archive of the OSPAAAL, Havana, Cuba.

57. *Tricontinental* 2 (1967): 43, Archive of the OSPAAAL, Havana, Cuba.

58. *Tricontinental* 6 (1968): 6; *Tricontinental* 2 (1967), 41, 43, 45, 47; *Tricontinental* 7 (1968), 92, Archive of the OSPAAAL, Havana, Cuba.

59. *Tricontinental* 3 (1967): 162–63, 165, 167, Archive of the OSPAAAL, Havana, Cuba.

60. *Tricontinental* 4–5 (1968): 52; *Tricontinental* 7 (1968): 118, 132, Archive of the OSPAAAL, Havana, Cuba.

61. *Tricontinental* 3 (1967): 65–68, Archive of the OSPAAAL, Havana, Cuba.

62. *Tricontinental* 4–5 (1968): 76; *Tricontinental* 8 (1968): 88; *Tricontinental* 13 (1969): 58; *Tricontinental* 15 (1969): 134, 137, Archive of the OSPAAAL, Havana, Cuba.

63. *Tricontinental* 18 (1970): 20, 22, Archive of the OSPAAAL, Havana, Cuba.

64. *Tricontinental* 4–5 (1968): 82, 86, 88, 90; *Tricontinental* 7 (1968): 147; *Tricontinental* 8 (1968): 18, 20, 22, 24, 26, 28, 30, 32, 34, Archive of the OSPAAAL, Havana, Cuba.

65. *Tricontinental* 6 (1968): 22, Archive of the OSPAAAL, Havana, Cuba.

66. *Tricontinental* 6 (1968): 26, 28, 30, Archive of the OSPAAAL, Havana, Cuba.

67. *Tricontinental* 6 (1968): 38, 40, Archive of the OSPAAAL, Havana, Cuba.

68. Amílcar Cabral, "Decididos a resistir," *Tricontinental* 8 (1968): 114–26, Archive of the OSPAAAL, Havana, Cuba.

69. *Tricontinental* 10 (1969): Archive of the OSPAAAL, Havana, Cuba.

70. Basil Davidson, "Los mercenarios del imperio," *Tricontinental* 11 (1969): 31–43, Archive of the OSPAAAL, Havana, Cuba.

71. *Tricontinental* 11 (1969): 34–36, Archive of the OSPAAAL, Havana, Cuba.

72. *Tricontinental* 12 (1969): front inside cover, Archive of the OSPAAAL, Havana, Cuba.

73. *Tricontinental* 23 (1971): front inside cover; *Tricontinental* 18 (1970): 97–100, Archive of the OSPAAAL, Havana, Cuba.

74. *Tricontinental* 2 (1967): 174–79, Archive of the OSPAAAL, Havana, Cuba.

75. *Tricontinental* 9 (1968): 116–19, Archive of the OSPAAAL, Havana, Cuba.

76. *Tricontinental* 13 (1969): 149–55, Archive of the OSPAAAL, Havana, Cuba.

77. See, for example, *Tricontinental* 7 (1968): 84, 150; *Tricontinental* 10 (1969): 98, 99, 102, 103, Archive of the OSPAAAL, Havana, Cuba.

78. *Tricontinental* 12 (1969): 97–120, Archive of the OSPAAAL, Havana, Cuba.

79. See, for example, *Tricontinental* 7 (1968): inside cover; *Tricontinental* 12 (1969): inside back cover; *Tricontinental* 15 (1969): inside back cover; *Tricontinental* 16 (1970): inside back cover; *Tricontinental* 17 (1970): 118–35, Archive of the OSPAAAL, Havana, Cuba. Margaret Peacock has illustrated the use of similar strategies in the Soviet Union in *Innocent Weapons: The Soviet and American Politics of Childhood in the Cold War* (Chapel Hill: University of North Carolina Press, 2014).

80. Lani Hanna, "Tricontinental's International Solidarity: Emotion in OSPAAAL as Tactic to Catalyze Support of Revolution," *Radical History Review* 136 (2020): 171.

81. *Tricontinental* 1 (1967): 5, Archive of the OSPAAAL, Havana, Cuba.

82. *Tricontinental* 26 (1971): 50, 52, Archive of the OSPAAAL, Havana, Cuba.

83. For more on the closure and legacy, see Camacho Padilla and Palieraki, "*Hasta Siempre*, OSPAAAL!"

84. *Tricontinental* 14 (1969): 42–82, Archive of the OSPAAAL, Havana, Cuba.

85. See, for instance, *Tricontinental* 11 (1969): 106, Archive of the OSPAAAL, Havana, Cuba. *Tricontinental* 14 (1969): 118, also has a reprint of a poster in solidarity with pan-Arabism featuring an ancient Egyptian hieroglyph of a seated woman bearing, instead of a spear, what appears to be a grenade launcher, with grenades and bullets.

86. See, with respect to Bolivia for example, *Tricontinental* 19–20 (1970): 110; in the same issue, with respect to Vietnam and Palestine, the inside back cover and back cover, Archive of the OSPAAAL, Havana, Cuba.

87. Helen Yaffe, *We Are Cuba! How a Revolutionary People Have Survived in a Post-Soviet World* (New Haven, CT: Yale University Press, 2020), 78. See also Myra Ann Houser, "Avenging Carlota in Africa: Angola and the Memory of Cuban Slavery," *Atlantic Studies* 12, no. 1 (2015): 50–66.

88. United Nations Press Section, Office of Public Information, "Statement by Secretary-General to Conference on Economic Co-operation among Developing Countries," United Nations Archives, New York, Series 273, Box 19, File 14, 1–5, 1.

89. Robert Self, "'To Plan Our Liberation': Black Power and the Politics of Place in Oakland, California, 1965–1977," *Journal of Urban History* 26, no. 6 (2000): 767. See also Cynthia A. Young, "Havana up in Harlem: LeRoi Jones, Harold Cruse and the Making of a Cultural Revolution," *Science and Society* 65, no. 1 (2001): 12–38.

90. Anne Garland Mahler, "The Global South in the Belly of the Beast: Viewing African American Civil Rights through a Tricontinental Lens," *Latin American Research Review* 50, no. 1 (2015): 95–116. Mahler refers to the work of Robert J. C. Young while suggesting that even current postcolonial theory can trace its origins to tricontinentalism through this vehicle. Robert J. C. Young, "Postcolonialism: From Bandung to the Tricontinental," *Historein* 5 (2005): 11–21.

91. This perspective has been common among scholars writing about Latin American involvement in Third Worldist institutions, conferences, and organizations

in the 1970s, and their collective pessimism is articulated well by Hugo Celso Felipe Mansilla, "Latin America within the Third World: The Search for a New Identity, the Acceptance of Old Contents," *Ibero-amerikanisches Archiv* 11, no. 2 (1985): 171–91.

92. For the full text of this speech translated into English, see "At the United Nations: October 12, 1979," speech of Fidel Castro Ruz, in *Fidel Castro Speeches: Cuba's Internationalist Foreign Policy, 1975–80*, ed. Michael Traber (Montreal: Pathfinder, 1981), 235–73. See also Corinne A. Pernet, "Shifting Position to the Global South: Latin America's Initiatives in the Early Years at the United Nations," in *Latin America 1810–2010: Dreams and Legacies*, ed. Claude Auroi and Aline Helg (London: Imperial College Press, 2011), 83–100.

Chapter 3. For Palestine in Argentina

1. Ted Swedenberg, "Bad Rep for a Neck Scarf?," *International Journal of Middle East Studies* 49, no. 1 (2009): 184–85.

2. Flyer, "Palestinos y argentinos: Los mismos enemigos, la misma lucha," Movimiento al Socialismo (Argentina) (MAS), 9 April 2002, "Politics in Argentina, 1943–2004, II," Box 2, Folder 2 of "Political Parties, Organizations and Movements," Princeton University collection of Latin American Political Ephemera, Dulles Library.

3. Sara Awartani, "In Solidarity: Palestine in the Puerto Rican Political Imaginary," *Radical History Review* 128 (2017): 215.

4. Alan O'Connor, "Punk Subculture in Mexico and the Anti-globalization Movement: A Report from the Front," *New Political Science* 25, no. 1 (2003): 46.

5. Jorge Nállim, "Del antifascismo al antiperonismo: Argentina Libre, Antinazi y el surgimiento del antiperonismo político e intelectual," in *Fascismo y antifascismo. Peronismo y antiperonismo. Conflictos políticos e ideológicos en la Argentina (1930–1955)*, ed. Marcela García Sebastiani (Madrid: Iberoamericana Vervuert, 2006); Mariano Plotkin and Ricardo González Leandri, eds., *Localismo y globalización: Apuntes para una historia de los intelectuales en Iberoamérica* (Madrid: Consejo Superior de Investigaciones Científicas, Instituto de Historia, 2000).

6. Ana Patricia Rodríguez uses the concept of "fiction finding" to help illustrate the concept of narrative construction in her work *Dividing the Isthmus: Central American Transnational Histories, Literatures and Cultures* (Austin: University of Texas Press, 2009), 11.

7. For greater detail on the origins of the Arab Argentine community, see Lily Pearl Balloffet, *Argentina in the Global Middle East* (Palo Alto, CA: Stanford University Press, 2020).

8. Palestinians fleeing the Six-Day War challenged this image of the Argentina-based diaspora, as for instance, in the two Gaza refugees accused of shooting at the Israeli embassy in Asunción, Paraguay, in 1970, whose trial revealed much about the dynamics of the Syrian-Lebanese diaspora's reactions to Palestinian militancy. See John Tofik Karam, "On the Trail and Trial of Palestinian Diaspora: Mapping South America

in the Arab-Israeli Conflict, 1967–1972," *Journal of Latin American Studies* 45, no. 4 (2013): 751–77.

9. For more on this topic, see Steven Hyland, "Margins of the Majar: Arabic-Speaking Immigrants in Argentina, 1880–1946" (PhD diss., Ohio State University, 2011).

10. Martín Bergel, *El oriente desplazado: Los intelectuales y los orígenes del tercermundismo en la Argentina* (Bernal: Universidad Nacional de Quilmes Editorial, 2015).

11. For more discussion of Latin America's response to the Palestine question at the United Nations, see Cecília Baeza, "América latina y la cuestión palestina (1947–2012)," *Araucaria* 14, no. 28 (2011): 111–31.

12. Raanan Rein, "Political Considerations and Personal Rivalries: Peronist Argentina and the Partition of Palestine," *Diplomacy and Statecraft* 8, no. 2 (1997): 125–47; Aaron Klieman, *Israel's Global Reach: Arms Sales as Diplomacy* (Oxford: Pergamon-Brassey, 1985); Ignacio Klich, "Arms for the Middle East and Argentina's Efforts at a Balances Approach to the Arab World and Israel," *Diplomacy and Statecraft* 7, no. 3 (1996): 704–28; Ignacio Klich and Jefferey Lesser, eds., *Arab and Jewish Immigrants in Latin America: Images and Reality* (London: Cass, 1998); Christina Civantos, *Between Argentines and Arabs: Argentine Orientalism, Arab Immigrants, and the Writing of History* (New York: State University of New York Press, 2006).

13. Balloffet, *Argentina in the Global Middle East*, 141.

14. Ignacio Klich, "The Chimera of Palestinian Resettlement in Argentina in the Early Aftermath of the First Arab-Israeli War and Other Similarly Fantastic Notions," *The Americas* 53, no. 1 (1996): 15–43. This possible solution to Palestinian displacement was also proposed after the Six-Day War; see Nur Masalha, "The 1967 Palestinian Exodus," in *The Palestinian Exodus, 1948–1998*, ed. Ghada Karmi and Eugene Coltran (Reading, UK: Ithaca Press, 1999), 63–108.

15. Adnan Musallam, "Palestinian Diaspora in Latin America: The Formative Stages, 19th Century to Early 20th Century," lecture, Bethlehem University, West Bank, 2006.

16. Ruben Sinay, *La verdad sobre el conflicto en el cercano oriente* (Buenos Aires: Editorial Documentos, 1967), Archivo Partido Comunista, Buenos Aires, Argentina. See also Ezequiel Fiszerman, "Entre Moscú y Europa: Israel como caso crítico de la vía socialista en la Argentina, 1946–1956," in *Israel-Palestine, una passion Argentina: Estudios sobre la recepción del conflicto árabe-israelí en la Argentina*, ed. Emmanual N. Kahan (Buenos Aires: Prometeo, 2016), 96.

17. Avner Yaniv, *P.L.O.: A Profile* (Jerusalem: Israel Universities Study Group for Middle Eastern Affairs, Attali Print Office, 1974), 5; Itamar Rabinovich, *Waging Peace: Israel and the Arabs, 1948–2003* (Princeton, NJ: Princeton University Press, 2004), 3.

18. "La crisis en el cercano: Confabulación imperialista," *Nuestra palabra*, no. 882 (30 May 1967), Archivo Partido Comunista, Buenos Aires Argentina.

19. See "Cuba: El alejamiento del Che Guevara y la cuestión de los exilados," *Palabra Obrera* 5 (January–February 1966): 27; "Cuba: La lucha contra la burocracia, una tarea decisiva," *Política Obrera* 7 (March 1968): 22–32; Centro de Documentación e Investigación de la Cultura de Izquierdas, Buenos Aires, Argentina. The PO was first

organized in 1964 as the Política Obrera; later, *Política Obrera* was also the title of one of the party's many periodicals, this one focused on trade union news.

20. Osvaldo Coggiola, *Historia del Trotskismo en Argentina y América Latina* (Buenos Aires: Ediciones Razón y Revolución, 2006), 198.

21. "El social imperialismo de la iqzuierda israeli," *Política Obrera* (26 June 1967): 5–6, Centro de Documentación e Investigación de la Cultura de Izquierdas, Buenos Aires, Argentina.

22. "La crisis en medio oriente," *Política Obrera* (19 July 1967): 4–5, 8, Centro de Documentación e Investigación de la Cultura de Izquierdas, Buenos Aires, Argentina.

23. Laura Schenquer and Liliana Mayer, "Tancerca y tanlejos: Israel en la mira de la prensa judeo-argentina durante la guerra deYom Kipur (1973)," in *Israel-Palestina: Una pasión argentina: Estudios sobre la recepción del conflicto árabe-israelí en la Argentina*, ed. Emmanuel N. Kahan (Buenos Aires: Prometeo, 2016), 155.

24. Maximiliano Jozami, "Argentine Left Parties and the 1967 Six-Day War through the Prism of Global Networks and South-South Connections," *Jahrbuch für Geschichte Lateinamerikas—Anuario de Historia de América Latina* 56 (2019): 28, 34.

25. Jeffrey Byrne, *Mecca of Revolution: Algeria, Decolonization, and the Third World Order* (London: Oxford University Press, 2016), 12.

26. Yaniv, *P.L.O.*, 41–42.

27. William R. Garner, "The Sino-Soviet Ideological Struggle in Latin America," *Journal of Inter-American Studies* 10, no. 2 (1968): 244–55. See also Jorge Castañeda, *Utopia Unarmed: The Latin American Left after the Cold War* (New York: Vintage, 1993); Jozami, "Argentine Left Parties," 18; "El conflicto cubano-chino," *Estragetia* 5 (April 1966): 6, Centro de Documentación e Investigación de la Cultura de Izquierdas, Buenos Aires, Argentina.

28. For a more detailed analysis of the international political dimension of the relations between Latin America and the Middle East, see Fehmy Saddy, ed., *Arab-Latin American Relations* (New Brunswick, NJ: Transaction, 1983); Regina Sharif, "Latin America and the Arab-Israeli Conflict," *Journal of Palestine Studies* 7, no. 1 (1977): 98–122.

29. Joseph Massad, "Conceiving the Masculine: Gender and Palestinian Nationalism," *Middle East Journal* 49, no. 3 (1995): 478.

30. Intelligence Report, Central Intelligence Agency, "The Sino-Soviet Split within Communist Movement in Latin America," ESAU 28, TS no. 196753, 15 June 1967, released 2007.

31. "¿Que hay detrás del complicito arabe israeli? Declaración del Comité Central del Partido Comunista," Buenos Aires, 7 June 1967, Archivo del Partido Comunista, Buenos Aires, Argentina.

32. Correspondence, Box 78, Folder "Varios resoluciones, Years 1958–1975," 1966, Archivo del Partido Comunista, Buenos Aires, Argentina.

33. Ambassador Abdel Khalek Hassouna, Secretary General of the League of Arab States, *A Short Guide to the League of Arab States* (Arab League Press and Information Department, 1965), 34–35.

34. "Hoy y aquí," *Nuestra Palabra*, no. 887 (4 July 1967), 1, Archivo del Partido Comunista, Buenos Aires, Argentina.

35. Report, "Informe sobre la posición a tomar con respecto al sionismo y problemática judia," Box 78, Folder "Varios resoluciones, Years 1958–1975," 1972, Archivo del Partido Comunista, Buenos Aires, Argentina.

36. Juan Abugattas, "The Perception of the Palestinian Question in Latin America," *Journal of Palestine Studies* 11, no. 3 (1982): 117–28.

37. Estela Valverde, "The Question of 'Argentinidad': The Self-Image of Arab and Jewish Ancestry in Recent Argentine Literature," in *Arab and Jewish Immigrants in Latin America: Images and Reality*, ed. Ignacio Klich and Jefferey Lesser (London: Cass, 1998), 189–203; Sergio Waisman, "*A Thousand and One Nights* in Argentina: Translation, Narrative and Politics in Borges, Puig, and Piglia," *Comparative Literature Studies* 40, no. 4 (2003): 351–71.

38. Malek Khoury, "Origins and Patterns in the Discourse of New Arab Cinema," *Arab Studies Quarterly* 27, nos. 1–2 (2005): 1–20.

39. Enrique Dickmann, *La Infiltración nazi-fascista en la Arentina* (Buenos Aires: Ediciones Sociales Argentinas, 1939), Centro de Documentación e Investigación de la Cultura de Izquierdas, Fondo Familia Dickmann. See also Enrique Dickmann, "Rindióse homenaje al Estado de Israel en la Casa del Pueblo," *El Socialista* 1, no. 4 (15 June 1948). For an analysis of orientalism in Dickmann's writings, see Maximiliano Jozami and Agustín Fertonani, "Un caso de orientalismo en la izquierda argentina: El Partido Socialista frente a la creación del Estado de Isarel," *CONTRA/RELATOS desde el Sur* 6, no. 7 (2010): 45–60.

40. Rodlofo Ghioldi, "El Gran octubre y su influencia en la argentina," Pamplet, Buenos Aires, 1977, NACLA papers, Princeton University. See also Ricardo Martínez Mazzola, "*Los Recuerdos de un militante socialista*, de Enrique Dickmann," *Políticas de la Memoria* 17 (Summer 2016–17): 44; Raanan Rein, *Populism and Ethnicity: Peronism and the Jews of Argentina* (Montreal: McGill-Queen's University Press, 2020), 130–31.

41. Mercedes Saborido, "El Partido Comunista Argentino y la Guerra de los Seis Días," *Revista Izquierdas* (12 April 2012): 68.

42. Lily Pearl Balloffet, "Argentine & Egyptian History Entangled: From Perón to Nasser," *Journal of Latin American Studies* 50, no. 3 (August 2018): 569.

43. Emmanuel N. Kahan, "Algunos usos del conflicto en Israel-Palestina en Argentina: Debates entorno al conflicto árabe-israelí entre el tercer peronismo y la última dictadura militar (1973–1983)," *Revista Nuevosmundos, Mundos nuevos* (2014), https://journals.openedition.org/nuevomundo/66778.

44. The Montoneros published a clandestine periodical, *Evita Montonera*, from 1975 to 1979.

45. *Militancia* 1, no. 29 (27 December 1973): 12–17.

46. *Militancia* 2, no. 33 (31 January 1974): 42–43, 47.

47. *Militancia* 2, no. 37 (14 March 1974): 30.

48. Movimiento Estudiantil, Federación Universitaria Argentina, n.d., NACLA papers, Princeton University.

49. "Ex-Pres. Juan Perón Denounces Anti-Zionist Ads in Argentine Press," *Daily News Bulletin* 39, no. 51 (14 March 1972), available through the Jewish Telegraphic Agency, http://pdfs.jta.org/1972/1972-03-14_051.pdf.

50. For more on this topic, see María Fernanda Alle, "Tuñón contra Borges: La division campo antiperonista en la segunda mitad de la década de 1950," *Acta Literaria* 59 (2019), https://scielo.conicyt.cl/scielo.php?script=sci_arttext&pid=S0717-68482019000200075; Luis Roniger and Leonardo Senkman, "Conspirationism, Synarchism, and the Long Shadow of Perón," *Journal of Modern Jewish Studies* 17, no. 4 (2018): 434–54.

51. John and Janet Wallach Papers, Princeton University Firestone Library, MC 220, Box 1, Folder "Background of PLO and Occupied Territories." Historian Jeffrey Lesser has written extensively about the Brazil UN vote.

52. Ivan Ivanovich Kovalenko and Rais Abdulkhakovich Tuzmukhamedov, *The Non-Aligned Movement: The Soviet View* (New York: Sterling, 1987), 59.

53. Jozami, "Argentine Left Parties," 23.

54. In her fascinating study of anti-Zionist Jewish youth activism, Beatrice Gurwitz describes this phenomenon as a "game of mirrors," an identity development process triggered by destabilizing metanarratives of the Cold War. See Beatrice Gurwitz, "From the New World to the Third World: Generation, Politics, and the Making of Argentine Jewish Ethnicity, 1955–1983" (PhD diss., University of California, Berkeley, 2012).

55. *Etgar Desafío*, no. 2 (July 1971), Archive of the Jabotinsky Institute, Tel Aviv, Israel.

56. *Etgar Desafío*, no. 2 (July 1971): 31–35, Archive of the Jabotinsky Institute, Tel Aviv, Israel.

57. *Etgar Desafío*, no. 4 (July 1972), inside front cover, Archive of the Jabotinsky Institute, Tel Aviv, Israel.

58. *Primera Plana*, 10 March 1964, 6.

59. *Leoplan* 18 IV, Central Zionist Archive, Jerusalem, Israel, 21.

60. Yaniv, *P.L.O.*, 43.

61. Neil C. Livingstone and David Halevy, *Inside the PLO: Covert Units, Secret Funds and the War against Israel and the United States* (New York: William Morrow, 1990), 141.

62. See also the excellent collection of essays edited by Emmanuel N. Kahan, *Israel-Palestina: Una pasión argentina: Estudios sobre la recepción del conflicto árabe-israelí en la Argentina* (Buenos Aires: Prometeo, 2016).

63. Michael Goebel, "A Movement from Right to Left in Argentine Nationalism? The Alianza Libertadora Nacionalista and Tacuara as Stages of Militancy," *Bulletin of Latin American Research* 26, no. 3 (2007): 362, 364.

64. Daniel Gutman, *Tacuara, historia de la primera guerrilla urbana argentina* (Buenos Aires: Ediciones B Argentina, 2003), 126.

65. Eduardo Weisz, *El PRT-ERP: Nueva Izquierda e Izquierda Tradicional*, 2nd ed., Cuaderno de Trabajo 30 (Buenos Aires: Centro Cultural de la Cooperación, 2004), 66.

See also Eduardo Weisz, *El PRT-ERP: Claves para una interpretación de su singularidad: Marxismo, internacionalismo y classismo* (Buenos Aires: Centro Cultural de la Cooperación, 2006), Ibero-Amerikanisches Institut, Berlin.

66. Gutman, *Tacuara*, 130.

67. Claudia Hilb and Daniel Lutzky, *La nueva izquierda argentina: 1960–1980 (Política y violencia)* (Buenos Aires: Centro Editor de América Latina, 1984), 19, 24, 43.

68. Paul Chamberlin, *The Global Offensive* (London: Oxford University Press, 2012), 19.

69. Chamberlin, *Global Offensive*, 64.

70. *Montoneros, El movimiento Peronista*, English-language solidarity pamphlet, 1977, 2, "Politics in Argentina, 1943–2004, II," Box 2, Folder 2 of "Political Parties, Organizations and Movements," Princeton University collection of Latin American Political Ephemera, Dulles Library.

71. Ibid.

72. Gustavo Vaca Narvaja and Fernando Frugoni, *Fernando Vaca Narvaja: Con igual ánimo, pensamiento político y biografía autorizada* (Buenos Aires: Colihue, 2002). For more on this, see Pablo Robledo, *Montoneros y Palestina* (Buenos Aires: Planeta Argentina, 2018).

73. Hilb and Lutzky, *La nueva izquierda argentina*, 156–57. For more on the Sandinistas and the PLO, see Federico Vélez, *Latin American Revolutionaries and the Arab World: From the Suez Canal to the Arab Spring* (New York: Routledge, 2017), 100–131.

74. Hilb and Lutzky, *La nueva izquierda argentina*, 158.

75. Héctor Germán Oesterheld and Leopoldo Durñona, *Latinoamérica y el Imperialismo: 450 años de Guerra, recopilación de la historieta aperecida entre 1973 y 1974 en el semanario "El Descamisado"* (Buenos Aires: Doeyo y Viniegra Editores, 2004), i.

76. Ibid., ii. All of Oesterheld's daughters were also killed by the Argentine state; two of them were pregnant at the time of their abduction.

77. Edward S. Milkenky, *Argentina's Foreign Policies* (Boulder, CO: Westview, 1978), 161–62. Under Isabel, relations soured, as Argentina failed to condemn Israel as racist at the 1975 NAM meeting in Lima and went on to purchase an Israeli ship-to-ship missile.

78. Ibid., 163–64.

79. David Sheinin, "Reading Kissinger's Avatars: Cold War Pragmatism in Argentina's Middle East Policy," in *The New Jewish Argentina*, ed. Raanan Rein and Adriana Brodsky (Boston: Brill, 2012), 270.

80. Gabriel Sued, "Vivir en un plan de lucha permanente," *La Nación*, 23 September 2012, https://www.lanacion.com.ar/politica/vivir-en-un-plan-de-lucha-permanente-nidi510997.

81. See "La Declaración de San Pablo (Brasil)," *Estudios Palestinos* 1, no. 1 (July–September 1984): 154–79.

82. Born into a Muslim family, Menem converted to Catholicism to pursue his political ambitions. In 1966, however, he married a Muslim woman in an Islamic ceremony.

83. See Carlos Escudé and Beatriz Gurevich, "Transnational Terrorism, Corruption and Erosion of State Authority: The Case of the 1992 and 1994 Attacks in Argentina," *Estudios Interdisciplinarios de América Latina* 4, no. 2 (2003): 127–48.

84. "Documentos Apropoados IV Congreso Nacional de la Corriente Patria Libre," 7 September 2003, 2, "Politics in Argentina, 1943–2004, II," Box 2, Folder 2 of "Political Parties, Organizations and Movements," Princeton University collection of Latin American Political Ephemera, Dulles Library.

85. *Socialismo o barbarie* 1, no. 1 (June 2000): cover, "Politics in Argentina, 1943–2004, II," Box 2, Folder 2 of "Political Parties, Organizations and Movements," Princeton University collection of Latin American Political Ephemera, Dulles Library.

86. Roberto Ramírez, "La justa ira de un pueblo ultrajado," *Socialismo o barbarie* 1, no. 4 (November 2000): 37, "Politics in Argentina, 1943–2004, II," Box 2, Folder 2 of "Political Parties, Organizations and Movements," Princeton University collection of Latin American Political Ephemera, Dulles Library.

87. Ibid., 39.

88. Ibid., 42.

89. Ibid., 44.

90. See Miguel Lamas, "Israel: Un Estado Genocida," *Alternativa socialista* 327 (10 April 2002): 6; Migel Lamas, "Escalada terrorista israelí," *Alternativa socialista* 325 (13 March 2002): 11, both in "Politics in Argentina, 1943–2004, II," Box 2, Folder 2 of "Political Parties, Organizations and Movements," Princeton University collection of Latin American Political Ephemera, Dulles Library.

91. Flyer, "Palestinos y argentinos: Los mismos enemigos, la misma lucha," MAS, 9 April 2002, "Politics in Argentina, 1943–2004, II," Box 2, Folder 2 of "Political Parties, Organizations and Movements," Princeton University collection of Latin American Political Ephemera, Dulles Library.

92. Bishara Bahbah, "Israel's Military Relationship with Ecuador and Argentina," *Journal of Palestine Studies* 15, no. 2 (1986): 76–101; Bishara Bahbah and Linda Butler, *Israel and Latin America: The Military Connection* (New York: St. Martin's, 1986); Benjamin Beit-Hallahmi, *The Israeli Connection: Who Israel Arms and Why* (London: Tauris, 1987); Milton Jamail and Margo Gutiérrez, *It's No Secret: Israel's Military Involvement in Central America* (Belmont, MA: American-Arab University Graduates Press, 1986); Jan Pieterse, "State Terrorism on a Global Scale: The Role of Israel," *Crime and Social Justice* 21/22 (1984): 58–80; Cheryl Rubernberg, "Israeli Foreign Policy in Central America," *Third World Quarterly* 8, no. 3 (1986): 896–915.

93. Miguel Lamas, "Israel: Un Estado Genocida" and "¡Fuera el ejército Israelí!," *Alternativa socialista* 327 (10 April 2002): 6–7, "Politics in Argentina, 1943–2004, II," Box 2, Folder 2 of "Political Parties, Organizations and Movements," Princeton University collection of Latin American Political Ephemera, Dulles Library. The PO also spearheaded the Movement for the Refoundation of the Fourth International, launching a conference in Buenos Aires in 2004, which included Partido Obrero Revolucionario from Chile, the Grupo de Acción Revolucionaria from Mexico, the Uruguayan

Partido de los Trabajadores, and Venezuela's Opción Obrera, along with parties from Europe.

94. "No a la agresión imperialista contra los pueblos árabes," *Quebracho* 5, no. 28 (October 2001): 14–15, "Politics in Argentina, 1943–2004, II," Box 2, Folder 2 of "Political Parties, Organizations and Movements," Princeton University collection of Latin American Political Ephemera, Dulles Library.

95. Pablo Abiad, "Esteche, el líder de Quebracho, fue procesado y sigue detenido," *Clarín*, 21 April 2007.

96. Cynthia y Sol, *El clave rojo*, September 2001, 3–7.

97. Carlos Marcelo Shäferstein, "Humberto Tumini," *Periodismo de verdad*, 27 July 2009, http://www.periodismodeverdad.com.ar/2009/07/27/humberto-tumini-el -paradigma-de-un-terrorista-que-se-desprendio-del-"kirchnerismo"-por-el-dr-carlos -marcelo-shaferstein/.

98. Humberto Tumini, "Gran Acto Popular, 17 años de Patria Libre," *En Marcha* 18, no. 217 (November 2004): 1, 6.

99. Claudia Cinatti, "Abajo la masacre de Sharon," *La Verdad Obrera*, 29 May 2004, 11.

100. Nicole Saffie Guevara and Lorenzo Agar Corbinos, "A Century of Palestinian Immigration to Chile: A Successful Integration," in *Latin American with Palestinian Roots*, ed. Viola Raheb (Beit Lahemk: Diyar Publishers, 2012), 63–80.

101. Juan Antonio Pacheco, "La prensa árabe en chile: Sueños y realidades árabes en un mundo nuevo," *Miscelánea de Estudios Árabes y Hebraicos, Sección Árabe-Islam* 55 (2006): 313. See also Lorenzo Agar Corbinos, "El comportamiento urbano de los migrantes árabes en Chile," *Revista EURE—Revista De Estudios Urbano Regionales* 9, no. 27 (1983): 73–84; Heba El-Attar, "Palestinian and Jewish Communal Press in Chile: The Case of Al-Damir and La Palabra Israelita," *Latin American and Caribbean Ethnic Studies* 6, no. 2 (2011): 189–206.

102. Antonia Rebolledo Hernández, "La 'Turcofobia': Discriminación anti-árabe en Chile, 1900–1950," *Historia* 28 (1994): 269.

103. Nadim Bawalsa, "Palestine West of the Andes," *NACLA Report on the Americas* 50, no. 1 (2018): 34–39.

104. Ceclia Baeza, "Palestinians in Latin America: Between Assimilation and Long-Distance Nationalism," *Journal of Palestine Studies* 43, no. 2 (2014): 61.

105. Brenda Elsey, *Citizens and Sportsmen: Fútbol and Politics in Twentieth-Century Chile* (Austin: University of Texas Press, 2011), 153.

106. "Solidaridad pasa a primer plano," *El Siglo*, 15 June 1968, 2, Archivo Nacional de Chile, Santiago, Chile; Peter Winn, *Weavers of Revolution: The Yarur Workers and Chile's Road to Socialism* (New York: Oxford University Press, 1989), 28.

107. The communist paper *El Siglo* kept close tabs on the reputation of Allende's reforms across the region: "Admiración mundial por el ejemplo de democracia que brinda Chile," *El Siglo*, 27 October 1970, 3; "Fidel: Chile lo recibira con los brazos abiertos," *El Siglo*, 8 November 1971, 1; Sergio Villegas, "Cuba y Chile: El gran abrazo

de la amistad," *El Siglo*, 2 January 1973, 7; "Cuba: Trabajadores aprueban solidaridad con Chile," *El Siglo*, 30 December 1972, 11; "Venezeula: La 'Nueva Fuerza' llama a solidarizar con Chile," *El Siglo*, 29 August 1972, 13; "Venezuela es solidaria de Chile," *El Siglo*, 8 February 1973, 16, Archivo Nacional de Chile, Santiago, Chile.

108. Joaquín Fermandois Huerta, "De una inserción a otra: Política exterior de Chile, 1966–1991," *Estudios Internacionales* 24, no. 96 (1991): 437. See also Alfredo Riquelme Segovia, "Los modelos revolucionarios y el naufraio de la vía chilena al socialismo," *Nuevo Mundo/Mundos Nuevos*, 27 January 2007, https://doi.org/10.4000/nuevomundo.10603.

109. Ashley Black, "Canto Libre: Folk Music and Solidarity in the Americas," in *The Art of Solidarity: Visual and Performative Politics in Cold War Latin America*, ed. Jessica Stites Mor and Maria del Carmen Suescun Pozas (Austin: University of Texas Press, 2018), 130–31. See also J. Patrice McSherry, *Chilean New Song: The Political Power of Music, 1960s–1973* (Philadelphia: Temple University Press, 2015). Examples of leftist news stories include "Nuevas manifestaciones de solidaridad con Vietnam," *El Siglo*, 13 May 1972, 7; "Chile entero repudia crímenes yanquis contra Vietnam," *El Siglo*, 19 December 1969, 9; "El pueblo chileno y el pueblo vietnamita," *El Siglo*, 3 May 1968, 2; "Volodia: 'Vietnam es también nuestra causa,'" *El Siglo*, 21 February 1968, 7; "Impresionante fue acto de solidaridad con Vietnam," *El Siglo*, 21 February 1968, 3; "Mañana cita de honor en solidaridad con Vietnam," *El Siglo*, 19 February 1968, 3; "Se crea fondo nacional de ayuda a Vietnam," *El Siglo*, 17 May 1972, 3, Archivo Nacional de Chile, Santiago, Chile.

110. "A reforzar la solidaridad con los pueblos arabes llamo el PCUS," *El Siglo*, 13 April 1971, 8; "La URSS continuara apoyando la justa causa de los pueblos árabes," *El Siglo*, 13 October 1971, 9, Archivo Nacional de Chile, Santiago, Chile.

111. Heba El-Attar, "Memorias acusticas palestino-chilenas: El caso de 'Palestina por Siempre,'" *Miscelánea de Estudios Árabes y Hebraicos, Sección Árabe-Islam* 68 (2019): 445–46.

112. "Guerrilleros palestinos atacan objectivo militar," *El Siglo*, 23 February 1970, 3; "Guerrilleros libran recias batallas contra tropas israelis," *El Siglo*, 18 February 1970, 3, Archivo Nacional de Chile, Santiago, Chile.

113. Union Nacional Arabe de Chile, "El Problema palestino, es problema de todo el mundo árabe," paid insert, *El Siglo*, 15 May 1970, 9, Archivo Nacional de Chile, Santiago, Chile.

114. Siri Schwabe, "Paradoxes of Erasure: Palestinian Memory and the Politics of Forgetting in Post-Dictatorship Chile," *Interventions* 20, no. 5 (2018): 657.

115. Ibid., 663.

116. David Lloyd and Laura Pulido, "In the Long Shadow of the Settler: On Israeli and U.S. Colonialisms," *American Quarterly* 62, no. 4 (2010): 792.

117. Ibid., 800.

118. David Featherstone, *Solidarity: Hidden Histories and Geographies of Internationalism* (London: Zed Books, 2012), 5.

119. Vélez, *Latin American Revolutionaries*, 172.

Chapter 4. Liberation Theology and Apartheid

1. Christian Smith, *Disruptive Religion: The Force of Faith in Social Movement Activism* (New York: Routledge, 1996).

2. Catalina Romero, "Globalization, Civil Society and Religion from a Latin American Standpoint," *Sociology of Religion* 62, no. 4 (Winter 2001): 475–90.

3. Paddy Kearney, *Guardian of the Light: Denis Hurley, Renewing the Church, Opposing Apartheid* (New York: Continuum, 2009), 108. See also Xavier Rynne, *Vatican Council II* (Maryknoll, NY: Orbis, 1999); René Latourelle, ed., *Vatican II: Assessment and Perspectives: Twenty-five Years After (1962–1987)*, 3 vols. (New York: Paulist Press, 1989).

4. For more on the anticommunist activities of the Catholic Church, see Pedro Ramet, ed., *Catholicism and Politics in Communist Societies* (Durham, NC: Duke University Press, 1990). Of particular interest in this volume is the discussion of Cuba's relationship after the revolution with the Holy See by Thomas Quigley, "The Catholic Church in Cuba," in *Catholicism and Politics in Communist Societies*, ed. Pedro Ramet (Durham, NC: Duke University Press, 1990), 296–312. Cuba was the only communist country to maintain continuous ties to the Vatican despite its repression of Catholic institutions and activities from 1961 to 1986. Quigley, "The Catholic Church in Cuba," 305.

5. Milagros Peña, *Theologies and Liberation in Peru: The Role of Ideas in Social Movements* (Philadelphia: Temple University Press, 1995), 53.

6. Enrique Dussel, "From the Second Vatican Council to the Present Day," in *The Church in Latin America, 1492–1992*, ed. Enrique Dussel (Maryknoll, NY: Orbis, 1992), 155.

7. Freire's groundbreaking work on the transformative role of education and pedagogy in challenging oppression, including his most famous work, *Pedagogy of the Oppressed* (1968), was published around this time and circulated widely in Catholic universities and other institutions of higher learning in Brazil and spread quickly to other parts of the region. It was translated into Spanish and English and found interested readers around the world, particularly in South Africa, where it was read and embraced by proponents of the black consciousness movement, including Stephen Biko. The black consciousness movement, however, predated English translations of Freire, and the influence of the movement on the reception of these ideas was critical to the context. See Daniel Magaziner, *The Law and the Prophets: Black Consciousness in South Africa, 1968–1977* (Columbus: Ohio University Press, 2010).

8. Luiz Alberto Gómez de Souza, "Latin America and the Catholic Church: Points of Convergence and Divergence (encontros e desencontros) 1960–2005," Helen Kellogg Institute for International Studies, Working Paper no. 334, February 2007, https://kellogg.nd.edu/sites/default/files/old_files/documents/334_0.pdf.

9. In 1910, the Vatican prohibited Catholics from participating in ecumenical organizations. However, the increasing organic interest of Catholic activists in connections with such meetings and organizations put pressure on the Church to eventually

reconsider this position. Graham Duncan and Anthony Egan, "The Ecumenical Struggle in South Africa: The Role of Ecumenical Movements and Liberation Organisations from 1966," *Studia Historiae Ecclesiasticae* 45, no. 1 (2019): 3.

10. Signatories included José N. Nasser, Rodolfo Ricciardelli, Justo Hilario Irazábal, Carlos A. Fugante, Telmo De Laurentis, Pedro Wurschmidt, Fransciso Mascialino, Juan R. Gómez, Belisario Tiscornia, Amado DIP [*sic*], Mario Chiefallo, Livio Inama, Manuel Pérez Vila, Luis Babín, "Comunicato sobre la preparación de la Asamblea Mundial de la Paz"; "1968 Convocatoria Conferencia por la Paz," Archive of the Partido Comunista, Buenos Aires, Argentina.

11. By 1979, the Sandinista revolution in Nicaragua drew renewed focus on conflicts in Central America and the role of Catholicism in supporting revolutionary activity. Already by 1965, Colombian priest Camilo Torres had joined the National Liberation Army and died fighting, and the work of activist priests Óscar Romero and Ernesto Cardenal influenced discussions about liberation theology significantly, which ultimately proved a fateful blow to the expansion of interest among many progressive Catholics. By the early 1980s, many liberation theologians faced formal suppression and correction from the Vatican; Pope John Paul II's view of socialist thought influenced his position and led to an "Instruction on Christian Freedom and Liberation" in 1986. For a detailed examination of the theological shifts throughout these years, see Philip Berryman, *Liberation Theology* (Philadelphia: Temple University Press, 1989).

Scott Mainwaring and Alexander Wilde define the progressive Church as follows: "a sector within the national Churches, roughly synonymous with other designations used by social scientists and theologians: the popular Church, the radical Church, the grass-roots Church, the Church of the poor, etc., However, the progressive Church is not a distinct entity, separate from the Church as a whole (the 'institutional' Church)." See "The Progressive Church in Latin America: An Interpretation," in *The Progressive Church in Latin America*, ed. Scott Mainwaring and Alexander Wilde (Notre Dame, IN: University of Notre Dame Press, 1989), 4–5.

12. Guillermo Cook, *The Expectation of the Poor: Latin American Base Ecclesial Communities in Protestant Perspective* (Maryknoll, NY: Orbis, 1985), 49; Christian Smith, *The Emergence of Liberation Theology: Radical Religion and Social Movement Theory* (Chicago: University of Chicago Press, 1991). See also Luis Alberto Gómez de Souza, "A caminhada de Medellín a Puebla," *Perspectiva teológica* 31, no. 84 (1999): 223–34; Enrique Correa and José Antonio Viera-Gallo, *Iglesia y dictadura* (Santiago: CESOC, Ediciones Chile y América, 1986); Emilio F. Mignone, *Iglesia y dictadura: El papel de la Iglesia a la luz de sus relaciones con el régimen militar* (Buenos Aires: Ediciones del Pensamiento Nacional, 1986).

13. Consejo Episcopal Latinoamericano (CELAM), *Evangelización en el presente y en el futuro de América Latina* (San Salvador: UCA Editores, 1979).

14. Kevin Coleman, "A Flamethrower to His Image," *Photography & Culture* 13, no. 2 (2020): 239–42.

15. John Burdick, *Legacies of Liberation: The Progressive Church in Brazil at the Start of a New Millennium* (Hampshire: Ashgate, 2004), xi. See also Cláudio Carvalhaes

and Fábio Py, "Liberation Theology in Brazil," *CrossCurrents* 67, no. 1 (March 2017): 157–79.

16. Originally coined by Gustavo Gutiérrez in *A Theology for Liberation: History, Politics and Salvation* (Maryknoll, NY: Orbis, 1971); this turn of phase became synonymous with this strand of social theology.

17. Burdick, *Legacies of Liberation*, 20.

18. John Burdick, "The Evolution of a Progressive Catholic Project: The Case of the Black Pastoral in Rio de Janeiro, Brazil," in *The Church at the Grassroots in Latin America: Perspectives on Thirty Years of Activism*, ed. John Burdick and W. E. Hewitt (Westport, CT: Praeger, 2000), 73.

19. Jerry Dávila, *Hotel Trópico: Brazil and the Challenge of African Decolonization, 1950–1980* (Durham, NC: Duke University Press, 2010), 218. It is worth noting that relations between Brazil and Angola were complicated because of the slave trade in the seventeenth through nineteenth centuries, which included Catholic complicity. See John Thornton, *The Congolese Saint Anthony: Dona Beatriz Kimpa Vita and the Antonian Movement, 1684–1706* (Cambridge: Cambridge University Press, 1998); James Sweet, *Domingos Álvares, African Healing, and the Intellectual History of the Atlantic World* (Chapel Hill: University of North Carolina Press, 2011).

20. Peña, *Theologies and Liberation in Peru*, 8.

21. Gustavo Morello, "Christianity and Revolution: Catholicism and Guerrilla Warfare in Argentina's Seventies," *Journal of Religion and Violence* 1, no. 1 (2013): 48–70. See also José Pablo Martín, *El Movimiento de Sacerdotes para el Tercer Mundo: Un debate argentine* (Buenos Aires: Editorial Guadalupe, 1992); Jeffrey Klaiber, *The Church, Dictatorships, and Democracy in Latin America* (Eugene, OR: Wipf and Stock/Orbis, 1998).

22. See Charles Villa-Vicencio, *A Theology of Reconstruction: Nation Building and Human Rights* (Cape Town: David Philip, 1992); Charles Villa-Vicencio, *Trapped in Apartheid: A Socio-Theological History of the English-Speaking Churches* (Cape Town: David Philip, 1998); Peter Walshe, "The Evolution of Liberation Theology in South Africa," *Journal of Law and Religion* 5, no. 2 (1987): 299–311; Peter Walshe, "South Africa: Prophetic Christianity and the Liberation Movement," *Journal of Modern African Studies* 29 (1991): 27–60.

23. Arthur Suzman, "South Africa and the Rule of Law," *South African Law Journal* 85, no. 2 (August 1968): 263, Brian Reid Papers Box 1 Acc. 92037–21.06, Folder "Left Wing Wins 1970s," Hoover Institution, Stanford University, California.

24. South African Institute on Race Relations, "The Native Laws Amendment Bill: Its Effect on Religious and Other Freedoms," Transvaal Printing & Photolithographers, April 1957, "South African Subject Collection," Box 3, Accession no. XX789–60.02/03, Folder "General Religion General," Hoover Institution, Stanford University, California.

25. "Minutes of the Executive Board of the American Committee on Africa," 11 March 1957, "Apartheid South Africa," Digital Archive, Michigan State University,

Lansing, http://kora.matrix.msu.edu/files/50/304/32-130-236C-84-PW%20ACOA%20 minutes%203-11-57%20°pt.pdf.

26. Catholic Action Department, "First National Conference of Catholic Action of the Clergy of South Africa, Held in Johannesburg, 23–27 February 1959," booklet, Pretoria, "Catholic Action" box, Archive of the Archdiocese of Cape Town, Cape Town, Western Cape, South Africa, 2. For a fascinating study of the Latin American face of the Catholic Action movement in Mexico, see Stephen Andes, "A Catholic Alternative to Revolution: The Survival of Social Catholicism in Postrevolutionary Mexico," *The Americas* 68, no. 4 (2012): 529–62; for background on South African Catholic activism, see Garth Abraham, *The Catholic Church and Apartheid: The Response of the Catholic Church in South Africa to the First Decade of National Party Rule 1948–1957* (Johannesburg: Ravan Press, 1989).

27. Catherine Higgs, "Silence, Disobedience, and African Catholic Sisters in Apartheid South Africa," *African Studies Review* 54, no. 2 (2011): 2. See also Abraham, *The Catholic Church and Apartheid*.

28. In the Western Cape in the 1940s and 1950s, the population was referred to as "Coloured," though I use the term "Black" to represent how they were more broadly included in this framework in the relevant discussion. However, it would not be entirely accurate to say that this Black population was Black African; the Western Cape has a distinct history of racial categorization. See Mohamed Adhikari, *Not White Enough, Not Black Enough: Racial Identity in the South African Coloured Community* (Columbus: Ohio University Press, 2005).

29. Tristan Anne Borer, *Challenging the State: Churches as Political Actors in South Africa, 1980–1994* (Notre Dame, IN: University of Notre Dame Press, 1998), 34.

30. Union of South Africa, Statutes of the Union of South Africa, Bantu Education Act, No. 47 of 1953, Digital Imaging South Africa Archive, 5 October 1953, 258–76, available online through Digital Innovation South Africa, https://www.sahistory.org.za/archive/bantu-education-act%2C-act-no-47-of-1953.

31. Trevor Verryn, "Catholic Bishops and Apartheid," in *Catholics and Apartheid Society*, ed. Andrew Prior (Cape Town: David Philip, 1982), 57.

32. Americans for South African Resistance, "Bulletin of the Campaign for the Defiance of Unjust Laws," *Bulletin*, no. 3 (18 July 1952), https://www.sahistory.org.za/sites/default/files/archive-files3/slsep88.7.pdf.

33. South African Council of Bishops, "South Africa and Apartheid," Pamphlet, 1991, Pretoria, Western Cape Provincial Council of Churches, box 263, Archive of the Archdiocese of Cape Town, Cape Town, Western Cape, South Africa, 6. See also Catherine Higgs and Jean N. Evans, "Embracing Activism in Apartheid South Africa: The Sisters of Mercy in Bophuthatswana, 1974–1994," *Catholic Historical Review* 94, no. 3 (2018): 500–521, whose findings confirm that prior to Vatican II, Catholic sisters also tended not to be activists.

34. Rynne, *Vatican Council II*, 46; for more on changes in the church, Vatican II, and the church in Southern Africa, see Elizabeth Foster, *African Catholic: Decolonization and the Transformation of the Church* (Cambridge, MA: Harvard University Press, 2019).

35. Rynne, *Vatican II*, 44, 89, 496.

36. Episcopal Churchmen for South Africa, "South Africa Bans Speech by American Civil Rights Leader," 30 August 1966, "Apartheid South Africa," Digital Archive, Michigan State University, http://kora.matrix.msu.edu/files/50/304/32-130-718-84-african_activist_archive-a0b5n5-a_12419.pdf.

37. Philippe Denis, "Archibishop Hurley's Strange Silence on Apartheid at Vatican II," *Ephererides Theologicae Lovanienses* 89, no. 4 (2013): 417.

38. For more information about the manner in which these interventions in social questions intersected with longer traditions of thought in Catholic doctrine, see Michael P. Hornsby-Smith, *An Introduction to Catholic Social Thought* (Cambridge: Cambridge University Press, 2006). After ten years of experimental status, the Pontifical Council for Justice and Peace was formalized in 1976.

39. Tracy Kuperus, "Building Democracy: An Examination of Religious Associations in South Africa and Zimbabwe," *Journal of Modern African Studies* 37, no. 4 (1999): 652.

40. For more on youth violence and religion in South Africa in the 1970s, see Jon Abbink, "Being Young in Africa: The Politics of Despair and Renewal," in *Vanguard or Vandals: Youth, Politics and Conflict in Africa*, ed. Jon Abbink and Ineke van Kessel (London: Brill Academic, 2005), 1–34; Motsoko Pheko, "40 Years After: Understanding the Soweto Uprising," *Pambazuka News*, 30 June 2016, https://www.sahistory.org.za/archive/40-years-after-understanding-soweto-uprising-motsoko-pheko-pambazuka-news-30-june-2016.

41. Clive Glaser, "Beyond the Legacy of 1976: Morris Isaacson High School, Popular Memory and the Struggle for Education in Central Soweto," *African Studies* 79, no. 1 (2020): 24. See also Pam Christie, *The Right to Learn: The Struggle for Education in South Africa* (Johannesburg: Ravan Press, 1991).

42. Higgs, "Silence, Disobedience," 11.

43. Margaret Kelly, "Letter All Archbishops, Bishops, and Priests, to All Justice and Peace Commissions," 24 October 1984, "Justice and Peace" box, Archive of the Archdiocese of Cape Town, Cape Town, Western Cape, South Africa.

44. "Letter to Archbishop McCann from Margaret Malherbe," 21 January 1974, "Justice and Peace" box, Archive of the Archdiocese of Cape Town, Cape Town, Western Cape, South Africa.

45. "Report of the Commission for Justice and Peace of the Archdiocese of Cape Town for the Year 1975," "Justice and Peace" box, Archive of the Archdiocese of Cape Town, Cape Town, Western Cape, South Africa.

46. By 1980, the Cape Town commission, somewhat dissatisfied with the appointed rather than elected membership, decided to restructure, appointing Sister Thora Pérez as chairperson.

47. "Report to Cardinal Owen McCann from Justice and Peace Commission of Cape Town," 7 February 1983, "Justice and Peace, Minutes 1975–1984" box, Archive of the Archdiocese of Cape Town, Cape Town, Western Cape, South Africa.

48. "Detention and Détente," 30 April 1976, published by the Christian Institute, was circulated by Margaret Malherbe to Catholic bishops in the short time between its embargo and its censorship in May 1976. "Detentions" Folder, "Situation in South Africa" Box, Archive of the Archdiocese of Cape Town, Cape Town, Western Cape, South Africa. This publication gave details on a set of ongoing trials and speculated on the fates of a handful of detainees, including various ANC leaders and the mysterious death in custody of ANC member Joseph Mdluli, held by Security Police under the Terrorism Act on 19 March 1976.

49. See, for example, "Letter to W.P.C.C. Justice and Reconciliation Commission from Sr. Margaret Malherbe," 19 December 1978; "Letter to Archbishop McCann from Margaret Malherbe" 24 October 1977, "Justice and Peace" box, Archive of the Archdiocese of Cape Town, Cape Town, Western Cape, South Africa.

50. For example, Margaret Malherbe, "Let's Respond to Our Bishops' Guidance," *Southern Cross*, 14 November 1976. "Justice and Peace" box, Archive of the Archdiocese of Cape Town, Cape Town, Western Cape, South Africa.

51. Higgs, "Silence, Disobedience," 9.

52. "Forced Removals, More than Hurt Feelings," *Pax*, no. 9 (August 1984), "Justice and Peace" box, Archive of the Archdiocese of Cape Town, Cape Town, Western Cape, South Africa.

53. "Report of the Meeting at the Salvo Centre, Landsdowne," 20 March 1979, "Justice and Peace" box, Archive of the Archdiocese of Cape Town, Cape Town, Western Cape, South Africa; "Report of the Commission of Justice and Peace of the Archdiocese of Cape Town during the Year 1973," "Justice and Peace" box, Archive of the Archdiocese of Cape Town, Cape Town, Western Cape, South Africa.

54. Margaret Malherbe, "Letter to Father Matthew," 31 February 1977, "Justice and Peace" box, Archive of the Archdiocese of Cape Town, Cape Town, Western Cape, South Africa.

55. Finbar Synnott, "Justice and Reconciliation in South Africa Report," *Pastoral Action*, no. 5, Pretoria, Pamphlet, "Justice and Peace" box, Archive of the Archdiocese of Cape Town, Cape Town, Western Cape, South Africa. As examples of this kind of work being done by women involved in and affiliated with the Black Sash, see Muriel Horrell, "The Group Areas Act," "Transvaal Advice Office," and Barbara Brock, *The Black Sash/Die Swart Serp*, July 1963, v. 9, no. 2, 9–13, 25–26, "Black Sash" Folder, Brian Reid Papers Box 1 Acc. 92037–21.06, Hoover Institution, Stanford University, California.

56. John F. Burns, "Catholic Defiance of Apartheid Stirs South Africa," *New York Times*, 6 February 1977, 14.

57. Letter to Archbishop Owen McCann from Margaret Malherbe, 5 October 1982, report and earlier correspondence attached, "Justice and Peace, Minutes 1975–1984" box, Archive of the Archdiocese of Cape Town, Cape Town, Western Cape, South Africa.

58. "Letter to Archbishop Owen McCann from Thora Pérez," report attached, 29 September 1981, "Justice and Peace, Minutes 1975–1984" box, Archive of the Archdiocese of Cape Town, Cape Town, Western Cape, South Africa.

59. South African Council of Bishops, "South Africa and Apartheid," Pamphlet, 1991, Pretoria, Western Cape Provincial Council of Churches, box 263, Archive of the Archdiocese of Cape Town, Cape Town, Western Cape, South Africa, 26.

60. The Ecumenical Association of Third World Theologians held its first meeting in 1976 and shortly thereafter began the work of publishing a biannual journal, *Voices from the Third World* (1978–85, 1999, 2004–6, 2009, 2011–present), published in Colombo, Sri Lanka, with a mission to expand coverage of voices and experiences of the poor and inform a broad global audience.

61. Letter to Archbishop Lawrence Henry, 18 March 2005, Western Cape Provincial Council of Churches, box 263, Archive of the Archdiocese of Cape Town, Cape Town, Western Cape, South Africa.

62. World Council of Churches, "The WCC and International Banking in Southern Africa," Docs. no. 31 and 32 revised (1974), Box 12 Accession no. XX789-60.02/03, Folder "Organizations Religious World Council of Churches," Hoover Institution, Stanford University, California. The document notes that it relies on data from "The Frankfurt Documents," produced by the Corporate Information Center Brief of July 1973, New York.

63. Richard Shorten, "Beyers Naudé and the Christian Institute," *Index on Censorship* 12, no. 5 (1983): 27. See also Retief Muller, "Beyers Naudé (1915–2004): Christianity, Violence, and Reconciliation in South Africa," *Theology Today* 72, no. 3 (2015): 299–311; Graham and Egan, "The Ecumenical Struggle," 9.

64. Southern Africa Committee, "A Monthly Survey of News and Opinion," *Southern Africa* 4, no. 5 (May 1971): 19, "Apartheid South Africa," Digital Archive, Michigan State University, http://kora.matrix.msu.edu/files/50/304/32-130-A0B-84-al.sff.document.nusa197105.pdf.

65. "Canadian Bank Loans to the Government of South Africa," Report, "Justice and Peace" box, Archive of the Archdiocese of Cape Town, Cape Town, Western Cape, South Africa. For more on this, see Michael Bueckert, "Boycotts and Revolution: Debating the Legitimacy of the African National Congress in the Canadian Anti-Apartheid Movement, 1969–94," *Radical History Review* 134 (2019): 96–115; John S. Saul, *On Building a Social Movement: The North American Campaign for Southern African Liberation Revisited* (Trenton, NJ: Africa World Press, 2017).

66. "Info '89 HAP," Pamphlet, "Justice and Peace, minutes 1975–1984" box, Archive of the Archdiocese of Cape Town, Cape Town, Western Cape, South Africa; C27, "Shell Shock" pamphlet, World Council of Churches, Box 12 Accession no. XX789-60.02/03, Folder "Organizations Religious World Council of Churches," Hoover Institution, Stanford University, California.

67. Staff, "The Case Against Liberation Theology," *New York Times*, sec. 6, 21 October 1984, 51.

68. Magaziner, *The Law and the Prophets*, 105–6. See also Philippe Denis, "Seminary Training and Black Consciousness in South Africa in the Early 1970s," *South African History Journal* 62, no. 1 (2010): 165.

69. Mokgethi Motlhabi, "Phases of Black Theology in South Africa: A Historical Review," *Religion & Theology* 16 (2009): 164; James Cone, *Black Theology and Black Power* (New York: Seabury, 1969) and *A Black Theory of Liberation* (Philadelphia: J. B. Lippincott, 1970), were crucial points of reference, but South African intellectuals quickly produced their own reflections on these issues in their South African context, notably Basil Moore's edited collection, *The Challenge of Black Theology in South Africa* (Atlanta: John Knox Press, 1974), and H. J. Becken, ed., *Relevant Theology for Africa* (Durban: Lutheran Publishing House, 1973). See also the discussion of Black theology as liberation theology in Emmanuel Martey, *African Theology: Inculturation and Liberation* (Maryknoll, NY: Orbis, 1993), and Gail M. Gerhard, *Black Power in South Africa: The Evolution of an Ideology* (Los Angeles: Greenberg, 1999).

70. Hashi K. Tarifa, *Black Nationalist Thought in South Africa* (London: Palgrave Macmillan, 2016), 27–28. See also Report of the Commission on "'The Christian Basis for Participation in the African Revolution,' of the All Africa Conference of Churches," Enugu, Nigeria (1965), IMBISA box, Archive of the Archdiocese of Cape Town, Cape Town, Western Cape, South Africa.

71. Nigel Gibson, "Black Consciousness 1977–1987: The Dialectics of Liberation in South Africa," *Africa Today* 35, no. 1 (1988): 11.

72. "Third Ordinary Synod of Bishops, 27 September–16 October 1974," South African History Archive, Religion and Churches Collection, Box 139, O.2.1, Collection AL2457, 2.1.5, Johannesburg, South Africa.

73. George Sombe Mukua, "The Establishment of the Black Catholic Clergy in South Africa from 1889 to 1957" (PhD diss., University of Natal, 2000), 289.

74. Finbar Synnott, "Justice and Reconciliation in South Africa Report," *Pastoral Action*, no. 5, Pretoria, Pamphlet, "Justice and Peace" box, Archive of the Archdiocese of Cape Town, Cape Town, Western Cape, South Africa; Bishop Pietro Buthelezi, "Statements on Black Consciousness and Human Rights," Pamphlet, Unity Publications, Durban, 1974, Box 12 Accession no. XX789-60.02/03, Folder "Organizations Religious World Council of Churches," Hoover Institution, Stanford University, California.

75. Verryn, "Catholic Bishops and Apartheid," 61.

76. Bishop Pietro Buthelezi, "Statements on Black Consciousness and Human Rights," Pamphlet, Unity Publications, Durban, 1974, Box 12 Accession no. XX789–60.02/03, Folder "Organizations Religious World Council of Churches," Hoover Institution, Stanford University, California.

77. Marjorie Hope and James Young, *South African Churches in a Revolutionary Situation* (Maryknoll, NY: Orbis, 1981), 154.

78. Hope and Young, *South African Churches*, 164. See also "Please Make the Church Available," Flyer, 1982, African Synod, IMBISA box, Archive of the Archdiocese of Cape Town, Cape Town, Western Cape, South Africa.

79. Patrick Noonan, *"They're Burning the Churches"* (Cape Town: Jacana, 2003).

80. Institute for Contextual Theology, "Institute for Contextual Theology: What It Is," Report, 1981, South African History Archive, Religion and Churches Collection, Box 136, O.2.1, Collection AL2457, 2.1, Johannesburg, South Africa.

81. Mike Deeb, "Pastoral Planning: Lessons from Latin America," *Grace and Truth*, no. 1 (1985): 37–44, South African History Archive, Religion and Churches Collection, Box 136, O.2.1, Collection AL2457, 2.1, Johannesburg, South Africa.

82. "Third Ordinary Synod of Bishops, 27 September–16 October 1974"; Stephen Naidoo, "Impressions of the 1983 Synod of Bishops," 5 January 1984, "African Synod, IMBISA" box, Archive of the Archdiocese of Cape Town, Cape Town, Western Cape, South Africa. See also "Minutes," Southern African Catholic Bishops' Conference, 5–12 February 1980, Waterkloof, Pretoria, South African History Archive, Religion and Churches Collection, Box 139, O.2.1, Collection AL2457, 2.1.5, Johannesburg, South Africa. These minutes include an extensive list of readings assigned for discussion among those present at a "War and Peace Seminar," which was part of the meetings.

83. He was arrested under the Terrorism Act due to his involvement "in the making of a British television film using factual information about living conditions in black resettlement areas which drew protest in England." Southern Africa Committee, "A Monthly Survey of News and Opinion," *Southern Africa* 4, no. 6 (June–July 1971): 31, "Apartheid South Africa," Digital Archive, Michigan State University, http://kora .matrix.msu.edu/files/50/304/32-130-AoC-84-al.sff.document.nusa197106.pdf.

84. Southern Africa Committee, "A Monthly Survey of News and Opinion," *Southern Africa* 4, no. 8 (October 1971), 30; "Apartheid South Africa," Digital Archive, Michigan State University, http://kora.matrix.msu.edu/files/50/304/32-130-AoE-84-al .sff.document.nusa197110.pdf, accessed 23 March 2020.

85. Margaret Kelly, "Letter All Archbishops, Bishops, and Priests, to All Justice and Peace Commissions," 24 October 1984, "Justice and Peace" box, Archive of the Archdiocese of Cape Town, Cape Town, Western Cape, South Africa.

86. Southern African Catholic Bishops' Council, "South Africa and Apartheid," Pamphlet, 1991, Pretoria, Western Cape Provincial Council of Churches, box 263, Archive of the Archdiocese of Cape Town, Cape Town, Western Cape, South Africa, 9.

87. Associated Press, "Brazilian Cardinal Forced to Cancel Visit to South Africa," 26 June 1985, https://apnews.com/f8bb3a5688a34dc2e4d931adb4d53f06.

88. George Mukuka, "'Black Man, You Are on Your Own,' Interview with Archbishop Peter F. Butelezi," *Grace and Truth* 3 (1997): 36–49. See also D. A. Kotzé, "Black Consciousness in South Africa," *South African Journal of Political Studies* 1, no. 1 (1974): 44–63; Peter John Butelezi, *Statement on Black Consciousness and Human Rights* (Pretoria: SACBC, 1976). In 1978, Butelezi was appointed archbishop of Bloemfontein.

89. Christian Institute, "Detention and Détente," 30 April 1976, "Detentions" Folder, "Situation in South Africa" Box, Archive of the Archdiocese of Cape Town, Cape Town, Western Cape, South Africa, 24–25.

90. World Council of Churches, "Communication," March 1973; World Council of Churches, "Press Release, 20 February 1974," South African Subject Collection, Box 12 Accession no. XX789-60.02/03, Folder "Organizations Religious World Council of Churches," Hoover Institution, Stanford University, California.

91. Don Morton, Tami Hultman, and Reed Kramer, "The Changing Situation in Southern Africa," prepared as part of a report by the World Council of Churches, April

1975, Box 12, Accession no. XX789-60.02/03, Folder "Organizations Religious World Council of Churches," Hoover Institution, Stanford University, California, 1–4.

92. "With One Voice," Report on Harare Follow-up, 11 January 1983, Box 12, Accession no. XX789-60.02/03, Folder "Organizations Religious World Council of Churches," Hoover Institution, Stanford University, California.

93. Paul Gifford, *The Religious Right in Southern Africa* (Harare: Baobab Books and University of Zimbabwe Publications, 1988).

94. Nolan's views are published in *God in South Africa: The Challenge of the Gospel* (Grand Rapids, MI: Eerdmans, 1988).

95. Catholic Defence League, "Sister Janice McLaughlin Still on the Way to Hell," *Candidus*, June–August 1979, 1–3, South African History Archive, Religion and Churches Collection, Box137, O.2.1, Collection AL2457, 2.1, Johannesburg, South Africa.

96. Borer, Challenging the State, 54.

97. Robert Dumas, Edward Adams, Khotso Kekana, and Ian Linden, "Report of the International Catholic Delegation to Namibia," 20–28 July 1989, South African History Archive, Religion and Churches Collection, Box 136, O.2.1, Collection AL2457, 2.1, Johannesburg, South Africa.

98. Western Cape Justice and Peace Commission, *Report on Namibia*, 1982, "Southern Africa and the Church" box, Archive of the Archdiocese of Cape Town, Cape Town, Western Cape, South Africa.

99. "Letter from Heinz Hunke," 16 December 1976, "Southern Africa and the Church" box, Archive of the Archdiocese of Cape Town, Cape Town, Western Cape, South Africa.

100. "Statement Issued by the Bishops' Conference of England and Wales on Southern Africa, Made at Their Low Week of 1985 Meeting," "Southern Africa and the Church" box, Archive of the Archdiocese of Cape Town, Cape Town, Western Cape, South Africa.

101. "Press Statement, Father H. Henning, Vicar-General of Diocese of Namibia," 16 April 1985, "Southern Africa and the Church" box, Archive of the Archdiocese of Cape Town, Cape Town, Western Cape, South Africa.

102. Joubert Malherbe, "'Get Political, Hurley Urges," *Rand Daily*, 21 August 1982; Ian Hobbes, "Bishops Vote to 'Understand' Armed Struggle," *The Argus*, 18 August 1988, 1, 4.

103. "Yet Another Agreed Statement, This Time on 'Scientific Socialism,'" *Approaches* Supplement, no. 69, "Southern Africa and the Church" box, Archive of the Archdiocese of Cape Town, Cape Town, Western Cape, South Africa.

104. Zambia Episcopal Conference, Christian Council of Zambia, and Zambia Evangelical Fellowship, "Marxism, Humanism, and Christianity: A Letter from the Leaders of the Christian Churches of Zambia to all their Members about Scientific Socialism," Pamphlet, August 1979, Lusaka, "Southern Africa and the Church" box, Archive of the Archdiocese of Cape Town, Cape Town, Western Cape, South Africa, 11.

105. "Love and Revolution," *Crisis News*, no. 21, April–May 1988, Cape Town, "Southern Africa and the Church" box, Archive of the Archdiocese of Cape Town, Cape Town, Western Cape, South Africa, 2.

106. "Committed Christian Takes Up Arms," *Crisis News*, no. 21, April–May 1988, Cape Town, "Southern Africa and the Church" box, Archive of the Archdiocese of Cape Town, Cape Town, Western Cape, South Africa, 10–11.

107. "Archbishop Hurley and Namibia," *War and Peace News*, Bulletin, no. 3 (April 1983), War and Peace Group, Diocese of Johannesburg, Johannesburg, 1; South African History Archive, Religion and Churches Collection, Box 139, O.2.1, Collection AL2457, 2.1.5, Johannesburg, South Africa.

108. "Testimony of Archbishop Denis Hurley," reprinted in Catholic Institute for International Relations, pamphlet, "Country and Conscience: South African Conscientious Objectors" (Catholic Institute for International Relations: London, 1988), 16–19, 17; South African History Archive, Religion and Churches Collection, Box 136, O.2.1, Collection AL2457, 2.1, Johannesburg, South Africa.

109. "Church and Conscience: A Collection of Church and Other Statements of Conscientious Objection in South Africa" (Methodist Church of Southern Africa, Christian Citizenship Department, Unity Publications: Durban, 1979), 5–7; South African History Archive, Religion and Churches Collection, Box 136, O.2.1, Collection AL2457, 2.1, Johannesburg, South Africa.

110. A Catholic perspective on the *New Nation* was published by the Commission of Studies of the Young South Africans for a Christian Civilization as a book titled *The "New Nation" and Liberation Theology: The Sad Journey of a Reader of the Newspaper Published by the Catholic Bishops' Publishing Co.* (Young South Africans for a Christian Civilization: Johannesburg, 1987), South African History Archive, Religion and Churches Collection, Box 136, O.2.1, Collection AL2457, 2.1, Johannesburg, South Africa. See Keyan G. Tomaselli and Ruth Teer-Tomaselli, "*New Nation*: Anarchronistic Catholicism and Liberation Theology," in *Contesting Media Power: Alternative Media in a Networked World*, ed. Nick Couldry and James Curran (Lanham, MD: Rowman and Littlefield, 2003), 195–208.

111. "Address of Pope John Paul II to the South African Catholic Bishops' Conference, Rome, November 1987," "Justice and Peace" box, Archive of the Archdiocese of Cape Town, Cape Town, Western Cape, South Africa.

112. SACBC, "Joint Letter on State Actions," signed by Reginald Orsmond, Denis Hurley, Peter Butelezi, George Daniel, Stephen Naidoo, Hans Brenninkmeijer, Michael O'Shea, and Zithulele Mvemve, "Justice and Peace" box, Archive of the Archdiocese of Cape Town, Cape Town, Western Cape, South Africa.

113. Allen Barnes, Commission for Justice and Peace of the Archdiocese of Cape Town, "Dear Father," Letter to churches, "Justice and Peace" box, Archive of the Archdiocese of Cape Town, Cape Town, Western Cape, South Africa. This action drew on support from the St. Francis Xavier Centre of Goa, India, which symbolically represented the connection between the mission societies of Portugal's former African colonies.

114. "State versus Church—1988, a Year of Increasing Conflict," in "Info '89 HAP," Pamphlet, "Justice and Peace, minutes 1975–1984" box, Archive of the Archdiocese of Cape Town, Cape Town, Western Cape, South Africa.

115. Father Michael Lapsley, "Amnesty: Forgiveness without Confession?" Pamphlet, Western Cape Provincial Council of Churches, 1995, Western Cape Provincial Council of Churches, box 263, Archive of the Archdiocese of Cape Town, Cape Town, Western Cape, South Africa, 5–9.

116. For more on Umkhonto we Sizwe, see Stephen R. Davis, *The ANC's War against Apartheid* (Bloomington: University of Indiana Press, 2018).

117. Karin Chubb, Mary Burton, and Jenny de Tolly, "The Black Sash," Pamphlet, n.d., Western Cape Provincial Council of Churches, box 263, Archive of the Archdiocese of Cape Town, Cape Town, Western Cape, South Africa, 16.

118. Published in Government Gazette Notices and Proclamations, 11196, 25 March 1988, by the South African Department of Justice.

119. South African Council of Churches, "The Mission of the South African Council of Churches in a Period of Political Transition in South Africa," Statement, Western Cape Provincial Council of Churches, box 263, Archive of the Archdiocese of Cape Town, Cape Town, Western Cape, South Africa. The SACC was founded in 1936 as the Christian Council of South Africa, an organization designed to coordinate activities of mutual interest, but in 1968, changing its name to the SACC, a new central mission was announced, taking on white power structures and eliminating apartheid. In 1978, a Namibian branch of the organization was created, with wide international support, which in 1983 began a social welfare branch, which provided legal aid and material support for political prisoners, detainees, refuges, and victims of drought. In September 1989, the WCC cosponsored a consultation in Harare, Zimbabwe, calling on churches to speak out against the South African government on the grounds of the dispossession, disenfranchisement, and exploitation of African peoples by the settler colonial state, using international law, historical contests over legal structures, and Organization of African Unity declarations, in addition to theological and moral arguments. See Harare Delegation, "With One Voice, Report on Harare Follow-Up Meetings," 13 January 1986, Box 12 Accession No. XX789–60.02/03, Folder "Organizations Religious World Council of Churches," Hoover Institution, Stanford University, California.

120. "Statement of a Consultation held at the Harare Sheraton on September 4 to 8 1989 on the Legitimacy of the South African Government," Pamphlet, "Justice and Peace" box, Archive of the Archdiocese of Cape Town, Cape Town, Western Cape, South Africa.

121. Consultation meeting minutes, 6–18 May 1990, Western Cape Provincial Council of Churches, box 263, Archive of the Archdiocese of Cape Town, Cape Town, Western Cape, South Africa.

122. Borer, *Challenging the State*, 17.

123. SACBC press release, Pretoria 5 August 1987, "South African Situation: Various Reports" box. Archive of the Archdiocese of Cape Town, Cape Town, Western Cape, South Africa, 5.

124. "Until Justice and Peace Embrace," Pamphlet, Western Cape Provincial Council of Churches, 1995, Western Cape Provincial Council of Churches, box 263, Archive of the Archdiocese of Cape Town, Cape Town, Western Cape, South Africa.

125. "Statement on Cape Peace Initiative," fax, April 28, 1999, Western Cape Provincial Council of Churches, box 263, Archive of the Archdiocese of Cape Town, Cape Town, Western Cape, South Africa.

126. "South Africa and the Church: Impulses for Ecumenical Action," Pamphlet, Western Cape Provincial Council of Churches, box 263, Archive of the Archdiocese of Cape Town, Cape Town, Western Cape, South Africa.

127. Lilian Calles Barger, *The World Came of Age: An Intellectual History of Liberation Theology* (New York: Oxford University Press, 2018), 262.

128. Jessica Alexis Jolicoeur Rich, "Organizing Twenty-First-Century Activism: From Structure to Strategy in Latin American Social Movements," *Latin American Research Review* 55, no. 3 (2020): 430.

129. Smith, *Emergence of Liberation Theology*, 218–19.

Conclusion

1. Robert Malley argues that we must recognize that the origins of *tiers mondisme* were not Arabic-speaking Algerians but the French intellectuals who offered the story of the revolution as a provocation to European democracies. He goes on to argue that this is why Algerian Third Worldist leaders were unable to resist the rise of Islamic nationalism. Robert Malley, *The Call from Algeria: Third Worldism, Revolution, and the Turn to Islam* (Berkeley: University of California Press, 1996), 78.

2. Yassin al-Haj Saleh, "A Critique of Solidarity," trans. Alex Rowell, *Al-Jumhuriya*, 16 July 2018, https://www.aljumhuriya.net/en/content/critique-solidarity.

3. Jeff Goodwin and James Jasper, "When and Why do Social Movements Occur: Introduction," in *The Social Movements Reader*, 2nd ed., ed. Jeff Goodwin and James Jasper (Oxford: Wiley-Blackwell, 2009), 11.

4. Steve Striffler, *Solidarity: Latin American and the U.S. Left in the Era of Human Rights* (London: Pluto Press, 2019), 23.

5. Ricardo de Titto, *El Pensamiento del socialism y la izquierda* (Buenos Aires: Editorial El Ateneo, 2010), 11.

6. Sachin Chaturvedi, "The Development Compact: A Theoretical Construct for South-South Cooperation," *International Studies* 53, no. 1 (2017): 28.

7. Vijay Prashad, *The Darker Nations: A People's History of the Third World* (New York: New Press, 2007), 276.

8. Jeffrey Byrne, "Africa's Cold War," in *The Third World in the Cold War*, ed. Robert J. McMahon (New York: Oxford University Press, 2013), 107.

9. Ruth Reitan, *The Rise and Decline of an Alliance: Cuba and African American Leaders in the 1960s* (East Lansing: Michigan State University, 1999), 92.

10. Teishan A. Latner, "Take Me to Havana! Airline Hijacking, U.S.-Cuba Relations, and Political Protest in Late Sixties' America," *Diplomatic History* 39, no. 1 (2015): 16.

11. Annie Jacobsen, *Area 51: An Uncensored History of America's Top Secret Military Base* (New York: Little, Brown, 2011), 380.

12. Edward N. Muller and Karl-Dieter Opp, "Rational Choice and Rebellious Collective Action," *American Political Science Review* 80, no. 2 (1986): 471.

13. Lara Putnam, *Radical Moves: Caribbean Migrants and the Politics of Race in the Jazz Age* (Chapel Hill: University of North Carolina Press, 2013), 230.

14. Betina Parry, "Resistance Theory/Theorizing Resistance: Or Two Cheers for Nativism," in *Rethinking Fanon: The Continuing Debate*, ed. Nigel C. Gibson (New York: Humanity Books, 1999), 240.

15. Tanya Harmer, *Allende's Chile and the Inter-American Cold War* (Chapel Hill: University of North Carolina Press, 2011), 3.

16. Striffler, *Solidarity*, 202.

17. Argus correspondent, "Bitter Vatican Reply to Israelis," *Argus*, 14 September 1982, 1, "South African Situation," Archive of the Archdiocese of Cape Town, Cape Town, Western Cape, South Africa.

18. Afua Cooper, Rinaldo Walcott, and Lekeisha Hughes, "Robin D. G. Kelley and Fred Moten in Conversation," *Critical Ethnic Studies* 4, no. 1 (2018): 167–68.

19. Laura Briggs, Gladys McCormick, and J. T. Way, "Transnationalism: A Category of Analysis," *American Quarterly* 60, no. 3 (2008): 641.

Bibliography

Archives

"Apartheid South Africa," Digital Archive, Michigan State University, Lansing

Archive of the Archdiocese of Cape Town, Cape Town

Archive of the Jabotinsky Institute, Tel Aviv

Archive of the Organización de Solidaridad con los Pueblos de Asia, África y América Latina (OSPAAAL), Havana

Archivo General de la Nación (AGN), Mexico City

Archivo Nacional de Chile, Santiago, Chile

Archivo del Partido Comunista, Buenos Aires

Central Zionist Archive, Jerusalem, Israel

Centro de Documentación e Investigación de la Cultura de Izquierdas, Buenos Aires

Cuban Heritage Collection, University of Miami Libraries

Departamento Diplomático, Sección de Archivo General, Secretaría de Relaciones Exteriores (SRE), Mexico City

Hoover Institution, Stanford University, Palo Alto

Ibero-Amerikanisches Institut, Berlin

Instituto de Investigaciones Jurídicas, Universidad Autónoma de México (IIJ-UNAM), Mexico City

John and Janet Wallach Papers, Princeton University Firestone Library, Princeton

Library of Congress, Palestine Poster Project Archives, Washington

North American Conference on Latin America Papers (NACLA), Princeton University, Princeton

Princeton University collection of Latin American Political Ephemera, Dulles Library, Princeton

Sam Slick Collection, University of New Mexico Library, Albuequerque

South African History Archive, Johannesburg

United Nations Archive, New York

Secondary Sources

Abbink, Jon. "Being Young in Africa: The Politics of Despair and Renewal." In *Vanguard or Vandals: Youth, Politics and Conflict in Africa*, edited by Jon Abbink and Ineke van Kessel, 1–34. London: Brill Academic, 2005.

Abraham, Garth. *The Catholic Church and Apartheid: The Response of the Catholic Church in South Africa to the First Decade of National Party Rule 1948–1957.* Johannesburg: Ravan Press, 1989.

Abugattas, Juan. "The Perception of the Palestinian Question in Latin America." *Journal of Palestine Studies* 11, no. 3 (1982): 117–28.

Abu Sitta, Salman. "Che Guevara in Gaza: Palestine Becomes a Global Cause." *Middle East Monitor*, 20 July 2015, 3–11.

Aceves Sepúlveda, Gabriela. *Women Made Visible: Feminist Art and Media in Post-1968 Mexico City.* Lincoln: University of Nebraska Press, 2019.

Adelman, Jeremy. *Sovereignty and Revolution in the Iberian Atlantic.* Princeton, NJ: Princeton University Press, 2006.

Adhikari, Mohamed. *Not White Enough, Not Black Enough: Racial Identity in the South African Coloured Community.* Columbus: Ohio University Press, 2005.

Agar Corbinos, Lorenzo. "El comportamiento urbano de los migrantes árabes en Chile." *Revista EURE—Revista De Estudios Urbano Regionales* 9, no. 27 (1983): 73–84.

Ahmed, Sara. *Strange Encounters: Embodied Others in Post-coloniality.* New York: Routledge, 2000.

Alessandrini, Anthony. "Fanon Now: Singularity and Solidarity." *Journal of Pan-African Studies* 4, no. 7 (2011): 52–74.

al-Haj Saleh, Yassin. "A Critique of Solidarity." Translated by Alex Rowell. *Al-Jumhuriya*, 16 July 2018. https://www.aljumhuriya.net/en/content/critique-solidarity.

Alle, María Fernanda. "Tuñón contra Borges: La division campo antiperonista en la segunda mitad de la década de 1950." *Acta literaria* 59 (2019). https://scielo.conicyt.cl/scielo.php?script=sci_arttext&pid=S0717-68482019000200075.

Alvarez, Sonia. "Translating the Global: Effects of Transnational Organizing on Local Feminist Discourses and Practices in Latin America." *Meridians* 1, no. 1 (2000): 29–67.

Andes, Stephen. "A Catholic Alternative to Revolution: The Survival of Social Catholicism in Postrevolutionary Mexico." *The Americas* 68, no. 4 (2012): 529–62.

Anguiano, Eugenio. "México y el Tercer Mundo: racionalización de una posición," in *Foro Internacional: Antología de estudios de política y relaciones internacionales*, edited by Elodie Brun and Humberto Garza Eliozondo, 4:15–158. Mexico City: El Colegio de México, 2019.

Anner, Mark S. *Solidarity Transformed: Labor Responses to Globalization and Crisis in Latin America.* Ithaca, NY: Cornell University Press, 2011.

Antognazzi, Irma, and María Felisa Lemos. *Nicaragua, el ojo del huracán revolucionario.* Buenos Aires: Nuestra América, 2006.

Appiah, Kwame. *Cosmpolitanism: Ethics in a World of Strangers.* New York: Norton, 2007.

Araujo, Ana Lucia. *Shadows of the Slave Past: Memory, Heritage, and Slavery.* New York: Routledge, 2014.

Archer, Julien. *The First International in France, 1864–1872: Its Origins, Theories and Impact.* Lanham, MD: University Press of America, 1997.

Armstrong, David. *Revolution and World Order: The Revolutionary State in World Order.* Oxford: Oxford University Press, 1993.

Aviña, Alexander. "An Archive of Counterinsurgency: State Anxieties and Peasant Guerrillas in Cold War Mexico." *Journal of Iberian and Latin American Research* 19, no. 1 (2013): 41–51.

Awartani, Sara. "In Solidarity: Palestine in the Puerto Rican Political Imaginary." *Radical History Review* 128 (2017): 199–222.

Baer, James A. *Anarchist Immigrants in Spain and Argentina.* Urbana: University of Illinois Press, 2015.

Baeza, Cecília. "América latina y la cuestión palestina (1947–2012)." *Araucaria* 14, no. 28 (2011): 111–31.

Baeza, Cecília. "Palestinians in Latin America: Between Assimilation and Long-Distance Nationalism." *Journal of Palestine Studies* 43, no. 2 (2014): 59–72.

Bahbah, Bishara. "Israel's Military Relationship with Ecuador and Argentina." *Journal of Palestine Studies* 15, no. 2 (1986): 76–101.

Bahbah, Bishara, and Linda Butler. *Israel and Latin America: The Military Connection.* New York: St. Martin's Press, 1986.

Balloffet, Lily Pearl. *Argentina in the Global Middle East.* Palo Alto, CA: Stanford University Press, 2020.

Balloffet, Lily Pearl. "Argentine & Egyptian History Entangled: From Perón to Nasser." *Journal of Latin American Studies* 50, no. 3 (2018): 549–77.

Balloffet, Lily Pearl, Fernando Camacho Padilla, and Jessica Stites Mor. "Pushing Boundaries: New Directions in Contemporary Latin America-Middle East History." *Jahrbuch für Geschichte Lateinamerikas—Anuario de Historia de América Latina* 56 (2019): 1–14.

Bartky, Sandra. *"On Solidarity and Sympathy" and Other Essays.* Lanham, MD: Rowman and Littlefield, 2002.

Basu, Amrita. "Globalization of the Local/Localization of the Global: Mapping Transnational Women's Movements." In *Feminist Theory Reader*, edited by Carole McCann Carole and Kim Seung-Kyung, 68–77. New York: Routledge, 2003.

Bawalsa, Nadim. "Palestine West of the Andes." *NACLA Report on the Americas* 50, no. 1 (2018): 34–39.

Bayertz, Kurt. "Four Uses of 'Solidarity.'" In *Solidarity: Philosophical Studies in Contemporary Culture*, edited by Kurt Bayertz, 3–28. London: Kluwer, 1999.

Becken, H. J., ed. *Relevant Theology for Africa.* Durban: Lutheran Publishing House, 1973.

Beit-Hallahmi, Benjamin. *The Israeli Connection: Who Israel Arms and Why.* London: Tauris, 1987.

Bergel, Martín. *El oriente desplazado: Los intelectuales y los orígenes del tercermundismo en la Argentina.* Quilmes: Editorial de la Universidad de Quilmes, 2015.

Berryman, Philip. *Liberation Theology.* Philadelphia: Temple University Press, 1989.

Black, Ashley. "Canto Libre: Folk Music and Solidarity in the Americas." In *The Art of Solidarity: Visual and Performative Politics in Cold War Latin America,* edited by Jessica Stites Mor and Maria del Carmen Suescun Pozas, 130–31. Austin: University of Texas Press, 2018.

Black, Ashley. "The Politics of Asylum: Stability, Sovereignty, and Mexican Foreign Policy in the Caribbean Basin, 1945–1959." PhD diss., Stony Brook University, 2018.

Blackburn, Robin. *The American Crucible: Slavery, Emancipation and Human Rights.* London: Verso, 2011.

Borer, Tristan Anne. *Challenging the State: Churches as Political Actors in South Africa, 1980–1994.* Notre Dame, IN: University of Notre Dame Press, 1998.

Borges Deminicis, Rafael, and Daniel Aarão Filho, eds. *História do anarquismo no Brasil.* Rio de Janeiro: EdUFF, 2006.

Borland, Katherine. "Traditions of Resistance, Expressions of Solidarity, and the Honduran Coup." In *The Art of Solidarity: Visual and Performative Politics in Cold War Latin America,* edited by Jessica Stites Mor and Maria del Carmen Suescun Pozas, 53–81. Austin: University of Texas Press, 2018.

Brands, Hal. *Latin America's Cold War.* Cambridge, MA: Harvard University Press, 2010.

Breitinger, Ekchardt. "Lamentations Patriotiques: Writers, Censors, and Politics in Cameroon." *African Affairs* 92 (1993): 557–75.

Brennan, James P. *Argentina's Missing Bones: Revisiting the History of the Dirty War.* Oakland: University of California Press, 2018.

Briggs, Laura, Gladys McCormick, and J. T. Way. "Transnationalism: A Category of Analysis." *American Quarterly* 60, no. 3 (2008): 625–48.

Brock, Lisa. "Back to the Future: African-Americans and Cuba in the Time(s) of Race." *Contributions in Black Studies: A Journal of African and Afro-American Studies* 12, no. 1 (1994): 1–24.

Bruey, Alison. *Bread and Justice: Grassroots Activism and Human Rights in Pinochet's Chile.* Madison: University of Wisconsin Press, 2018.

Brysk, Alison. "From Above and Below: Social Movements, the International System, and Human Rights in Argentina." *Comparative Political Studies* 26, no. 3 (1993): 259–85.

Brysk, Alison. *The Politics of Human Rights in Argentina: Protest, Change, and Democratization.* Stanford, CA: Stanford University Press, 1994.

Buchenau, Jürgen, and Gilbert M. Joseph. *Mexico's Once and Future Revolution: Social Upheaval and the Challenge of Rule since the Late Nineteenth Century.* Durham, NC: Duke University Press, 2013.

Bueckert, Michael. "Boycotts and Revolution: Debating the Legitimacy of the African National Congress in the Canadian Anti-Apartheid Movement, 1969–94." *Radical History Review* 134 (2019): 96–115.

Burden-Stelly, Cherisse. "Reclaiming the Tricontinental: Transnational Solidarity and Contemporary Struggles." *Black Perspectives*, 9 November 2018.

Burdick, John. "The Evolution of a Progressive Catholic Project: The Case of the Black Pastoral in Rio de Janeiro, Brazil." In *The Church at the Grassroots in Latin America: Perspectives on Thirty Years of Activism*, edited by John Burdick and W. E. Hewitt, 71–84. Westport, CT: Praeger, 2000.

Burdick, John. *Legacies of Liberation: The Progressive Church in Brazil at the Start of a New Millennium.* Hampshire: Ashgate, 2004.

Burton, Julianne. "Film and Revolution in Cuba: The First Twenty-Five Years." In *New Latin American Cinema*, vol. 2, *Studies of National Cinemas*, edited by Michael T. Martin, 123–42. Detroit: Wayne State University Press, 1997.

Butelezi, Peter John. *Statement on Black Consciousness and Human Rights.* Pretoria: SACBC, 1976.

Byrne, Jeffrey. "Africa's Cold War." In *The Third World in the Cold War*, edited by Robert J. McMahon, 101–23. New York: Oxford University Press, 2013.

Byrne, Jeffrey. *Mecca of Revolution: Algeria, Decolonization, and the Third World Order.* London: Oxford University Press, 2016.

Calandra, Benedetta, and Marina Franco. *La guerra fría cultural en América Latina.* Buenos Aires: Biblos, 2012.

Calderón, Fernando, and Elizabeth Jelin. *Clases y movimientos sociales en América Latina: Perspectivas y realidades.* Buenos Aires: Centro de Estudios de Estado y Sociedad, 1987.

Calles Barger, Lilian. *The World Came of Age: An Intellectual History of Liberation Theology.* New York: Oxford University Press, 2018.

Calvo González, Patricia. "La Organización Latinomamericana de Solidaridad (OLAS) a través del boletín de información de su comité organizador (1966–1967)." *Revista de Historia Social y de las Mentalidades* 22, no. 1 (2018): 155–85.

Camacho Padilla, Fernando. "Las relaciones entre Latinoamérica e Irán durante la última década de la dinastía Pahleví." *Jahrbuch für Geschichte Lateinamerikas—Anuario de Historia de América Latina* 56 (2019): 66–96.

Camacho Padilla, Fernando. "The Swedish Chilean Society: Fascist Solidarity with Pinochet's Chile in Sweden." In *Making Sense of the Americas: How Protest Related to America in the 1980s and Beyond*, edited by Jan Hansen, Christian Helm, and Frank Reichherzer, 131–50. Chicago: Campus Verlag, 2015.

Camacho Padilla, Fernando, and Eugenia Palieraki. "*Hasta Siempre*, OSPAAAL!" *North American Congress on Latin America Report on the Americas* 51, no. 4 (2019): 410–21.

Canton Navarro, José C., and Arnaldo Silva León. *Historia de Cuba 1959–1999: Liberación nacional y socialism.* Havana: Editorial Pueblo y Educación, 2009.

Cardoso, Ruth. "Popular Movements in the Context of the Consolidation of Democracy." Working Paper Series, Helen Kellogg Institute for International Studies, 120 (March 1989).

Carnovale, Vera. "El PRT-ERP en el exilio: Armas, comunismo y derechos humanos." *Revista de Historia* 15 (2014): 1–28.

Carr, Barry. "Pioneering Transnational Solidarity in the Americas: The Movement in Support of Augusto C. Sandino 1927–1934." *Journal of Iberian and Latin American Research* 20, no. 2 (2014): 141–52.

Carr, Barry, and Steve Ellner, eds. *The Latin American Left: From Allende to Perestroika.* Boulder, CO: Westview, 1993.

Carvalhaes, Cláudio and Fábio Py. "Liberation Theology in Brazil." *CrossCurrents* 67, no. 1 (March 2017): 157–79.

Castañeda, Jorge. *Utopia Unarmed: The Latin American Left after the Cold War.* New York: Vintage, 1993.

Castillo, Manuel Ángel. "El dilema del retorno o la permanencia de los refugiados guatemaltecos en México: Una reflexión veinte años después." In *El retorno: Migración económica y exilio político en América Latina y España*, edited by Alicia Gil Lázaro, Aurelio Martín Nójera, and Pedro Pérez Herrero, 75–89. Madrid: Cátedra del Exilio, Institutio de Estudios Latinoamericanos, 2013.

Castillo, Manuel Ángel, and Fabienne Venet. "Migraciones internacionales." In *Los grandes problemas de México*, 3:195–226. Mexico City: Colegio de Mexico, 2010.

Cesana, Roberta. *"Libri necessary": Le edizioni letterarie Feltrinelli (1955–1965).* Milan: Edizioni Unicopli, 2010.

Cezar Miskulin, Silvia. "O ano de 1968 em Cuba: Mudanças na política internacional e na política cultural." *Esboços* 15, no. 20 (2008): 47–66.

Chamberlin, Paul. *The Global Offensive.* London: Oxford University Press, 2012.

Chanan, Michael. *Cuban Cinema.* Minneapolis: University of Minnesota Press, 2004.

Chaplin, Tamara, and Jadwiga Pieper Mooney, eds. *The Global 1960s: Convention, Contest, and Counterculture.* New York: Routledge, 2018.

Chaturvedi, Sachin. "The Development Compact: A Theoretical Construct for South-South Cooperation." *International Studies* 53, no. 1 (2017): 15–43.

Chomsky, Aviva, and Steve Striffler. "Reply: Solidarity Latin America Solidarity: The Colombian Coal Campaign." *Dialectical Anthropology* 32 (2008): 191–96.

Christie, Pam. *The Right to Learn: The Struggle for Education in South Africa.* Johannesburg: Ravan Press, 1991.

Civantos, Christina. *Between Argentines and Arabs: Argentine Orientalism, Arab Immigrants, and the Writing of History.* New York: State University of New York Press, 2006.

Cobb, Russell. "The Politics of Literary Prestige: Promoting the Latin American 'Boom' in the Pages of *Mundo Nuevo*." *A Contra corriente: A Journal on Social History and Literature in Latin America* 5, no. 3 (2008): 75–94.

Coleman, Kevin. "A Flamethrower to His Image." *Photography & Culture* 13, no. 2 (2020): 239–42.

Coggiola, Osvaldo. *Historia del Trotskismo en Argentina y América Latina.* Buenos Aires: Ediciones Razón y Revolución, 2006.

Cone, James. *Black Theology and Black Power.* New York: Seabury, 1969.

Cone, James. *A Black Theory of Liberation.* Philadelphia: Lippincott, 1970.

Consejo Episcopal Latinoamericano (CELAM). *Evangelización en el presente y en el futuro de América Latina.* San Salvador: UCA Editores, 1979.

Cook, Guillermo. *The Expectation of the Poor: Latin American Base Ecclesial Communities in Protestant Perspective*. Maryknoll, NY: Orbis, 1985.

Cooper, Afua, Rinaldo Walcott, and Lekeisha Hughes. "Robin D. G. Kelley and Fred Moten in Conversation." *Critical Ethnic Studies* 4, no. 1 (2018): 154–72.

Cornell, Sarah E. "Citizens of Nowhere: Fugitive Slaves and Free African Americans in Mexico, 1833–1857." *Journal of American History* 100, no. 2 (2013): 351–74.

Correa, Enrique, and José Antonio Viera-Gallo. *Iglesia y dictadura*. Santiago: CESOC, Ediciones Chile y América, 1986.

Corrigan, Lisa M. "Cross-Pollinating the Revolution: From Havana to Oakland and Back Again." *Journal of Postcolonial Writing* 50, no. 4 (2014): 452–65.

Cortina Orero, Eudald. "Internacionalismo y revolución sandinidta: Proyecciones militantes y reformulaciones orgánicas en la izquierda revolucionaria argentina." *Estudios interdisciplinarios de América Latina y el Caribe* 28, no. 2 (2017): 80–103.

Coutaz, Pierre. "Regards sur le Movement Syndical International." *Recherches internationales* 112 (2018): 81–85.

Craib, Raymond. *Cartographic Mexico: A History of State Fixations and Fugitive Landscapes*. Durham, NC: Duke University Press, 2004.

Craven, David. *Art and Revolution in Latin America, 1910–1990*. New Haven, CT: Yale University Press, 2002.

Craven, David. "Latin American Posters: Public Aesthetics and Mass Politics." In *Latin American Posters: Public Aesthetics and Mass Politics*, edited by Russ Davidson, 15–19. Santa Fe: Museum of New Mexico Press, 2006.

Cushing, Lincoln. "Republic of Cuba, 1959." In *Communist Posters*, edited by Mary Ginsburg, 321–67. London: Reaktion Books, 2020.

Cushing, Lincoln. *¡Revolución! Cuban Poster Art*. San Francisco: Chronicle, 2003.

Cushing, Lincoln, ed. *Visions of Peace and Justice*. Vol. 1, *San Francisco Bay Area, 1974–2007*. Berkeley, CA: Inkworks Press, 2007.

Dávila, Jerry. *Hotel Trópico: Brazil and the Challenge of African Decolonization, 1950–1980*. Durham, NC: Duke University Press, 2010.

Davis, Stephen R. *The ANC's War against Apartheid*. Bloomington: University of Indiana Press, 2018.

de Laforcade, Geoffroy, and Kirwin Shaffer, eds. *In Defiance of Boundaries: Anarchism in Latin American History*. Gainesville: University of Florida Press, 2015.

de la Mora Valencia, Rogelio. "Intelectuales guatemaltecos en México: Del movimiento Claridad al antifascismo, 1921–1939." *Signos históricos* 14, no. 27 (2012): 104–37.

de la Torre, Verónica. "La acción colectiva transnacional en las acción colectiva de los movimientos sociales y de las Relaciones Internacionales." *CONfines de relaciones internacionales y ciencia política* 7, no. 14 (2011): 45–72.

della Porta, Donatella, ed. *Solidarity Mobilizations in the "Refugee Crisis."* New York: Palgrave Macmillan, 2018.

de Titto, Ricardo. *El Pensamiento del socialismo y la izquierda*. Buenos Aires: Editorial El Ateneo, 2010.

Demers, Maurice. *Connected Struggles: Catholics, Nationalists, and Transnational Relations between Mexico and Quebec, 1917–1945.* Montreal: McGill-Queen's University Press, 2014.

Denis, Philippe. "Archibishop Hurley's Strange Silence on Apartheid at Vatican II." *Ephererides Theologicae Lovanienses* 89, no. 4 (2013): 411–24.

Denis, Philippe. "Seminary Training and Black Consciousness in South Africa in the Early 1970s." *South African History Journal* 62, no. 1 (2010): 162–82.

Dorais, Geneviève. "Indo-America and the Politics of APRA Exile, 1918–1945." PhD diss., University of Wisconsin, 2014.

Drinot, Paulo. *The Allure of Labor: Workers, Race, and the Making of the Peruvian State.* Durham, NC: Duke University Press, 2011.

Dumois, Conchita, and Gabriel Molina. *Jorge Ricardo Masetti, el Comandante Segundo.* Havana: Editorial Capitán San Luis, 2012.

Duncan, Graham, and Anthony Egan. "The Ecumenical Struggle in South Africa: The Role of Ecumenical Movements and Liberation Organisations from 1966." *Studia Historiae Ecclesiasticae* 45, no. 1 (2019): 1–28.

Durkheim, Émile. *The Division of Labor in Society.* Translated by W. D. Halls. 1893. Reprint, New York: Free Press, 2014.

Dussel, Enrique. "From the Second Vatican Council to the Present Day." In *The Church in Latin America, 1492–1992*, edited by Enrique Dussel, 153–82. Maryknoll, NY: Orbis, 1992.

Eckmann, Teresa. "The Latin American Poster: Image, Message, and Means." In *Latin American Posters: Public Aesthetics and Mass Politics*, edited by Russ Davidson, 35–49. Santa Fe: Museum of New Mexico Press, 2006.

El-Attar, Heba. "Memorias acusticas palestino-chilenas: El caso de 'Palestina por Siempre.'" *Miscelánea de Estudios Árabes y Hebraicos, Sección Árabe-Islam* 68 (2019): 441–50.

El-Attar, Heba. "Palestinian and Jewish Communal Press in Chile: The Case of Al-Damir and La Palabra Israelita." *Latin American and Caribbean Ethnic Studies* 6, no. 2 (2011): 189–206.

Elsey, Brenda. "'As the World Is My Witness': Popular Culture and the Chilean Solidarity Movement, 1974–1987." In *Human Rights and Transnational Solidarity in Cold War Latin America*, edited by Jessica Stites Mor, 177–208. Madison: University of Wisconsin Press, 2013.

Elsey, Brenda. *Citizens and Sportsmen: Fútbol and Politics in Twentieth-Century Chile.* Austin: University of Texas Press, 2011.

Elsey, Brenda. "Cultural Ambassadorship and the Pan-American Games of the 1950s." *International Journal of the History of Sport* 33, nos. 1–2 (2016): 105–26.

Escudé, Carlos, and Beatriz Gurevich. "Transnational Terrorism, Corruption and Erosion of State Authority: The Case of the 1992 and 1994 Attacks in Argentina." *Estudios Interdisciplinarios de América Latina* 4, no. 2 (2003): 127–48.

Estradet, Víctor. *Memorias del Negro Pedro: Tupamaros en la revolución Sandinista.* Montevideo: Fin de Siglo, 2013.

Faligot, Roger. *Tricontinentale: Quand Che Guevara, Ben Barka, Cabral, Castro et Hô Chi Minh préparaient la révolution mondiale (1964–1968).* Paris: La Découverte, 2013.

Featherstone, David. *Solidarity: Hidden Histories and Geographies of Internationalism.* London: Zed Books, 2012.

Fermandois Huerta, Joaquín. *Chile y el mundo, 1973–1975.* Ediciones Universidad Católica de Chile: Santiago, 1985.

Fermandois Huerta, Joaquín. "De una inserción a otra: Política exterior de Chile, 1966–1991." *Estudios Internacionales* 24, no. 96 (1991): 433–55.

Fernández, Damián J. "Fiction and Nonfiction: Problems in the Study of Cuban Foreign Policy." *Latin American Research Review* 25, no. 3 (1990): 237–47.

Fernández, Paula Daniela. "Fora o imperialismo da América Central, el caso de la solidaridad brasileña con la revolución sandinista." *Revista de la Red de Intercátedras de Historia de América Latina Contemporánea* 2, no. 2 (2015): 94–113.

Figueiredo de Castro, Ricardo. "A Frente Unica Antifascists e o antifascism no Brasil, 1933–1934." *Topoi* 3, no. 5 (2002): 354–88.

Fiszerman, Ezequiel. "Entre Moscú y Europa: Israel como caso crítico de la vía socialista en la Argentina, 1946–1956." In *Israel-Palestine, una passion Argentina: Estudios sobre la recepción del conflicto árabe-israelí en la Argentina,* edited by Emmanual N. Kahan, 75–98. Buenos Aires: Prometeo, 2016.

Forbis, Melissa. "After Autonomy: The Zapatistas, Insurgent Indigeneity, and Decolonization." *Settler Colonial Studies* 6, no. 4 (2016): 365–38.

Foster, Elizabeth. *African Catholic: Decolonization and the Transformation of the Church.* Cambridge, MA: Harvard University Press, 2019.

Fox, Claire. *Making Art Panamerican: Cultural Policy and the Cold War.* Minneapolis: University of Minnesota Press, 2015.

Gandhi, Leela. *Affective Communities: Anti-colonial Thought, Fin-de-Siècle Radicalism, and the Politics of Friendship.* Durham, NC: Duke University Press, 2006.

García, María Cristina. *Seeking Refuge: Central American Migration to Mexico, the United States, and Canada.* Berkeley: University of California Press, 2006.

Garcia-Bryce, Iñigo. "Transnational Activist: Magda Mortal and the American Popular Revolutionary Alliance (APRA), 1926–1950." *The Americas* 70, no. 4 (2014): 677–706.

Garner, William R. "The Sino-Soviet Ideological Struggle in Latin America." *Journal of Inter-American Studies* 10, no. 2 (1968): 244–55.

Geggus, David P. *The Impact of the Haitian Revolution in the Atlantic World.* Columbia: University of South Carolina Press, 2001.

George, Edward. *The Cuban Intervention in Africa, 1965–1991: From Che Guevara to Cuito Cuanavale.* London: Routledge, 2005.

Gerhard, Gail M. *Black Power in South Africa: The Evolution of an Ideology.* Los Angeles, Greenberg, 1999.

Gibson, Nigel. "Black Consciousness 1977–1987: The Dialectics of Liberation in South Africa." *Africa Today* 35, no. 1 (1988): 5–26.

Gifford, Paul. *The Religious Right in Southern Africa.* Harare: Baobab Books and University of Zimbabwe Publications, 1988.

Gillingham, Paul, and Benjamin T. Smith. "Paradoxes of Revolution." In *Dictablanda: Politics, War, and Culture in Mexico, 1938–1968*, edited by Paul Gillingham and Benjamin T. Smith, 1–44. Durham, NC: Duke University Press, 2014.

Glaser, Clive. "Beyond the Legacy of 1976: Morris Isaacson High School, Popular Memory and the Struggle for Education in Central Soweto." *African Studies* 79, no. 1 (2020): 21–36.

Gleijeses, Piero. *Conflicting Missions: Havana, Washington, and Africa, 1959–1976.* Chapel Hill: University of North Carolina Press, 2002.

Gliejeses, Piero. *Visions of Freedom: Havana, Washington, Pretoria, and the Struggle for Southern Africa.* Chapel Hill: University of North Carolina Press, 2013.

Goebel, Michael. "A Movement from Right to Left in Argentine Nationalism? The Alianza Libertadora Nacionalista and Tacuara as Stages of Militancy." *Bulletin of Latin American Research* 26, no. 3 (2007): 356–77.

Goldfarb, Jeffrey C. "Media Events, Solidarity, and the Rise and Fall of the Public Sphere." *Media, Culture, and Society* 40, no. 1 (2018): 118–21.

Gómez Chacón, César. *Cuito Cuanavale: Viaje al centro de los heroes.* Havana: Editorial Letras Cubanas, 1989.

Gómez de Souza, Luiz Alberto. "A caminhada de Medellín a Puebla." *Perspectiva teológica* 31, no. 84 (1999): 223–34.

Gómez de Souza, Luiz Alberto. "Latin America and the Catholic Church: Points of Convergence and Divergence (encontros e desencontros) 1960–2005." Working Paper Series, Helen Kellogg Institute for International Studies, 334 (February 2007). https://kellogg.nd.edu/sites/default/files/old_files/documents/334_0.pdf.

Goodwin, Jeff, and James Jasper. "When and Why Do Social Movements Occur: Introduction." In *The Social Movements Reader*, 2nd ed., edited by Jeff Goodwin and James Jasper, 9–14. Oxford: Wiley-Blackwell, 2009.

Gordon Wellen, Michael. "Pan-American Dreams: Art, Politics, and Museum-Making at the OAS, 1948–1976." PhD diss., University of Texas at Austin, 2012.

Gosse, Van. "Active Engagement: The Legacy of Central American Solidarity." *North American Conference on Latin America* 28, no. 5 (1995): 22–29.

Gosse, Van. *Rethinking the New Left: An Interpretative History.* New York: Palgrave Macmillan, 2005.

Gould, Carol C. "Transnational Solidarities." *Journal of Social Philosophy* 38, no. 1 (2007): 148–64.

Gould, Jeffrey. "Solidarity under Siege: The Latin American Left, 1968." *American Historical Review* 114, no. 2 (2009): 348–75.

Gould, Jeffrey. *Solidarity under Siege: The Salvadoran Labor Movement, 1970–1990.* Cambridge: Cambridge University Press, 2019.

Grandin, Greg. "Human Rights and Empire's Embrace." In *Human Rights and Revolutions*, 2nd ed., ed. Jeffrey N. Wasserstrom, Lynn Hunt, Marilyn B. Young, and Gregory Grandin, 191–212. New York: Rowman and Littlefield, 2007.

Grandin, Greg. "Living in Revolutionary Time: Coming to Terms with the Violence of Latin America's Long Cold War." In *A Century of Revolution: Insurgent and Counterinsurgent Violence in Latin America's Long Cold War*, edited by Greg Grandin and Gilbert M. Joseph, 1–44. Durham, NC: Duke University Press, 2011.

Green, James N. "Clerics, Exiles, and Academics: Opposition to the Brazilian Military Dictatorship in the United States, 1969–1974." *Latin American Politics and Society* 45, no. 1 (2003): 87–117.

Green, James N. "The Emergence of the Brazilian Gay Liberation Movement, 1977–1981." *Latin American Perspectives* 21, no. 1 (1994): 38–55.

Green, James N. *We Cannot Remain Silent: Opposition to the Brazilian Military Dictatorship.* Durham, NC: Duke University Press, 2008.

Greene, Julie. *The Canal Builders: Making America's Empire at the Panama Canal.* New York: Penguin Press, 2009.

Guerra, Lillian. *Visions of Power in Cuba: Revolution, Redemption and Resistance, 1959–1971.* Chapel Hill: University of North Carolina Press, 2012.

Guidry, Frank. *Forging Diaspora: Afro-Cubans and African Americans in a World of Empire and Jim Crow.* Chapel Hill: University of North Carolina Press, 2010.

Gurwitz, Beatrice. "From the New World to the Third World: Generation, Politics, and the Making of Argentine Jewish Ethnicity, 1955–1983." PhD diss., University of California, Berkeley, 2012.

Gutman, Daniel. *Tacuara, historia de la primera guerrilla urbana argentina.* Buenos Aires: Ediciones B Argentina, 2003.

Gutiérrez, Gustavo. *A Theology for Liberation: History, Politics and Salvation.* Maryknoll, NY: Orbis, 1971.

Habermas, Jürgen. "Justice and Solidarity: On the Discussion Concerning Stage 6." *Philosophical Forum* 21, no. 12 (1989): 32–52.

Hanna, Lani. "Tricontinental's International Solidarity: Emotion in OSPAAAL as Tactic to Catalyze Support of Revolution." *Radical History Review* 136 (2020): 169–84.

Hansen, Jan, Christian Helm, Frank Reichherzer, eds. *Making Sense of the Americas: How Protest Related to America in the 1980s and Beyond.* Chicago: Campus Verlag, 2015.

Harmer, Tanya. *Allende's Chile and the Inter-American Cold War.* Chapel Hill: University of North Carolina Press, 2011.

Harmer, Tanya, and Alfredo Riquelme Segovia, eds. *Chile y la Guerra Fría global.* Santiago, RIL Editores, 2014.

Harto de Vera, Fernando. "La URSS y la revolución sandinista: Los estrechos límites de la solidaridad soviética." *Cuadernos África América Latina* 7 (1992): 87–93.

Hatzky, Christine. *Cubans in Angola: South-South Cooperation and Transfer of Knowledge, 1976–1991.* Madison: University of Wisconsin Press, 2014.

Hatzky, Christine. "Cuba's Concept of 'Internationalist Solidarity': Political Discourse, South–South Cooperation with Angola, and the Molding of Transnational Identities." In *Human Rights and Transnational Solidarity in Cold War Latin America*, edited by Jessica Stites Mor, 143–76. Madison: University of Wisconsin Press, 2013.

Hatzky, Christine, and Jessica Stites Mor. "Solidarity in Latin America: Contexts and Research Paradigms." *Journal of Iberian and Latin American Research* 20, no. 2 (2014): 127–40.

Hechter, Michael. *Principles of Group Solidarity.* Berkeley: University of California Press, 1987.

Helm, Christian. "'The Sons of Marx Greet the Sons of Sandino': West German Solidarity Visitors to Nicaragua Sandinista." *Journal of Iberian and Latin American Research* 20, no. 2 (2014): 153–70.

Henighan, Stephen. "The Cuban Fulcrum and the Search for a Transatlantic Revolutionary Culture in Angola, Mozambique and Chile, 1965–2008." *Journal of Transatlantic Studies* 7, no. 3 (2009): 233–48.

Hernández Padilla, Salvador. *El magonismo: Historia de una passion libertaria, 1900–1922.* Mexico City: Ediciones Era, 1988.

Herzog, Melanie. "'My Art Speaks for Both My Peoples': Elizabeth Catlett in Mexico." In *Art of Solidarity: Visual and Performative Politics in Cold War Latin America*, edited by Jessica Stites Mor and Maria del Carmen Suescun Pozas, 23–52. Austin: University of Texas Press, 2018.

Higgs, Catherine. "Silence, Disobedience, and African Catholic Sisters in Apartheid South Africa." *African Studies Review* 54, no. 2 (2011): 1–22.

Higgs, Catherine, and Jean N. Evans. "Embracing Activism in Apartheid South Africa: The Sisters of Mercy in Bophuthatswana, 1974–1994." *Catholic Historical Review* 94, no. 3 (2018): 500–521.

Hilb, Claudia, and Daniel Lutzky. *La nueva izquierda argentina: 1960–1980 (Política y violencia).* Buenos Aires: Centro Editor de América Latina, 1984.

Hinderliter, Beth. "An International Alliance of 'Colored Humanity': Robert Williams in Asia." *Journal of Postcolonial Writing* 50, no. 4 (2014): 437–51.

Hirsch, Steven, and Lucien van der Walt, eds. *Anarchism and Syndicalism in the Colonial and Post-Colonial World, 1870–1940.* Leiden: Brill, 2010.

Hobson, Emily. *Lavender and Red: Liberation and Solidarity in the Gay and Lesbian Left.* Oakland: University of California Press, 2016.

Hooker, Juliet. *Race and the Politics of Solidarity.* London: Oxford University Press, 2009.

Hope, Marjorie, and James Young. *South African Churches in a Revolutionary Situation.* Maryknoll, NY: Orbis, 1981.

Hornsby-Smith, Michael P. *An Introduction to Catholic Social Thought.* Cambridge: Cambridge University Press, 2006.

Houser, Myra Ann. "Avenging Carlota in Africa: Angola and the Memory of Cuban Slavery." *Atlantic Studies* 12, no. 1 (2015): 50–66.

Hyland, Steven. "Margins of the Majar: Arabic-Speaking Immigrants in Argentina, 1880–1946." PhD diss., Ohio State University, 2011.

Imaz, Cecilia. *La práctica del asilo y de refugio en México.* Mexico City: Potrerillos Editores, 1995.

Jabary Salamanca, Omar, Mezna Qato, Kareem Rabie, and Sobhi Samour. "Past Is Present: Settler Colonialism in Palestine." *Settler Colonial Studies* 2, no. 1 (2012): 1–8.

Jacobsen, Annie. *Area 51: An Uncensored History of America's Top Secret Military Base.* New York: Little, Brown, 2011.

Jamail, Milton, and Margo Gutiérrez. *It's No Secret: Israel's Military Involvement in Central America.* Belmont, MA: American-Arab University Graduates Press, 1986.

Jasiewicz, Krzystof. "Problems of Postcommunism: From Solidarity to Fragmentation." *Journal of Democracy* 3, no. 2 (1992): 55–69.

Jelin, Elizabeth. *Constructing Democracy: Human Rights, Citizenship, and Society in Latin America.* New York: Routledge, 2019.

Johns, Rebecca A. "Bridging the Gap between Class and Space: U.S. Worker Solidarity with Guatemala." *Economic Geography* 74, no. 3 (1998): 252–71.

Jolicoeur Rich, Jessica Alexis. "Organizing Twenty-First-Century Activism: From Structure to Strategy in Latin American Social Movements." *Latin American Research Review* 55, no. 3 (2020): 430–44.

Jozami, Maximiliano. "Argentine Left Parties and the 1967 Six-Day War through the Prism of Global Networks and South-South Connections." *Jahrbuch für Geschichte Lateinamerikas—Anuario de Historia de América Latina* 56 (2019): 15–41.

Jozami, Maximiliano, and Agustín Fertonani. "Un caso de orientalismo en la izquierda argentina: el Partido Socialista frente a la creación del Estado de Isarel." *CONTRA/ RELATOS desde el Sur* 6, no. 7 (2010): 45–60.

Kahan, Emmanuel N. "Algunos usos del conflicto en Israel-Palestina en Argentina: Debates entorno al conflicto árabe-israelí entre el tercer peronismo y la última dictadura militar (1973–1983)." *Revista Nuevosmundos, Mundos nuevos* (2014). https:// journals.openedition.org/nuevomundo/66778.

Kahan, Emmanuel N., ed. *Israel-Palestina: una pasión argentina: Estudios sobre la recepción del conflicto árabe-israelí en la Argentina.* Buenos Aires: Prometeo, 2016.

Kalt, Monica. *Tiersmondismus in der Schweiz der 1960er und 1970er Jahre. Von der Barmherzigkeit zur Solidarität.* Bern: Lang, 2010.

Kearney, Paddy. *Guardian of the Light: Denis Hurley, Renewing the Church, Opposing Apartheid.* New York: Continuum, 2009.

Keck, Margaret, and Kathryn Sikkink. *Activists beyond Borders: Advocacy Networks in International Politics.* Ithaca, NY: Cornell University Press, 1998.

Keller, Renata. *Mexico's Cold War: Cuba, the United States, and the Legacy of the Mexican Revolution.* Cambridge: Cambridge University Press, 2015.

Kelley, Robin D. G. *Freedom Dreams: The Black Radical Imagination.* Boston: Beacon, 2002.

Kelley, Sean. "'Mexico in His Head': Slavery and the Texas-Mexico Border, 1810–1860." *Journal of Social History* 37, no. 3 (2004): 709–23.

Kelly, Patrick William. "The 1973 Chilean Coup and the Origins of Transnational Human Rights Activism." *Journal of Global History* 8, no. 1 (2013): 165–86.

Khouri, Kristine, and Rasha Salti, eds. *Past Disquiet: Artists, International Solidarity and Museums in Exile.* Warsaw: Museum of Modern Art, 2019.

Khoury, Malek. "Origins and Patterns in the Discourse of New Arab Cinema." *Arab Studies Quarterly* 27, nos. 1–2 (2005): 1–20.

Kiddle, Amelia. "Between Two Revolutions: Cultural Relations between Mexico and Cuba." *Jahrbuch für Geschichte Lateinamerikas—Anuario de Historia de América Latina* 54 (2017): 108–28.

Kiddle, Amelia. *Mexico's Relations with Latin America during the Cárdenas Era.* Albuquerque: University of New Mexico Press, 2016.

Klaiber, Jeffrey. *The Church, Dictatorships, and Democracy in Latin America.* Eugene, OR: Wipf and Stock/Orbis, 1998.

Klich, Ignacio. "Arms for the Middle East and Argentina's Efforts at a Balances Approach to the Arab World and Israel." *Diplomacy and Statecraft* 7, no. 3 (1996): 704–28.

Klich, Ignacio. "The Chimera of Palestinian Resettlement in Argentina in the Early Aftermath of the First Arab-Israeli War and Other Similarly Fantastic Notions." *The Americas* 53, no. 1 (1996): 15–43.

Klich, Ignacio, and Jefferey Lesser, eds. *Arab and Jewish Immigrants in Latin America: Images and Reality.* London: Cass, 1998.

Klieman, Aaron. *Israel's Global Reach: Arms Sales as Diplomacy.* Oxford: Pergamon-Brassey, 1985.

Komter, Aafke Elisabeth. "The Disguised Rationality of Solidarity: Gift Giving in Informal Relations." *Journal of Mathematical Sociology* 25, no. 4 (2001): 385–401.

Kotzé, D. A. "Black Consciousness in South Africa." *South African Journal of Political Studies* 1, no. 1 (1974): 44–63.

Kovalenko, Ivan Ivanovich, and Rais Abdulkhakovich Tuzmukhamedov. *The Non-Aligned Movement: The Soviet View.* New York: Sterling, 1987.

Kruijt, Dirk. "Cuba and the Latin American Left: 1959–Present." *Estudios Interdisciplinarios de América Latina y el Caribe* 28, no. 2 (2017): 30–53.

Kunzle, David. "Public Graphics in Cuba: A Very Cuban Form of Internationalist Art." *Latin American Perspectives* 2, no. 4 (1975): 89–109.

Kuperus, Tracy. "Building Democracy: An Examination of Religious Associations in South Africa and Zimbabwe." *Journal of Modern African Studies* 37, no. 4 (1999): 643–68.

Laitinen, Arto. "From Recognition to Solidarity: Universal Respect, Mutual Support, and Social Unity." In *Solidarity: Theory and Practice*, edited by Arto Laitinen and Anne Birgitta Pessi, 126–54. Lanham, MD: Lexington Books, 2014.

Latner, Teishan A. "'Assata Shakur Is Welcome Here': Havana, Black Freedom Struggle, and U.S.-Cuba Relations." *Souls* 19, no. 4 (2017): 455–77.

Latner, Teishan A. *Cuban Revolution in America: Havana and the Making of a United States Left, 1968–1992.* Chapel Hill: University of North Carolina Press, 2018.

Latner, Teishan A. "Take Me to Havana! Airline Hijacking, U.S.-Cuba Relations, and Political Protest in Late Sixties' America." *Diplomatic History* 39, no. 1 (2015): 16–44.

Latourelle, René, ed. *Vatican II: Assessment and Perspectives: Twenty-Five Years After (1962–1987).* 3 vols. New York: Paulist Press, 1989.

LeFeber, Walter. *Inevitable Revolutions: The Unites States in Central America.* 2nd ed. New York: Norton, 1993.

Lida, Clara. *Inmigración y exilio: Reflexiones sobre el caso español.* Mexico City: Siglo Veintiuno Editores, 1997.

Lida, Clara. "La España perdida que México ganó." *Letras libres* (May 2003): 30–33.

Livingstone, Neil C., and David Halevy. *Inside the PLO: Covert Units, Secret Funds and the War against Israel and the United States.* New York: William Morrow, 1990.

Lloyd, David, and Laura Pulido. "In the Long Shadow of the Settler: On Israeli and U.S. Colonialisms." *American Quarterly* 62, no. 4 (2010): 795–809.

Loomis, James A. *Revolution of Forms: Cuba's Forgotten Art Schools.* 2nd ed. Princeton, NJ: Princeton Architectural Press, 2011.

López Blanch, Hedelberto. *Cuba: Pequeño gigante contra el apartheid.* Buenos Aires: Acercándonos Editorial, 2015.

López de la Torre, Carlos Fernando. "Encuentros solidarios en épocas revolucionarias: La Revolución Cubana y el Frente Sandinista de Liberación Nacional ante la causa Palestina." *Crítica y Emancipación* 7, no. 14 (2015): 45–106.

Luis, Roger Ricardo. *Prepárense a vivir: Crónicas de Cuito Cuanavale.* Havana: Editora Política, 1989.

Lutan, Rusli, and Fan Hong. "The Politics of Sport: GANEFO—A Case Study." *Sport in Society* 8, no. 3 (2011): 425–39.

Magaziner, Daniel. *The Law and the Prophets: Black Consciousness in South Africa, 1968–1977.* Columbus: Ohio University Press, 2010.

Mahler, Anne Garland. *From the Tricontinental to the Global South: Race, Radicalism, and Transnational Solidarity.* Durham, NC: Duke University Press, 2018.

Mahler, Anne Garland. "The Global South in the Belly of the Beast: Viewing African American Civil Rights through a Tricontinental Lens." *Latin American Research Review* 50, no. 1 (2015): 95–116.

Mainwaring, Scott, Eduardo Viola, and Rosa Cusminsky. "Los nuevos movimientos sociales, las culturas políticas y la democracia: Brasil y Argentina en la década de los ochenta." *Revista Mexicana de Sociología* 47, no. 4 (1985): 35–84.

Mainwaring, Scott, and Alexander Wilde. "The Progressive Church in Latin America: An Interpretation." In *The Progressive Church in Latin America*, edited by Scott Mainwaring and Alexander Wilde, 1–37. Notre Dame, IN: University of Notre Dame Press, 1989.

Malley, Robert. *The Call from Algeria: Third Worldism, Revolution, and the Turn to Islam.* Berkeley: University of California Press, 1996.

Mansilla, Hugo Celso Felipe. "Latin America within the Third World: The Search for a New Identity, the Acceptance of Old Contents." *Ibero-amerikanisches Archiv* 11, no. 2 (1985): 171–91.

Marañón, Boris, ed. *Solidaridad económica y potencialidades de transformación en América Latina.* Buenos Aires: CLACSO, 2012.

Marchesi, Aldo. "Revolution beyond the Sierra Maestra: The Tupamaros and the Development of a Repertoire of Dissent in the Southern Cone." *The Americas* 70, no. 3 (2014): 523–53.

Marchesi, Aldo. "Southern Cone Cities as Political Laboratories of the Global Sixties: Montevideo (1962–1968); Santiago de Chile (1969–1973); Buenos Aires (1973–1976)." *Estudios interdisciplinarios de América Latina y el Caribe* 28, no. 2 (2017): 54–79.

Marchesi, Aldo. "Writing the Latin American Cold War: Between the 'Local' South and the 'Global' North." *Estudos Históricos* 30, no. 60 (2017): 187–202.

Markarian, Vania. *Left in Transformation: Uruguayan Exiles and the Latin American Human Rights Networks, 1967–1984.* New York: Routledge, 2005.

Markarian, Vania. *Uruguay, 1968: Student Activism from Global Counterculture to Molotov Cocktails.* Oakland: University of California Press, 2016.

Marshall, T. H., and Tom Bottomore. *Citizenship and Social Class.* London: Pluto Press, 1987.

Martey, Emmanuel. *African Theology: Inculturation and Liberation.* Maryknoll, NY: Orbis, 1993.

Martín, José Pablo. *El Movimiento de Sacerdotes para el Tercer Mundo: Un debate argentine.* Buenos Aires: Editorial Guadalupe, 1992.

Martín Álvarez, Alberto, and Eduardo Rey Tristán. "La oleada revolucionaria latinoamericana contemporánea, 1959–1996." *Naveg@mérica: Revista electrónica editada por la Asociación Española de Americanistas* 9 (2012): 1–36.

Martín Álvarez, Alberto, and Eduardo Rey Tristán, eds. *Revolutionary Violence and the New Left: A Transnational Perspective.* New York: Routledge, 2017.

Martínez Mazzola, Ricardo. "*Los Recuerdos de un militante socialista,* de Enrique Dickmann." *Políticas de la Memoria* 17 (Summer 2016–17): 41–50.

Martínez Viademonte, José Augustín. *El derecho de asilo y el regimen internacional de refugiados.* Mexico City: Ediciones Botas, 1961.

Masalha, Nur. "The 1967 Palestinian Exodus." In *The Palestinian Exodus, 1948–1998,* edited by Ghada Karmi and Eugene Coltran, 63–108. Reading, UK: Ithaca Press, 1999.

Massad, Joseph. "Conceiving the Masculine: Gender and Palestinian Nationalism." *Middle East Journal* 49, no. 3 (1995): 467–83.

Mateos, Abdón. *La batalla de México: Final de la guerra civil y ayuda a los refugiados, 1939–1945.* Madrid: Alianza, 2009.

Matthews, Gelien. *Caribbean Slave Revolts and the British Abolitionist Movement.* Baton Rouge: Louisiana State University Press, 2006.

McCormick, Gladys. "The Last Door: Political Prisoners and the Use of Torture in Mexico's Dirty War." *The Americas* 74, no. 1 (2017): 57–81.

McGee Deutsch, Sandra. "The New School Lecture 'An Army of Women': Communist-Linked Solidarity Movements, Maternalism, and Political Consciousness in 1930s and 1940s Argentina." *The Americas* 75, no. 1 (2018): 95–125.

McSherry, J. Patrice. *Chilean New Song: The Political Power of Music, 1960s–1973.* Philadelphia: Temple University Press, 2015.

Melgar Bao, Ricardo. "The Anti-Imperialist League of the Americas between the East and Latin America." *Latin American Perspectives* 35, no. 2 (2008): 9–24.

Melgar Bao, Ricardo. *Redes e imaginario del exilio en México y América Latina, 1934–1940.* Buenos Aires: Ediciones Libros en Red, 2003.

Mignone, Emilio F. *Iglesia y dictadura: El papel de la Iglesia a la luz de sus relaciones con el régimen military.* Buenos Aires: Ediciones del Pensamiento Nacional, 1986.

Milkenky, Edward S. *Argentina's Foreign Policies.* Boulder, CO: Westview, 1978.

Mohanty, Chandra. *Feminism without Borders: Decolonizing Theory, Practicing Solidarity.* Durham, NC: Duke University Press, 2000.

Montes, Verónica, and María Dolores Paris Pombo. "Ethics of Care, Emotional Work, and Collective Action of Solidarity: The Patronas in Mexico." *Gender, Place and Culture* 26, no. 4 (2019): 559–80.

Moore, Basil, ed. *The Challenge of Black Theology in South Africa.* Atlanta: John Knox Press, 1974.

Moore, Carlos. "Afro-Cubans Push Back." *Journal of Pan African Studies* 4, no. 2 (2010): 457–61.

Moore, Carlos. *Castro, The Blacks, and Africa.* Los Angeles: University of California Press, 1988.

Morales Muñoz, Daniela. *El exilio brasileño en México durante la dictadura militar, 1964–1979.* Mexico City: SRE, 2018.

Morell Otero, Grethel. "Absolut Revolution: Revisitando la imagen cubana de los años 60 (1959–1969)." *Discursos fotográficos* 5, no. 7 (2009): 57–76.

Morello, Gustavo. "Christianity and Revolution: Catholicism and Guerrilla Warfare in Argentina's Seventies." *Journal of Religion and Violence* 1, no. 1 (2013): 48–70.

Motlhabi, Mokgethi. "Phases of Black Theology in South Africa: A Historical Review." *Religion & Theology* 16 (2009): 162–80.

Moyn, Samuel. *Human Rights and the Uses of History.* London: Verso Books, 2014.

Mukuka, George. "'Black Man, You Are on Your Own,' Interview with Archbishop Peter F. Butelezi." *Grace and Truth* 3 (1997): 36–49.

Muller, Dalia. *Cuban Émigrés and Independence in the Nineteenth-Century Gulf World.* Chapel Hill: University of North Carolina Press, 2017.

Muller, Edward N., and Karl-Dieter Opp. "Rational Choice and Rebellious Collective Action." *American Political Science Review* 80, no. 2 (1986): 471–87.

Muller, Retief. "Beyers Naudé (1915–2004): Christianity, Violence, and Reconciliation in South Africa." *Theology Today* 72, no. 3 (2015): 299–311.

Musallam, Adnan. "Palestinian Diaspora in Latin America: The Formative Stages, 19th Century to Early 20th Century." Lecture, Bethlehem University, West Bank, 2006.

Nállim, Jorge. "Antifascismo, revolución y Guerra Fría en México: La revista América, 1940–1960." *Latinoamérica: Revista de Estudios Latinoamericanos* 70 (2019): 93–123.

Nállim, Jorge. "Del antifascismo al antiperonismo: *Argentina Libre, Antinazi* y el surgimiento del antiperonismo político e intelectual." In *Fascismo y antifascismo: Peronismo y antiperonismo: Conflictos políticos e ideológicos en la Argentina (1930–1955),* edited by Marcela García Sebastiani, 77–105. Madrid: Iberoamericana Vervuert, 2006.

Nickel, James W., and Eduardo Viola. "Integrating Environmentalism and Human Rights." *Environmental Ethics* 16, no. 3 (1994): 265–73.

Nolan, Albert. *God in South Africa: The Challenge of the Gospel.* Grand Rapids, MI: Eerdmans, 1988.

Noonan, Patrick. *"They're Burning the Churches."* Jacana: Cape Town, 2003.

O'Connor, Alan. "Punk Subculture in Mexico and the Anti-globalization Movement: A Report from the Front." *New Political Science* 25, no. 1 (2003): 43–53.

Oesterheld, Héctor Germán, and Leopoldo Durñona. *Latinoamérica y el Imperialismo: 450 años de Guerra, recopilación de la historieta aperecida entre 1973 y 1974 en el semanario "El Descamisado."* Buenos Aires: Doeyo y Viniegra Editores, 2004.

Ojeda Gómez, Mario. "México ante los Estados Unidos en la coyuntura actual." In *Foro Internacional: Antología de estudios de política y relaciones internacionales*, edited by Elodie Brun and Humberto Garza Eliozondo, 4:159–90. Mexico City: El Colegio de México, 2019.

Olcott, Joclyn. *International Women's Year: The Greatest Consciousness-Raising Event in History.* London: Oxford University Press, 2017.

Olesen, Thomas. *International Zapatismo: The Construction of Solidarity in the Age of Globalization.* London: Zed Books, 2005.

Olivaries, Edmundo. *Pablo Neruda: Los caminos de América; Tras las huellas del poeta itinerante III (1940–1950).* Santiago: LOM Ediciones, 2014.

Orwell, George. "You and the Atom Bomb." *Tribune*, 19 October 1945. https://www.orwellfoundation.com/the-orwell-foundation/orwell/essays-and-other-works/you-and-the-atom-bomb/.

Ostrom, Elinor. *Governing the Commons: The Evolution of Institutions for Collective Action.* Cambridge: Cambridge University Press, 1990.

Pacheco, Juan Antonio. "La prensa árabe en chile: sueños y realidades árabes en un mundo nuevo." *Miscelánea de Estudios Árabes y Hebraicos, Sección Árabe-Islam* 55 (2006): 277–322.

Parry, Betina. "Resistance Theory/Theorizing Resistance: Or Two Cheers for Nativism." In *Rethinking Fanon: The Continuing Debate*, edited by Nigel C. Gibson, 215–50. New York: Humanity Books, 1999.

Pastorino, Ana María, and M. Raquel Ippoliti. "A propósito del Asilo Diplomático." *Revista de la Facultad de Derecho* 47 (2010): 1–37.

Peacock, Margaret. *Innocent Weapons: The Soviet and American Politics of Childhood in the Cold War.* Chapel Hill: University of North Carolina Press, 2014.

Pelant, Matyáš, "Czechoslovakia and Brazil 1945–1989." *Central European Journal of International & Security Studies* 7, no. 3 (2013): 96–117.

Peña, Milagros. *Theologies and Liberation in Peru: The Role of Ideas in Social Movements.* Philadelphia: Temple University Press, 1995.

Pensado, Jaime. *Rebel Mexico: Student Unrest and Authoritarian Political Culture during the Long Sixties.* Palo Alto, CA: Stanford University Press, 2015.

Pensado, Jaime, and Enrique Ochoa, eds. *Mexico beyond 1968: Revolutionaries, Radicals, and Repression during the Global Sixties and Subversive Seventies.* Tucson: University of Arizona Press, 2018.

Pereyra, Daniel. *Del Moncada a Chiapas. Historia de la lucha armada en América Latina.* Madrid: Libros de la Catarata, 1994.

Pereyra, Daniel Ezequiel. "Sociological Textbooks in Argentina and Mexico." *Current Sociology* 56, no. 2 (2008): 267–87.

Perla, Héctor, Jr. "La revolución nicaragüense y la solidaridad internacional." In *Nicaragua y el FSLN (1979–2009): ¿Qué queda de la revolución?*, edited by Salvador Martí i Puig and David Close, 117–136. Barcelona: Edicions Bellaterra, 2009.

Perla, Héctor, Jr. "Si Nicaragua Venció, El Salvador Vencerá: Central American Agency in the Creation of the U.S.–Central American Peace and Solidarity Movement." *Latin American Research Review* 43, no. 2 (2008): 136–58.

Pernet, Corinne A. "Shifting Position to the Global South: Latin America's Initiatives in the Early Years at the United Nations." In *Latin America 1810–2010: Dreams and Legacies*, edited by Claude Auroi and Aline Helg, 83–100. London: Imperial College Press, 2011.

Petersson, Fredrik. "Hub of the Anti-Imperialist Movement: The League against Imperialism and Berlin, 1927–1933." *Interventions: International Journal of Postcolonial Studies* 16, no. 1 (2014): 49–71.

Pettinà, Vanni. "Global Horizons: Mexico, the Third World, and the Non-Aligned Movement at the Time of the 1961 Belgrade Conference." *International History Review* 38, no. 4 (2016): 741–64.

Pieper Mooney, Jadwiga. "Forging Feminisms under Dictatorship: Women's International Ties and National Feminist Empowerment in Chile, 1973–1990." *Women's History Review* 19, no. 4 (2010): 613–30.

Pieterse, Jan. "State Terrorism on a Global Scale: The Role of Israel." *Crime and Social Justice*, nos. 21/22 (1984): 58–80.

Pitman, Thea, and Andy Stafford. "Introduction: Transatlanticism and Tricontinentalism." *Journal of Transatlantic Studies* 7, no. 3 (2009): 197–207.

Plotkin, Mariano, and Ricardo González Leandri, eds. *Localismo y globalización. Apuntes para una historia de los intelectuales en Iberoamérica.* Madrid: Consejo Superior de Investigaciones Científicas, Instituto de Historia, 2000.

Popescu, Monica. "On the Margins of the Black Atlantic: Angola, the Eastern Bloc, and the Cold War." *Research in African Literatures* 45, no. 3 (2014): 91–109.

Power, Margaret. "The U.S. Movement in Solidarity with Chile in the 1970s." *Latin American Perspectives* 36, no. 6 (2009): 46–66.

Power, Margaret, and Julie A. Charlip. "On Solidarity." *Latin American Perspectives* 36, no. 6 (2009): 3–9.

Prashad, Vijay. *The Darker Nations: A People's History of the Third World.* New York: New Press, 2007.

Putnam, Lara. *Radical Moves: Caribbean Migrants and the Politics of Race in the Jazz Age.* Chapel Hill: University of North Carolina Press, 2013.

Quigley, Thomas. "The Catholic Church in Cuba." In *Catholicism and Politics in Communist Societies*, edited by Pedro Ramet, 296–312. Durham, NC: Duke University Press, 1990.

Rabinovich, Itamar. *Waging Peace: Israel and the Arabs, 1948–2003*. Princeton, NJ: Princeton University Press, 2004.

Ramet, Pedro, ed. *Catholicism and Politics in Communist Societies*. Durham, NC: Duke University Press, 1990.

Randall, Margaret. *Exporting Revolution: Cuba's Global Solidarity*. Durham, NC: Duke University Press, 2017.

Rebolledo Hernández, Antonia. "La 'Turcofobia': Disriminación anti-árabe en Chile, 1900–1950." *Historia* 28 (1994): 249–72.

Redmond, Shana L. *Anthem: Social Movements and the Sound of Solidarity in the African Diaspora*. New York: New York University Press, 2014.

Reeves, Michelle Denise. "Extracting the Eagle's Talons: The Soviet Union in Cold War Latin America." PhD diss., University of Texas at Austin, 2014.

Rein, Raanan. "Political Considerations and Personal Rivalries: Peronist Argentina and the Partition of Palestine." *Diplomacy and Statecraft* 8, no. 2 (1997): 125–47.

Rein, Raanan. *Populism and Ethnicity: Peronism and the Jews of Argentina*. Montreal: McGill-Queen's University Press, 2020.

Reitan, Ruth. *The Rise and Decline of an Alliance: Cuba and African American Leaders in the 1960s*. East Lansing: Michigan State University Press, 1999.

Retamozo, Martín. "Movimientos sociales, política y hegemonía en Argentina." *Polis: Revista Latinoamericana* 28 (2011). http://journals.openedition.org/polis/1249.

Reyes, Miguel Angel. "La cultura de la revolución en los Andes: Aproximación a las relaciones transnacionales entre el M-19 y AVC en la década de 1980." *Estudios interdisciplinarios de América Latina y el Caribe* 28, no. 2 (2017): 104–28.

Richard, Nelly. "Cultural Peripheries: Latin America and Postmodernist De-Centering." *boundary 2* 20, no. 3 (1993): 156–61.

Rieiro, Anabel, ed. *Gestión Obrera: Del fragmento a la acción colectiva*. Montevideo: Nordan, 2010.

Rinaldo Fanesi, Pietro. "El exilio antifascista en América Latina: El caso mexicano." *Estudios interdisciplinarios de América Latina y el Caribe* 3, no. 2 (2015).

Riquelme Segovia, Alfredo. "Los modelos revolucionarios y el naufraio de la vía chilena al socialismo." *Nuevo Mundo/Mundos Nuevos*, 27 January 2007. https://doi.org/10.4000/nuevomundo.10603.

Rivera Mir, Sebastián. "El otro exilio Chileno en México y Guatemala, 1948–1951; Militancia transnacional en los orígenes de la Guerra Fría." *Historia* 50, no. 1 (2017): 209–40.

Robledo, Pablo. *Montoneros y Palestina*. Buenos Aires: Planeta Argentina, 2018.

Rodríguez, Ana Patricia. *Dividing the Isthmus: Central American Transnational Histories, Literatures and Cultures*. Austin: University of Texas Press, 2009.

Rodríguez de Ita, Guillermo. "Tres asilos otorgados por México a un mismo antitrujillista." *Tzintzun: Revista de Estudios Históricos*, no. 52 (2010): 101–42.

Rodríguez Munguía, Jacinto. *La otra guerra secreta: Los archivos prohibidos de la prensa y el poder*. Mexico City: Random House, 2007.

Rojas Mira, Claudia Fedora. "El exilio político chileno: La Casa de Chile en México, 1973–1993, Una experiencia singular." PhD diss., Universidad de Santiago de Chile, 2013.

Romero, Catalina. "Globalization, Civil Society and Religion from a Latin American Standpoint." *Sociology of Religion* 62, no. 4 (Winter 2001): 475–90.

Roniger, Luis, and Leonardo Senkman. "Conspirationism, Synarchism, and the Long Shadow of Perón." *Journal of Modern Jewish Studies* 17, no. 4 (2018): 434–54.

Rorty, Richard. *Contingency, Irony, and Solidarity.* Cambridge: Cambridge University Press, 1989.

Rosemblatt, Karin. *The Science and Politics of Race in Mexico and the United States, 1910–1950.* Chapel Hill: University of North Carolina Press, 2018.

Rosenblum, Beth Tamar. "OSPAAAL Posters and the Cuban Vanguard Aesthetic." Master's thesis, University of California at Los Angeles, 2005.

Rosenthal, Anton. "Radical Border Crossers: The Industrial Workers of the World and Their Press in Latin America." *Estudios Interdisciplinarios de América Latina y el Caribe* 22, no. 2 (2011): 39–70.

Ross, Kristin, *May '68 and Its Afterlives.* Chicago: University of Chicago Press, 2002.

Ruíz Guerra, Rubén. *Mas allá de la diplomacia: Relaciones de México con Bolivia, Ecuador y Perú.* Mexico City: SRE, 2007.

Rubernberg, Cheryl. "Israeli Foreign Policy in Central America." *Third World Quarterly* 8, no. 3 (1986): 896–915.

Rupprecht, Tobias. *Soviet Internationalism after Stalin: Interaction and Exchange between the USSR and Latin America during the Cold War.* Cambridge: Cambridge University Press, 2015.

Rynne, Xavier. *Vatican Council II.* Maryknoll, NY: Orbis, 1999.

Saborido, Mercedes. "El Partido Comunista Argentino y la Guerra de los Seis Días." *Revista Izquieras* (12 April 2012): 52–70.

Saddy, Fehmy, ed. *Arab-Latin American Relations.* New Brunswick, NJ: Transaction, 1983.

Saffie Guevara, Nicole, and Lorenzo Agar Corbinos. "A Century of Palestinian Immigration to Chile: A Successful Integration." In *Latin American with Palestinian Roots*, edited by Viola Raheb, 63–80. Beit Lahem: Diyar Publishers and Create Space Independent Publishing Platform, 2012.

Salazkina, Masha. "Moscow-Rome-Havana: A Film-Theory Road Map." *October* 139 (2011): 97–116.

Saldívar, Martha Vanessa. "From Mexico to Palestine: An Occupation of Knowledge, a Mestizaje of Methods." *American Quarterly* 62, no. 4 (2010): 821–33.

Salem, Sara. "On Transnational Feminist Solidarity: The Case of Angela Davis in Egypt." *Signs: Journal of Women in Culture and Society* 43, no. 2 (2018): 245–67.

Sánchez Barría, Felipe. "'En la lucha contra el imperialismo, México y Chile de Pie': Salvador Allende en la política tercermundicsta de Luis Echeverría en la guerra fría interamericana." *Foro Internacional* 54, no. 4 (2014): 954–91.

Sánchez García, Darío Gabriel, Iraida María Calzadilla Rodríguez, and Ramón Cabrales Rosabal. "Anatomía del Fotoperiodismo Cubano." *Alcance: Revista Cubana de Información y Comunicación* 8, no. 20 (2019): 104–17.

Sanders, Sara Katherine. "The Mexican Student Movement: National Protest Movements in International and Transnational Contexts." In *Human Rights and Transnational Solidarity in Cold War Latin America*, edited by Jessica Stites Mor, 74–99. Madison: University of Wisconsin Press, 2013.

Saney, Isaac. "African Stalingrad: The Cuban Revolution, Internationalism, and the End of Apartheid." *Latin American Perspectives* 33, no. 5 (2006): 81–117.

Sarmiento, Nicole. "Cuba and the South African Anti-Apartheid Struggle." *Links: International Journal of Socialist Renewal*, 21 January 2010, 1–6.

Saul, John S. *On Building a Social Movement: The North American Campaign for Southern African Liberation Revisited*. Trenton, NJ: Africa World Press, 2017.

Schenquer, Laura, and Liliana Mayer. "Tancerca y tanlejos: Israel en la mira de la prensa judeo-argentina durante la guerra deYom Kipur (1973)." In *Israel-Palestina: Una pasión argentina: Estudios sobre la recepción del conflicto árabe-israelí en la Argentina*, edited by Emmanuel N. Kahan, 151–69. Buenos Aires: Prometeo, 2016.

Scholz, Sally. *Political Solidarity*. University Park: Pennsylvania University Press, 2008.

Schreiber, Rebecca M. *Cold War Exiles in Mexico: U.S. Dissidents and the Culture of Critical Resistance*. Minneapolis: University of Minnesota Press, 2008.

Schuyt, Kees. "The Sharing of Risks and the Risks of Sharing: Solidarity and Social Justice in the Welfare State." *Ethical Theory and Moral Practice* 1 (1998): 297–311.

Schwabe, Siri. "Paradoxes of Erasure: Palestinian Memory and the Politics of Forgetting in Post-Dictatorship Chile." *Interventions* 20, no. 5 (2018): 651–65.

Segre, Roberto. *Diez años de arquitectura revolucionaria en Cuba*. Havana: Ediciones Union, 1969.

Self, Robert. "'To Plan Our Liberation': Black Power and the Politics of Place in Oakland, California, 1965–1977." *Journal of Urban History* 26, no. 6 (2000): 759–92.

Serrano Migallón, Fernando. *El asilio político en México*. Mexico: Editorial Porrúa, 1998.

Sharif, Regina. "Latin America and the Arab-Israeli Conflict." *Journal of Palestine Studies* 7, no. 1 (1977): 98–122.

Sheinin, David. "Reading Kissinger's Avatars: Cold War Pragmatism in Argentina's Middle East Policy." In *The New Jewish Argentina*, edited by Raanan Rein and Adriana Brodsky, 263–92. Boston: Brill, 2012.

Shorten, Richard. "Beyers Naudé and the Christian Institute." *Index on Censorship* 12, no. 5 (1983): 27.

Shuler, Jack. *Calling Out Liberty: The Stono Slave Rebellion and the Universal Struggle for Human Rights*. Jackson: University Press of Mississippi, 2009.

Sikkink, Katherine. *The Justice Cascade: How Human Rights Prosecutions Are Changing World Politics*. New York: Norton, 2011.

Sikkink, Katherine, and Carrie Booth Walling. "The Impact of Human Rights Trials in Latin America." *Journal of Peace Research* 44, no. 4 (2007): 427–45.

Simpson, Bradley. "Southeast Asia in the Cold War." In *The Cold War in the Third World*, edited by Robert J. McMahon, 48–66. New York: Oxford University Press, 2013.

Sinay, Ruben. *La Verdad sobre el conflicto en el cercano oriente*. Buenos Aires: Editorial Documentos, 1967.

Slobodian, Quinn. *Foreign Front: Third World Politics in the Sixties West Germany*. Durham, NC: Duke University Press, 2012.

Smith, Christian. *Disruptive Religion: The Force of Faith in Social Movement Activism*. New York: Routledge, 1996.

Smith, Christian. *The Emergence of Liberation Theology: Radical Religion and Social Movement Theory*. Chicago: University of Chicago Press, 1991.

Smith, Christian. *Resisting Reagan: The U.S. Central America Peace Movement*. Chicago: University of Chicago Press, 1996.

Sombe Mukua, George. "The Establishment of the Black Catholic Clergy in South Africa from 1889 to 1957." PhD diss., University of Natal, 2000.

Spivak, Gayatri. "Bonding in Difference, Interview with Alfred Arteaga (1993–1994)." In *The Spivak Reader*, edited by Donna Landry and Gerald MacLean, 15–28. New York: Routledge, 1996.

Stermer, Dugald, and Susan Sontag. *The Art of Revolution: 96 Posters from Cuba*. London: Pall Mall, 1970.

Stites Mor, Jessica. "Circum-Caribbean Development and Transnational Solidarity: Perspectives from a Post-Development Research Paradigm." *Canadian Journal of Latin American and Caribbean Studies* 38, no. 2 (2013): 279–81.

Stites Mor, Jessica. "Introduction: Situating Transnational Solidarity within Human Rights Studies of Cold War Latin America." In *Human Rights and Transnational Solidarity in Cold War Latin America*, edited by Jessica Stites Mor, 3–18. Madison: University of Wisconsin Press, 2013.

Stites Mor, Jessica. "The Question of Palestine in the Argentine Political Imaginary: Anti-Imperialist Thought from Cold War to Neoliberal Order." *Journal of Latin American and Iberian Research* 20, no. 2 (2014): 183–97.

Stites Mor, Jessica, ed. *Solidarity and Human Rights in Cold War Latin America*. Madison: University of Wisconsin Press, 2013.

Stites Mor, Jessica. *Transition Cinema: Political Filmmaking and the Argentine Left since 1968*. Pittsburgh: University of Pittsburgh Press, 2012.

Stites Mor, Jessica, and Maria del Carmen Suescun Pozas. "Transnational Pathways of Empathy in the Americas." In *The Art of Solidarity: Visual and Performative Politics in Cold War Latin America*, edited by Jessica Stites Mor and Maria del Carmen Suescun Pozas, 1–22. Austin: University of Texas Press, 2018.

Stratta, Fernando, and Marcelo Barrera. "¿Movimientos sin clases o clases sin movimiento? Notas sobre la recepción de la teoría de los Movimientos Sociales en la Argentina." *Conflicto social* 2, no. 1 (2009): 118–34.

Striffler, Steve. "Latin American Solidarity: Human Rights and the Politics of the US Left." In *The Palgrave Encyclopedia of Imperialism and Anti-Imperialism*, edited by Immanuel Ness and Zak Cope, 859–75. London: Palgrave Macmillan, 2015.

Striffler, Steve. *Solidarity: Latin America and the US Left in the Era of Human Rights.* London: Pluto, 2019.

Sullivan, Frances Peace. "'For the Liberty of the Nine Boys in Scottsboro and Against Yankee Imperialist Domination in Latin America': Cuba's Scottsboro Defense Campaign." *Canadian Journal of Latin American and Caribbean Studies* 38, no. 2 (2013): 282–92.

Suriano, Juan. *Anarquistas: Cultura y política libertaria en Buenos Aires, 1880–1910.* Buenos Aires: Ediciones Manantial, 2001.

Suzman, Arthur. "South Africa and the Rule of Law." *South African Law Journal* 85, pt. 2 (August 1968): 261–71.

Svampa, Maristella. "Protesta, movimientos sociales y dimensiones de la acción colectiva en América Latina." Lecture presented at the "Jornadas de Homenaje a Charles Tilly," Universidad Complutense de Madrid-Fundación Carolina, 7–9 May 2009.

Swedenberg, Ted. "Bad Rep for a Neck Scarf?" *International Journal of Middle East Studies* 49, no. 1 (2009): 184–85.

Sweet, James. *Domingos Álvares, African Healing, and the Intellectual History of the Atlantic World.* Chapel Hill: University of North Carolina Press, 2011.

Sznajder, Mario, and Luis Roniger. *The Politics of Exile in Latin America.* Cambridge: Cambridge University Press, 2009.

Taoua, Phillis. "The Anti-Colonial Archive: France and Africa's Unfinished Business." *SubStance* 32 (2003): 146–64.

Tarifa, Hashi K. *Black Nationalist Thought in South Africa.* London: Palgrave Macmillan, 2016.

Thornton, John. *The Congolese Saint Anthony: Dona Beatriz Kimpa Vita and the Antonian Movement, 1684–1706.* Cambridge: Cambridge University Press, 1998.

Tinsman, Heidi. *Buying into the Regime: Grapes and Consumption in Cold War Chile and the United States.* Durham, NC: Duke University Press, 2014.

Todd, Molly. *Beyond Displacement: Campesinos, Refugees, and Collective Action in the Salvadoran Civil War.* Madison: University of Wisconsin Press, 2010.

Todd, Molly. "'We Were Part of the Revolutionary Movement There': Wisconsin Peace Progressives and Solidarity with El Salvador in the Reagan Era." *Journal of Civil and Human Rights* 3, no. 1 (2017): 1–56.

Tofik Karam, John. "On the Trail and Trial of Palestinian Diaspora: Mapping South America in the Arab-Israeli Conflict, 1967–1972." *Journal of Latin American Studies* 45, no. 4 (2013): 751–77.

Tolliver, Julie-Françoise. "Césaire/Lumumba: A Season of Solidarity." *Journal of Postcolonial Writing* 50, no. 4 (2014): 398–409.

Tomaselli, Kevan G., and Ruth Teer-Tomaselli. "*New Nation*: Anarchronistic Catholicism and Liberation Theology." In *Contesting Media Power: Alternative Media in a Networked World*, edited by Nick Couldry and James Curran, 195–208. Lanham, MD: Rowman and Littlefield, 2003.

Torregrosa, Gabriela. "François Maspero, retrato de un editor." *Trama and Texturas* 28 (2015): 113–22.

Torres, Cesar R., and Bruce Kidd. "Introduction: The History and Relevance of the Pan-American Games." *International Journal of the History of Sport* 33, nos. 1–2 (2016): 1–5.

Traber, Michael, ed. *Fidel Castro Speeches: Cuba's Internationalist Foreign Policy, 1975–80*. Montreal: Pathfinder, 1981.

Tyler, Ronnie C. "Fugitive Slaves in Mexico." *Journal of Negro History* 57, no. 1 (1972): 1–12.

Ulianova, Olga. "La Unidad Popular y el golpe militar en Chile: Percepciones y análisis soviéticos." *Estudios públicos* 79 (2000): 83–171.

Vaca Narvaja, Gustavo, and Fernando Frugoni. *Fernando Vaca Narvaja: Con igual ánimo, pensamiento político y biografía autorizada*. Buenos Aires: Colihue, 2002.

Valverde, Estela. "The Question of 'Argentinidad': The Self-Image of Arab and Jewish Ancestry in Recent Argentine Literature." In *Arab and Jewish Immigrants in Latin America: Images and Reality*, edited by Ignacio Klich and Jefferey Lesser, 189–203. London: Cass, 1998.

Vaois Gitersos, Terry. "The Sport Scramble for Africa: GANEFO, the IOC, and the 1964 Africa Games." *Sport in Society* 14, no. 5 (2011): 645–59.

Vaughan, Mary Kay. "Mexico, 1940–1968 and Beyond: Perfect Dictatorship? Dictablanda? or PRI State Hegemony?" *Latin American Research Review* 53, no. 1 (2018): 167–76.

Vázquez Olivera, Mario, and Fabián Campos Hernández. "Solidaridad transnacional y conspiración revolucionaria: Cuba, México y el Ejército Guerrillero de los Pobres de Guatemala, 1967–1976." *Estudios interdisciplinarios de América Latina y el Caribe* 30, no. 1 (2019): 72–95.

Vélez, Federico. *Latin American Revolutionaries and the Arab World: From the Suez Canal to the Arab Spring*. London: Ashgate, 2016.

Verryn, Trevor. "Catholic Bishops and Apartheid." In *Catholics and Apartheid Society*, edited by Andrew Prior, 54–66. Cape Town: David Philip, 1982.

Vieira, Manuel Adolfo. *Derecho de asilo diplomático*. Montevideo: Facultad de Derecho de la Universidad de la República, 1961.

Villa-Vicencio, Charles. *A Theology of Reconstruction: Nation Building and Human Rights*. Cape Town: David Philip, 1992.

Villa-Vicencio, Charles. *Trapped in Apartheid: A Socio-Theological History of the English-Speaking Churches*. Cape Town: David Philip, 1998.

Waisman, Sergio. "*A Thousand and One Nights* in Argentina: Translation, Narrative and Politics in Borges, Puig, and Piglia." *Comparative Literature Studies* 40, no. 4 (2003): 351–71.

Walker, Louise. "Spying at the Drycleaners: Mexico City." *Journal of Iberian and Latin American Research* 19, no. 1 (2013): 52–61.

Walshe, Peter. "The Evolution of Liberation Theology in South Africa." *Journal of Law and Religion* 5, no. 2 (1987): 299–311.

Walshe, Peter. "South Africa: Prophetic Christianity and the Liberation Movement." *Journal of Modern African Studies* 29 (1991): 27–60.

Weisz, Eduardo. *El PRT-ERP: Claves para una interpretación de su singularidad: Marxismo, internacionalismo y classismo*. Buenos Aires: Centro Cultural de la Cooperación, 2006.

Weisz, Eduardo. *El PRT-ERP: Nueva izquierda e izqueirda tradicional*. 2nd ed. *Cuaderno de Trabajo* 30. Buenos Aires: Centro Cultural de la Cooperación, 2004.

Westad, Odd Arne. *The Global Cold War: Third World Interventions and the Making of Our Times*. Cambridge: Cambridge University Press, 2007.

Weyland, Kurt. *Bounded Rationality and Policy Diffusion: Social Sector Reform in Latin America*. Princeton, NJ: Princeton University Press, 2009.

Wimberley, Dale W. "Setting the Stage for Cross-Border Solidarity." *Labor Studies Journal* 34, no. 3 (2009): 318–38.

Winn, Peter. *Weavers of Revolution: The Yarur Workers and Chile's Road to Socialism*. New York: Oxford University Press, 1989.

Wollny, Hans. "México y el reto del asilo: Una visión desde afuera." *Verfassung und Recht in Übersee/Law and Politics in Africa, Asia and Latin America* 23, no. 4 (1990): 374–96.

Yaffe, Helen. *We Are Cuba! How a Revolutionary People Have Survived in a Post-Soviet World*. New Haven, CT: Yale University Press, 2020.

Yaniv, Avner. *P.L.O.: A Profile*. Jerusalem: Israel Universities Study Group for Middle Eastern Affairs, Attali Print Office, 1974.

Yankelevich, Pablo. *México, país refugio: La experiencia de los exilios en el siglo XX*. Mexico City: Plaza y Valdés, 2002.

Yankelevich, Pablo. "Los rostros de Jano: Vigilancia y control de los exiliados latinoamericanos en México (1960–1980)." *Estudios Interdisciplinarios de América Latina y el Caribe* 30, no. 1 (2019): 125–57.

Yankelevich, Pablo, and María Luisa Tarres. *En México, entre exilios: Una experiencia de sudamericanos*. Mexico City: Plaza y Valdés, 1998.

Young, Cynthia A. "Havana up in Harlem: LeRoi Jones, Harold Cruse and the Making of a Cultural Revolution." *Science and Society* 65, no. 1 (2001): 12–38.

Young, Cynthia A. *Soul Power: Culture, Radicalism, and the Making of a U.S. Third World Left*. Durham, NC: Duke University Press, 2006.

Young, Robert J. C. "Postcolonialism: From Bandung to the Tricontinental." *Historein* 5 (2005): 11–21.

Zagaris, Bruce, and Julia Padierna Peratta. "Mexico-United States Extradition and Alternatives: From Fugitive Slaves to Drug Traffickers—150 Years and Beyond the Rio Grande's Winding Courses." *American University International Law Review* 12, no. 4 (1997): 519–627.

Zolov, Eric. "¡Cuba sí, Yanquis no! The Sacking of the Instituto Cultural México-Norteamericano in Morelia, Michoacán, 1961." In *In from the Cold: Latin America's New Encounter with the Cold War*, edited by Gilbert M. Joseph and Daniela Spenser, 214–52. Durham, NC: Duke University Press, 2008.

Zolov, Eric. "Introduction: Latin America in the Global Sixties." *The Americas* 70, no. 3 (2014): 349–62.

Zolov, Eric. *The Last Good Neighbor: Mexico in the Global Sixties.* Durham, NC: Duke University Press, 2020.

Zourek, Michal. "Czechoslovak Policy towards Chile in the 1970s and 1980s." *Canadian Journal of Latin American and Caribbean Studies* 39, no. 2 (2014): 211–28.

Index

antiapartheid, 62, 132, 144–45, 147, 155, 161, 174; and Catholic activism, 146; movement, 23, 137

anticapitalism, 8, 29, 121

anticolonialism, 53, 55, 62, 79–80, 104, 135, 149, 169

anticommunism, 132, 134, 183n76

antifascism, 7–8, 100

anti-imperialism, 17, 27, 29, 55, 59, 85, 103, 109, 116, 124, 126, 128, 132, 150, 174

antiracism, 53, 59, 62, 79, 85, 137, 150, 154

antisemitism, 105, 108–11, 113, 134

anti-Zionism, 110, 113

apartheid, 21, 23, 62, 64, 68, 96, 128, 132, 138, 140, 144–45, 148, 153–54, 161–64, 173, 220n119; laws, 139, 154, 156; state (South Africa), 23, 138, 141, 147, 158, 161–62, 164

APRA (Alianza Popular Revolucionaria Americana) (Peru), 32, 85

Arab-Israeli conflict, 63, 104, 107

Arab-Israeli War (1948), 63, 105, 121

Arab League, 22, 102–3, 105, 109, 113, 117–18; First Summit, 105

Arab Spring, 169, 173

Arab states, 64, 104, 106, 109, 114, 118. *See also* League of Arab States

Arafat, Yasser, 65, 99–100, 105–7, 109, 113–15, 117–18, 123–24, 126–27, 174

Archivo General de la Nación (AGN) (Mexico), 21–22

Arévalo, Juan José, 41

Argentine: leftists, 22, 99–100, 102, 104–6, 116, 120, 128; military, 113, 116–17; socialists, 107–8. *See also* Communist Party: Argentina

Argentines, 23, 49, 54, 99–100, 102–4, 106, 114, 118–21, 128–30

Arguedas Mendieta, Antonio, 36–37

artists, 57–59, 65, 69, 78–79, 98, 107

Asia, 10, 22, 51–52, 62, 105, 154, 165, 169

Asociación Argentina de Solidaridad, 119

Asociación Mutual Israelita Argentina, 123

associations, civic, 100, 125, 127, 132; religious, 140, 164

asylum, 31–39, 42, 45–46, 49–50, 136; diplomatic, 32–34, 42; laws, 27, 28, 46, 173; political, 19, 31, 33, 36, 38–39, 43, 46–47, 50, 173, 191n85; territorial, 33, 46

asylum seekers, 27, 31, 33–36, 38, 42–43, 45–46, 49, 185n9, 192n89; Chilean, 32, 41–42, 48; political, 21–22, 27, 29, 34, 38, 41–42, 45, 188n48

authoritarianism, 15, 30, 43–44, 129

autonomy, 15, 34, 36, 39, 105; legal, 26; political, 100

Azanian People's Organisation (Zimbabwe), 163

Balfour Declaration, 121

Bandung Conference. *See* Afro-Asian Solidarity Conference

Bantu Education Act, 140

Baraka, Amiri (LeRoi Jones), 68

Barnet, Miguel Ángel, 3, 4, 174, 175n1

Baxter, Joe, 113–14

Bay of Pigs, 54

Belafonte, Harry, 68

Belgrade (Yugoslavia, now Serbia), 54, 169

Ben Barka, Mehdi, 55

Ben Bella, Ahmed, 54–55

Berlin (Germany), 23, 135

Betancourt, Iván, 148

Biko, Stephen, 209n7

Birri, Fernando, 79, 107

bishops, 132, 134–37, 139–42, 144–45, 154–56, 159, 161; Black, 150; councils, 132

Bishops' Council of England and Wales, 159

Black Bishops Solidarity Group, 150

Central Intelligence Agency (CIA), 36–37, 41, 56
Central Zionist Organization, 113
Césaire, Aimé, 193n2
Charlip, Julie, 10
Chávez, Hugo, 122
Chile, 10–11, 28–29, 31, 39–50, 102, 114, 116, 125–27, 132, 137, 147, 167, 174, 192–93n99, 206–7n93; citizens, 21–22, 28, 40, 42–48, 50, 125, 127–28, 185n9, 193n100; exiles from, 28, 41–45, 47–49; military coup, 39; solidarity movement, 28, 41, 47, 50, 173
China, 53, 106, 110, 114
Chomsky, Aviva, 11
Christian Council of South Africa. See SACC
Christian Institute, 145, 147, 154–56
Christians, 103, 125, 135, 174
churches, 131–48, 150, 152–57, 159–60, 162–64, 166, 174, 209–10n9, 220n119; institutional, 165, 210n11; leaders, 147, 162, 165; national, 142, 150, 210n11. See also Catholic Church
CIA (Central Intelligence Agency), 36–37, 41, 56
Cienfuegos Gorriarán, Osmany, 55
citizens, 172; marginalized, 37; Mexican, 28, 34, 43, 45; South African, 160; U.S., 170, 184n1
citizenship, 8–9, 37, 45, 63, 100, 125, 128; Black, 140; Cuba, 65; political, 8–9; rights, 15, 128, 140; women's, 8
Clarke, Maura, 148
clergy, 138, 140, 146, 148, 150; Catholic, 135, 147, 165
Club Fotográfico de Cuba, 78
COBEM (Comitê dos Brasileiros Exilados no México), 44–45
Cold War, 7–9, 11, 13, 17, 31, 44, 52, 106–9, 118, 167–68, 171–72, 194n11, 204n54
Colombia, 10, 32, 58, 99, 120, 131

colonialism, 6, 8, 59, 63, 68, 80, 108, 110, 114, 120, 122, 128, 131, 145; discourses of, 14; French, 63; ongoing, 59, 62, 109
colonization, 6, 55, 91, 121, 129
Comisión Mexicana de Ayuda a Refugiados, 50
Comitê dos Brasileiros Exilados no México (COBEM), 44–45
Comité de Solidaridad y Apoyo al Pueblo Peruano, 38
Comité de Solidaridad y Apoyo a Chile, 40
Commission for Mutual Economic Assistance, 173
Communist International, 6, 8, 13, 53
Communist Party: Argentina, 8, 104, 106, 107, 110, 129; Mexico, 32, 40, 43; Chile, 40, 44, 126; Cuba, 55, 56; Israeli, 106; Soviet Union, 126
Conference of Latin American Bishops, 131–32, 136, 145; meeting in Puebla, Mexico (1979), 136–37, 145–46
Conference on Economic Co-operation, 96
Congo, 54, 63, 65, 80, 82, 84, 141
Congreso Cultural de la Habana, 59
consciousnesses: political, 19–20, 82, 88, 95, 110; revolutionary, 51, 57
Consejo Episcopal Latinoamericano (CELAM), 134–35, 136, 165
Convención de Caracas, 31, 34
coups, military, 21, 29, 36, 38, 54, 119, 135. See also under Chile
crises, 13, 28, 49, 100, 109, 118, 120–22, 124, 128–29, 170, 174; economic, 170; environmental, 16; financial, 119–20, 124, 174; political, 20
Crisis News (Western Province Council of Churches publication), 160
Cristero War (Mexico), 131
Crowley, Donald, 36
Cuba, 8, 27, 31, 37, 48, 51–59, 62–65, 68, 78–79, 86, 96–97, 100, 113–15, 126–27,

Evaristo Arns, Paul, 156
exiles, 6, 19, 28, 32, 41–43, 45–46, 48, 51, 108–9, 136, 146, 155–56, 158, 162–64; communities, 28, 38, 42, 44, 47, 179–80n36, 182n60; political, 32, 46, 50; radical, 28–29

Falklands War, 118, 119
Fanon, Frantz, 80, 149
fascism, 107, 123, 134
Al-Fatah, 105–7, 114–15, 118, 127
Federación de Entidades Argentino-Palestinas, 119, 127
Federación Latinoamericana de Periodistas, 46
Federación Universitaria Argentina, 107
Feltrinelli, Giangiacomo, 80
Fernandes, Carlos Augusto, 33
filmmakers, 79, 107, 114, 197–98n53
films, 56, 79, 82, 107, 114, 170–71
Firmenich, Mario Eduardo, 115
FORA (Federación Obrera Regional Argentina), 7
Forman, James, 86
France, 7, 41, 48, 53, 189–90n61
Francis (pope), 174
Franco, José Luciano, 95
Freire, Paulo, 135, 209n7
FRELIMO (Frente de Libertação de Moçambique), 88, 156
Frente Antiimperialista y por el Socialismo (Argentina), 109
Frente de Libertação de Moçambique (FRELIMO), 88, 156
Frente Revolucionario Indo-americano Popular, 105
Frente Sandinista de Liberación Nacional (FSLN) (Nicaragua), 87, 115
Frolinat, 113
FSLN (Frente Sandinista de Liberación Nacional) (Nicaragua), 87, 115. See also Sandinistas

Gaddafi, Muammar, 117
Gallardo Vasquez, Guillermo, 192n89
Games of the New Emerging Forces (GANEFO), 57
GANEFO (Games of the New Emerging Forces), 57
García Robles, Alfonso, 46
Garland Mahler, Anne, 97
Garvey, Marcus, 149
Gaxiola, Javier, 192n89
Gaza, 65, 99, 114, 129, 200–201n8
Geneva Convention, 40
geographies, 4, 6, 24, 41, 97
Germany, 48, 107, 150, 156; Nazi Germany, 122
Getino, Octavio, 107
Giannoni, Jorge, 114
globalization, 8, 11
global sixties, 17–18, 27, 169
Global South, 4–5, 7, 12, 17, 20, 48, 51–52, 96, 120–21, 131, 155, 167–69, 172–73
Goemans, Loek "Louise," 143
González Casanova, Pablo, 43
González Rostgaard, Alfredo J., 56
González Videla, Gabriel, 40–41
Goss, Jean, 145
Gosse, Van, 9–10
Goss-Mayr, Hildegard, 145–46
Goulart, João, 38
Gould, Jeffrey, 11
governance, 15, 48, 141, 165; democratic, 133
Gramar, Roberto, 110
Guatemala, 38, 191n83, 41; civil war in, 11; Guatemala City, 38
Guevara, Ernesto "Che," 36–37, 55, 58, 65, 80, 85–86, 106, 124, 135
Gurwitz, Beatrice, 204n54
Gutiérrez, Gustavo, 134–37, 150, 153, 155, 166, 211n16

Habermas, Jürgen, 13
Hadouchi, Olivier, 193n3

Harmer, Tanya, 173
Havana (Cuba), 22, 31, 51–52, 55, 58, 64, 78, 96, 109, 113, 170–71
Havana Convention on Asylum (1928), 32
Haya de la Torre, Víctor Raúl, 31–34, 37–39
Hennemann, Franziskus, 139
hierarchies, 132, 139, 141, 150, 171, 174
historians, 3, 6, 14, 16–17, 23, 29, 171–72
histories, 3, 8–10, 14, 17, 28, 41, 58, 68, 87, 95, 99, 125, 129, 167–74, 188n49 (chap. 1)
Ho Chi Minh, 58–59, 65, 80, 126
Hooker, Juliet, 14, 18
Hornsby-Smith, Michael P., 213n38
human rights, 8–11, 33, 48, 64, 91, 119–20; abuses of, 38, 42, 119, 134, 136, 147, 162
Hunke, Heinz, 159
Hurley, Denis, 141–42, 155, 159, 160, 161, 162
Hurley, Jeremy, 155

ICAIC (Instituto Cubano del Arte e Industria Cinematográficos), 56–57, 79, 82
ICT (Institute of Contextual Theology), 151–52
ideologies, 7, 9–11, 20, 33, 52, 56–57, 85, 91, 97, 100, 110–11, 122, 137, 173
images, 31, 47, 52, 57–59, 65, 68, 78, 80, 82, 85–88, 91, 95, 108, 121–22, 200–201n8
IMBISA (Inter-Regional Meeting of the Bishops of Southern Africa), 144, 154, 155
imperialism, 5, 12, 29, 42, 45–46, 51–52, 58, 68, 78, 86, 97, 100, 103–5, 106, 110–11, 116, 122–23, 127–29, 135, 141, 146, 171; Arab, 109; French, 82; global, 99; ongoing, 87; Portuguese, 87; social, 104; South African, 23; Soviet,

106; U.S., 10, 31, 37, 55, 62, 120, 123, 134, 185n9
indigenous: groups, 12, 15, 39, 116; peoples, 11, 38, 131
injustice, 3, 13, 16, 116, 144; economic, 135–36, 152; social, 143, 150; socio-economic, 131, 135
Institute of Contextual Theology (ICT), 151–52
Institute of Palestine Studies, 118
Instituto Cubano del Arte e Industria Cinematográficos (ICAIC), 56–57, 79, 82
intellectuals, 6, 58–59, 65, 78, 86, 100, 103, 107, 109, 134; French, 221n1
International Commission for Justice and Peace, 144
internationalism, 11, 17, 19, 52, 55, 58, 110, 125–26, 131, 146, 169; communist, 8; revolutionary, 96, 170
internationalist, 3, 50–51, 55–56, 80, 86, 91, 96, 106, 109, 118, 127, 130–31, 137, 168, 185n9; leftists, 52, 103, 133; vision, 123
Inter-Regional Meeting of the Bishops of Southern Africa (IMBISA), 144, 154, 155
Intifada, 119, 121
Irani National Front, 113
Iraq, 104, 106, 120, 123
Irish Republican Army, 113
Israel, 23, 57, 63, 64, 85, 103–4, 106–7, 110, 113, 115, 120, 121, 122, 124, 129, 145, 205n77; state, 63, 99, 104–5, 107–8, 129
Israeli Communist Party, 106
Israel-Palestine conflict, 23, 110, 118, 130
Italy, 80, 110, 113
Ivens, Joris, 79
Izquierda Cristiana de Chile, 44
Izquierda Socialista, 118
Izquierda Unida, 122

Pontifical Council for Justice and Peace, 138, 142. *See also* Justice and Peace Commissions

PO (Partido Obrero) (Argentina), 104–5, 110, 118, 201–2n19, 206–7n93

Popular Front for the Liberation of Palestine, 115, 127. See also *Prensa Obrera*

poster art, political, 52, 56–59, 62, 65, 68, 86–87, 96; Cuban, 56–62

Power, Margaret, 10

Prensa Latina (news agency), 54

Prensa Obrera (PO publication), 118–19

Pretoria (South Africa), 156–57, 162

PRI (Partido Revolucionario Institucional) (Mexico), 30, 37–41, 44–47, 49–50

priests, 134, 136–37, 145, 150, 155

prisoners, political, 11, 43, 100, 138, 143, 220n119

PRM (Partido de la Revolución Mexicana), 30

PRN (Partido Revolucionario Nacional) (Mexico), 30

Proença Sigaud, Geraldo de, 134

protests, 4–5, 7, 10, 30, 33, 38, 46, 99, 107, 109, 122, 140, 142–44, 147, 150, 155, 164, 217n83; popular, 30, 137

PRT (Partido Revolucionario de los Trabajadores) (Argentina), 105–7, 114; ERP-PRT, 114

PS (Partido Socialista) (Argentina), 104–7, 129, 135

Pueblo Peruano (group), 38

Puente, Luis de la, 85

Puerto Rico, 59, 100

Puig, Manuel, 107

Putnam, Lara, 172

Quebracho (Movimiento Patriótico Revolucionario Quebracho) (Argentina), 122–23

Quigley, Thomas, 209n4

Rabasa, Emilio, 42

race, 12, 14, 137, 150, 155; relations, 8, 59, 138, 144, 149

racial: equality, 59, 150; inequality, 59, 68

racism, 51, 53, 59, 64, 68, 110, 122, 135, 142–43, 149, 154, 156, 170–71, 205n77; institutionalized, 59, 139

radicalism, 39, 49; left-wing, 80; political, 113

Radical Revolutionary Youth (Chile), 44

RAU (República Árabe Unida), 113

Reagan, Ronald, 11

Red de Mujeres Solidarias (Argentina), 124

Reed, John, 80

Reeves, Ambrose, 138

reforms, 13, 22, 25, 28–30, 37, 48, 131, 134, 140, 173; agrarian, 126; legal, 31–32, 34–35

refugees, 49–50, 64, 189–90n61, 191n83; political, 28, 188n49

regimes, 5, 7, 9, 17, 28, 58, 91, 104, 132, 155, 162, 170; military, 11, 78, 116, 118–19, 132, 147, 185n9

religious: associations, 140, 164; institutions, 34, 132–33; organizations, 132, 164. *See also under* repression

repression, 13, 32, 41, 45, 109, 118, 123, 129, 136, 170, 209n4; political, 6, 153; religious, 110

resistance, 4, 9, 12, 20, 25–26, 42, 55, 68, 82, 87–88, 106–8, 114–15, 119, 127, 132, 140, 150, 152–54, 164, 169, 171–73, 184n3; cultural, 129; financial, 121; hemispheric, 46; ideological, 95; leftist, 107; nonviolent, 145; ongoing, 57; organized, 24, 139; peaceful, 144; popular, 122; radical, 105

revolution, 3, 10, 27, 29–30, 41, 49, 51–52, 54, 56–59, 65, 78–79, 85, 87, 96–97, 160, 209n4, 221n1; permanent, 96. *See also under the following*: Algeria; Cuba; Mexico; movements

Yom Kippur War, 63
Young, Cynthia, 11
Young African Religious Movement, 142
Young Christian Students (South Africa), 155
Young Christian Women (South Africa), 145
Young Christian Workers (South Africa), 150, 155, 157
Young Lords, 11

Zagaris, Bruce, 184n3
Zambia, 160
Zanzibar, 54
Zimbabwe, 145–46, 155, 157–58, 162, 220n119. *See also* Rhodesia
Zimbabwe News (Patriotic Front newspaper), 157
Zionism, 63, 65, 107–11, 113, 121, 129
Zulu, Alpheus, 149
Zulu, Lawrence, 149
Zuno de Echeverría, María Esther, 41

Critical Human Rights